FILMMA

ed

ANTHONY SLIDE

Perpetually Cool

The Many Lives of Anna May Wong (1905–1961)

Anthony B. Chan

Filmmakers Series, No. 103

The Scarecrow Press, Inc.
Lanham, Maryland • Toronto • Plymouth, UK
2007

SCARECROW PRESS, INC.

Published in the United States of America
by Scarecrow Press, Inc.
A wholly owned subsidary of
The Rowman & Littlefield Publishing Group, Inc.
4501 Forbes Boulevard, Suite 200, Lanham, Maryland 20706
www.scarecrowpress.com

Estover Road
Plymouth PL6 7PY
United Kingdom

British Library Cataloguing in Publication Information Available

The hardback edition of this book was previously cataloged by the Library of
Congress as follows:

Chan, Anthony B.
    Perpetually cool : the many lives of Anna May Wong, 1905–1961 / Anthony
B. Chan.
        p. cm.—(Filmmakers series ; no. 103)
    Includes bibliographical references and index.
        1. Wong, Anna May, 1905–1961. 2. Motion picture actors and actresses—
United States—Biography. I. Title. II. Series.
PN2287.W56C48 2003
791.43'028'092273—dc21   2003007801
    ISBN-13: 978-0-8108-4789-7 (hardcover : alk. paper)
    ISBN-10: 0-8108-4789-2 (hardcover : alk. paper)
    ISBN-13: 978-0-8108-5909-8 (pbk : alk. paper)
    ISBN-10: 0-8108-5909-2 (pbk : alk. paper)

To
All those Chinese girls
adopted by non-Chinese families.

May they find strength in
being Chinese.

CONTENTS

Part III. Life Is Cinema

PREFACE

In the age of exclusion in Chinese America (1882–1943) and Chinese Canada (1923–1947), Chinese individuals with a strong sense of empowerment in the European American media were almost nonexistent until Chinese America's first movie star, Anna May Wong (1905–1961), or Wong Liu Tsong (Yellow Frosted Willow), appeared in *Shanghai Express* (1932). According to my relatives in Victoria, British Columbia, and Shanghai, Wong captivated the Chinese everywhere just by being there. No Asian American female film star has ever equaled her prolific career in film, stage, vaudeville, radio, and television before or after her death in 1961.

My parents, Steven and Rosy, were married in the same year that *Shanghai Express* appeared in theaters in Victoria and Vancouver. Born and raised in Canada and members of a merchant class in Chinese Canada, one of their few sources of entertainment was the movie theater. Like many Chinese in North America, the films they eagerly awaited, cherished, and from which they could escape the repercussions of the Great Depression and the consequences of racist acts were those that revealed people who actually looked like them. Anna May Wong was clearly one of those who looked like them.

Watching her repartee with Shanghai Lily and Mrs. Haggarty in *Shanghai Express* was almost like watching one of their neighbors on the wide screen.

Here was a yellow woman holding her own against two white women. It was truly an extraordinary sight that almost never happened in the icy reality of interracial relationships, in which no yellow person could think or act equally to a white person in the 1930s. That Wong as Hui Fei, a Chinese, could brazenly speak in such a witty and cool manner while exuding a controlled rationality in this mind game was even more astonishing to Chinese living in a North America that precluded and subordinated them with discriminatory legislation and overt hostility.

For my parents and their generation, Anna May Wong was always an integral part of the family. Since she was the only female Chinese American film actress in Hollywood who actually became world famous, she eventually became an icon to the people of Chinese North America. Yet when her cinematic career as a lead performer ended with *The Lady from Chungking* (1942), her image disappeared. It was as if she were an apparition that appeared in more than sixty films and then evaporated like a short-lived butterfly.

In Hong Kong, where I worked as a television journalist, documentary filmmaker, and anchor from 1986 to 1987, the cinema is an integral part of the entertainment world. Newspaper articles sometimes referred to Anna May Wong as a Chinese American actress in the context of overseas Chinese film production originating from Hollywood. In the political environment of the 1980s, during which Hong Kong was conditioning itself to the fate of discovering its Chinese roots again as this city-state began its reintegration with China, I realized that the story of Anna May Wong was in fact the story of Chinese America discovering itself. She was the startling flash point in a Chinese America that sought agency and empowerment.

It was not until I began teaching documentary film production and Asian media systems at the University of Washington in 1991 that I thought to explore the possibility of a biography of Anna May Wong. I wondered why there had not been any extensive study of such a movie icon. As the first major Chinese American film star from Hollywood, her impact on Asian America was obvious. But only a paucity of movie-driven articles and her short memoir existed on "Yellow Frosted Willow."

Sidetracked by my book *Li Ka-shing: Hong Kong's Elusive Billionaire* (1996), a four-part documentary film series on Asian Americans in Vietnam, and various administrative and teaching duties at the university, I began researching the Anna May Wong biography in earnest only in 1999. The wealth of material in English-, French-, and Japanese-language newspapers, her memoir, and her own writings, especially during her sojourn in China in 1936 and collections at the New York Public Library, the Margaret Herrick Library of the Academy of Motion Picture Arts and Sciences, and the Library of the

British Film Institute, revealed a complex, witty, and sophisticated Asian American woman whose powerful intelligence, gift for languages, extraordinary ability to market her persona, and Daoist capacity to understand the world on her own terms transcended race, ethnicity, and citizenship. Although the research material was extraordinarily rich, many of her films simply no longer existed. Fortunately, the film that revealed her first lead role, *The Toll of the Sea* (1922); her portrayal of the Mongol spy in *The Thief of Bagdad* (1924), which catapulted her to international fame; her finest and last silent film, *Piccadilly* (1929); and her tour de force performance in *Shanghai Express* (1932) were readily available. The textual analysis of these and other films such as *A Study in Scarlet* (1933), *Chu Chin Chow* (1934), and *The Lady from Chungking* (1942) divulged a penchant for perfection, a deft handling of difficult lines, a willingness to upstage the lead performers, a natural ability to consume the latest fashions as if they were simply tight body wear, and the capacity to exude a feverish sexuality. This was often exemplified by a hip, cool demeanor that beckoned and captivated the audience.

Writers will often mention that the act of writing is the act of exploration and discovery. This book is no exception, as I discovered through the act of examining Wong's life and career. She represented every Chinese who lived and worked in North America and who longed to come to terms with being Chinese in a Western country.

Writing is essentially a solitary endeavor, but the production of a book is not. Many people helped in the completion of this work. Many thanks to my research assistants at the University of Washington: Leah Altaras, Christy Aquino, Travis Brown, Cheryl Chu, Leah dela Cruz, Wai Ho, Melissa Lankhaar, Hazel Lin, Robert Newell, and Lauren Robison. Special thanks to Asako Yanai, who translated several passages from the Japanese. Thanks also to the University of Washington for granting me a ten-week sabbatical leave during which I was able to research and write the chapter entitled "'Yellowface,' Masks, and Stereotypes," and to the staff at the university's interlibrary loan division. As cinema studies librarian, Glenda Pearson was especially helpful. Albert L. Sampson of Seattle University and Kevin Kawamoto provided insightful editorial comments.

At Scarecrow Press, it was a pleasure to work with the noted film historian Anthony Slide, editor of the Filmmakers series. His vast cinematic knowledge helped to make this a better book. I also thank editors Rebecca Massa and Jason Proetorius for their work in the completion of this publishing endeavor.

A contemplative home life is essential to productive writing endeavors. My companion of more than twenty years, Professor Wei Djao of North Seattle Community College, has always been there. Her book, *Being Chinese: Voices from the Diaspora* (University of Arizona Press, 2003), was the main intellectual inspiration behind this biography of Anna May Wong. Her good humor and meals of drunken pork tenderloin and lion heads also sustained me. With excursions into her own ethnicity, identity, and self-actualization, our daughter, Lian Djao Chan, witnessed all of our creative machinations. Life is good, with no complaints when the act of creation can be exhibited and maintained.

INTRODUCTION

"Lotus Flower," "China Doll," and "Dragon Lady" are just a few of the stereotypical appellations attached to Anna May Wong by European American and European producers, directors, critics, and journalists. As the first and most famous Chinese American movie star in the history of cinema, she was more than the images she portrayed in her films, stage productions, vaudeville acts, and radio and television shows over forty-two years. Wong was the first internationally acclaimed Asian American female film star. She mesmerized audiences from Hollywood and London to Berlin, Paris, and Vienna with more than sixty films. Her stage career took her to Australia, Austria, Denmark, Italy, Scotland, Sweden, and Switzerland. Even more remarkable, she sometimes performed in the languages of the countries in which she worked. Her spoken German was legendary. Her cinematic demeanor was detached, cool, and hip. The woman had style!

This is a multifaceted story of the star as she grew up in Los Angeles during a time of social and political ferment when the Chinese revolution touched California. This period also was marked by the development of the Los Angeles laundry industry, which helped sustain her family, as well as by the emergence of Hollywood as a viable career alternative for some Asian Americans.

Perpetually Cool is presented in three parts. The first chapters of part 1 chronicle Anna May Wong's life from her birth in Los Angeles, to her performance in early Hollywood films and her work in Berlin, London, and Paris during the 1920s, to her return to Hollywood in major films during the 1930s. She subsequently returned to London film studios for three films, followed by a contract with Paramount studios.

This biography is also the story of the patriotism of one Asian American woman who worked tirelessly against fascism during World War II. In addition to fund-raising, she starred in war films during the 1940s. In her final acting years from 1951 to 1960, Wong performed on television and was set to star in the movie version of *Flower Drum Song* when she died.

In part 2 Anna May Wong begins her enduring attachment to China and experiences life in Shanghai and other parts of Asia. The opening chapter is the story of seeking her roots when she ventured to China to discover that part of herself that was missing during her time in the United States. She lost her restlessness and was able to transcend her ethnicity, race, and citizenship. The later chapters reveal life in Shanghai and a philosophy based on family ties. In addition, Anna May Wong came to understand her place in the universe and began to think and live as a Daoist.

Part 3 concludes the book with textual analyses of Wong's signature films, from *The Toll of the Sea* (1922), *The Thief of Bagdad* (1924), and *Piccadilly* (1929) to *Shanghai Express* (1932), *A Study in Scarlet* (1933), *Chu Chin Chow* (1934), and *The Lady from Chungking* (1942). What resonates in all her films are the insidious racist ideologies of "Yellowface" and "Orientalism." Understanding these ideologies helps place her work in the context of forces that hampered her aspirations and career. Yet they helped Wong to understand the cinematic nature of European America, the pull of China, and her place on Earth.

In the context of the unequal treatment fostered by "Yellowface" and "Orientalism," readers will note that I mainly use the term "European Americans" to refer to "white" Americans. In the United States, where race matters, this is an attempt to equalize terminology and to level the semantic playing field. Hitherto "white" Americans, denoting color, were juxtaposed against "Chinese" Americans, "Asian" Americans, or "African" Americans, revealing a geography and/or culture. By emphasizing "color" against "geography" and "culture," the term "white" American became unique and extraordinary. It was glaringly unequal in terms of common prerequisites of demarcation. In fact, the term "white" was a representation of power and authority, whereas "nonwhites" were essentially powerless and subordinated. Representing "white" Americans as "European" Americans brings them into the common family of geography and culture. They become part of a European geographical and cultural heritage in the same manner as Asian Americans are part of an Asian geographical and cultural heritage.

This book is an original and significant contribution to the cultural and film histories of the United States and to the cinematic development of Asian America and Asian American studies. From her first unbilled appearance in *The Red Lantern* in 1919 to her final role in the television series *Danger Man* in 1961, Wong transcended silent films, talkies, the London and New York stage, vaudeville, musical revues, and television. Magazines voted her the best-dressed woman in the world and the most beautiful Chinese woman on Earth. Heretofore, there has been no work of such magnitude about the first major Asian American female film star in the world.

This biography is informed by the theories of Edward Said, Michael Omi, Howard Winant, Antonio Gramsci, Stuart Hall, and David Wellman. Methodologically, it follows Robert Yin's case study research design. The book examines data gathered mainly from Anna May Wong's memoir, film articles, extensive interviews in newspaper stories, and extant copies of her films.

Perpetually Cool is timely not only because it examines the life, times, and body of work of the first and most famous Asian American female film star of the United States and even Europe, but also because it is written from a uniquely Asian American perspective and sensibility. This then is the story of a remarkable Asian American actor, writer, and philosopher with political substance, whose legendary humor was always filled with pithy advice.

PART I

LIVING GLOBALLY

ONE

LOS ANGELES:
A CHINESE AMERICAN CHILDHOOD

In 1904, Los Angeles was entering an era in which it would go from being a small, laid-back, palm-tree-lined Western city with big ambitions to a big city with bloated needs and gargantuan appetites. This transformation was energized by a mammoth oil boom between 1899 and 1900, which not only attracted a variety of characters like car dealers, gamblers, hookers, land speculators, lawyers, and prospectors from across America all scratching for a buck, but also new service enterprises like caterers, hotels, restaurants, and merchandise wholesalers.

Before the discovery of oil by Edward L. Doheny (1856–1935), the most widely speculative money explosion had been in real estate. Between 1887 and 1888, the buying and selling of land attracted a vast influx of people from other states and countries. Along with the salubrious weather, horizontal terrain, and wide stretches of land, the enormous fortunes from the "black gold" and gas discoveries and real estate speculation propelled Los Angeles into a fixation with the motor car. The twentieth century embarked on a glorious future, with the automobile as the chief mode of transportation. By 1905 more vehicles were found in the city than in any other community in the United States. In 1916 there were fifty-five thousand cars in Los Angeles county, one for every thirteen inhabitants.[1]

But Los Angeles was neither self-absorbed nor isolationist. In 1887, 2,212 carloads of citrus fruit were shipped to the frozen Midwestern and Eastern states and abroad. The city of Los Angeles alone had 700,000 orange trees.[2] Hunger for citrus fruit in the frozen climes of the United States swelled the incomes of the likes of orange king William Wolfskill and his estate as well as his industry colleagues to $15 million annually. Other products in the food industry also exploded. By 1919 sugar beets yielded an annual profit of $1,300,000, vegetables $1,800,000, dried fruits $6,640,000, and butter $1,525,000.[3] Bank deposits in the city grew from $4 million before the booms to an annual average of more than $25 million beginning in 1905.[4] Between 1900 and 1912 bank clearings in Los Angeles grew from $123 million to $1.25 billion.[5]

From 1890 to 1900 Los Angeles's populace ballooned from 50,395 to 102,479. By 1904 the population was more than 160,000. While this new city on the make doubled its population, the number of Chinese Americans limped from 1,871 in 1890 to 2,111 in 1900. Of that number, 225 were born in the United States. An increase of 240 people in ten years attests to the effects of the Exclusion Act of 1882, a legalized elimination of the Chinese in America. By 1910 the population of the Chinese in Los Angeles had slipped to 1,967, a decrease of 144 people. Of that number, 473 were born in the United States.[6] No doubt some of this collapsing populace in the city and the decimation of Chinese American communities in the country also resulted from the Scott Act of 1888, which denied Chinese American residents with permanent addresses the right of reentry to the United States after a brief sojourn visiting families in China or other places overseas.

Despite the Exclusion Act, a European American device to wipe out the number of Chinese in the United States, Chinese Americans remained steadfast in their attempts to live and prosper in the new world. Chinese American laborers knew that the European American laws to exclude them meant that families with wives and children could never flourish. In 1904, Chang Kiu Sing succinctly proclaimed, "they call it exclusion, but it is not exclusion. It is extermination."[7]

At the dawn of 1904 the Chinese American community in Los Angeles was under intense siege. It needed to redefine itself, establish a new identity, and create a more vibrant future, especially after the 1871 Los Angeles lynchings, when nineteen Chinese men and boys were viciously murdered by a rampaging European American mob. That violent event, the result of some European Americans bent on robbing Chinese American merchants, as well as other acts of terror against Chinese Americans nationwide, eventually culminated in federal legislation in 1882 that banned Chinese immigrants from the United States. In 1902 the law was made permanent.[8]

The physical and legal attacks against Chinese Americans disrupted many families, causing schisms between the women and children in China and the men in Chinese America. Chinese American families with fathers, mothers, and especially children were a rarity not only in Los Angeles but also across the country. Any family in Chinese America was to be cherished. The birth of a Chinese American child was usually a cause for celebration, even though it might not appear to be so in the beginning. Anna May Wong recalled:

> My sister was named Wong Lew (Liu) Ying, but her arrival was not the signal for any rejoicing in the family. In fact, when father found out that his first child was a girl he was so disgusted that he didn't come home for days, mother says. And when he did come home, he wouldn't even look at the baby for some time. Lew Ying was certainly considered a loss.
>
> Then to make matters worst [sic], I was born second in the family, on January 3, 1905. Not only did my father have two girls on his hands, but mother, my sister and I all contracted the measles as a crowning insult. It is a wonder that father ever did get over that. Luckily he had four sons born later, or he might never have been reconciled to his Los Angeles family.[9]

According to the Western calendar, Anna May Wong was born in 1905.[10] Her Chinese name at birth was Wong Liu Tsong, translated as Yellow Frosted Willow. However, the fact that her birth date, January 3, came before the Chinese New Year, which was often between January 23 and February 21, meant that she was born in the Chinese year 1904. Because of this, Wong was born in the Year of the Dragon (1904) and not in the Year of the Snake (1905). That she became a "dragon lady" in some of her films was mere coincidence; it had nothing to do with her year of birth and its attachment to the "dragon" year. This was a fact that would have been lost on the European American directors in their zeal to characterize Wong as a conniving, manipulative, and unscrupulous Chinese femme fatale in films.

During the year of Wong's birth, the Los Angeles Chinese community did not crumble even under the threat of annihilation as a result of various European American acts of law and physical brutality. It continued to be a regional center for Chinese politics. In fact, such small entrepreneurs as Sam Sing Wong (1858–1949), Anna May Wong's father, intersected with China's reformers, revolutionaries, and antiexclusionists. In many ways, the Los Angeles Chinese community, which was a significant player in the overseas Chinese diaspora, was a product of the clash between China and the West during the nineteenth century.

CHINESE POLITICS

The cataclysmic event of the Opium Wars (1839–1842) defines China even today. With the Qing Dynasty (1644–1911) mortally wounded by Western military power, contending forces like reformers and revolutionaries inevitably appeared to either rejuvenate or replace the foreign Manchu monarchy. One of these reformers was the constitutionalist Liang Qichao (1873–1929), who traveled for seven months in 1903 to three Canadian cities and twenty-eight cities and towns in the United States to learn about North American culture and government while soliciting Chinese American support. Invited by the *Baohuang hui* (Protect the Emperor Society), a reformist, antirevolutionary group, Liang visited Los Angeles on October 22, 1903, and other Chinese communities, with a prolonged stay in San Francisco.[11] In his travel memoir, *Xin dalu youji jielu (Selected Memoirs of Travels in the New World)*, he expressed disgust especially with the filth of San Francisco Chinatown and slammed the Chinese Americans for being too regional and not nationalistic enough. He also derided the Chinese Americans who:

> can be clansmen, but not citizens. I believe this all the more since my travels in America. There you have those who have left villages and taken on the character of individuals and come and go in the most free of the great cities and enjoy all that they have to offer, and still they cling to the family and clan systems to the exception of no other things.[12]

Obviously for Liang Qichao this seven-month sojourn did not reveal the true nature of the lives of Chinese Americans in the United States, who had to contend with its discriminatory laws and European American violence. Rather than seek out the root cause of the state of Chinese America, Liang simply blamed its inhabitants for their sorry plight. No doubt merchants and business owners like Sam Sing Wong received these elitist words with either indifference or disdain.

The most direct impact of Liang Qichao's visit on Los Angeles was his endorsement of the Western Military Academy, founded by Homer Lea (1876–1912) in 1902. With tuition and supplies paid for by the Qing government through the Chinese Consolidated Benevolent Association or the Chinese Six Companies in San Francisco, the academy trained a total of 120 Chinese cadets. Located at 627 West Olympic Boulevard in Los Angeles, its avowed aim was to provide Western military education to Chinese officers for the Imperial Army in China. In other cities like Boston, Chicago, Denver, New York, Philadelphia, and St. Louis, European American officers were dispatched

by the Brigade Headquarters in Los Angeles to drill companies of Chinese recruits. In 1905 the first fifty-eight graduates of the Western Military Academy
with training in modern European American drill, troop deployment, and lo-
gistics marched in the Tournament of Roses Parade in Pasadena.[13]
    With the Western Military Academy acting as a publicity arm of the *Bao-
huang hui* as well as training Chinese cadets, Chinese America was more inclined to support the reform movement rather than the revolutionary cause of
Sun Wen (Sun Yat-sen, 1866–1925), the inspirational father of the Chinese
Republic. In 1906 the revolutionaries could only attack the reformists through
their Hong Kong–based newspaper, *China Daily.*
    The debate over which group should revitalize China played well in Chi-
nese America across the United States. In Los Angeles, where Lea's Western
Military Academy played a prominent role among some European Americans,
the constitutional monarchists of the *Baohuang hui* had legitimate foreign support. The capitalist ideas of the Protect the Emperor Society resonated with
many Chinese American merchants and entrepreneurs. But by 1908 Chinese
Americans were cognizant of Liang Qichao's elitist and condescending attitude
to them, as revealed in his *Selected Memoir.* The revolutionaries were beginning
to infiltrate many quarters of Chinese society, especially the government armies
in Wuhan. More important, Sun Wen's band of iconoclasts became more adept
at organizing infrastructure, gathering support, and raising funds. Many Chinese Americans began to perceive the revolutionaries as a viable and distinct
alternative to the Qing Dynasty, which had done little to protect them against
racist European American laws and physical violence.
    Homer Lea also began to see the withering of Chinese American support
for the *Baohuang hui.* In 1908, when Sun Wen visited Los Angeles, Lea offered
him his support.[14] After the Wuhan uprising, which precipitated the fall of the
Qing Dynasty on October 10, 1911, the revolutionaries, now firmly organized
in the *Zhonghua gemingdang* (Chinese Revolutionary Party), descended on
Canada and the United States, seeking support and funds. Even the cofounder
of the Chinese Republic, Huang Xing (1874–1916), visited Los Angeles in
1914 to solicit money and to pay his respects to the wife of Homer Lea, who
became a widow in 1912.[15]

ANTIEXCLUSION BOYCOTT

While the Protect the Emperor Society and the Chinese Revolutionary Party
brought China's politics into the lives of Chinese Americans, the antiexclusion

crusade of Reverend Ng Poon Chew (Wu Panzhao, 1866–1931), which began in 1904, revealed the extent of Chinese and Chinese American rage against an unjust and thoroughly racist piece of legislation. No exclusion act has ever been passed in Congress against any other racial or ethnic group in the United States. At the age of fifteen, Ng Poon Chew emigrated to the United States in 1881, one year before the Exclusion Act was promulgated. While working as a house boy in San Francisco and San Jose, he studied English. With his scholarly inclinations, vast interest in ideas, and a penchant for advocacy and social change, he eventually became a Presbyterian minister before settling in Los Angeles in 1894. To introduce Christianity to Chinese Americans, the Presbyterian church board appointed him minister of the Chinese Presbyterian Mission at 214 North San Pedro, where he began to formulate his ideas about the injustice and unfairness of the European American exclusion laws. To disseminate these provocative notions about immigration, Chew founded the *Chung Sai Yat Po (Chinese Western Daily)* in 1898. This was the first Chinese-language newspaper that would be read widely throughout Chinese America until 1946.[16] At first the tabloid was very tame, with stories about Presbyterianism and Christianity. By 1904 the paper reflected Chew's increasingly progressive ideas against European American exclusionists and their actions.[17] His anger was succinctly revealed in the following diatribe:

> [W]e are now stuck with an Agreement, nominally to protect the Chinese in the United States, but [which] in fact attacks Chinese, whether they are merchants or officials, teachers, students or tourists, [they] are reduced to the status of dogs in America. The dogs must have with them necklaces [their registration] which attest to their legal status before they are allowed to go out [into the streets]. Otherwise they would be arrested as unregistered, unowned wild dogs and would be herded into a detention camp. . . . This is analogous to the present plight of the Chinese in America. Though the treaty was designed to prohibit labor and protect officials, students and merchants, now the U.S. Government is attempting to expel all Chinese.[18]

Assisted by journalist Patrick Joseph Healy, Ng Poon Chew wrote *Statement for Non-Exclusion*. He advocated that China boycott such products as cotton cloth and kerosene coming from the United States. Chinese Americans, especially in San Francisco, took up his call for a ban on American products in China and in Chinese America unless the laws excluding Chinese immigrants to the United States were rescinded.[19] As the main advocate of the antiexclusion campaign, Chew traveled across the country in 1905 urging people to support the boycott while slamming the European American exclusion laws. He was even able to speak to the House of Representatives and was granted an audience with President Theodore Roosevelt. This sideshow of meeting European American politicians, however, was merely to placate the Chinese forces of the boycott. In 1906 the U.S. government not only ignored entreaties by Ng Poon Chew and the Qing representatives but also dismissed the efforts by the Chinese Six Companies in San Francisco, which had established the Anti-Treaty Society *(Juyue zongju)*. If China, which was in a semicolonial situation in the early twentieth century, had been in a more powerful position, and Chinese Americans had had a larger population, more money, and more political clout, the results would have been different.

CHINESE LOS ANGELES

During the early 1900s, when Anna May Wong entered the world, the global politics and immigration conflicts that linked China to the United States and demanded fundamental social and political change were prevalent in Chinese Los Angeles. The community was developing its own unique culture, with a Chinese-language newspaper that became the cornerstone of news from China and Chinese America. A telephone exchange helped bring people together in a more convenient and speedier way. Three temples provided institutionalized worship, and a Chinese theater offered Chinese opera with twenty-five performers to the approximately two thousand Chinese Americans living in the six blocks that would be known as Chinatown. The theater group was the Jok Wah Ming Company from Hong Kong and was housed on Court Street.[20] For a small populace with such cultural institutions, social activism, and political dimensions, Chinese Los Angeles at the turn of the twentieth century sustained a vital and energetic community.

In 1900 there were two or three Chinese restaurants. By 1910 eateries had expanded to fifteen establishments. From three produce houses out of forty-three in the city, Chinese American produce companies exploded to seventeen out of a total of 155 in 1910.[21] No doubt the establishment of the City Market, incorporated on April 13, 1909, helped the produce market in Chinese Los Angeles. More Chinese Americans held shares (40,885) in the enterprise than any other ethnic group. Led by produce dealer Louie Gwan, this was the first attempt at organizing a business venture in the Chinese community on such a large scale.[22] By 1922 there were 184 shops owned by Chinese Americans. By 1923 there were "four large warehouses in the district, a large garage, two small factories, and several wholesale houses."[23] With the advent of Hollywood and the movies, this vital, energetic segment of Chinese America would become part of a new European American industry.

Within this growing Chinese American community, the Chinese Six Companies, based in San Francisco, advocated on behalf of the people and businesses in Chinese America from 1860 to 1910. Until the establishment of an effective Chinese embassy in Washington, D.C., it served not only as the arbitrator in major disputes consigned by regional associations but also as the formal registrar of all Chinese Americans in the West. Throughout its history the Chinese Six Companies fought against European American anti-Chinese laws in numerous court appearances. It organized many campaigns, protests, and boycotts against injustices suffered by Chinese Americans. It also shipped bones back to China, hired private police and security to protect Chinese businesses, and helped the Qing and Republican governments establish Chinese-language schools in Chinese America. In 1913 it succeeded in breaking the stronghold of criminal elements like the *tongs* (organized gangs) by negotiating a Chinese Peace Society. Until 1910, when the Chinese Chamber of Commerce was established, the Chinese Six Companies also intervened in business disputes. No doubt entrepreneurs like Anna May Wong's father, Sam Sing Wong, were influenced by this powerful capitalist regulator.[24]

As a leading member of Chinese Los Angeles by virtue of his ownership of a laundry, Sam Sing Wong was well aware of the political dynamics, social innuendos, cultural forces, and commercial constraints that affected his family. The visits of Liang Qichao, Sun Wen, and Huang Xing to Los Angeles exposed the grim politics of China to Chinese Americans, who often cynically viewed the arrival of these luminaries as merely a plea for cash donations. Ng Poon Chew, however, was a genuine political crusader working tirelessly and spending his own money on a cause that affected all Chinese Americans.

LAUNDRIES

As the proprietor of a business, Sam Sing Wong and his fellow laundry owners were often targeted for funds by the reformers and revolutionaries. If these Chinese iconoclasts did not approach Sam Sing Wong individually, they would have negotiated through his occupational guild, the Chinese Laundry Alliance.[25] This business association was essential for entrepreneurs like Sam Sing Wong, who needed regulations to protect them from competing among themselves. Individual laundries were allocated to certain areas. In San Francisco, businesses could not be less than ten doors from each other. This stress on competitive distance was probably in effect in Los Angeles as well and may explain why Sam Sing Wong's laundry was on North Figueroa Street, some blocks away from the main Chinese American business community. The guild also served its members by threatening force or violence against freelance rivals who were without guild sanction. In addition to setting competitive limits so that everyone would prosper, the laundry guild attempted to protect its members from the racist sentiments of European Americans.[26] The guild even went to court against unjust laws. In 1911, Los Angeles enacted a zoning ordinance banning laundries from specific districts.[27] Since many Chinese American laundries were already flourishing in these areas, this demonstrated blatant racial discrimination. The lawsuits of Quong Wo, Sam Kee, and Hop Wah against these regulations[28] attracted the attention of Los Angeles's Chinese laundry workers and owners, including Anna May Wong's father.

As a business, the laundry trade was easily established and accessible. After the Chinese were driven out of work by European Americans in cigar factories, fruit farms, gold mines, jute and woolen mills, railroad track labor, and road repair and construction, what was left was washing clothing, peddling vegetables, or setting up an eatery. Traditionally women's work, the occupation of washing clothing did not attract macho European American men, who feared a loss in social standing if they opened a washhouse. Without much choice, Chinese American men filled this need for clean clothes. By 1890, sixty-four hundred Chinese Americans worked in laundries across California. Since China had no public washhouses, many learned the trade in the United States by apprenticing at a laundry or working as a house servant in a European American residence.[29]

As a service trade, laundry attracted the ambitious and agile bent on carving out a living on their own. Many Chinese Americans had no choice but to engage in self-employment. The start-up cost was usually from $75 to $200 depending on the rent and equipment. A small empty store or an annex in an otherwise occupied shop would suffice as a locale. Access to a steady source of water, enough soap (usually Swift Pride Washing Powder),[30] serviceable irons, a wood stove that generated enough heat to boil water and heat the irons, a trough to eliminate soiled water, laundry wringers, areas to dry the clothing, and a sign to advertise prices and hours of business were other necessities.[31] In 1896 there were thirty-five laundries in Los Angeles owned by many with the surnames Wong or Lew.[32] No doubt Sam Sing Wong was one of the thirty-five.

Without access to European American banks or lending institutions, capital was often raised through the Chinese Six Companies or, in the case of Sam Sing Wong, through his friendly family association, the *Wong Kong Har Tong,* which included those with the surnames Wong and Ng.[33] The Wong family association was the largest in Canada and the United States. While Anna May Wong may not have called upon this association during her travels throughout North America, she certainly had access to its many branches by virtue of her surname and her father's family affiliations.

With support from family associations and the occupational guild, the laundry trade could provide a living wage of from $50 to $70 weekly for its proprietors.[34] Between the 1880s and the early twentieth century, these wash-houses formed the bulk of the commercial activity in Chinese California. Customers were usually European Americans, bringing in much sought after revenue from outside the Chinese American community.[35]

By the time Anna May Wong and her sister Lulu and brother James were hauling soiled laundry to their father's North Figueroa Street shop, it was a thriving business.[36] If Sam Sing Wong's business approached the occupational standard of the early-twentieth-century Chinese American laundry, the personnel inside the establishment would include two or three hired help as well as Wong himself. Their tasks were separated into washing, ironing, and delivering. "The bigger laundries had large cylindrical dryers while the smaller ones hung their clothes outside to dry. Everything was ironed by hand. Tall cast-iron stoves were constantly fueled by wood or gas to keep the irons hot. When an iron resting on a stove top became cool, the laundryman returned it to the stove then grabbed another iron next to it. As many as a dozen irons would be resting on the stove ready for use."[37]

EARLY DAYS

The activities of the laundry played an influential part in Anna May Wong's early upbringing. She experienced the daily toil and long hours of her parents as they attempted to stave off poverty in European America. This type of work with its small monetary rewards and strenuous labor convinced Wong that this life was not for her. It was probably not the wish of her parents, either.

Besides the everyday drudgery of laundry work, Anna May Wong, as a child of Chinese America, was connected to the politics of China with its reformers and revolutionaries and the politics of the antiexclusion movement in Chinese America by the fact that her parents and their friends and acquaintances were part of the Chinese Los Angeles. She may not have understood the nuances of these political dimensions as a young Chinese Californian, but they would always be part of her Chinese American culture and may have even contributed to her eagerness to visit China and absorb its culture in 1936.

As the second daughter of Sam Sing Wong and Gon Toy Lee, she was the favorite of her father. In later years she described her childhood feelings for her father:

> My father, whose name is Wong Sam Sing [the last name comes first in Chinese] stayed in Michigan Bluffs working in the mines, until he was nineteen years old. He must have been very popular with the children of the town, for when I was a little girl he showed me a lot of pictures taken with them gathered around him. I was very jealous, having always been my father's favorite daughter, and tore the pictures up! I didn't want any rivals for my father's affection.[38]

Wong's family came from the *Taishan* district (*Taishan,* also known as *Sunning* and *Xinning*[39]) in Guangdong province. Her grandfather, Leung Chew Wong, arrived in the United States during the 1850s as part of the great wave of Chinese immigration that exploded from 20,026 in 1852 to 63,000 in 1870.[40] Like the other economic refugees from China, Wong was attempting to escape the devastation of the Taiping Rebellion (1854–1860). Much of the famine and destruction that resulted from this civil war occurred in central and southern China.[41] Wong went straight to Michigan Bluffs outside of Sacramento, where gold had been discovered at John Sutter's Mill in 1848. There Wong opened a store with four other Chinese immigrants. The place doubled as a gambling outlet at night. Before he drowned trying to save a woman who had fallen into a well, Wong and his wife had given birth in 1858 to Anna May Wong's father in Michigan Bluffs.[42]

Sam Sing Wong worked in the mines until the age of nineteen. When he went to China is unclear, but it is known that he was thirty-one when he married his first wife in *Taishan* in 1889. His son by his first wife was born in 1890. He soon returned to California and married a second time. His first wife and son remained in China. Between the births of his first son in 1890 and his first daughter in 1900, he and his Oakland-born Chinese American wife, Gon Toy Lee, moved to Los Angeles.[43] Gon Toy Lee was born in 1887.[44] She was in her early teens when she married Sam Sing Wong, probably in 1900. While living in Los Angeles, Wong rented a building and established a laundry at 241 North Figueroa Street, five to six blocks west of central Chinese Los Angeles, which was bounded by Macy, Alameda, Aliso, and Los Angeles Streets.[45]

NORTH FIGUEROA STREET NEIGHBORHOOD

The laundry was the key to the Wong's family prosperity and stability in an increasingly hostile and unfriendly European America. The business was prosperous enough that the family took a house on Flower Street rather than live on the premise of the laundry, which was common in other Chinese American households with businesses. Sam Sing Wong and Gon Toy Lee were also preparing for a family. Later they returned to live in the North Figueroa Street residence.

As a family unit, Sam Sing Wong and Gon Toy Lee flourished with the birth of daughter Liu Ying, or Lulu, in 1900, Liu Tsong, or Anna May (who was born in the Flower Street, house), in 1905, and the family's first son, James Norman, in 1907. A second son, Frank, was born in 1913, a third daughter, Liu Heung or Mary, in 1915, and a third son, Roger, in 1916. A fourth daughter, Meahretta, or Margaretta, was born in 1920 but died while still an infant, and in 1922 the fourth son, Richard, came into the family.[46]

Since the family lived and worked in the Flower Street and North Figueroa Street neighborhood outside of the main Chinese American community, their friends and neighbors reflected global America. As the only Chinese American family in the North Figueroa Street neighborhood block, the Wong family was surrounded by neighbors who came originally from England, French Canada, Germany, Mexico, Poland, Russia, and Spain. As a child Anna May Wong interacted daily with her Chinese American family and children from Canada, Europe, and South America.[47] She recalled:

> Probably my earliest memory is of playing with some English children who lived next door to us for several years. Until I went to public school it never occurred to me that I wasn't of the same nationality as all the children in the neighborhood. We all played games together and romped with no thought of color or creed to disturb us.[48]

Anna May Wong was popular enough with the neighborhood children that she was even invited into their homes. On one occasion her discovery of a piano at the home of one of her playmates left her bemused:

> I remember, though, that I was very shy as a little child. I had been taught to be decorous, and to carry myself with dignity. [At one house I] became interested in their piano. The mother of the family said that I might touch the black and white keys which particularly enchanted me. So I climbed up on the piano stool. I must have perched on one edge of the stool, for suddenly to my consternation and dismay, I toppled over onto the floor, stool and all.

I was covered with humiliation. I felt that I was disgraced forever, in the home of my friends and that probably I would not be permitted to play with them anymore, because of such undignified conduct. What would my parents say when they found out that I had tumbled off a piano stool and gone sprawling on the floor, before the mother of my playmates? Was this the way Wong Lew Song (Wong Liu Tsong) rewarded her parents, when they sought to make a proper little girl of her?

Probably an American child would have laughed, or cried over her bruises, would have blamed the piano stool for falling over her. But with the Chinese child, I had behaved, according to my upbringing, in an unbecoming manner. I had disgraced myself and my family. It was a tragedy to me, and though I was such a tiny child, I have never forgotten it.[49]

Fearing the loss of her neighborhood playmates, Anna May Wong afterwards went gingerly around them for awhile.[50] "Luckily, my playmates didn't view the accident in so serious a light. I was too embarrassed to approach them for several days, but presently found, to my great relief, that even a girl who fell off a piano stool might still play with them."[51]

SCHOOL DAYS

Lulu and Anna May Wong were brought up speaking English as a way of communicating with their English-speaking neighborhood pals. Anna May said that she "spoke English from my earliest childhood, and when my sister and I were old enough, we entered the California Street School, one of the public schools in Los Angeles."[52] Since California Street was one of the major intersections of North Figueroa Street, where the family laundry was located, this school was within easy walking distance for Lulu and Anna May and accepted Chinese American students. Despite the racist laws and negative attitudes against the evolution of Chinese American families in the United States, by 1929 elementary schools such as the California Street School and the Macy Street School, as well as Custer Avenue Intermediate and Lincoln High Schools, all accepted Chinese American students. By then more than two out of three school-aged Chinese Americans attended Los Angeles public schools.[53]

At many of these European American public schools Chinese children were given Western first names as the very first symbol of assimilation into the larger culture. Thus the oldest Wong sister, Liu Ying, may have been given the name Lulu by a European American teacher. No Chinese would have given the name Lulu to Liu Ying because the name "Liu" was the generational name for all the daughters of Sam Sing Wong and Gon Toy Lee. That was why Anna May was Liu Tsong and Mary was Liu Heung. The teachers at the elementary school where Liu Heung attended may have given her the name Mary. Liu Tsong, however, was not given the name Anna May Wong by a teacher at the California Street School. Wong recalled that the "doctor who brought me into the world named me 'Anna'; my Chinese name is Tsong. When I was old enough to begin to think about a career, I added 'May' to 'Anna' partly because we (daughters) had all four letter names and I wanted to be different and partly because it made a prettier signature."[54] She also remarked that "I liked the suggestion of springtime in 'May.'"[55]

LEARNING MUCH

The California Street School provided Lulu and Anna May with ample opportunities to learn about European America and its many quirks. At first the two sisters looked forward with much anticipation to school. Anna May said, "I was going to enjoy school very much. I would learn my lessons well, and be an obedient student, so that my teachers as well as my parents would feel that I fully appreciated my opportunities."[56] Valuing education, their parents were very helpful. Wong enthused:

> I was very much thrilled to be going to school, not realizing that it was going to mean torture to me before very long. My parents brought me slates, pencils and books with pictures of bright red apples and gaily colored birds and goodness knows what all, in them. I learned the alphabet, and how to write 'This is a Cat. This is a Dog!' I learned to write my name, laboriously, in English. With a whole-souled devotion, I bent over my books as, I had been taught, a proper student should do.[57]

While growing up around the Figueroa Street laundry, Wong understood the value of diversity. She was surrounded by it. She later explained:

> Having played with white children, it seemed perfectly natural to be surrounded by them in school. I had straight black hair and black eyes. They had brown, blond or red hair, hazel or gray eyes. This meant nothing to me. The children in school looked just about like my playmates next door. I was certain that I would enjoy knowing them, when I overcame my shyness enough to mingle with them. They could come to my house and, if they

liked, play with my toys. My mother would give them cookies. My father would always welcome them, even show them the delightful mysteries of the laundry. My father has always been kind to children.[58]

While walking home one day the two sisters were deep in thought about the day's activities, musing about the delights of learning and chatting about their hopes of acquiring knowledge and experience that would help them become successful and earn their parents' praise. Anna May and Lulu had not yet made any friends at the school. It was still early in the school year. But they were optimistic that this would be just a matter of time.

Then came the knife stab which, even today, has left a scar on my heart. A group of little boys, our schoolmates, started following us. They came nearer and nearer, singing some sort of a chant. Finally, they were at our heels.

"Chink, Chink, Chinaman," they were shouting, "Chink, Chink, Chinaman."

They surrounded us. Some of them pulled our hair, which we wore in long braids down our backs. They shoved us off the sidewalks, pushing us this way and that, and all the time keeping up their chant: "Chink, Chink, Chinaman. Chink, Chinaman."

When finally they had tired of tormenting us, we fled for home, and once in our mother's arms we burst into bitter tears. I don't suppose either of us cried so hard in our lives, before or since.[59]

This first racial incident that Lulu and Anna May Wong experienced was almost a rite of passage for young Chinese Americans growing up in European America. No Chinese American entering European America has ever escaped it. European American attempts to demean, degrade, and assert power seemed to be the experience in both overt and subtle ways of every young Chinese American outside of Chinatown. As Wong sought roles in her film career, she began to experience European American racism in more indirect ways, like being passed over for obvious Asian roles that went to a "Yellowface" Myrna Loy in *The Crimson City* (1928) or Luise Rainer as O-lan in *The Good Earth* (1937). Being shunted aside in Hollywood was almost like reliving the early chants of "Chink, Chink, Chinaman."

Lulu and Anna May Wong asked their father why the "little boys [had] pulled our hair, driven us from the sidewalk?"[60] The sisters noted that their father was forlorn to discover that his eldest children had experienced racism so early in their lives. With one on each of his knees, he explained to them that those remarks were meant to shame them because they were Chinese Americans. But he insisted that they should "be proud always of our people and our race. Then he told us that our position in an American community must at times be a difficult one. Perhaps it was just as well for us to find this out now, while we were still young."[61] He said, "accept everything in life as it comes. Hold no malice in your hearts toward anyone."[62]

When she was in her late teens Anna May Wong would not heed her father's advice about "accepting everything in life and holding no malice in her heart." Her decisive action at such a young age would galvanize her attitude to racist acts. She called this event one of the "psychological mileposts" in her life, and she ceased to be on "the defensive":

> When I was about 17, a truck came booming down the street and the driver yelled for me to get out of the way. He called me "Chink." To my surprise I blazed back a remark equally insulting at him and he wilted. That was the turning of a corner for me.[63]

Even at such an early age, Wong was developing the street smarts that would carry her to international fame. As a woman and a person of color in European America, she knew that if she did not speak up on her own behalf, no one would. Even if the notion of Chinese Americans as "model minority" had been prevalent at that time, Wong would never have qualified.

MISSION SCHOOL

The name calling, tormenting, and meanness that Lulu and Anna May's European American male classmates subjected them to continued when they returned to the California Street School the next day. They were pinched, pushed, and slapped. Even the European American girls joined in and made sport of the Wong sisters, who turned the other cheek in the grand Christian manner and suffered in stoic silence. Since the European American teachers never intervened to stop the racial bullying, every day became an escalation of this schoolyard intimidation. Anna May Wong remembered that "we lived in such terror that we couldn't keep our minds on our lessons. We became ill with fright. All of our bright dreams of making friends with our schoolmates, of standing well in our lessons, of winning the approbation of our teachers vanished. We were just two hunted, tormented little creatures, and presently our parents realized that they must find some escape for us."[64]
If the Wong girls' European American classmates were intent on driving out this modicum of diversity at the California Street School, they succeeded. But the more terrifying aspect of this story that has haunted many other Chi-

nese Americans in public schools was the overt approval of racial activities by the teachers and administrators.

Sam Sing Wong and Gon Toy Lee were searching for other educational possibilities in Los Angeles. Certainly they believed in the efficacy and usefulness of education, which could open doors to a better life for their children. If they had been the usual conservative and traditional Chinese or Chinese American parents, they would not have stretched their attention and resources for mere daughters. In the idealized version of Chinese life, a family based on patriarchal relationships was the norm. Daughters were often educated, but only in domestic skills like cooking and sewing as prerequisites to their inevitable marriage. But the family of Sam Sing Wong and Gon Toy Lee was atypical. The parents nurtured both daughters and sons in their pursuit of a good life in the United States.

Finally they discovered that the Chinese Mission School in Chinatown would take their two daughters as students. This new school gave the Wong sisters their first glimpse of Chinese Los Angeles as they studied and played with other Chinese American children. As the major vehicle for converting the Chinese and Chinese Americans to Christianity, mission schools played a large part in the dissemination of the English language and European American culture. In 1923 Nora Sterry, principal of the Macy Street School in Chinatown, observed that "the mission schools, which are largely attended during the day by the younger children, have night classes for adults. These classes, which have been in existence for nearly half a century, have been of great civic value in as much as they taught English to many men."[65]

At the Chinese Mission School, Lulu and Anna May studied the same curriculum as that found at the California Street School. But this segregated school was completely Chinese American. Among the more common subjects, they were given a generous dose of arithmetic, English, geography, and history by European American teachers. To inculcate them with the culture of European America, students were smacked with a ruler if they spoke Chinese. Anna May later exclaimed that "right and left, we were smashing the traditions of our forefathers."[66]

The daily operation of a typical mission school was routine and structured. In a 1926 *Los Angeles Times* story, Myra Paule wrote that "one boy wrestles with fractions, another scratches his head over complicated verbs of the English language which stick out their tongues at rules. The smaller girls learn to sew and sing psalms. Unfortunately, at the same time, they find 'American' names more euphonious. Tea of the olive skin becomes Joan; Oi is Rose."[67]

At the Chinese Mission School in 1912 the Wong sisters most likely encountered similar experiences as those Chinese American students in 1926.

Anna May in particular refused to attend the sewing circle. She remembered that, "I handled my needle awkwardly, stuck it in my finger instead of the doily on which I was laboring, and finally gave up in disgust."[68] Instead, she gravitated to baseball and was considered a "slugger" with the rest of the "home run hitters." She shot marbles with the boys. But after classes ended, the Wong sisters returned to Figueroa Street and the family laundry. Anna May lamented that she could not play shuttlecock with her pals from Chinatown.[69]

CHINESE SCHOOL

Between 1912 and 1917 Lulu and Anna May Wong had the opportunity to see their schoolmates after their classes at the Chinese Mission School, which finished at 3:00 P.M. But this was not to play shuttlecock or any other games. Their father decided that "something must be done with so an unnatural daughter"[70] (Anna May), with her penchant for European American games. So he sent both daughters to Chinese school, which emphasized the learning of not only *Guangdong hua* (Cantonese) but also Chinese culture and civilization.

Unlike the mission schools, Chinese language and heritage schools originated in 1848 in the United States. Informal Cantonese language classes were taught to both adults and children across Chinese America. In 1884 the Chinese Six Companies started the Qing school, with tuition adjusted to a parent's economic situation. At fifty cents a month, even the poorest family could send their children to school. Reminiscent of the curriculum found in Qing China, it was taught by teachers who were licentiates with degrees equivalent to the B.A. or provincial graduates with degrees similar to the Western M.A. Without access to quality European American schools, students in Chinese America were given the opportunity to study for the same provincial and central examinations as students in China. Chinese education in San Francisco in particular was to provide recruits to the Qing bureaucracy.[71]

It was not until 1905 that the Qing government dispatched an envoy to determine the actual language needs of the Chinese American communities.[72] In 1908 Liang Jinggui headed a delegation to provide curricular advice to leaders in Chinese America. Chinese-language schools opened in Sacramento, New York, and later San Francisco. These schools were set up because Chinese American leaders saw a real need for teaching the Chinese language in the United States rather than compelling those Chinese Americans born in the United States to return to China for their education. From a commercial perspective, spoken Chinese was also needed to conduct business in the Chinese American communities across the country.[73] With rampant racial discrimination against Chinese Americans in the European American workplace, even those with university degrees from institutions in the United States needed proficiency in the Chinese language to secure vocational opportunities in Chinese America.[74]

Lulu and Anna May attended Chinese school in Los Angeles for five years after their regular classes at the Chinese Mission school adjourned for the day. That was a total of ten hours of education per day, with the day beginning at nine in the morning and ending at seven in the evening. Besides learning to read, write, and speak the southern Chinese dialect of Cantonese, they were also exposed to the Chinese classics and history. The Wong sisters began to understand the importance of family values and their relationship with each other and with society. The standard Chinese school curriculum included the *Trimetrical Classic,* the *Thousand Words Classic,* and the *Incentive to Study.* Later students would open the pages of the *Four Books* and *Five Classics* of Kong Qiu (551–479 B.C.E.), also known as Confucius in the West. In those books they would learn the efficacy of the Five Relationships, filial piety *(xiao),* and practical learning.[75] These philosophical tracts and Wong's later excursions into Daoism helped shape her philosophy of life.

The teacher of Chinese language and culture was sometimes as grim as the extent of the curriculum. For many Chinese American students, he was a bane to be endured. Wong revealed that "the teacher sat at his desk, a bamboo stick beside him. If one of the pupils showed signs of restlessness or disobedience, whack went the stick across the hands of the offender. Serious disobedience was punished in a severe manner—and not across the hands either."[76]

By the time Lulu and Anna May began attending Chinese school, the Qing Dynasty had collapsed in 1911 and a new Republic of China emerged a year later. Chinese teachers who were Confucian scholars with a license or provincial degrees were now anachronistic in China but even more so in Chinese America. If any were employed at the local school in Chinese San Francisco or Los Angeles, they were put in charge of the education of children born in the United States whose attendance at Chinese school was more at the will of the parents than a result of the enthusiasm of the young. Anna May, however, empathized with the plight of the Chinese teacher in Chinese America. She exclaimed that he certainly "doesn't have it as easy as American teachers do. Not only did he have to devote nearly every hour of every day to teaching, but he lived in a small room partitioned off at the back of the school room. Here he cooked his own meals, and slept. There certainly wasn't much variety in his life. It's not much wonder that he was often stern with us and whacked us with the bamboo stick."[77] Even at the age of twelve or thirteen, Anna May Wong understood life's hardships and vagaries.

At times, the Wong sisters considered Chinese school as a period of play, whenever they could manage any type of recreation within a ten-hour school day. Only thirty minutes, from 3:00 to 3:30 in the afternoon, was allowed outside of school. That was the time it took to walk from the Chinese Mission School to the Chinese school, with only a pause to gulp down a bowl of noodles bought at a nearby cafe for five cents.

Every day in Chinese Los Angeles meant new adventures. Anna May saw the real Chinatown, not the stereotypical one depicted in the media or existing in the minds of outsiders. She was an insider in the life of Chinese America. She revealed that:

> Going to Chinese school, I met many children who lived down in Chinatown. I played in the streets, I mingled with the people there, and so to me it does not seem the mysterious place that it does to Americans. I accepted it as a matter of course—the narrow streets lined with grimy buildings, the shops where Chinese herbs and drugs were sold, the gambling places where white men and Chinese mingled, the overcrowded tenements where the Chinese lived, sometimes entire families in one room, the gaily painted chop-suey restaurants with their lanterns a soft, many colored blur in the dark.
>
> I was glad my parents didn't live in Chinatown, but only as any child might be glad to live in a house with lawns and gardens around it rather than a crowded tenement.[78]

Going to school in Chinese Los Angeles had one distinct advantage over attending school in another suburb or even another city. That was the presence of Hollywood, and Wong took advantage of all that Tinseltown had to offer. It was in Chinatown that she first nurtured the astonishing and untraditional idea of becoming a movie star.

NOTES

1. Paul C. Johnson, ed., *Los Angeles: Portrait of an Extraordinary City* (Menlo Park, Calif.: Lane Magazine and Book Company, 1968), 21. For the land boom, see Lynn Bowman, *Los Angeles: Epic of a City* (Berkeley, Calif.: Howell-North Books, 1974), 186–87.

2. Harry Carr, *Los Angeles: City of Dreams* (New York: Grosset & Dunlap, 1935), 197.

3. Carr, *Los Angeles,* 197.

4. Charles D. Willard, *The Herald's History of Los Angeles City* (Los Angeles: Kingsley-Barnes & Neuner, 1901), 351–52.

5. Louis B. Perry, *A History of the Los Angeles Labor Movement, 1911–1941* (Berkeley: University of California Press, 1963), 5.

6. Figures from 1890 to 1904 are from the United States Department of Commerce, Bureau of Census, eighth through sixteenth censuses, 1860–1940, cited in Roberta S. Greenwood, *Down by the Station: Los Angeles Chinatown, 1880–1933* (Los Angeles: University of California, Institute of Archaeology, 1996), 9. See also Christopher Rand, *Los Angeles: The Ultimate City* (New York: Oxford University Press, 1967), 34; William Mason, "The Chinese in Los Angeles," *Museum Alliance Quarterly* 6, no. 2 (1967): 16.

7. Chang, cited in Victor Nee and Bret de Bary, *Longtime Californ': A Documentary Study of an American Chinatown* (New York: Pantheon Books, 1973), 55.

8. Peter C. Y. Leung, *One Day, One Dollar: Locke California and the Chinese Farming Experience in the Sacramento Delta* (El Cerrito, Calif.: Chinese/Chinese American History Project, 1984), 6.

9. Anna May Wong, "The True Life Story of a Chinese Girl," *Pictures* (August 1926 and September 1926), at http://www.mdle.com/Classic Films/Feature Star/star49e2.htm (accessed 31, July 1998).

10. Some sources still give 1907 as the year of Anna May Wong's birth. This discrepancy may have come from her obituary in the *New York Times,* which stated that she was born in 1907. "Anna May Wong Is Dead at 54: Actress Won Fame in '24," *New York Times,* 4 February 1961, 3. Since then, many works have cited her birth date erroneously as 1907, including Helen Zia and Susan G. Gall, eds., *Notable Asian Americans* (Detroit: Gale Research, 1995), 414; Geraldine Gan, *Lives of Notable Asian Americans* (New York: Chelsea House, 1994), 83–91.

11. Key Ray Chong, *Americans and Chinese Reform and Revolution, 1898–1922* (Lanham, Md.: University Press of America, 1984), 52–55.

12. Liang Qichao, *Xin dalu youji jielu* (*Selected Memoirs of Travels in the New World*), 122, cited in K. Scott Wong, "Chinatown: Conflicting Images, Contested Terrain," *MELUS* 20, no. 1 (spring 1995): 4.

13. Liang Qichao, *Xin dalu youji jielu* (*Selected Memoirs of Travels in the New World*), 68–72, cited in Wong, "Chinatown," 4; L. Eve Armentrout Ma, *Revolutionaries, Monarchists, and Chinatowns* (Honolulu: University of Hawaii Press, 1990), 108–13; Bowman, *Los Angeles,* 340.

14. Ma, *Revolutionaries,* 132.

15. Chun-tu Hsueh, *Huang Hsing and the Chinese Revolution* (Stanford, Calif.: Stanford University Press, 1961), 171.

16. Greenwood, *Down by the Station,* 29. For an extensive analysis of Ng Poon Chew's *Chung Sai Yat Po,* see Sun Yumei, "From Isolation to Participation: *Chung Sai Yat Po [Chinese Western Daily]* and San Francisco Chinatown, 1900–1920" (Ph.D. dissertation, University of Maryland, 1999).

17. Greenwood, *Down by the Station,* 28–29; Corinne K. Hoexter, *From Canton to California: The Epic of Chinese Immigration* (New York: Four Winds Press, 1976), 188–89; Elmer C. Sandmeyer, *The Anti-Chinese Movement in California* (Urbana: University of Illinois Press, 1973), 111.

18. Ng Poon Chew, cited in Hoexter, *From Canton to California,* 189.

19. Ma, *Revolutionaries,* 33–34, 100.

20. For population figure, see Thomas A. McDannold, "Development of the Los Angeles Chinatown, 1850–1970" (master's thesis, California State University, Northridge, June 1973), 21; for Chinese Los Angeles, see J. M. Scanland, *Los Angeles Times,* 9 May 1926; Frank J. Taylor, "The Bone Money Empire," *Saturday Evening Post* (24 December 1932): 48; Franklin S. Clarke, "Seats Down Front," *Sunset Magazine* 54 (April 1925): 33; Bruce Hensell, *Sunshine and Wealth: Los Angeles in the Twenties and Thirties* (San Francisco: Chronicle Books, 1984), 90.

21. Mason, "Chinese in Los Angeles," 16.

22. George Yee and Elsie Yee, "The Chinese and the Los Angeles Produce Market," *Gum Saan Journal* 9, no. 2 (1986): 5–8.

23. Nora Sterry, "Housing Conditions in Chinatown Los Angeles," *Journal of Applied Sociology* 7, no. 2 (November–December 1922): 74.

24. William Hoy, *The Chinese Six Companies: A Short, General Historical Resume of Its Origin, Function, and Importance in the Life of the California Chinese* (San Francisco: The Consolidated Benevolent Association [the Chinese Six Companies], 1942), 19–23.

25. Greenwood, *Down by the Station,* 21.

26. Thomas Chinn, ed., *A History of the Chinese in California: A Syllabus* (San Francisco: Chinese Historical Society of America, 1974), 63; Paul Ong, "An Ethnic Trade: The Chinese Laundries in Early California," *The Journal of Ethnic Studies* 8, no. 4 (winter 1981): 103.

27. Los Angeles California Ordinance 21, 996 (new series), 1911, cited in David E. Bernstein, "Lochner, Parity and the Chinese Laundry," *William and Mary Law Review* 41 (December 1999): 19.

28. Los Angeles Ordinance, cited in Bernstein, "Lochner, Parity," 41.

29. Paul Ong, "Chinese Laundries as an Urban Occupation in Nineteenth Century California," *The Annals of the Chinese Historical Society of the Pacific Northwest* (1983): 72.

30. Roberta S. Greenwood, "The Overseas Chinese at Home: Life in Nineteenth Century Chinatown in California," *Archaeology* 31, no. 5 (September–October 1978): 44.

31. Garding Lui, *Inside Los Angeles Chinatown* (Los Angeles: n.p., 1948), 186–87; Wen-hui Chen, "Changing Socio-Cultural Patterns of the Chinese Community in Los Angeles" (Ph.D. dissertation, University of Southern California, 1952), 336–37; Ronald Takaki, *Strangers from a Different Shore* (Boston: Little, Brown, 1989), 93.

32. Lui, *Inside Los Angeles Chinatown,* 187–89; Chinn, *History of the Chinese,* 63; "How It Is Done," *The Land of Sunshine* 6 (December 1896): 58; McDannold, "Development of the Los Angeles Chinatown," 47.

33. Lui, *Inside Los Angeles Chinatown,* 142–43; Ivan Light, *Ethnic Enterprise in America* (Berkeley: University of California Press, 1972), 23–27; Milton Barnett, "Kinship as a Factor Affecting Cantonese Economic Adjustment in the US," *Human Organization* 19 (1960): 41.

34. Lui, *Inside Los Angeles Chinatown,* 188.

35. Ong, "An Ethnic Trade," 96.

36. Rob Wagner, "Two Chinese Girls . . . ," Stenographic Notes of a Recent Broadcast, *Script* 14, no. 390 (November 21, 1936): 4, 28, cited in Karin Janis Leong, "The China Mystique: Mayling Soong Chiang, Pearl S. Buck and Anna May Wong" (Ph.D. dissertation, University of California, Berkeley, spring 1999), 349–50.

37. Lani Ah Tye Farkas, *Bury My Bones in America* (Nevada City: Carl Mautz, 1998), 79.

38. Wong, "True Life Story of a Chinese Girl."

39. For more on the other four counties, see Lynn Pan, ed., *The Encyclopedia of the Chinese Overseas* (Singapore: Archipelago Press, 1998), 35.

40. Takaki, *Strangers from a Different Shore*, 79.

41. For a succinct analysis of the Taiping Rebellion and its impact on central and southern China, which was the key motivating factor persuading Chinese workers and merchants to immigrate to Southeast Asia, North America, and parts of Africa, Australia, and South America, see Anthony B. Chan, *Gold Mountain: The Chinese in the New World* (Vancouver, B.C.: New Star Books, 1983), 33–36.

42. According to "Funeral for Father of Anna May Wong," *San Francisco Chronicle,* 14 October 1949, 5, Sam Sing Wong was ninety-one when he died in Los Angeles in 1949. If that is correct he was born in 1858.

43. Leong, "The China Mystique," 346.

44. For details of Gon Toy Lee's birth and death, see "Injuries Fatal to Mrs. Wong," *Los Angeles Times,* 12 November 1930, 5.

45. For the proximity of North Figueroa Street and Sam Sing Wong's laundry business to the center of Chinese Los Angeles, see the map of Los Angeles Chinatown in Lui, *Inside Los Angeles Chinatown,* 7.

46. In 1931 when Anna May Wong returned from her first sojourn in Europe, she was met by James at the Los Angeles railroad station. He had just graduated with a master's from the University of Southern California, which would put his age at twenty-four, if the normal duration of two years for the completion of a master's immediately following the bachelor's is assumed. Also greeting Anna May were Frank, who had just graduated from high school, making him eighteen in 1931; Roger, who was fifteen; and Richard, who was nine. "Screen Star Has Her Homecoming After Much Delay," *Seattle Daily Times,* 6 September 1931, 14. A 1920 census recorded a daughter born to Sam Sing Wong and Gon Toy Lee named Meahretta, or Margaretta, who was never mentioned by Anna May Wong, probably because she died as a newborn. Leong, "The China Mystique," 117 n 6.

47. Bureau of the Census, *Thirteenth Census of the United States, 1910 Population, Los Angeles County, CA, April 16, 1910,* United States Department of Commerce and Labor; Bureau of the Census; *Fourteenth Census of the United States, 1920 Population, Los Angeles County, CA, January 19, 1920,* United States Department of Commerce and Labor, cited in Leong, "The China Mystique," 346, n. 8, 347, nn. 9, 10.

48. Wong, "The True Life Story of a Chinese Girl."

49. Wong, "The True Life Story of a Chinese Girl."

50. Helen Carlisle, "Velly Muchee Lonely," *Motion Picture Magazine* 34, no. 2 (March 1928): 101.

51. Carlisle, "Velly Muchee Lonely," 101.

52. Carlisle, "Velly Muchee Lonely," 101.

53. Greenwood, *Down by the Station,* 29–30.

54. Wong, cited in Alice Tildesley, "I Am Lucky That I Am Chinese," *San Francisco Chronicle,* 3 June 1928, 3.

55. Wong, cited in Harry Carr, "I Am Growing More Chinese—Each Passing Year!" *Los Angeles Times,* 9 September 1934, 3.

56. Wong, "The True Life Story of a Chinese Girl."

57. Wong, "The True Life Story of a Chinese Girl."

58. Wong, "The True Life Story of a Chinese Girl."

59. Wong, "The True Life Story of a Chinese Girl."

60. Wong, "The True Life Story of a Chinese Girl."

61. Wong, "The True Life Story of a Chinese Girl."

62. Wong, "The True Life Story of a Chinese Girl."

63. Wong, cited in Carr, "I Am Growing More Chinese," 3.

64. Wong, cited in Carr, "I Am Growing More Chinese," 3.

65. Nora Sterry, "Social Attitudes of Chinese Immigrants," *Journal of Applied Sociology* (July–August 1923), 326–27.

66. Wong, "The True Life Story of a Chinese Girl."

67. Myra Paule, "Chinese Mission Times Amid Squalor," *Los Angeles Times,* 24 January 1926, 20.

68. Paule, "Chinese Mission," 20.

69. Wong, cited in Tildesley, "I Am Lucky That I Am Chinese," 3.

70. Wong, cited in Tildesley, "I Am Lucky That I Am Chinese," 3.

71. Chinn, *History of the Chinese in California,* 68; Charles M. Wollenberg, *All Deliberate Speed* (Berkeley: University of California Press, 1978), 29–32; Hoy, *Six Companies,* 1–29.

72. Theresa Hsu Chao, "Chinese Heritage Community Language Schools in the United States," in *A View from Within: A Case Study of Chinese Heritage Community Language Schools in the United States,* ed. Xueying Wang (Washington, D.C.: National Foreign Language Center, 1997), 4.

73. Yuen Chih Yuen, "A Story of the Education of Chinese Immigrants," *Chung Sai Yat Po,* 26 December 1947 to January 1948, cited in Chen, "Changing Socio-Cultural Patterns," 303.

74. Kim Fong Tom, "Functions of Chinese Language Schools," *Sociology and Social Research* 25 (July 1941): 561.

75. Chinn, *History of the Chinese in California,* 69; Nee and de Bary, *Longtime Californ',* 151.

76. Wong, "The True Life Story of a Chinese Girl."

77. Wong, "The True Life Story of a Chinese Girl."

78. Wong, "The True Life Story of a Chinese Girl."

TWO

HOLLYWOOD: FILM APPRENTICESHIP

Two years after the birth of Anna May Wong, the idea of motion pictures as an industry swept into Los Angeles in the obscure personalities of Francis Boggs (1870–1911) and Thomas Persons in 1907. Employed by the Selig Company in Chicago, their December train ride into California was the final step in the completion of a one-reeler, *The Count of Monte Cristo*. With the Midwest caked in a white winter, Boggs as director and Persons as cinematographer were seeking suitable external venues for their summer scenes. The primitive lighting and cameras were not conducive to summer scenes in a Chicago studio. The next best thing, therefore, was actually to go shoot the summer scenes in either Florida or California. But Florida was always boringly the same. In California, there were choices. Filmmakers could choose such varied terrain as deserts, forests, lakes, and mountains for their locations. Oil patches, orchards, wineries, and urban locales like Chinese Los Angeles and traffic scenes with numerous automobiles were other possible visuals. Of course none of these locations was ever in snow drifts or torrential rainfall.

That Boggs left the Chicago performers out in the cold while he hired a Los Angeles cast to replace them did little for continuity in the film. Having different performers playing the same roles at different periods in filming might have been disconcerting for the audience. But the cinema was such a craze in

1907 that producing any film was almost like having a license to print money. Producers figured that if they filmed it, the people would come. Not only did *The Count of Monte Cristo* improve the profit margin of the Selig Company, but it was the first picture ever shot in California. This began the Hollywood movie industry.[1]

By the time Wong encountered cinema, Adolph Zukor (1873–1976) had already shown *Queen Elizabeth* (1912), one of the first acclaimed dramatic films. She may not have seen this film, but she was a witness to many scenes shot for other Hollywood pictures. She remembered:

> We were always thrilled when a motion picture company came down into Chinatown to film scenes for a picture. I would play hookey from school to watch them at work, though I knew I would get a whipping from my teacher, and later from my father, for it. I would worm my way through the crowd and get as close to the cameras as I dared. I'd stare and stare at these glamorous individuals, directors, cameramen, assistants, and actors in grease-paint, who had come down into our section of town to make movies.[2]

The first Hollywood actress that she saw performing take after take on location in Chinese Los Angeles was Mae Murray (1883–1965) in *To Have and To Hold* (1916).[3] Wong was dazzled by her performance but was perplexed by the dirty, ragged clothing that Murray wore. She recalled that she

> couldn't figure out at the time that she was dressed that way because of the character she was portraying in the picture. To me, she should have been all dressed up in ermine, and blazing with diamonds. So this was the way a movie star looked! I was quite disgusted. We children talked about it for days. Yet my first ambition to become a film actress myself was born at this time. Perhaps I thought I'd show Miss Murray how a movie star should dress. She little realized what was going on in the mind of the serious, silent little Chinese girl who watched her at work.[4]

From merely watching scenes being shot and performers working their characters, Wong developed a plan that would eventually take her to a Hollywood studio, Paramount, where she would sign multipicture deals, and to German and British studios where she would become a global celebrity with fame and fortune at her heels. The first step in her cinematic education was simply to watch films and discover camera work, character development, dramatic nuances, scene transitions, and story line. She reasoned, what better school for an aspiring movie star than the pictures themselves?

Yes, I would become a movie star too. Having made up my mind to this, the next step was to watch motion pictures on the screen. There were, and still are, a great many motion picture theaters on Main Street, not far from Chinatown. They're not very stylish places. No thought is given to ventilation or comfortable seating. An electric piano furnishes the music, and with many of the pictures, the titles are run in Spanish, as the audiences are composed largely of Mexicans, many of whom do not read English.[5]

At the age of eleven Wong began cutting classes so that she could become immersed in the making of motion pictures on location in Chinese Los Angeles. Then she began skipping more school to attend the movies. Paying a nickel for each show, she sat enchanted by the performances of Ruth Roland (1892–1937) in *The Red Circle* (1915) and Pearl White (1889–1938) in *The Perils of Pauline*. Attendance was becoming a habit. Roland was her idol, and Wong would sit through more than one performance so that she could learn as much as possible about film acting.[6] By the time she had watched the same Ruth Roland characters on screen two or three times, Wong had memorized the animation, emotions, nuances, and body language of Roland's acting.

Wong vividly remembered what she did after she had thoroughly digested Ruth Roland's acting technique:

And then I would rush home and do the scenes I had witnessed before a mirror. I would register contempt, shame, reproach, joy and anger. I would be the pure girl repulsing the evil suitor, the young mother pleading for her baby, the vampire luring her victim.

One day, I was doing a big crying scene before my mirror when my mother walked into the room. She must have been amazed to see me with tears streaming down my face clutching a bit of lingerie to my bosom, but she said nothing. She was very considerate of one whom she must have thought at least peculiar. She left the room without a word.[7]

If Gon Toy Lee was silent about her second daughter's play acting, Wong's brother James was not. She remembered:

Using my bed for a stage, I arranged the tiny dolls and made up all sorts of dramas of my own. When my brother Jimmy got old enough, I pressed him into service and we acted plays that I made up. Jimmy, being all boy, finally struck and refused to play act any more.[8]

Besides witnessing actual scenes being shot in Chinatown locales and sitting entranced at the Plaza Theater while watching Ruth Roland, Pearl White,

Mae Murray, and Wallace Reid (1891–1923) perform, Wong also went to the source for guidance and knowledge. While on shooting breaks she would pester the directors, cinematographers, and even the property men with her many questions about the business. Around the location shoots and studio lots she became well known as the "curious Chinese child." But most of the Hollywood people had a schedule to meet and therefore had little time for an eleven-year-old, even during their slow periods. Stars like Mae Murray kept to themselves in their limousines while they waited for their scenes.[9]

JAMES WANG AND *THE RED LANTERN*

While Anna May Wong cruised the Chinatown locations soaking in all the acting nuances and techniques in early Hollywood, there was a small group of Chinese American film performers in Los Angeles who already played a variety of parts in movies with themes about China. Such films as *The Chinese Lily* (1914), *The Yellow Traffic* (1914), *The War of the Tongs* (1917), *Mystic Faces* (1918), and *City of Dim Faces* (1918) accentuated the "Yellow Peril" stereotype and negative images of the Chinese as opium addicts, white slavers, lawbreakers, thugs, and debauchers. In *City of Dim Faces,* a Christian minister turned actor was one of the Asian American cast. Like Ng Poon Chew, James Wang was a Christian minister who immigrated to the United States in the 1880s. For creative and intelligent individuals like Chew and Wang, the ministry was the quickest and surest avenue to developing their talents as social or theatrical performers. While Chew's stage was the political arena, Wang looked to the cinema for his expression.

James Wang traveled widely in search of roles and was not averse to playing evil characters. Because of this, movie directors in Chicago and New York were willing to hire him to portray Chinese villains.[10] In 1919 he was in two important films about the Chinese. His first such role was as the Buddhist priest in D. W. Griffith's *Broken Blossoms,* starring Lillian Gish as Lucy, the young waif, and Richard Barthelmess in "Yellowface" as the emasculated Cheng Huan. Strangely, Griffith never acknowledged Wang as the temple priest but did reveal Moon Kwan as his technical adviser in the credits.[11]

In 1918 Chinese Los Angeles was the site for the most extravagant Chinese epic yet produced. This was Alla Nazimova's interpretation of the Boxer Rebellion in *The Red Lantern* (1919). Since James Wang had now relinquished his Baptist collar for the occupation of actor, casting agent, and technical adviser, Albert Capellani hired him to work in all those roles. In particular, he was summoned to produce up to three hundred Chinese or Asian extras as lantern carriers and five hundred in other roles. Wong remembered:

> My first opportunity to work in a picture came in 1918. Nazimova was filming *The Red Lantern* and she was using a good many Chinese as extras in the picture. James Wang, a friend of my father's, who has worked in a good many motion pictures, took me out to the Metro studio and introduced me to the assistant director. You can imagine how thrilled I was when the assistant director accepted me. To actually be working with Nazimova exceeded all my wildest hopes. The studio was an enchanted fairyland to me, and though I was only an extra, I felt sure that I'd see my name in electric lights before long.[12]

Wong also recalled that James Wang told her: "Your eyes are large and your features stand out clearly. There is no reason why you should not make good if you are willing to work hard. You will do."[13] When she heard these encouraging words, Wong remembered, "I felt flattered until I learned that he had just had an order for 600 Chinese actors in a hurry and hadn't been able to find but fifty."[14]

Chosen by Capellani to play a lantern carrier, Wong admitted that she was not only excited by the prospect of a first movie but also "felt the responsibility for the whole movie industry on my shoulders."[15] She also wanted to act like a film star:

> I had noticed that actresses were "made up" on the sets, so I produced a grand scenic version of myself. I borrowed my mother's rice powder rag and fairly kalsomined my face. With the most painstaking effort, I managed to curl my straight Chinese hair. As a finish[ing] touch, I took one of our Chinese red papers, wet it and rubbed off the color onto my lips and cheeks.
>
> The director looked at me with astonishment and gasped: "Good God!" Two costume women, under his orders, seized me, rubbed off my fine red cheeks and washed down my hair until they got the curl out of my hair.

With such care by Albert Capellani and the introduction by James Wang, Anna May Wong's first taste of show business was the thrill of a lifetime, especially for the fourteen-year-old daughter of a laundryman. But what she may have been even more enthusiastic about was the stipend that went with the work as an extra. Chinese American extras were paid $7.50 per day. That was $1.50 more than European American extras, especially in films with a Chinese or Chinese American story line.[16] After *Broken Blossoms* and *The Red Lantern,* an outburst of "yellow" movies crept into the movie theaters. Now audiences could choose from among *The Pagan God* (1919), *Crooked Streets* (1920), *Dinty* (1920), *The Yellow Typhoon* (n.d.), *The Invisible Hand* (1919–1920), *The First Born* (1921), *Shame* (1921), *The Toll of the Sea* (1922), *Drifting* (1923), and *The Purple Dawn* (1923).

Audiences could also select *Lotus Flower* (1921) for their entertainment. This was one of the first films in Chinese America completely financed by Chinese American entrepreneurs. The Wah Ming Motion Picture Company, or James B. Leong Productions, produced the film from an original story by Leong But-Jung (James B. Leong, 1889–1967). The Shanghai-born Leong's sole purpose for setting up his production house was to make films with only positive images of the Chinese. Wong's inspiration, James Wang, was a member of the cast. Unfortunately for Chinese America, Leong's Wah Ming Motion Picture Company lasted for just one motion picture.[17]

THE FIRST MOVIES

In 1919, when Wong first tasted Hollywood show business, Chinese Los Angeles was creating its own entertainment vehicles. In this whirlwind of cinematic activity, she was savoring her role as lantern bearer in *The Red Lantern* and continued to dream the big dream of becoming a Hollywood movie star. When *The Red Lantern* was finally released for public screening, Wong was one of the first to see the picture. What she saw might have dampened the enthusiasm of even the most ardent movie apprentice. But this "curious Chinese child" was not to be dissuaded by her first stab at fame. She recalled that

> in the flu epidemic when Nazimova was making *The Red Lantern*, I had my first chance as an extra. I was enchanted. Afterward I saved up my pennies, going without lunch for more than a week to take five girl friends up to the top gallery of the old California Theater on Main Street to witness my triumph. I bought a balcony seat to see how I would look on the screen. I watched the picture eagerly, anxiously then despairingly. I could not find myself at all. All we saw were three dim Chinese girls walking by with lanterns. "Which one is you?" my girl friends asked. "I . . . I don't know." I faltered. "I think I must be the outside one."[18]

If she had been one of only three extras Wong might have been able to discover herself in *The Red Lantern*. But she was one of three hundred extras, each with a similar costume, and she became just one anonymous Chinese American girl in a sea of lantern carriers.[19] Although Wong was unable to pick herself out of a cast of exotic extras, movie directors Marshall Neilan, Colin Campbell, and Fred Niblo had different perceptions. They saw something special in the Chinese American fourteen-year-old with the large eyes and ambition to burn. Even though they only cast her as an extra in *Dinty* (1920), *The First Born* (1921), and *Mother O'Mine* (1921), respectively, Marshall Neilan was so captivated by Wong that he wrote the part of Toy Sin in *Bits of Life* (1921) especially for her. Now not only could she identify herself in the picture, she was even in the credits!

By 1921 Wong had already been allowed by her father to leave Chinese school behind because she had fallen ill under the strain of the regimented, ten-hour school days. She had completed her middle school education at the California Street School, where she returned with Lulu for the fifth grade in 1916. None of the catcalls and abusive language continued at that school. Wong also became less interested in athletics. She revealed that:

> As I grew older, I lost much of my tomboyishness that had made [me] such a good baseball player in my kid days, and tried to be as dignified as possible.
>
> But the boys in the Chinese school always thought of me more as a pal than a girl to be admired. These boys were in the habit of sending "love letters" to the girls they liked, the notes being carried back and forth by younger pupils. But not one of the boys ever sent me a love letter! I felt very unhappy over this for a time, especially so because my sister received dozens of notes, but presently I gave up bothering about it and lost interest in the boys entirely. After all, I had a career ahead of me. I was going to be a movie star.[20]

The irony was that these pubescent Chinese American lads had absolutely no idea that Anna May Wong would become a huge Hollywood star. She was even proclaimed in 1934 by the Mayfair Mannequin Society of New York to be the "world's best dressed woman" amid much controversy, especially from Alma Whitaker of the *Los Angeles Times,* who remarked:

> There are a lot of Hollywood charmers to challenge Anna May Wong's new won sartorial supremacy. Since the Mayfair Mannequin Academy of New York, on a poll of costume designers of many countries, voted Anna May "The best dressed woman in the world," opinion has buzzed mightily. Dangerous laurels, Anna May.[21]

In 1938 *Look* magazine proclaimed her the "world's most beautiful Chinese girl."[22] She would be admired by countless men and women throughout the Western world and much of Asia, including China, Hong Kong, Japan, and the Philippines. In Europe she would be received by royalty. Lulu, the sister who received numerous love letters, was Anna May's alter ego and companion in Europe and Asia. Lulu's sole film credit was a role in *Eskimo* (1934).

But in 1916 stardom was simply a foolish childhood dream, even more so for a child of color living in European America. That year all Anna May Wong was concerned about was shedding formal schooling from her responsibilities and concerns. After leaving the California Street School at the age of fifteen, when she had already appeared as a Hollywood extra, she enrolled at Los Angeles High School, where she majored in art. Wong remembered that "my two years at the old Los Angeles High School were perhaps the happiest years I've known."[23] Besides attending classes regularly, she excelled in tennis, winning singles and doubles in the school tournament. But she fell ill again on an excursion with her high school classmates to a Mount Baldy girl's camp. Having missed several months of school and with Hollywood movie directors beckoning her, Wong decided to leave Los Angeles High School with two years remaining to graduate. At sixteen she had already appeared in several pictures. She was so focused in her ambition and possessed such a strong belief in her own innate abilities that this Chinese American woman named "Yellow Frosted Willow" was ready to take on Hollywood on her own terms.[24]

Anna May Wong was no stranger to hard work and long hours. She had worked at her father's washhouse almost since the day she could haul laundry. At fourteen she was working at Hollywood's Ville de Paris when James Wang approached her about a job as an extra in *The Red Lantern*.[25] In 1919 Sam Sing Wong had found secretarial work for his daughter in hopes that she would find a worthy occupation after graduating from high school. With such a steady job, he reasoned that she could work and save a little, thus exhibiting an industriousness and thrift that would attract a Chinese American suitor, eventually resulting in a traditional wedding and children.[26] But marriage was hardly on Wong's life agenda. With an impending career in the movies, she succinctly stated her opinion of Chinese American women who had married, just before she set sail to Europe with her sister, Lulu, in 1928:

> The girls I went to school (Chinese school) with have married and seem to hit it off in the free and easy American style. But already they have many heirs to worship at the grave. Chinese girls in this country try to be American on the outside; they wear American clothes or if they wear Chinese costume, I noticed that they have discarded the trousers for the short skirts! Most of them have bobbed their hair and they look at me in a strange manner because my hair is long. They have marcel waves and permanent waves

and their heads [look] like American heads at a little distance. But they cannot change inside.[27]

Marriage was certainly on her parents' minds. Like many traditional fathers who worried about their daughters' future, Sam Sing Wong believed that
a good, steady job, especially in European America, was an apprenticeship for
a possible courtship and wedding. Unfortunately for this parental ambition,
Anna May proved to be absolutely incompetent at shorthand. Luckily for her
film ambitions, she was told by her boss not to return after a week of dicta-
tion.[28] Bad shorthand may have saved this ambitious Chinese American
woman from a conventional Chinese American marriage that held little prom-
ise of a good life or even an interesting one in European America.

After quitting high school in 1921, teenage Wong, who was now five
feet, seven inches tall, modeled furs at several trendy Los Angeles furriers in
between acting jobs.[29] Her parents were so proud of her work as an elegant
model, mainly because it was not acting, that her father once clipped out an
advertisement of Wong attired in a magnificent mink coat in the rotogravure
section of a Los Angeles Sunday paper. Even though she was not hired for
any substantive parts in Hollywood movies, Wong was getting some decent
work as a glamorous model. This exposed her physical attributes not only to
the Los Angeles rich and famous but also to movie directors and producers
and the Los Angeles reading public. That she was modeling highly expensive
and fancy clothing was in itself astonishing because being a model was one
of the excluded classes of people. In this case, one Chinese American
woman's looks and appearance transcended racial barriers. Wong was probably not surprised by her father's clipping out the newspaper's advertisement,
but the reaction her father got to what he did with the item was amusing.
Wong remembered:

> My father was so impressed by my elegance that he cut the picture out and
> sent it to my half-brother in China who had never seen me.
> My brother wrote back: "Tsong is indeed very beautiful but please send
> me the dollar watch on the back of the picture."
> The moral of this story—and Confucius never said it—is: "a fur coat
> doesn't tick."[30]

This story illustrates Wong's legendary humor, a quality that would assist her
through some of her toughest times in Hollywood.

By 1921 Anna May Wong was ready for a more challenging but not nec-
essarily a starring role. She had apprenticed in films, gaining recognition in the

credits as Lotus Blossom in *Shame* (1921) and Toy Sing in *Bits of Life* (1921). The opportunity for a meatier part came in 1922, when she made cinematic history at the age of seventeen. Director Chester Franklin selected her to star in the first two-color Technicolor film, *The Toll of the Sea* (1922), photographed with red and green filters. Written by Frances Marion, the picture was an adaptation of *Madame Butterfly*, with the predictable sacrifice by the heroine, Lotus Flower, played by Wong.[31]

Recognizing her talents in *The Toll of the Sea*, Hollywood's greatest bankable male performer at that time, Douglas Fairbanks, cast Wong in the role of the Mongol spy and infiltrator in his spectacular film *The Thief of Bagdad* (1924). Although many Chinese Americans thought Wong's part was demeaning, this film propelled her to international fame. Her father gave his parental consent to Fairbanks allowing his nineteen-year-old daughter to wear a revealing costume as the princess's handmaid.[32] In an interview with the *New York Times*, Douglas Fairbanks remarked:

> Then there was the trouble with Anna May Wong who impersonated the Mongol slave. Anna is a very hard worker and usually a modest little person. But she chanced to say one day that her name meant "Two Yellow Willows" and a publicity man who had only half heard what she said sent out a yarn saying that Anna May Wong meant "Two Yellow Widows." It took some time to tell her that it was in error, and I finally, even then, had to write a letter to her honored parents before she would agree to put on the Mongol slave costume, which, as you will see, is not much of a job, seeing that Mongol slaves are merely attired for comfort.[33]

Amusingly, the "modest little person" to whom Fairbanks referred was, at five feet, seven inches, taller than the star himself.

That she needed her parents' permission to dress in a provocative way in *The Thief of Bagdad* illustrated that Wong still relied on them for support. Although she sought her parents' approval, she knew that they initially did not approve of her career as a movie actress. It was alien to them, beyond their comprehension. During her second role as an extra in Marshall Neilan's *Dinty* (1920), her mother said to her, "Anna May, I wish you would not have so many photographs taken. Eventually you may lose your soul."[34] Wong's response was respectful but firm. She said that "I couldn't tell my mother that her religion and superstitious beliefs were a lot of bunk. That would be cruel. So, I just tried to explain to her that my life must be lived along different lines than hers had been. It might not be a happier life, but that was for time to tell. It was my life."[35] Even then, Wong was planning to leave the family home.

BEYOND *THE THIEF OF BAGDAD*

Just after the completion of *The Thief of Bagdad,* Wong moved out of the North Figueroa Street household and into her own apartment. She became a European American flapper with collegiate clothes to match and "spoke the slang of day-after-next."[36] During this period, she also experienced her first real taste of Tinseltown treachery and duplicity.

Immediately following the release of *The Thief of Bagdad* in March 1924, Wong's sizzling performance attracted not only such directors as George B. Seitz and Herbert Brenon, who cast her respectively in *The Fortieth Door, The Alaskan,* and *Peter Pan,* but also self-promoters like Forrest B. Creighton. Her interaction with Creighton, which led to a superior court ruling, demonstrated clearly that even at nineteen years old, Wong was not the dainty, deferring, giggling, hand-over-mouth Asian woman often portrayed by Western media with "Orientalist" stereotypical attitudes toward people of color. Her career was her business, and she was tenacious at defending it, even slapping affidavits against her nemeses.

In March 1924 Wong and her manager, George M. Martin, signed an agreement in Los Angeles with Forrest B. Creighton stipulating that the promoter would raise $400,000 in thirty days to bankroll "The Anna May Wong Productions."[37] Since this was to be a film series of productions accentuating "ancient Chinese legends," Wong was obviously looking to cash in on her ethnic heritage. With "The Anna May Wong Productions," her business acumen was being developed.

According to Creighton, however, his copy of the agreement revealed that Anna May Wong had signed a three-year service contract as well as a partnership agreement. It also stated that the actress was liable for certain debts Creighton might incur. Upon hearing of Creighton's duplicity, Wong immediately filed three affidavits. She and George M. Martin contended that Creighton's current contract had been reconfigured without their consent. Even the $400,000 figure that he was to raise for "The Anna May Wong Productions" had been suspiciously omitted.

In the meantime, Forrest B. Creighton was exploiting the fact that he had Anna May Wong's signature on a contract to produce "ancient Chinese legends." This turned out to be a ploy to entice potential investors in "The Anna May Wong Productions" as an eminently profitable enterprise. Creighton even told Wong that M. S. Jung and Louis E. Mauthe would be two of the main backers for this film series. However, in an affidavit Jung denied that he was ever a financial supporter, while Mauthe lamented that "through fraud and misrepresentation" by Creighton, he did put up money for incorporating the enterprise and other legal expenses.

Upon hearing from Wong that Creighton's "plan was to use her name in a stock-selling venture for his own benefit," Superior Judge Roche issued a temporary injunction. This prohibited Creighton from continuing with "The Anna May Wong Productions." Faced with devastating evidence against him, Creighton eventually backed off from representing Wong's "ancient Chinese legends" series.[38] This episode was another part of her apprenticeship in the commercial realities of Hollywood as she sought to navigate her cinematic career among cutthroats and shady characters. With this legal experience lodged in her psyche, she never hesitated to sue any interloper who might damage her career.

While the legal wrangling after *The Thief of Bagdad* was obviously disconcerting, Anna May Wong's 1924 film work following her performance in Douglas Fairbanks's extravaganza was equally dismal. *The Fortieth Door* and *The Alaskan,* especially, were hardly exceptional films, and the acclaim she received for *The Thief of Bagdad* seemed short-lived. In fact, she may have discovered the old Hollywood adage that "you're only as good as your last performance."

If the immediate period after *The Thief of Bagdad* in 1924 was disheartening for the aspiring actress, the year 1925 was devastating. She was cast in only one film, *Forty Winks.* At the age of twenty, Wong was fast on her way to becoming a has-been.

Yet knowing European American Hollywood's penchant for extolling whiteness as a key determinant to stardom, Chinese America's first movie star already had a definite plan to forestall her early demise in Tinseltown. Besides her unyielding ambition, uncommon good looks, multiple talents, and exemplary work ethic, Wong also had plenty of perseverance and a natural inclination to learn new things.

THEATER AND VAUDEVILLE

Even before her role as the adventuress Annabelle Wu in *Forty Winks,* cinematic work was so uncertain that Wong decided that theatrical performances would not only help pay the rent but also provide a new direction in her acting career. She debuted at San Francisco's Orpheum Theater in January 1925 with her first onstage work as a "speaking actress."[39] In addition to film performances, Wong wanted to expand her repertoire in speaking parts. She may not have known that talking pictures would debut two years later with *The Jazz Singer* (1927), but she was astute enough to realize that she needed venues for new work. Her first stab at theatrical performances was an attempt to reposition herself in this fast-changing business of theater and motion pictures. That meant acquiring live acting, dancing, and singing experience that would benefit her onstage and perhaps in "talkies" when that form of cinematic productions became an eventuality. She may have realized the limitations of silent films even at the age of twenty and decided to seize every opportunity to expand her theatrical resume. Anna May Wong's vaudeville act at the Orpheum Theater consisted of a Chinese lullaby and a popular ditty called "Sally." She was adamant in developing this side of her career. She proclaimed:

> If I go on with the act, and I think now that I shall, I will put in a Nautch dance after the lullaby, and perhaps do a short dramatic recitation. I love dramatic things, and I have picked out several little poems that I should like to do. I am doing this vaudeville engagement as a step toward real dramatic work. I have always wanted to act in serious plays. I hope I shall have the opportunity some day to do them. In the studio one can act only before the other workers, and can't get the effect. I think I like the stage better.[40]

Wong's penchant for theater work was not only an aesthetic and professional decision but also a survival tactic to remain in the profession of acting. She realized early on that European American Hollywood, with its racial bias in favor of "whiteness," would cause her great difficulties in furthering her career. She exclaimed that "it is hard to get into pictures, but it is harder to keep in them. Of course, it is nice enough if one gets a five-year contract as some of the actors do, but freelancing which I do, is not easy. You see there are not many Chinese parts."[41] As Wong was eventually to learn, even with an abundance of Chinese or Asian roles, the entrenched idea of "Yellowface" in European American popular culture would prevent her from landing plum parts.

Wong's live theatrical experience in San Francisco later expanded into a small vaudeville troupe, which toured the Midwest in the spring of 1925. As part of the Cosmic Production Company, she accompanied Harry Anderson, Jack Daugherty (1895–1938), D. S. Fridner, Edna Gregory (1905–1965), Helen Holmes (1893–1950), Cullen Landis (1895–1975), Ruth Stonehouse (1892–1941), and Harry L. Tighe, the company's president, to Kansas, Nebraska, and Iowa. The business manager of the tour was H. A. de Veaux.[42]

Wong was in the midst of performers who could supply her with real-world knowledge about the stage and the world of film. A high school dropout at the age of sixteen, Wong undoubtedly never envisioned that four years later she would be in another, more relevant, and more demanding "school" where the curriculum was as varied as the teachers. Always a quick study, she constantly asked questions and learned as much as her waking hours permitted.

These veteran performers dispensed information and wisdom not only about acting in theater and film but also about the realities of the business. Certainly the acclaim for her roles as Lotus Flower in *The Toll of the Sea* and the Mongol spy and infiltrator in *The Thief of Bagdad* gave her some leverage among her more experienced colleagues as they traveled from California to Kansas, Nebraska, and Iowa.

The Midwest in the spring can be as enticing as its breathtaking sunsets and vast open plains. For Wong this was an opportunity to see a bit of the United States, expand her repertoire, and experience the working nature of a road show. Although there might have been some small theatrical triumphs, the company fell into a few misfortunes because of ineffective advance publicity and faulty financial management.

In Kansas City, Kansas, the company was booked to play at the city's convention hall. A marching band and a police escort traveled with the performers to the hall. It was to be an extravaganza the likes of which the municipality of Kansas City had never seen. But what was missing from the whole scenario were just those seeing customers, at $2 a person. In a hall with a capacity of eighteen thousand, not one seat was taken, much to the astonishment and disillusionment of Wong and her fellow performers. Only the media were present. Understanding the theatrical adage of "better negative reviews than no reviews," the Cosmic Production Company performed its acts in front of a few journalists and maybe even members of the marching band and the local Kansas City constabulary.[43]

Atkinson, Kansas, the next stop, was little better with its sparse crowds. Surely, the performers reasoned, Omaha, Nebraska, across the state line, would yield more positive results. While the production quality of the vaudeville was professional and entertaining, the financial side was not as robust. After the performers had left for Des Moines, Iowa, the Hotel Fontannelle called the city's local police to arrest Wong and her theatrical colleagues for running out on their hotel bill of $237. What transpired was that the business manager, H. A. de Veaux, had paid for only his own expenses at the hotel.[44] Whether he simply neglected to pay the bill of the rest of the production company or pocketed the budgeted amount, no one will ever know. Through his lack of action, twenty-year-old Wong was facing imprisonment.

After the company's members were transported to the local Des Moines jailhouse, de Veaux finally paid the delinquent $237. Arguing that they had suffered from "false" arrest and the humiliating episode of being paraded to the jail, the performers contemplated suing the hotel for $70,000. The owner of the company, Harry L. Tighe, said that "he felt partially responsible for the 'shameful' publicity given his company and laid all the blame on 'poor management' and financial difficulties arising therefrom of which neither he nor any of his companions were aware."[45] Following the release of Wong and her fellow actors, Tighe promptly fired de Veaux and declared that the tour would continue.

BACK TO HOLLYWOOD

With the vaudeville experience under her belt, Anna May Wong returned to screen acting in 1926 with small "Orientalist" parts as Nan Lo in *Fifth Avenue,* Ohtai in *A Trip to Chinatown,* Oneta in *The Desert's Toll,* and a lead role in *The Silk Bouquet,* also known as *The Dragon Horse.* For about three years, Wong, as a flapper, had pursued assimilation into European American culture with the same tenacity that she pursued her film career. But with such a failure on the road, the continuation of banal roles, and weariness of her flapper life, Wong returned to the family's North Figueroa residence in 1926 with the encouragement of her father. He built her a separate apartment behind the laundry and there she received visitors, plotted the next steps in her cinematic career, and enjoyed the support of her immediate family.

Adopting more Chinese dress, she basked in the intimacy of her parents and siblings. More important, she was reunited with her favorite sister, Lulu. Wong told Alice Tildesley of the *San Francisco Chronicle,* "I believe close quarters promote sympathy and understanding. Lives are interwoven. What affects one affects all and much opportunity is to be had for learning the Chinese virtue, compassion. Yes, I tell you, I am lucky that I am Chinese."[46]

Returning to the family home on North Figueroa Street was almost as if she had never left. In 1923 Wong said that

> some girls might get upset about the laundry. Not for me. Pictures are fine, and I'm getting along all right, but it's not so bad to have the laundry in the back of you, so you can wait and take good parts and be independent when you're climbing. Not to have to worry about where your next meal is coming from. My oldest brother—there are eight of us in the family—went to China and he saw me in a picture [probably *The Toll of the Sea*] and he wrote to mama to take me out quick. But mama didn't pay any attention to him. And I'm keeping right on.[47]

From 1927 on, Wong was indeed "keeping right on." She appeared in *The Chinese Parrot* (1927), directed by the German artist Paul Leni, who may have been the conduit to her film career in Germany. She also performed in *Driven from*

Home (1927); *Mr. Wu* (1927); *Old San Francisco* (1927); a short comedy with Stan Laurel and Oliver Hardy entitled *Why Girls Love Sailors* (1927); and *The Devil Dancer* (1927), with the "shimmy queen," Gilda Gray, with whom she would later work in the British production *Piccadilly* (1929), and with Clive Brook, the male star of *Shanghai Express* (1932), which would become the signature film of Chinese America's foremost film star. Other fillers included *Streets of Shanghai* (1927), *Across to Singapore* (1928), *The Crimson City* (1928), and *Chinatown Charlie* (1928).

With only supporting roles in Hollywood movies in the offing, Wong was open to work elsewhere. Impressed by her performance in *The Thief of Bagdad,* which was also acclaimed in Europe, German director Richard Eichberg made her an offer that she could not refuse. She became a global star who would act with Laurence Olivier and perform in British English, German, and French. In fact, her first talking picture was *The Flame of Love* (1930), directed by Eichberg for London's British International Pictures.

Emerging from the confines of a North Figueroa Street laundry and Los Angeles mission schools, Wong would dance and drink to the music of Duke Ellington at parties with British royalty.[48] She would be acquainted with the very rich and famous and with femme fatales like Marlene Dietrich and Leni Riefenstahl.

It was at the Berlin Press Ball in 1928 that Alfred Eisenstaedt took the famous photos of the three young actresses each making cinematic history in her own way.[49] From 1928 to 1930, Anna May Wong was the toast of Europe, because nothing like her unique Chinese Californian persona had ever been seen. With her black hair, un-European looks, statuesque figure, and ability to wear the latest fashions with sophistication, grace, and panache, she represented to Europe a new Chinese woman hitherto unseen and unimagined. Unlike the usual peasant wives of the few Chinese merchants in Europe, Wong personified the cool and detached. She embodied the hipster, the modern, and the new world. She certainly was not the type of Chinese woman to which Europeans were accustomed. In one dramatic gesture of venturing to Europe, she shattered traditional stereotypes of Chinese and Asian women as submissive and reactive.

At the age of twenty-three, she left one-dimensional Los Angeles behind for the richness of Europe and the world.

NOTES

1. Remi A. Nadeau, *Los Angeles: From Mission to Modern City* (New York: Longmans, Green, 1960), 204–5.

2. Anna May Wong, "The True Life Story of a Chinese Girl," *Pictures* (August 1926, September 1926), at http://www.mdl.com/Classic Films/Feature Star/star49e2.htm (accessed 31 July 1998).

3. Helen Carlisle, "Velly Muchee Lonely," *Motion Picture Magazine* 34, no. 2 (March 1928): 41.

4. Wong, "The True Life Story of a Chinese Girl."

5. Wong, "The True Life Story of a Chinese Girl."

6. Alice Tildesley, "I Am Lucky That I Am Chinese," *San Francisco Chronicle*, 3 June 1928, 3.

7. Wong, cited in Tildesley, "I Am Lucky That I Am Chinese," 3.

8. Wong, cited in Harry Carr, "I Am Growing More Chinese—Each Passing Year!," *Los Angeles Times,* 9 September 1934, 3.

9. Betty Willis, "Famous Oriental Stars Return to the Screen," *Motion Picture Magazine* 42, no. 3 (October 1931): 44; Wong, "The True Life Story of a Chinese Girl."

10. Kevin Brownlow, *Behind the Mask of Innocence: Sex, Violence, Prejudice, Crime, Films of Social Conscience in the Silent Era* (Berkeley: University of California Press, 1990), 332.

11. Brownlow, *Behind the Mask,* 327.

12. Wong, "The True Life Story of a Chinese Girl."

13. James Wang, cited in Tildesley, "I Am Lucky That I Am Chinese," 3; Wong, cited in Carr, "I Am Growing More Chinese," 3.

14. Wong, cited in Carr, "I Am Growing More Chinese," 3.

15. Wong, cited in Carr, "I Am Growing More Chinese," 3.

16. Brownlow, *Behind the Mask,* 330.

17. Brownlow, *Behind the Mask,* 330–32.

18. This description of the first time Anna May Wong watched herself on screen with her five girlfriends is a composite of quotations from Wong, cited in Tildesley, "I Am Lucky That I Am Chinese," 3; Wong, cited in Carr, "I Am Growing More Chinese," 3.

19. Geraldine Gan, *Lives of Notable Asian Americans* (New York: Chelsea House, 1994), 84.

20. Wong, "The True Life Story of a Chinese Girl."

21. Alma Whitaker, "Which Star Really Deserves Best Dressed Woman Title? Studio Designers and Stars Themselves Can't Agree Who's 'It,' Though Contenders Aren't Lacking," *Los Angeles Times,* 28 October 1934, 2.

22. "The World's Most Beautiful Chinese Girl," *Look* (1 March 1938): front cover, 37–38.

23. Wong, "The True Life Story of a Chinese Girl."

24. Wong, "The True Life Story of a Chinese Girl."

25. Hans J. Wollstein, *Vixens, Floozies and Molls: 28 Actresses of Late 1920s and 1930s Hollywood* (Jefferson, N.C.: McFarland, 1999), 248.

26. Willis, "Famous Oriental Stars," 44.

27. Wong, cited in Tildesley, "I Am Lucky That I Am Chinese," 3.

28. Helen Zia and Susan G. Gail, eds., *Notable Asian Americans* (Detroit: Gale Research, 1995), 414.

29. Barrie Roberts, "Anna May Wong: Daughter of the Orient," *Classic Images* 270 (December 1997): 20; Philip Leibfried, "Anna May Wong," *Films in Review* (n.d.): 148.

30. Wong, cited in Michel Mok, "Anna May Wong, with Chinese Courtesy, Makes a Newspaper Photographer Blush," *New York Post,* 26 April 1939, 25.

31. Tom Collins, "The Reel Thing: Resurrecting 'Lost' Films," *Wall Street Journal,* 12 March 1985, 12; Cari Beauchamp, *Without Lying Down: Frances Marion and the Powerful Women of Early Hollywood* (New York: Scribner, 1997), 143.

32. "Troubles of a Bagdad Thief," *New York Times,* 16 March 1924, 5; Wollstein, *Vixens,* 249.

33. Fairbanks, cited in "Troubles of a Bagdad Thief," 5.

34. Gon Toy Lee, cited in Wong, "The True Life Story of a Chinese Child."

35. Wong, "The True Life Story of a Chinese Girl."

36. Tildesley, "I Am Lucky That I Am Chinese," 3.

37. "Chinese Movie Star Accuses Film Partner," *San Francisco Chronicle,* 18 July 1924, 9.

38. "Chinese Movie Star," 9.

39. George C. Warren, "Anna May Is Pure Delight," *San Francisco Chronicle,* 22 January 1925, 11.

40. Wong, cited in Warren, "Anna May," 11.

41. Wong, cited in Warren, "Anna May," 11.

42. "Picture Actors Jailed in Omaha Board Bill Dispute May Sue Hotel for $70,000," *San Francisco Chronicle,* 6 March 1925, 4; Wollstein, *Vixens,* 250.

43. Wollstein, *Vixens,* 250.

44. "Picture Actors Jailed in Omaha Board Bill Dispute," 4.

45. "Picture Actors Jailed in Omaha Board Bill Dispute," 4.

46. Wong, cited in Tildesley, "I Am Lucky That I Am Chinese," 3.

47. Anna May Wong, cited in Mary Winship, "The China Doll," *Photoplay* 24, no. 1 (June 1923): 35.

48. Stuart Nicholson, *A Portrait of Duke Ellington: Reminiscing in Tempo* (London: Pan Books, 1999), 143.

49. For the actresses in various Eisenstaedt poses, see Wolfgang Jacobsen, Hans Helmut Prinzler, and Werner Sudendorf, eds., *Film Museum Berlin* (Berlin: Nicolai, 2000), 170; "World's Most Beautiful Chinese Girl," 37; Vincent Sneed, *China Doll Special* (spring 1992): n.p.

THREE

BERLIN: SPEAKING PARTS

Anna May Wong's trek to Berlin with her sister, Lulu, in March 1928[1] was courtesy of a generous five-picture film contract from Richard Eichberg (1888–1953). Leaving the optimism and warmth of a Los Angeles that was beginning to emerge as a major force in California's economic, political, and social life, she entered into a city and country still smarting from the "syphilitic peace"[2] of the Treaty of Versailles. As the capital of Weimar Germany, Berlin took the brunt of the losses sustained in World War I. It was a depressed place with little optimism. A city augmented by drab gray streets and alleyways that appeared to beckon more to statues of dead military heroes than to the war survivors, Berlin was reminiscent of the Prussian state of Bismarck with its conventional manners, orderly ways of human interaction, formal dress, and an acquiescence to power and authority. But that was just a cover-up.

After four years of war, a large section of republican Berlin was ready to party. While the excesses of the war and Germany's abysmal defeat would germinate a social and political revolution that culminated in an Adolph Hitler, Berlin was also a pleasure palace that rivaled only Shanghai of the 1930s. Drugs, fashionable perversions, free love and sexual gratification of all kinds and gender, whores in velvet jackboots, and readily available pornography in cabarets, clubs, and coffeehouses pervaded the nightlife into the mornings.

In a city of 4.3 million, Anna May Wong, at the age of twenty-three, and her sister, now twenty-eight, were just two of the 150,000 foreigners seeking celebrity, money, or simply a good time. As an aspiring Chinese American actress whose skimpy attire in *The Thief of Bagdad* (1924) attracted many onlookers including Richard Eichberg, Wong was a natural addition to the raucous, seemingly endless parade of pleasure seekers operating at full speed. Like terminally ill cancer patients, these Berliners seemed bent on cashing in on their dormant hedonism as if some catastrophe were lurking in the shadows. Little did they know that those dark men in jackboots would eventually come out into the light with their swastikas and billy clubs and brutalize a world and several generations.

But this was Berlin in 1928, and Anna May Wong knew nothing of Hitler or his murderers. Nor did she care. This was her first time away from her home in Los Angeles, and she was poised to take every opportunity to further her cinematic career. For a laundryman's daughter previously cloistered in a suffocating and narrowly confined Chinese America, the move to Berlin expanded Wong's scope to a new global level of awareness. At the Berlin Press Ball in 1928, where she stood gazing at the Associated Press camera of Alfred Eisenstaedt (1898–1995), accompanied by the two German divas, Marlene Dietrich (1901–1992) and Leni Riefenstahl (1902–), it was obvious that being in Berlin was an auspicious and a delightful occasion for Wong.

CINEMATIC GLOBALIZATION

If Josef von Sternberg (1894–1969) was Marlene Dietrich's mentor and confidant, who helped establish her career as the consummate German femme fatale in such films as *The Blue Angel* (1931), *Morocco* (1930), *Shanghai Express* (1932), *Blond Venus* (1932), and *The Scarlet Empress* (1934), Richard Eichberg was the closest thing to a mentor and adviser that Anna May Wong had. Both von Sternberg and Eichberg came from rich Germanic backgrounds. But Eichberg lacked one major facet that could have furthered Wong's film career. He did not have a cache of Hollywood backers that could develop a performer's career like that which von Sternberg had possessed at Paramount studios.

What Eichberg offered Wong was not only a five-picture deal but also the chance to star before a vast European audience. Germany had the most self-contained and innovative production unit in continental Europe. It had a sophisticated viewing audience that was highly developed as a profitable market.[3] In the Western world in the late 1920s and early 1930s, only the German market could rival the British production houses. Germany and Britain were the chief moviemaking countries in Europe. Along with the United States, they captured almost all of the Western world's cinematic entertainment market.

When Wong arrived in Berlin, Eichberg, as a director, was already part of a multinational and "pan-European" cinematic arrangement with British International Pictures (BIP). This was an important media venture established by John Maxwell (d. 1940), a major player in British film distribution as head of Wardour films. He began BIP by acquiring British National studios at Elstree in 1927. In the same year, BIP seized a majority stake in Suedfilm, one of Germany's major distributors. Because of the lack of readily available studio facilities in Britain, contrasted with the many German production houses, BIP's aim was to produce films in Germany through Suedfilm and simultaneously provide multilingual productions of films with similar story lines. This would consolidate the British–German connection. This was the first direct penetration of the European film market by a major British film studio. BIP's expansion into the European market was further enhanced when it scored major distribution arrangements with such firms as Sascha in Austria in 1928 and Stefano Pittaluga in Italy a year later.[4] Films starring Anna May Wong could be seen in Britain, Germany, Austria, and Italy. This would add to Wong's international persona and exposure.

BIP's attempt at a pan-European conglomerate was one of the first modern attempts at media globalization. The company knew that Hollywood was the most formidable world player in the film industry. Going alone with merely British studios would not alter this supremacy. But learning from Tinseltown and casting some of its most talented performers, such as Tallulah Bankhead (1902–1968), Lionel Barrymore (1878–1954), and Gilda Gray, as well as using directors like Harry Lachman (1886–1975) and Tim Whelan (1893–1957), might make a crack in the cinematic armor of the United States. BIP also had European stars like the Hungarian Maria Corda (b. 1902), the South African Syd Chaplin (1885–1965), the Dane Carl Brisson (1893–1958), the German Anny Ondra (1902–1987), and the Russian Olga Tschechorva (1897–1980), a niece of Anton Chekhov (1860–1904).[5] BIP was becoming just as international as Hollywood.

In 1933, along with Associated British Cinemas, BIP became Associated British Picture Corporation. It also established its own distribution arm in Hollywood. This was World Wide Pictures, which was to finance the production of Anna May Wong's Sherlock Holmes venture, *A Study in Scarlet* (1933). Wong's venture in Berlin, therefore, was more than just working with Richard Eichberg on five films. The contacts she made would augur well for her future prospects.

SONG (1928)

The first Eichberg–Wong collaboration was *Song,* known in German as *Schmutziges Geld* and adapted from a novel by Karl Vollmoeller (1878–1948). Opened in Berlin on July 30, 1928, it was first translated as *Dirty Money* from the French title, *Argent Maudit.* When *Song* was released in London, it was called *Show Life.* For its New York premiere, it was titled *Wasted Love.*[6] It was produced at a Suedfilm studio in Neubabelsberg. Wong portrayed a biracial German–Malayan character named Song, who becomes entangled with a would-be painter, John Houben, played by Heinrich George (1893–1946). In his day job, Houben works as a knife thrower in a cabaret act. When Song and Houben meet, she immediately falls for him and the tale of unrequited love between an Asian woman and a European man begins yet again. This role was not the first of this type Wong had played. In her initial starring role in *The Toll of the Sea* (1922), Wong's character, Lotus Flower, like Song, died because of her love for a non-Asian lover. Whereas Lotus Blossom walks into the raging sea, thus ending her life, Song falls spectacularly on one of her own upright knives during a lapse in concentration while performing her Orientalist saber dance at the Palace Hotel. She becomes frightened at the sight of the menacing Houben advancing toward her.

Reviews

Song was an unqualified hit in Germany. Although reviewers in Berlin stressed Wong's "Chinese" background, they noted the film's global attraction.[7] Wong was proclaimed the foundation of the film. In fact, *Lichtbildbuhne* enthused that "this German film will, in its success, announce the glory of Anna May Wong throughout the world as one of the greatest film artists."[8] They also referred to her as "this exquisite Oriental maiden," "porcelain loveliness," and "exotic pulchritude."[9] All these affirmations of Wong's star quality had the newspaper *8-Uhr-Abendblatt* gushing even to the point of declaring her German in a pre-Aryan period, when ethnic diversity, especially in Berlin, remained a worthwhile objective. It exalted: "Anna May Wong is ours now and we won't let her go."[10]

British reviewers also praised her performance. The film was first shown in London in September 1928. *The Bioscope* critic described Wong's subtle performance as a masterpiece.[11] In class-conscious Britain, *Kinematograph Weekly* proclaimed that a better class of people would attend the showings. It condescendingly remarked that *Show Life* was not the type of film that a coarse popular audience like the working class could appreciate, especially Wong's deliberate performance enhanced by an actual, linear story line.[12] With such critical acclaim from German and British reviewers, the cinematic prospects of Los Angeles's first Asian American film star seemed endless.

Personal Reflections

Anna May Wong's performance in *Song* was the second turning point in her life. Her first had occurred when she was about seventeen. Lashing back verbally at racist insults by a truck driver in Los Angeles, she demonstrated that she could stand her ground against bigotry. That was the first defining moment when she decided not to endure racist remarks or actions.[13] The second was in Germany. She remarked:

> My next milepost was in Berlin. The first picture in which I appeared made a hit. Crowds waited in the lobby for me to come out. Weaving my way through that pack of admiring fans, I seemed suddenly to be standing at one side watching myself with complete detachment. It was my Chinese soul coming back to claim me. Up to that time I had been more of an American flapper than Chinese. That was also the turning of a corner.[14]

Leaving the United States was good not only for her career but also for her psyche. She was beginning to develop her own agency and empower herself as a woman and a person of color. Wong was entering a stage of success that she had never experienced in European America. Her self-confidence as a film performer certainly soared, but it was her value as a woman and Asian American that was to evolve in Europe. This would sustain her throughout the hardships in the United States that would surely come again. But now at the age of twenty-three, she was savoring the delights of Berlin. The Germans even called her "Maia" Wong because they felt that "Anna" was far too Scandinavian.[15]

PAVEMENT BUTTERFLY (1929)

Wong's next German film was also a resounding success. Shot at a Suedfilm studio as *Grossstadtschmetterling,* it was also known in German as *Asphaltschmetterling* and *Die Fremde.* The picture showcased her modeling talents as she wore the current fashions from Paris. This BIP production, entitled *Pavement Butterfly* and *City Butterfly* for the English-speaking market, was another example of how European studios attempted to exalt fashion as spectacle, thus creating a specific style.[16] Just before returning to Berlin for *Pavement*

Butterfly, Wong completed production at London's Elstree studios in the starring role in *Piccadilly* (1929). As Shosho, she wore the latest London fashions, setting forth a sophisticated femme fatale whose actions move the story line to its final conclusion.

Pavement Butterfly was set in Nice along the French Riviera with a bohemian backdrop of artists, dancers, performers, and gangsters. This cinematic motif of potential danger, sex, and violence coupled with Parisian fashions and avant garde sophistication provided conventional European audiences with a peek into a forbidden world. Playing an "Orientalist" show performer, emphasizing the inaccessibility of a biracial romance between her character and those played by the French actor Gaston Jacquet and the Polish performer Alexander Granach (1890–1945), Wong brought an added complication to the racial firewall of this French "floating world." As the exotic Other, her cinematic role was to captivate, titillate, and sensationalize the possibility of miscegenation.

Reviews

Like *Song, Pavement Butterfly* was purely a vehicle for Anna May Wong to display her celebrity. But the bar was now raised. Critics applauded her performance, but with a caveat. *Variety* exclaimed that "Richard Eichberg's last film with Anna May Wong, *Song,* was a good money maker. This time he has not caught her personality and her exotic charms half as completely. It's just a conventional film story which could have been played by any girl of any race."[17] What this meant was that Eichberg failed to bring out her exotic qualities, her "Chineseness," her differences. These were central to cinematic success. The reviewer at *Film-Kurier* had similar opinions. But he wanted to see more action: "The Eichberg team did not dare to let a happy white man share the same bed as the undressed body of a Mongolian woman. The erotic hypocrisy of this German Anna May Wong film could have originated in an English boarding school for girls."[18]

THE FLAME OF LOVE (1930)

In Richard Eichberg's final film with Wong (produced in three versions), the opportunity for her character, Hai-tang, to find romance with a European in an obvious kissable embrace was recorded in the English-language version of *The Flame of Love.* This was also her first English-language talking picture. Codirected by Walter Summers (1896–1973), the film was also called *The Road to Dishonor*. John Longden (1900–1971) had the honor of being the first male actor on screen to smack the lips of Chinese America's foremost movie queen.[19] Contrary to the *Film-Kurier* critic, or perhaps because of his comments, protracted miscegenation via a kiss highlighted *The Flame of Love*. According to the reporter, Audrey Rivers, "even [Greta] Garbo [1905–1990] herself was never more thoroughly kissed! The critics made a big fuss about it and the controversy raged for days in the newspapers."[20] Since miscegenation was frowned upon in the British empire, especially in the colonies where the superiority of the white race was always proclaimed, the embrace and kiss between an Englishman and an Asian woman were sacrilegious even in a film set in Russia. The penalty for such a transgression could only result in the death of the woman.

Screen Deaths for Anna May Wong

The three versions of *The Flame of Love* were produced at Elstree studios in London. In the German interpretation, entitled *Der Weg zur Schande* or *Hai Tang*, Eichberg was solo director. Wong learned enough German to move the story to its final death scene conclusion. In the French-language production, *L'amour maitre des choses*, Tunis-born film entrepreneur Jacques Haik (1893–1950) and his production house Establissements Jacques Haik, founded in 1924, provided the distribution in France. With codirector Jean Kemm (d. 1939), Eichberg's French version opened on September 19, 1930, at the Colisee in Paris. In *L'amour maitre des choses*, Wong mastered enough French to perform her role as Hai-tang.

The three stories described Hai-tang as a member of a dance troupe touring Czarist Russia. In the three versions, her fate is to fall for a Russian officer, played by John Longden, Francis Lederer (1899–2000), and Robert Ancelin in the English, German, and French versions, respectively. Like Lotus Blossom, Song, and Shosho, Hai-tang commits the unpardonable act of interracial romance. As a self-sacrificing dancer, she allows herself to be seduced by the Grand Duke to save her brother from the firing squad.[21] In *L'amour maitre des choses*, it is her father whom she must rescue from execution.[22] With her family members finally safe from Russian brutality, "having previously offered her virtue on the altar of paternal (and fraternal) love, the girl is now free to sacrifice her own life on the altar of pure love for the young Russian officer." Since these three films centered on the "illicit" love affair between a yellow and a white, the cinematic denouement inevitably ended with the death of the yellow woman.

Despite the actual text of the stories, Wong's inaugural work in talking pictures was remarkable because it involved a Chinese American from California acting in three European languages. This demonstrated a creative flexibility and adaptation. When she starred in the German films, critics remarked that "her German is too perfect. She must have had a double."[23] But when they found out that she learned German "studying six hours for many weeks," the critics later revised their criticisms.[24]

Reviews

Unlike *Song* and *Pavement Butterfly,* English and German critics panned the three versions of *The Flame of Love* as cinema. Although Wong was lauded for her acting and spoken words in English, the criticisms centered on the flaccid story line and the unconvincing performances of the other actors. German reviewers were less enamored with her German diction. In fact, it seemed that the Germans were not yet convinced that talking pictures were valuable cinematic assets, especially for an actress like Wong, who has always been noted for her silent film prowess and repertoire.[25] The reviewer at *Film-Kurier* was especially cutting:

> It is interesting to see how well the producer Eichberg has understood the English mentality: eroticism without sex appeal, exoticism without miscegenation; instead, tender melodies are played on the piano in a homely setting. Hai-Tang's lover is her brotherly friend, he watches her dancing, alluringly undresses, but apart from that—nothing happens between them. This is truly English.[26]

As for the French company, Establissements Jacques Haik, it declined any further coproductions with Richard Eichberg. No doubt the bad reviews played a part in this decision, but in 1931 it was revealed that the Courvoisier Bank, which was underwriting Jacques Haik and his production houses in the Paris suburbs of Courbevoie and La Garenne, had collapsed into bankruptcy.[27]

Despite the critics' negative reactions to Wong's initial talking pictures, the opportunities in Berlin for a twenty-five-year-old Chinese American actress from Los Angeles were unprecedented. They demonstrated that Europeans were willing to accommodate a young Asian American's cinematic aspirations as an international performer. Certainly there was the commercial interest of BIP to establish a European union of film production and distribution. But the fact that Richard Eichberg provided Wong with the vehicle to global stardom represented a cosmopolitan attitude to race and gender. More significantly, German critics called for more reality-based stories with genuine physical interaction between yellow women and white men to be played in human ways. Their contempt for English film productions that were based on emasculated love relationships smacked more of their own arrogance than an understanding of the British inability to even mount a truthful yellow–white romantic liaison with kissing, hugging, and bedding. Like Americans, the British also censored any films that extolled miscegenation. Any hint of yellow–white, brown–white, or black–white romantic relationship always resulted in the death of the woman of color, never the white man. Racial purity was the key to British cinematic prohibition. This was especially relevant since Britain had an empire full of yellow, brown, and black people. To allow British filmmakers to show a yellow, brown, or black woman in a loving embrace with a white man would have damaged the empire's exalted notion of its own racial superiority. Such a consensual romantic liaison would imply equality. In the cinematic case of Wong, since she was very much a woman and a leading cinematic performer, stories without love relationships were improbable and unlikely to generate any profits.

Anna May Wong's celebrity and potential to enhance the bottom line were not lost on British producers when she and Lulu arrived in Berlin in 1928. Almost immediately after the release of *Song,* BIP, which was part of the coproduction firm that involved Richard Eichberg, contracted her to play Shosho in *Piccadilly* (1929). Shot at the Elstree studio, this was Wong's only silent film made in London. But because of its enormous popularity in Britain, it landed the daughter of Chinese America a leading role in a London stage play. Like the initial reception for her films, the atmosphere and publicity surrounding the play were almost stories in themselves.

NOTES

1. Tim Bergfelder, "Negotiating Exoticism: Hollywood, Film Europe and the Cultural Reception of Anna May Wong," in *"Film Europe" and "Film America," Cinema, Commerce and Cultural Exchange, 1920–1939,* ed. Andrew Higson and Richard Maltby (Exeter, England: University of Exeter Press, 1999), 307; John Scott, "European Bouquets Get Notice: Chinese Flapper Crashes Continent Before Finding Recognition Here," *Los Angeles Times,* 23 August 1931, 2.

2. Joachim C. Fest, *Hitler,* trans. Richard and Clara Winston (New York: Vintage, 1974), 98.

3. Andrew Higson, "Polygot Films for an International Market: E. A. Dupont, the British Film Industry, and the Idea of a European Cinema, 1926–1930," in Higson and Maltby, *"Film Europe" and "Film America,"* 286.

4. Higson, "Polygot Films," 286.

5. Tom Ryall, "A British Studio System: The Associated British Picture Corporation and the Gaumont British Picture Corporation in the 1930s," in *The British Cinema Book,* ed. Robert Murphy (London: British Film Institute, 1997), 29.

6. Garth Pedlar, "Anna May Wong in 'Show Life,'" *Classic Images* (April 1985): 28; "Song," *New York Times,* 14 November 1928, 24; "Berlin Praises Miss Wong," *Variety,* 14 November 1928, 26.

7. "Berlin Praises Miss Wong," 26.

8. *Lichtbildbuhne,* August 25, 1928, cited in Bergfelder, "Negotiating Exoticism," 310.

9. "Berlin Praises Miss Wong," 26.

10. *8-Uhr-Abendblatt,* cited in Bergfelder, "Negotiating Exoticism," 310.

11. *The Bioscope,* 19 September 1928, cited in Bergfelder, "Negotiating Exoticism," 310.

12. *Kinematograph Weekly,* 20 September 1928, cited in Bergfelder, "Negotiating Exoticism." 310.

13. Wong, cited in Harry Carr, "I Am Growing More Chinese—Each Passing Year!" *Los Angeles Times,* 9 September 1934, 3.

14. Wong, cited in Carr, "I Am Growing More Chinese," 3.

15. Scott, "European Bouquets Get Notice," 2.

16. For a provocative study on style as spectacle, see Sarah Berry, *Screen Style: Fashion and Femininity in 1930s Hollywood* (Minneapolis: University of Minnesota Press, 2000), 47–93.

17. "City Butterfly," *Variety,* 8 May 1929, 34.

18. *Film-Kurier,* April 11, 1929, cited in Bergfelder, "Negotiating Exoticism," 311.

19. Audrey Rivers, "Anna May Wong Sorry She Cannot Be Kissed," *Movie Classics* (November 1939): 39.

20. Rivers, "Anna May Wong," 39.

21. Marjory Collier, "The Chinese Girl: East Meets West in Anna May Wong," *The Picturegoer* (May 1930): 26–27.

22. For a complete French version, see "Hai-Tang," *Variety,* 8 October 1930, 23.

23. Wong, cited in Scott, "European Bouquets Get Notice," 2.

24. Wong, cited in Scott, "European Bouquets Get Notice," 2.

25. Bergfelder, "Negotiating Exoticism," 313.

26. *Film-Kurier,* 27 February 1930, cited in Bergfelder, "Negotiating Exoticism," 313.

27. "Jacques Haik," *Les Independants du premier siecle, Biographies,* n.d., at http://www.lips.org/bio_Haik_GB.asp (accessed 5 October 2001).

FOUR

LONDON: LIVE STAGE

A damp early spring evening on March 14, 1929, in London did not deter the crowd waiting anxiously outside the New Theater as the cast of *The Circle of Chalk* left the building. Like any veteran dramatic star, Anna May Wong waited until all the supporting players exited first. Leaving just before her was her costar, a beginning actor who in the 1920s simply wanted to be seen on stage anywhere and everywhere.[1] Although Laurence Olivier (1907–1989) would eventually receive world acclaim for his many distinguished stage and cinematic performances and even a lordship, at this time he walked unnoticed past the adoring crowd into a waiting taxi. As his vehicle left the New Theater, he might have wondered why a British stage audience was waiting for a Chinese American movie star from California.

Even for London's theatergoers with investments in stocks, March 14, 1929, was not a time to wonder or to worry. It was six months until Black Thursday, when the world would stagger from the crash of the New York Stock Exchange and the end of the hedonistic Roaring Twenties. Now the hip London theater crowd had no inkling of the Great Depression. Rather, thoughts turned to the new play, *The Circle of Chalk,* opening that evening at the New Theater in the theatrically congested West End.

It was a gala occasion because a movie star from the United States was the leading lady. Waiting for Wong outside were "the young men who wore their best clothing, combing their hair and knotting and reknotting their ties. Some of the women wore a uniform hairstyle, their locks sheared off in geometric bangs in front and cut long and straight in the back imitating their idol."[2] Years later, she reminisced that:

> In 1929, I was in *The Circle of Chalk* with Laurence Olivier. At night, at the stage door, people waited for me. Did they wait for Olivier? Never. I would walk outside into the fog or rain, and they would be there—young men in their tuxedos, young women with their bangs cut straight and blunt. Those young men lusted for me. Those young women tinted their faces ivory with powder, hoping to duplicate my complexion.[3]

At the time of the staging of *The Circle of Chalk* in 1929, Wong was just a twenty-four-year-old movie star who looked a lot younger, as Asian women often do. She was really too young to be an idol. But she was, as she mingled and joked with her British public while signing autographs. In 1924 Anna had been nineteen years old and looked even younger. But she had stolen scenes from Douglas Fairbanks (1883–1939) in *The Thief of Bagdad*. This was the film that got Wong noticed, and it would catapult her to international fame. Now fans in the English-speaking world would jostle in crowds just to get a brief glimpse of the film star who happened to be of Chinese ancestry.

What was remarkable about *The Circle of Chalk* was that Wong would continue to portray an Asian woman on stage as if this were her birthright emanating from her American film roles as a Chinatown resident: Lotus Blossom, Lotus Flower, daughter of a sinister Asian physician, Zira, Keok (an Inuit), Tiger Lily, Annabelle Wu (an adventuress), Nan Lo (a prostitute), Ohtai, a Nautch dancer, Loo Song, Delamar, Sada, Su Quan, and Su.[4] In fact, Wong was the quintessential Asian everywoman of the 1920s in Hollywood. Being Asian, it was almost as if she were ageless. Certainly the audience never really noticed whether she were nineteen or twenty-four. It was the fact that she was an Asian woman portraying Asian characters that drew the people to her. They had never seen anyone like Wong before, and they were mesmerized. Eventually she would bring those roles played in silent American films to the London stage, where she portrayed a teahouse girl in a Basil Dean production of *The Circle of Chalk*. This time, she would speak.

That Basil Dean (1887–1978) selected Wong to play the female lead in one of his stage plays was a testimony to her acting prowess and fame even though she had acted only in essentially low-budget or B-movies in Hollywood. His first preference was always "for an actress, almond-eye[d], if possible to impart some degree of atmosphere into the part of Chang Hi-Tang, meaning the Flower."[5]

As one of Britain's foremost stage directors, theatrical managers, and impresarios, Dean, a former actor, was among the first to produce and direct sound, or talking, pictures in the country. His theatrical influence was so enormous that he became director on May 8, 1929, of Associated Talking Pictures Limited. One of Britain's first sound film companies, it later became Ealing Studios.

As a theatrical producer of such renown, Dean had his pick of plays. In 1929 he became enamored of *The Circle of Chalk* as a theatrical vehicle. The play itself originated from the Yuan Dynasty (1271–1368). The fact that the Yuan was a foreign monarchy founded and ruled by the Mongol leader Kublai Khan (1215–1294) and his descendants may have accounted for *The Circle of Chalk's* fascination for Dean. As a highly creative, innovative, and inquisitive producer, Dean wanted to expand his theatrical repertoire to include an Asian vehicle. *The Circle of Chalk* gave him that opportunity.

Ever since the publication of *The Travels of Marco Polo* (originally called *A Description of the World*) in 1299 and its subsequent English translations, especially the authoritative London edition by William Marsden (1754–1836) published in 1818, the popular image of China in Europe and especially Britain as well as the United States was that portrayed by the Venetian Marco Polo (1254–1329) and his merchant father, Nicholas.[6] For the Polos, who traveled extensively through Yuan China for seventeen years, that country was a Mongol, and therefore a foreign, controlled China, not a Chinese or Han China. Was it any wonder then that Wong's role in *The Thief of Bagdad* was that of a Mongol agent?

In dynasties before and after the Yuan, members of the Chinese literati as the best class were nurtured and conditioned to sit for the government examinations to fill positions in the federal civil service and the provincial and municipal bureaucracies. The educated Chinese held political office and therefore political power and authority. But during the Yuan, the educated Chinese were never trusted by the Mongol rulers, who sectioned off the populace into four classes. At the top were the Mongols: royalty, aristocracy, administrators, military commanders, and retainers, followed by the *semu*, or people with colored eyes from the western regions and the western Xia. The Han Chinese of the north, including the Qidans and Nuxhens who lived in the Huanghe valley, ranked third, with the Han Chinese of the south and other nationalities living south of the Chiangjiang valley dragging in the rear.[7] Of course without the support of the Chinese landowning or gentry class and the elite classes of other nationalities, Mongol rule would have been doomed.

The exclusion of the Chinese literati from government office could have presented a simmering danger for the Mongol rulers without an outlet for its restless and prodigious energies and creativeness. To counteract possible sources of rebellion and sedition, Kublai Khan established the Imperial Academy as an institutional expression for indigenous Chinese literary energy and pursuits.[8] In doing so, the Yuan Dynasty became one of the great eras of drama in Chinese civilization. Unlike European drama, Chinese theater was based on dramatic ballads that combined acting, dancing, singing, and even acrobatics as well as spoken lines.[9] In fact, prose and poetry were essential parts of the storytelling, with the actors performing on a projecting platform that was reminiscent of the Elizabethan apron stage. There were also elaborate costumes with almost no scenery. Like most Elizabethan plays, music as the basis or background for songs, sonnets, and alarms in Chinese drama was also essential.[10] Out of this tradition came *The Circle of Chalk.*

Besides the possibility of a box office success, the fact that much in Yuan drama seemed similar to English theater may have been another reason why Basil Dean began considering *The Circle of Chalk* as a British stage production. Part of a Yuan dramatic repertory called *A Hundred Pieces*, the play[11] passed through several reincarnations before it reached the audience at the New Theater in 1929.

In 1832 a French academic in Chinese studies first translated the original document into a non-Chinese language. Invited by the editorial board of John Murray Publishers with financial backing from the Oriental Translation Fund of Great Britain and Ireland, Stanislas Julien (1832–1874) produced *Hoei-lan-ki, ou l'histoire du cercle de craie, drama en prose et en vers.* Once the French version had become public, Alfred Henshke (1890–1928), a left-leaning poet, penned an adaptation called *Der Kreidekreis.* Better known by his pseudonym, Klabund, this Berlin-based lyric author was enamored of *The Circle of Chalk's* interplay between prose and poetry. Since he was not a scholar of Chinese literature and had little knowledge of the sensibilities of Chinese culture, Klabund wrote in two new protagonists. Now there was a pimp named Tong and a prince who later became emperor. (The latter, named Po, was played by Laurence Olivier in "Yellowface" when the play was produced by Dean.) Finally in 1929 James Laver (1899–1975) of the Victoria and Albert Museum translated *Der Kreidekreis* into English as *The Circle of Chalk: A Play in Five Acts Adapted from the Chinese by Klabund.*[12] From Laver's publication, Basil Dean took the play to production at the New Theater.

With the introduction of a pimp and therefore a prostitute euphemistically called a teahouse girl, there was an obvious sexual overtone injected into this adaptation of a heroic Yuan drama. Before seeking financial backing, Dean submitted *The Circle of Chalk* informally to Lord Cromer, Britain's theatrical censor.

Cromer replied that "although it may not come direct from Shanghai, its gesture is too distinctly from that neighborhood. Consequently, I fear the circle I am bound to draw must be of blue pencil rather than of chalk."[13] Lord Cromer seemed to equate anything Chinese with Shanghai's reputation as a city of vice, vermin, voracious greed, and volcanic sin. *The Circle of Chalk,* with its plot of intrigue, treachery, prostitution, and a murder trial, did nothing to dispel that notion.

Dean resubmitted the play to Cromer with some changes in hopes of getting a reversal. His banker partner, George Ansley, was enthusiastic about this much translated and adapted Yuan play. So was Lady Wyndham, owner of the New Theater. Now money and a place to stage the play were available. In the meantime, Dean began devising the stage for production. He also cast about for a female lead.

In 1929 British International Pictures was just completing its shooting of *Piccadilly* starring Anna May Wong as Shosho, paramour to the lead character. Although this was Wong's first major British motion picture, her fame preceded her in Europe as she was coming off a triumphant collaboration with the German director Richard Eichberg in the 1928 film *Song.* In 1929 Wong starred in Eichberg's *Pavement Butterfly.* Impressed by these highly touted credits, Basil Dean discovered a Chinese American film star in Germany to play his Chang Hi-Tang in *The Circle of Chalk.* No doubt Wong's international film celebrity enhanced her attraction for Basil Dean, who remarked:

> The principal part in the film *(Piccadilly)* was taken by a young Chinese [American] actress, Anna May Wong, who had made a considerable success—her first—with Douglas Fairbanks in the *Thief of Baghdad* [sic]. She was receiving tremendous publicity, and, judging by the press photographs, was a celestial beauty. After the usual tussle with her agent, I engaged her while she was still filming.

The photographs did not lie. Wong was certainly lovely to look at and possessed natural grace of movement.[14]

Basil Dean met Wong while she was shooting the London scenes of *Piccadilly.* He liked what he saw. More important, he was convinced that Wong was made for the part because she had acted in a German production of *The Circle of Chalk* two months earlier.[15] Because of Wong's good looks and persona, low and resonating voice, box office reputation, and experience in the play itself, Dean was convinced that he had a hit on his hands after a string of flops. One major characteristic that Dean did not expect from Wong was her high intelligence. She also demonstrated a strong work ethic and instinctual predilection for stage drama. Dean soon discovered that she not only had an almost obsessive passion to act, she also liked to read. To familiarize herself with British literature, she even studied Bertrand Russell's *Essay on China* before the first rehearsals. The British press ate this up.[16]

Wong was surprised to be chosen by Basil Dean as the female lead in a London stage play. She admitted: "I thought they would not like the idea of a Hollywood film player appearing on the stage—but they fooled me completely. I was lucky enough to be signed up almost immediately in London for the leading role in a play translated from the Chinese, *The Circle of Chalk*. There were more than twenty actresses after the part."[17]

As for the play itself, once the censors approved it, Basil Dean began to delegate the work of designing the costumes, lighting, scenery, and sound. Because of the Chinese "flavor" of the play, the sets were elaborate. To Aubrey Hammond (1893–1940), his designer, Dean's directives were exacting:

> Begin by enclosing the stage space in a box as wide as the proscenium arch itself: swing doors right and left at the back for entrances and exits; ceiling, walls, floors, all in black lacquer; in the center of the stage an oblong turntable on which the various scenes—the tea house, the magistrate's court, etc.—can be built back to back. The final scene, the throne room of the Imperial Palace, will occupy the whole platform; all this inner scenery to be painted and decorated in Chinese red lacquer and gold except the journey in the snowstorm; we'll play that against a blue-green back cloth with coolies throwing white confetti up in the air to represent the snow.[18]

As for the instrumentals and songs, Dean realized that he needed some Chinese-sounding music that was pleasing to the European ear. He summoned composer Ernest Irving, with whom he had worked on other plays, to accomplish this. Irving's eccentricities proved equal to the task:

> His orchestra included many strange instruments: gongs, drums of various kinds, a cello adapted for the purposes of the b-chord fiddle of China, a marimba, and a heckelphone: He was greatly tickled at being able to unearth this rare instrument.[19]

With the key technical and musical components in place, Dean began rehearsing this Chinese folk drama, which evoked the struggles of the common Chinese people in Yuan times. The play evolved around the selling of sixteen-year-old Hi-Tang (played by Wong) by her mother, Mrs. Chang, to Tong, a teahouse (brothel) proprietor. While in the teahouse, Hi-Tang meets Po, the prince and heir to the dynastic throne. She also meets Ma, the greedy and evil member of the landed gentry, or Mandarin, who bankrupted her father and drove him to his death. Outbidding Prince Po in an informal auction, Ma buys Hi-Tang to be his second wife. After a year in a household shared with the first Mrs. Ma, Hi-Tang conceives a son. Since the first Mrs. Ma is barren, Ma decides to divorce his first wife. This proves to be his undoing, as he is soon poisoned by the first Mrs. Ma, who pins the blame on Hi-Tang. As the police take Hi-Tang to jail, she cries for her child. Mrs. Ma replies, "Your child! You are mad or worse. She has no child. The child in this house is my child, mine and Mr. Ma's. She was only its nurse."[20]

To determine the true mother of the child, Po, who is now emperor, chosen from among "fifty imperial princes," decides to place the child in a chalk circle. He then orders Hi-Tang and Mrs. Ma to pull the child from the circle. The one who does is the true mother of the child. Hi-Tang, however, exclaims:

> I fear your Majesty's anger. You glower upon me like a wolf or tiger, ready to devour me if I do not obey you. But I cannot do it. I bore this child under my heart for nine months. Nine months have I lived with him, nine months longer than other people. I have known all sweetness with him, and all bitterness without him. When it was cold, I warmed his tiny limbs. His joints are so tender and brittle that I should break them if I pulled to my side as hard as that woman pulls to hers. The arms of a child are as tender and brittle as stems of straw or hemp. If the child can only be won by pulling out his arms, only she can pull him out of the circle who has never felt the pains of a mother for her child.[21]

This speech convinces the emperor that Hi-Tang did not poison Ma. He then extracts a confession from Mrs. Ma that she was indeed the murderess. During the final curtain, the emperor proclaims that Hi-Tang will be his wife and empress. As a play about justice, *The Circle of Chalk* was consistent with the didactic objectives of Chinese theater. It was a representative example of a Yuan drama that was "often highly moral in its teachings, setting good over evil in a most forceful manner."[22]

As a story of intrigue, jealousy, greed, and murder, the tale was gripping but inauthentic. Critics laughed at the conclusion that a Chinese emperor would actually take a former whore and widow as his bride. The dialogue smacked of fortune cookie messages with such delights as, "I am your most unworthy servant," and "May a thousand mosquitoes buzz in his brain, and a thousand wasps sting his eyes and blind him!" There were also gems like these: "I am honored, Mrs. Chang, that you should have thought of me first," and "I swear by the bones of my ancestors."[23] There were also direct references to Kwanyin, the goddess of mercy (in the play, she was the goddess of cleansing)[24] and to Chinese men with "pigtails." However "pigtails" were only present in

China during the Qing Dynasty as a symbol of Chinese subjugation to the Manchu rulers and not in the Yuan period from which *The Circle of Chalk* received its inspiration. The play closed after eight weeks.[25] For many critics, it was eight weeks too long. Laurence Olivier overdid his makeup and was peculiar in his lackluster movements, gestures, and speech. Of the future Lord Olivier, one critic wrote, "Here he had become what he had always wanted to be, a leading man in the West End. And he was practically throwing away the opportunity to expand himself. It wasn't that Larry was bad because he had insufficient talent and couldn't help it. It was as if he was being bad deliberately."[26]

As the producer, Basil Dean was more circumspect. He remarked that "Laurence Olivier in a gorgeous primrose silk robe as the Prince, spoke, sang and made love delightfully, although at this period of his career overinclined to reticence."[27] Olivier actually had a severe case of laryngitis, and his singing suffered to such an extent that a critic from the *Daily Express* wrote that Olivier "should not be allowed to sing and neither should Miss Wong."[28]

As for Laurence Olivier's leading lady, Anna May Wong, an American critic named Trask wanted a stereotype of the dainty China doll rather than a well-acted protagonist. No doubt he was disturbed that a woman with an Asian face could speak English with an American accent. He wrote, "her voice is guttural and uncultivated in comparison to the lightness and delicacy of her bodily makeup. Instead of a high bell-like quality with a slight Oriental accent, she has the tone quality of a middle western high school girl. Anna in talkers will not be the same as Anna of the silent screen."[29] Even Basil Dean was taken aback by that American voice. He wrote:

> But oh! that California accent! As thick as the smog that now smothers their cities. Try as she might—and she did try—Anna May couldn't get rid of it. In Berlin they had made no complaint. After all, why should they? She was making a silent film. There was miscalculation on my part, too. I had not realized the strong prejudice, amounting almost to total rejection in some cases of the American accent in English plays at that time, just as the British accent was resented on Broadway. Now both have become internationalized. I was out of sort with my own folly in engaging a silent film actress when any attractive English ingenue with good voice and gesture might well have carried the production to success.[30]

Another critic said that "as soon as the great Anna May opened her mouth, her squeaky American voice shattered any attempt at illusion."[31]

Not all was lost, however. Wong did impress. Dean exclaimed that "in the event, Anna May failed to make Chang Hi-Tang comprehensible either to the stalls or gallery, save in the ecstatic movements of the Lotus dance which she did to perfection. This was pure Chinese and the audience recognized its integrity at once."[32] *The Evening Standard's* Hubert Griffith also wrote that the dancing was a "triumph" while the *Daily Mail's* Alan Parson said he liked it "immensely."[33] A critic from the *Morning Post* was moved to write:

> Not only is *The Circle of Chalk* a success that does credit to everyone concerned, but it is also a peculiarly personal one to Miss Anna May Wong, the little Chinese film star. Miss Wong shows herself—in spite of a frank, but pretty American accent—a perfect little artist—graceful, appealing and intelligent.[34]

Despite the negative reviews of her opening night performance, the "production was cheered from every quarter of the house." Wong even spoke to the audience in Cantonese, causing one critic to proclaim that "her reception was tremendous and her little speech of thanks in Chinese captured the more an audience that was already won. She sings too, as beautifully as could be and dances 'such a way.'"[35]

Despite the critics' lukewarm reception of Wong's initial London stage play, she profited immensely from this experience. She remarked: "I found it difficult at first to act on the stage without a director always in front of me, as we have in the studios. Of course, Mr. Dean directed us for weeks of rehearsal, but when the performance came, he was not there at the front of the stage, and I was lost for a time. Acting before an audience puts a person on her own, and in time I became used to being alone."[36]

EUROPEAN SOCIETY AND A FEW LESSONS

As a consummate professional, Anna May Wong accepted the praise with humility. But the negative remarks galvanized the twenty-four-year-old into improving herself. She hired an English elocution teacher from Oxford University to study voice and to eliminate the Midwestern or California accent that underlay her monotonous projection.[37] While taking intensive English voice instruction at 200 guineas a lesson, she stayed in a flat on Park Lane after a stint at the Claridge's Hotel.[38] Her network of friends and admirers grew. To a standing ovation, "her elegance and beauty stopped Parliament when she walked into the visitor's gallery."[39] She even met the Prince of Wales. The king's sister visited her in her dressing room after one of her performances of *The Chalk Circle*.[40] Wong was amused by all this attention.

There was a rumor that she was to be presented to the British court. Her response was:

> No Chinese woman has ever been introduced at the English Court. It would have been nice, but I left London too early. Among all these men who were so kind, there were some who wanted to marry me. I might have brought home a title if I had chosen! Englishmen are not like Americans. They have traveled a great deal in the Orient, and many of them have brought wives from China, or Arabia or India back to conservative England.[41]

England and London would always remain special places in Wong's heart and mind. She remembered that "that early stay in England was a wonderful experience for me. The English are a cool, detached, broad-minded people. I made warm friendships that helped me. I studied German, French and music."[42] In fact, her cool, detached demeanor on-screen and off seemed to have developed from her days in London and Berlin. Her matter-of-fact style smacked more of London, Berlin, and Paris than Hollywood or Los Angeles.

As she socialized with Europeans and worked on films in Britain and Germany, Wong began to evolve into a sophisticated Chinese American woman with upper-class social manners, an upper-class British accent, and elegant attire to match. In fact, she "became known as one of the best dressed women in Mayfair."[43] Her time in London was one of her many highlights in Europe. She reflected "that sometimes it happens that when you are very happy within yourself, you radiate that feeling and attract happy people to you. I had a very marvelous time socially in London. Many of the finest people became my friends and were wonderful to me."[44]

Despite the accolades, the demands of her European films and stage performances caused Wong to seek a respite from the pressures of work. After rounds of many parties, she needed relief from celebrity. She recalled:

> There was a lot of hard work and finally I decided to go to a sanatorium and rest. The head doctor told me they would not take a patient for less than a fortnight. I assured him that I would be there at least that long. But four days after my arrival, there came a frantic wire which insisted that I attend the world premiere of a German film *(The Flame of Love)* which was opening in Zurich. So, that rest period was a short one.[45]

Besides performing in German, Wong also learned French and performed in *L'amour maitre des choses* (1930). That she was able to overcome language barriers and cultures while projecting her unique persona and style onstage and in film demonstrated that she was not merely a performer from the United States.

Rather, her capacity to work and live in many cultures showed her resilience, adaptability, and a constant search for newness. Moreover, this Asian American woman's fluency in two major European languages was not just a feat of linguistic agility but also an accomplished act of cinematic dexterity. She became the first Chinese American movie star of international proportions who was comfortable in French, German, Austrian, and British films and theater. Her ability to readily access foreign languages and cultures showed her remarkable intelligence and range. In many ways, her internationalism reflected an early twentieth-century impulse in the United States to become more global, especially after World War I and the admonition by Woodrow Wilson (1856–1924) to European Americans to become less isolated and more worldly. By being global, Wong also transcended being merely a national of the United States.

Her portrayal of the Chinese woman in British-, French-, and German-language films was always a Europeanized version of the Chinese and China as exotic, inscrutable, mysterious, and the Other. The image of the Chinese and China was grounded in little more than a European distortion of reality. Without the foreign languages, Europe's perspective of Wong could almost be a carbon copy of that revealed in European American theater and films. Despite the stereotypes, racist hiring policies, and racial illusions that affected her career in many negative ways, from being denied important starring roles to a twisted representation of China and the Chinese, Wong never wavered in her quest for personal agency. The discrimination against her as a Chinese American and as a woman was not a deterrent in her individual quest for empowerment. It was as if she had taken Woodrow Wilson's political rhetoric of self-determination to heart by recognizing only its human, psychological, and cultural attributes.

Wong's European experience was the defining moment in her film career as she realized that her reach could extend beyond Hollywood. It demonstrated to her that she needed to recondition her voice with a slight British accent now that sound pictures were beginning to take hold of the public's imagination. Meeting Europeans of wealth and status provoked this daughter of a Los Angeles laundry owner to dress elegantly, engagingly, and sometimes provocatively. While in Europe Wong, with her intuitive sense of public relations, re-created herself as a performer to whom absolutely no one would ever feel indifferent.

REFLECTIONS

After working in the three versions of *The Flame of Love,* Anna May Wong returned to the United States and a lengthy run as Minn Lee in the Broadway play *On the Spot.* While acting in the play at the Curran Theater in San Francisco, she reflected on her life in Europe to reporter George C. Warren:

> I know now that I was very young when I went to Europe. Yes, I was young in feeling and understanding. But I found myself there. A person must be alone to find herself. If I had remained in Los Angeles, I should perhaps still be immature, for the daily habits of life prevent meditation and study. These I found time for in Europe where there is no routine of home life. I was alone and on my own. For one thing, I learned to think of others. When I was at home, I was selfish and thought only of myself.[46]

While in Europe, Wong also dealt with the race question. She remarked that:

> There's one reason why I was so happy there. Of course, it depends a lot upon who you are. People who might ordinarily have racial feeling would make an exception in the case of a celebrity. But there, everyone was lovely to me.
>
> That is not always true of America. But what difference does it make. People like that who would be rude and unkind, you wouldn't wish to know them anyway, so it doesn't matter.[47]

Anna May Wong's initial experience in Europe was certainly a defining moment in her evolution as a film actress, stage performer, world traveler, and intelligent, active human being. But more important, it gave her a clarity of purpose and an agency that would empower her as she returned to the United States to face the continuing burden of race in Hollywood. She would spend the early 1930s working in *Daughter of the Dragon* (1931); costarring in *Shanghai Express* (1932), one of her most enduring signature films; and starring in *A Study in Scarlet* (1933). She also returned to London for three more films, *Tiger Bay* (1933), *Chu Chin Chow* (1934), and *Java Head* (1934). Along with the acclaim for *Shanghai Express,* those British films helped net her a contract from Paramount that resulted in *Limehouse Blues* (1934); *Daughter of Shanghai* (1937); *Dangerous to Know* (1938), which was a film version of *On the Spot; King of Chinatown* (1939); and *Island of Lost Men* (1939). Wong would also work extensively in stage productions, vaudeville, and nightclub acts.

NOTES

1. Foster Hirsch, *Laurence Olivier* (Boston: Twayne, 1979), 22.
2. Neil Okrent, "Right Place, Wong Time," *Los Angeles Magazine* (25 May 1990): 84.

3. Cited in Lisa See, "Anna May Speaks (From the Grave)," in *On Gold Mountain* (New York: St. Martin's Press, 1995), 226. See's account of what Anna May Wong might have said is compiled from interviews and other sources.

4. These roles were in *Dinty* (1920), *Shame* (1921), *The Toll of the Sea* (1922), *Drifting* (1923), *The Fortieth Door* (1924), *Peter Pan* (1924), *Forty Winks* (1925), *Fifth Avenue* (1926), *A Trip to Chinatown* (1926), *The Chinese Parrot* (1927), *Mr. Wu* (1927), *Why Girls Love Sailors* (1927), *The Devil Dancer* (1927), *Streets of Shanghai* (1927), and the *Crimson City* (1928).

5. Basil Dean, *Mind's Eye: An Autobiography, 1927–1972,* vol. 2 of *Seven Ages* (London: Hutchinson, 1973), 67.

6. *The Travels of Marco Polo* (Hertfordshire, England: Wordsworth Classic, 1997), xv. For an account of the impact of *The Travels of Marco Polo* on China, see Shen Fuwei, *Cultural Flow Between China and Outside World Throughout History* (Beijing: Foreign Language Press, 1996), 170–76.

7. *Chinese History: From Primitive Society Down through the Qing Dynasty* (Beijing: China Reconstructs Press, 1988), 127–28.

8. Li Hsing-tao, *The Story of the Circle of Chalk: A Drama from the Old Chinese,* trans. Frances Hume (London: Rodale Press, 1954), 5–6.

9. Bai Shaoyi, *An Outline History of China* (Beijing: Foreign Language Press, 1982), 300.

10. Gwyn Williams, in Li, *Story of the Circle of Chalk,* 7.

11. Of the one hundred Yuan plays, only four in French translation ever reached Europe in the eighteenth and early nineteenth centuries: *L'Orphelin de la famille Tchao,* trans P. Premare; *Le Viellard qui obtient un fils* and *Les chagrins du palais de Han,* trans. M. Davis; and Stanislas Julien's *Le Cercle de Craie.* James Laver, *The Circle of Chalk: A Play in Five Acts Adapted from the Chinese by Klabund* (London: William Heinemann, 1929), ix.

12. Laver, *Circle of Chalk.*

13. Lord Comer to Basil Dean, in Dean, *Mind's Eye,* 64.

14. Dean, *Mind's Eye,* 67.

15. "All for Mr. Wallace: A Chinese Actress Reaches Broadway, and If She Is Not Wong, Sue Her," *New York Times,* 16 November 1930, 4.

16. Dean, *Mind's Eye,* 67.

17. Wong, cited in John Scott, "European Bouquets Get Notice: Chinese Flapper Crashes Continent Before Finding Recognition Here," *Los Angeles Times,* 23 August 1931, 2.

18. Dean, *Mind's Eye,* 65.

19. Dean, *Mind's Eye,* 66.

20. Mrs. Ma, cited in Laver, *Circle of Chalk,* 49.

21. Hi-Tang, cited in Laver, *Circle of Chalk,* 103.

22. William Dolby, *A History of Chinese Drama* (New York: Barnes & Noble, 1976), 67.

23. Cited in Laver, *Circle of Chalk,* 4, 6, 7, 69.

24. Cited in Laver, *Circle of Chalk,* 20.

25. "All for Mr. Wallace," 4.

26. Cited in Thomas Kiernan, *Sir Larry: The Life of Laurence Olivier* (New York: Times Books, 1981), 61.

27. Dean, *Mind's Eye,* 68.

28. Cited in Dean, *Mind's Eye,* 69; Donald Spoto, *Laurence Olivier: A Biography* (New York: HarperCollins, 1992), 51; Anthony Holden, *Olivier* (London: Weidenfeld & Nicolson, 1998), 53.

29. Cited in Barrie Roberts, "Anna May Wong: Daughter of the Orient," *Classic Images* 270 (December 1997): 21.

30. Dean, *Mind's Eye,* 67–68.

31. Cited in Holden, *Olivier,* 53.

32. Dean, *Mind's Eye,* 68.

33. Cited in Dean, *Mind's Eye,* 68.

34. S.R.L, cited in Philip Leibfried, *Anna May Wong (1905–1961),* 1999, at http://annamaywong.com/biography.htm (accessed 2 January 2000).

35. Leibfried, *Anna May Wong.*

36. Wong, cited in George C. Warren, "Anna May Wong Returns a Poised Cosmopolite," *San Francisco Chronicle,* 4 October 1931, D1.

37. Roberts, "Anna May Wong," 21. See also Shirley Jennifer Lim, "Girls Just Wanna Have Fun: The Politics of Asian American Women's Public Culture, 1930–1960" (Ph.D. dissertation. University of California, Los Angeles, 1998), 81; Scott, "European Bouquets Get Notice," 2.

38. Judy Chu, "Anna May Wong," in *Counterpoint: Perspectives on Asian America,* ed. Emma Gee (Los Angeles: Asian American Center, 1976), 286.

39. Cited in Lim, "Girls Just Wanna Have Fun," 81.

40. Betty Willis, "Famous Oriental Stars Return to the Screen," *Motion Picture Magazine* (October 1931): 90.

41. Audrey Rivers, "Anna May Wong Sorry She Cannot Be Kissed," *Movie Classics* (November 1939): 39.

42. Wong, cited in Henry Carr, "I Am Growing More Chinese—Each Passing Year!" *Los Angeles Times,* 9 September 1934, 3.

43. James Robert Parish and William T. Leonard, eds., "Anna May Wong," in *Hollywood Players: The Thirties* (New Rochelle, N.Y.: Arlington House, 1976), 534.

44. Wong, cited in Willis, "Famous Oriental Stars," 90.

45. Wong, cited in Scott, "European Bouquets Get Notice," 2.

46. Wong, cited in Warren, "Anna May Wong Returns a Poised Cosmopolite," D1.

47. Wong, cited in Willis, "Famous Oriental Stars," 90.

FIVE

THE JOURNEY ENDS HALFWAY

The highlight of Anna May Wong's initial European sojourn was her success as the female lead in *The Flame of Love,* her first talking picture. Revamped as *Hai-Tang* with Wong speaking German and *L'amour maitre des choses,* in which she had a French-speaking role as Hai-tang, the fact that she was cast almost simultaneously in three similar roles attests to her box office prominence and celebrity. Although her stature as the star was clearly defined, Wong was always seeking other work. During the production of Richard Eichberg's trilogy, she also performed in one of Britain's first screen musicals.[1]

ELSTREE CALLING (1930)

Directed in part by Alfred Hitchcock (1899–1980), *Elstree Calling* was a film revue with nineteen musical and comedy sketches. In it Wong acted, danced, and performed with such British notables as Donald Catthrop (1888–1940), Bobbie Comber (1890–1942), Cicely Courtneidge (1893–1980), Will Fyffe (1885–1947), Tommy Handley (1894–1949), and Lily Morris (1884–1952). In particular, Wong played Katherine in a satire of *The Taming of the Shrew.*[2]

In the revue, comedian "Little" Teddy Brown (1900–1946) offered his own brand of racist humor with a comment on Jewish avarice. He announced, "Here is the Hebrew Parade, to the bank, to the bank."[3] Shot in twelve days and translated into eleven languages, *Elstree Calling* was released in the United States on September 29, 1930. It was enlivened with risqué performances by the Berkoff Dancers, Charlot Girls, and Adelphi Girls. *Elstree Calling* was also a *Piccadilly* homecoming of sorts for Wong since Hannah Jones, who played Bessie, and Jameson Thomas, who starred as Valentine Wilmot, were also in the cast. By the time *Elstree Calling* was released, Wong was already well into her next performance. In Austria she starred in a Viennese operetta with acting, dancing, and singing that delighted the German-speaking audience. In fact, *Springtime,* or *Tschuin Tschi* (1930), was Wong's stage debut, and she wrote all the parts in the German language.[4] Although her German was fluent, Wong admitted that "I suffered stage fright the moment I started speaking German and felt as if it were my first appearance anywhere, but now, after this wonderful reception, I cannot go back to earth!"[5] Even her new German friends were astonished by her spoken German after a full conversation with Wong. Before that, they thought that her German film was dubbed by a native speaker.[6]

Artists and critics were enraptured by her performance. Felix Weiss (1907–) sculpted a bust of her head, which was eventually included in a collection of Chinese ethnography at a Vienna museum.[7] One film critic enthused that "Fraulein Wong had the audience perfectly in her power and the unobtrusive tragedy of her acting was deeply moving, carrying off the difficult German speaking part very successfully."[8]

Although *Springtime* ran for ten months, Wong was not pleased with her performance.[9] She admitted that "it wasn't very good, but the Viennese are enthusiastic people."[10] Wong continued, "[A]fter the first performance, men and women both rushed back stage. Ladies kissed my hand (imagine my embarrassment) and one little girl asked me for the stocking I wore the first night of the show. She said if she wore them, they would bring her good luck."[11]

Even though the adulation of Europeans was unconditional, strong, and intense, Wong was homesick for Los Angeles and her family. She left Europe with her sister and companion, Lulu, on her first return voyage to the United States in 1930. After three years abroad, she was a major star. Her plan was to spend a short visit with family in California and then make a quick return to Europe where the producers, directors, and audiences always welcomed her.[12] With her first European performances, however, Wong had developed such an iconic status that contracts were offered to her even before she landed in New

York. Although she was not overtly seeking work from the European American stage or Hollywood, she was made an offer that she could not refuse.

ON THE SPOT (1930)

While traveling aboard the Cunarder *Aquitania* steaming across the Atlantic Ocean, stage director Lee Ephraim sent Wong a telegram imploring her to accept the role of Minn Lee in Edgar's Wallace's stage play *On the Spot*.[13] She would replace Marie Carroll.[14] After auditioning three European American actresses who "were not sufficiently Oriental," Ephraim decided to forego the "Yellowface" charade so common among Western directors. He rushed down to meet Wong at the New York docks with a script in one hand and a contract in the other. During the customary search of her luggage by customs officials she agreed to Ephraim's contractual terms.[15]

Despite the fact that Wong would perform an "Orientalist" and therefore an exotic role as the mistress of a Chicago mobster named Tony Perrelli, played by Crane Wilbur (1886–1973), this was an opportunity to star in a major New York play on Broadway. It was not an opportunity to turn down. Although she was described by Brooks Atkinson of the *New York Times* as Perrelli's "inscrutably loyal Chinese jade,"[16] the role of Minn Lee was a part in which she sought to expand beyond the cliché of an "Oriental" sexual handmaiden serving her European American lover and gangster boss. The play itself was not simply a typical rendition of a "China doll," written by a hack playwright, calling for Wong to express femme fatale dramatics.

It was, in fact, a major melodrama by Edgar Wallace (1875–1932), one of the literary world's foremost playwrights and novelists, whose reputation was secure by 1930. With five million copies of his books sold annually, he was at the zenith of his creative and intellectual powers. On the other hand Wong, a child of Chinese America, was merely an aspiring actress attempting to prove herself in her first Broadway play.

Edgar Wallace's *On the Spot* was conceived while the British writer was in Chicago during the autumn of 1929 having lunch with local journalists and visiting police departments:

> He was shown (Al) Capone's headquarters, the Hotel Lexington (which possessed the features of so many of the mysterious establishments in his own thrillers, since though a gang stronghold it was still used as a middle-class hotel by unsuspecting provincials); the flower-shop where Dion O'Banion was "put on the spot"; restaurants where rival gangs had settled

their differences with machine-guns; the garage which had been the scene of the St. Valentine's Day massacre. He was also driven around the old "red light" district, where every house had been an open brothel until the police drove prostitution underground, and had new and flourishing bawdy houses pointed out to him in the suburb of Cicero.[17]

From a day of listening to tales of gangland killings and intrigues, Wallace had the basis for a play. He wrote *On the Spot* in four days and nights at his home in England.[18] His biographer, Margaret Lane, called *On the Spot* the best play Edgar Wallace had ever written.[19]

Wong already knew about *On the Spot* because it had premiered in London while she was working on her own productions in 1930. In fact, she "attended the melodrama over there with him" and was considering the notion of playing Minn Lee even then.[20] Meeting Wallace for lunch in the summer of 1930, she was at the height of hipness and savvy chic. With a dash of "Oriental" wisdom and a reference to her own ethnicity and cultural heritage, she remarked to the *New York Herald Tribune* reporter:

> The exceedingly busy Mr. Wallace like the eternal beaver he is, could grant me only an hour for lunch. During that time he invented three new plots, two for books and one for a play. He insisted on beginning to work on them at once, knowing that it is always well to follow one path to the end. I'm sure the Son of Heaven had three men in mind when he created Mr. Wallace.[21]

After her stint in Europe, Wong had developed her own theatrical persona to such an extent that she was no longer a Chinese American pretending to be a European American flapper. In fact, she became quintessentially Anna May Wong. This was to be her greatest and most enduring role, playing herself. Understanding perfectly that she lived and worked in a European American and wholly European artistic environment with its inclination to "Yellowface" and racist stereotyping, Wong played the role of the sage Chinese female with "celestial" references when the circumstances warranted it. She could also evoke her California and Western being. This was all too clear to an astute *New York Herald Tribune* journalist, who remarked:

> Then there's her slang. When the use of Americanisms seemed proper, in a situation, she discloses an amazing knowledge of the *patois;* and she will use a French or German word if it describes better than another language.[22]

By the time Wong was immersed in her first rehearsals for *On the Spot,* she had already attained a definite agency in her career and approach to life. While others would have influence on her acting career, she was now the sole agent of her destiny. At the age of twenty-five she was discovering herself as Anna May Wong. Her European sojourn was part of this discovery.

The advent of her agency and a firm belief in her abilities, talents, and place in the theatrical world as a no-nonsense actress was evident in her dealings with Lee Ephraim. As director of an Edgar Wallace play, Ephraim made it abundantly clear during one of the first rehearsals that this role of Minn Lee was of such magnitude that Wong ought not to take it lightly. Replying in an equally concise manner, Wong said, "Quite true. But one actor does not make a play."[23]

In another exchange, Ephraim insisted that Minn Lee's stage crossing reflect the "short, hesitant steps" either of a *geisha* girl or Cho Cho San in Paramount's *Madame Butterfly* (1915). Wong's retort was that the notion of the "short, hesitant steps" was found only in Japan. There was a huge difference between the way women walked in Japan and China. She emphasized that no Chinese woman ever walked like a *geisha*. Ephraim gave in, and Wong as Minn Lee walked across the stage in a normal manner as any Chinese woman would.[24]

Wong's Broadway debut was at the Forrest Theater on October 29, 1930. It was a smashing success, with 167 performances in New York and across the United States.[25] While the play was praised for Wong's virtuoso performance, what was more gratifying was the fact that her sister, Mary, was cast as her understudy.[26] By the end of January 1931, Wong had exhausted *On the Spot* and was replaced by Kay Strozzi (1899–1996).[27]

From 1928 to 1930, Wong's European triumph had been shared with her elder sister, Lulu. Now Mary was part of her first Broadway success. With both Wong sisters associated with the female lead in the play, the nation's theater audiences were able to witness some of the other acting talents in Sam Sing Wong's family. By October 10, 1931, after eleven months of performances, *On the Spot* closed in San Francisco at the Curran Theater.[28] It was a splendid triumph for Anna May Wong, spoiled only by the death of her mother, Gon Toy Lee, in a car accident in front of the family house in Los Angeles during her New York engagement in November 1930. Wong sued the driver, Joe Rondoni, for negligence, but the court threw out the suit. Witnesses told police that Gon Toy Lee "had stepped back in front of his automobile and that he was unable to avoid striking her."[29]

FEMININITY

During a period of free time from her stage performance as Minn Lee in *On the Spot* in San Francisco, Wong appeared before a gathering of three hundred women. As an actress whose beauty was a major selling point in her celebrity, she had many opportunities to speak to women about femininity, beauty, and how to enhance their otherwise mundane lives with cosmetics. Sponsored by the *San Francisco Chronicle* and scheduled at the Jane Friendly Lounge in the newspaper's building, the program emphasized:

> One particular phase of Miss Wong's talk will be her theory of what actually constituted Oriental beauty. The fine points of Celestial comeliness make up a sadly neglected subject. She also will discuss the feminine preparations for the stage and the street.[30]

Beginning with a remembrance of starstruck childhood days in her North Figueroa Street home, Wong told of her first encounter with makeup, involving Chinese red paper, white rice powder, and "a hoard of burned matches."[31] But here, her counsel to the crowd was simple. She gave a word or two of advice to her audience on street and daytime use of cosmetics. It all simmered down to three rules: use powder the exact shade of the skin, blend color with powder with the utmost care, and use makeup so that it will be as inconspicuous as possible.[32]

Although the ethnicity of these three hundred women was not noted, many in the audience were presumably Asian American women interested in glamorizing their ordinary lives and discovering what actually constituted "Oriental" beauty from a noted Asian American woman whose career depended on her beauty. The use of Wong's fame and celebrity was one of the ways in which the cosmetics industry, in tandem with newspapers, promoted nonessential products in a society becoming increasingly dependent on conspicuous consumption. Asian American women were a natural target in a city like San Francisco, which had a large Asian presence. Like the selling of Asian and Asian American stereotypes in films and stage plays, Wong endorsed products through her lectures and appearances. Selling merchandise, like selling herself, was just part of being a film star and another way to enhance her marketability.

Wong's presence as a global performer resonated with audiences in Asia, Australia, Europe, and North America. As the most famous Asian American female star in the history of film, she was closely tied to Hollywood's version of femininity. But even though that femininity depicted a European American ideal of beauty, the cosmetics industry, with its almost intuitive sense of profitability, often utilized performers of color to sell its merchandise.[33] The color of money was never restricted by race or ethnicity in the marketing of beauty aids for women. During the 1930s Max Factor was especially innovative in the adaptation of its products to a woman's eye, hair, and skin color. In particular, "cosmetic advertising of the 1930s certainly utilized stereotypes (popular makeup products used 'Tropical,' 'Chinese,' and 'Gypsy' colors), but the advertising was, nevertheless, significant because it described beauty in terms of multiple points on a spectrum, rather than a single monochromatic deal."[34]

After her femininity lecture and the closing of *On the Spot* in San Francisco, Wong began work on two Paramount productions, *Daughter of the Dragon* and *Shanghai Express.* Her superb performance in *Shanghai Express,* however, was not enough to persuade the studio to renew her contract. While Marlene Dietrich went on to star in Paramount's *Blond Venus* (1932) with Cary Grant (1904–1986), Wong signed with World Wide Pictures to play Mrs. Pyke in a Sherlock Holmes thriller called *A Study in Scarlet.* But this film was not enough work. After her first series of European films with Eichberg, Dupont, and Hitchcock from 1928 to 1930, Wong realized that Hollywood was not her only source of income. By 1932 she was contemplating performing in films and onstage on a global scale.

VAUDEVILLE

Before shooting began on *A Study in Scarlet* in California, Wong worked the vaudeville circuit. Actor Dick Powell (1904–1963) introduced her at the Mastbaum Theater in Philadelphia in a musical revue in which she sang "Boys Will Be Girls and Girls Will Be Boys." After thunderous applause, Wong expressed her "thanks" in Cantonese Chinese, French, German, English, and even Yiddish.[35] In July 1932 she entertained a New York audience at the grandiose Capitol Theater with an intimate seating capacity of eight hundred. Established in 1921, this was one of New York's finest live theaters, "with its Venetian marble floor, its wainscoting and stairs of light, clouded marble and its circular ceiling, which features eight inlaid panels, and a glittering dome of Bohemian cut glass."[36]

In the New York show Wong's fellow entertainers were stars such as Jack Benny (Benjamin Kubelsky, 1894–1974), who acted as master of ceremonies; Jean Hersolt (1886–1956); Una Merkel (1903–1982); and Abe Lyman (1897–1957) with his Hollywood Orchestra. Augmenting this live revue, called *Hollywood on Parade,* was the MGM feature *Unashamed.* Dancing, singing, acting, and reciting a Chinese poem constituted some of Wong's performances. Her Chinese poem later became part of a series of shorts titled *Hollywood on Parade.*

Bland Johansen wrote in the *New York Mirror* that the "Capitol never was offered a stage show as elaborate and as entertaining as its current *Hollywood on Parade*. It's a $5.50 review, brisk, tuneful, colorful, loaded with laughs, rich in personalities."[37] During this tour, Una Merkel and Wong became such fast friends that Philippa, a columnist at the *Hong Kong Sunday Herald,* revealed that "Anna May Wong's special Hollywood friend is Una Merkel—a darling girl, she says: sympathetic, sincere, and as natural off the screen as on."[38]

"WINDSOR EXPRESS"

But before March 1932, when Wong's vaudeville troupe arrived in Philadelphia,[39] Wong would encounter neither sympathy, sincerity, nor applause. When the itinerary called for a stopover in Windsor, Ontario, she ventured across to the Detroit train station to visit with some friends. When she attempted to leave Detroit to reboard her train in Windsor, Canadian immigration officials stopped her at the border. The reason was succinctly stated by Inspector O. G. Adams, inspector at Windsor: "Chinese must enter Canada through designated ports of entry of which Windsor is not one."[40] Wong had no choice but to continue on to New York through the United States. No measure of Hollywood stardom could provide immunity from Canadian racism in the 1930s. By the time the tour stopped at the Capitol Theater in New York during the summer of 1932, the Windsor episode was merely a minor irritant.

A EUROPEAN RETURN

A Study in Scarlet was released in the United States in April 1933 and in Britain in January 1934.[41] Distributed by Fox Film Corporation, this Sherlock Holmes film was seen by many people in Europe and North America, including Canada.

Following *A Study in Scarlet,* Anna May Wong signed a three-picture British deal to star in *Tiger Bay* (1933), *Chu Chin Chow* (1934), and *Java Head* (1934). Recognizing her global celebrity in these films and the acclaim she had garnered in *Shanghai Express,* Paramount was quick to offer her the leading female role in *Limehouse Blues* (1934). There were also parts in *Daughter of Shanghai* (1937) and *Dangerous to Know* (1937).[42] But before working on the latter two films, Wong brought her vaudeville stage show to theaters in Italy, Switzerland, Spain, Scandinavia, France, Scotland, Ireland, and England. The Italian tour was especially lengthy, and she learned Italian. She was quoted as saying that "one third of her act will be spoken in that tongue with the naive suggestion that she hopes they'll understand her."[43] Her vaudeville tour began in Torino, moved to Rome, Naples, Palermo, Messina, Catania, and then returned to Rome, followed by stints in Florence, Milan, Venice, Trieste, Torino again, and finally Genoa.

In February 1935 Wong took her act to the National Scola Theater in Copenhagen. In March she performed in Switzerland, and during the entire month of April she worked in Paris.[44] She later vacationed in Germany and France and then returned to London.[45] During this period Wong was offered the title role of Lady Precious Stream in a Broadway production by Morris Gest (1881–1942), who had been following her career ever since he was the impresario for the New York premiere of *The Thief of Bagdad*. Later he was keenly interested in the success of the talking version of *Chu Chin Chow* because he had staged a Broadway production of the operetta from 1917 to 1918. But in 1935 Wong told Gest that although she "was simply enchanted by the play," she was "so buried in other work," such as the extensive European tour, that she had to decline.[46]

After the exhausting European tour, Wong returned to the United States to begin preparing for the experience of a lifetime in China while taking a respite from Hollywood. The maturity that was consolidated by her time in China was evident in her later films, in which she played women with recognizable and legitimate professions. While Wong portrayed heroines like Hu Fei in *Shanghai Express* and Zahrat in *Chu Chin Chow* with cinematic and theatrical conviction, her roles during the late 1930s were played with wisdom, humanity, and conviction that revealed an inspired and irreverent persona without self-doubt or regret.

THE BEST YEARS

By the time she returned to the United States from China in November 1936, Wong had entered into one of her most productive film stages, with a multipicture contract from Paramount. She had already starred in *Limehouse Blues* (1934) and would play leading roles in *Daughter of Shanghai* (1937), *Dangerous to Know* (1938), *King of Chinatown* (1939), and *Island of Lost Men* (1939). Just before working on *Daughter of Shanghai,* she was signed by the *Royal Gelatin Hour* to play a young woman returning from China after many years in the United States.[47] Aired on NBC's WCAF, this dramatization was based on her China sojourn of eleven months.

Between *Dangerous to Know* and *King of Chinatown,* Wong starred in *When Were You Born* (1938) for Warner Bros. The character Mary Lee Ling, an astrologist, was almost a parallel to the character Charlie Chan, a detective. In fact, Warner Bros. was contemplating a mystery series similar to the Chan episodes, with Wong as the astrologist who could predict the future and therefore foretell likely murders, thievery, and assorted illegal misdeeds while charting the stars. Paying Wong a sum of $5,250 for three weeks' work in *Where Were You Born,* the studio envisioned an option for six pictures over five years.[48] Although it was innovative and audacious because it called for an authentic Asian American female to star in a Hollywood series, little of consequence resulted from this notion of a woman playing a sleuth. This revolutionary idea of an Asian American woman investigator would finally take shape with Wong playing a detective in a 1951 Du Mont television series called *The Gallery of Mme. Liu Tsong.*

A BIZARRE TWIST

The end of the 1930s was a stellar period for Anna May Wong. Her career was never better. But in the spring of 1937 a crazed stalker named A. M. Foote began sending threatening letters to Wong and Irene Mayer Selznick (1907–1990), wife of Hollywood producer David O. Selznick (1902–1965). Declaring himself the attempted assassin of Los Angeles District Attorney Buron Fitts (1895–1971), who was wounded close to his home in March 1937, Foote warned Wong that:

> Unless you come down to my room immediately with $20,000, you will be disfigured and your father will be crippled and others close to you will be included. First call my number, Trinity 6931, and ask for me, Dr. A. M. Foote. You don't need to lose the $20,000. It is a mere guarantee of cooperation to the fullest extent on your part.[49]

Targeting Irene Mayer Selznick, who was also the daughter of MGM movie mogul Louis B. Mayer (1885–1957), with a note demanding $20,000 in "unmarked bills on pain of death to her young sons and her father,"[50] seemed to fit in with Foote's cinematic ambitions. He fancied himself a modern Jesus Christ. His note continued:

> I will play the part of Jesus Christ as I look just like him. I strike quick like I did to Buron Fitts when he took a warning from me as other warnings. Had I desired to kill him I could have done so. I added to his injuries. Look at him. That's you if you do not comply.
>
> . . . A. M. Foote, M.D.[51]

Foote then insisted that MGM also cast evangelist Aimee Semple McPherson and a Dr. McCoy in his picture about Jesus Christ. To confuse the matter, this A. M. Foote sent a third letter to a chiropractor named E. J. Foote and demanded that the latter Foote receive the $20,000 each from Wong and Selznick and wait for further instructions. The threats to Wong continued into April 1937.[52]

Captain Clyde Plummer, head of the Los Angeles police investigation, never discovered why Wong was selected to receive the brunt of Foote's madness. Certainly her association with MGM and its main principals, Irene Mayer Selznick, David O. Selznick, and Louis B. Mayer, was tenuous. The film version of *The Good Earth*, for which she auditioned, was backed by MGM, but she had no role in that picture. In the three MGM films in which she had a part, Wong played minor characters: Oneta in *The Desert's Toll* (1926), Loo Song in *Mr. Wu* (1927), and a cameo in *Hollywood Party* (1937). Therefore, she had no real connection with MGM. The role MGM played in this extortion case was certainly pertinent because of its vast movie production potential in the mind of A. M. Foote. But the choice of Wong by the "man who would be Christ" may just have been random.

THE 1940s

From 1937 to the 1940s, global warfare was interrupting the making and distribution of films. The Japanese atrocities in China hardened Wong's political attitude. She began searching for different roles. Besides being lent to Warner Bros., Wong played diplomat Lois King in Columbia Pictures's *Ellery Queen's Penthouse Mystery* (1941).

Between 1937 and 1942 Wong appeared in nine films, with cameos in *Hollywood Party* (1937) and *Chinese Garden Festival* (1940). She portrayed positive roles as the filial daughter of a slain Chinatown elder, a daughter (Kim Ling) of a general, a physician (Dr. May Ling), and a diplomat (Lois Ling), as well as an astrologist (Mary Lee Ling). In *Dangerous to Know,* she portrayed the female role of Lan Ying (Minn Lee in *On the Spot*), mistress to Stephen Recka, played by Akim Tamiroff (1899–1972).

As well as making many films during these five years, Wong also worked the theatrical and vaudeville circuits. In 1937 she played the female lead in *Princess Turandot* at the Westport Country Playhouse. The *White Plains Reporter* enthused that she was "delightful in the natural role of the Princess." The reviewer continued that "her breeding" was the chief attraction in a role that only Wong could have played with authenticity.[53] Two years later, she took her vaudeville act to Australia and New Zealand with the agent, Tivoli Theaters, Ltd., booking her opening performance in Melbourne in June.[54] Following this tour she played opposite Vincent Price (1911–1993) in *Turandot* in 1940.[55] Two years later she worked the fashion circuit with "her Chinese girls," staging a show of "ancient and modern costumes," for W & J Sloane, a San Francisco department store.[56]

Positive roles continued in 1942, when she signed a four-picture contract with Producers Releasing Corporation, with *The Devil's Sister* scheduled to be the first production.[57] Because of funding problems, however, the film company was able to release only *Bombs Over Burma* (1942) and *The Lady from Chungking* (1942), with Wong playing Lin Ying, an educator, and Kwan Mei, a guerrilla leader, respectively. During the late 1940s a new player emerged as a dramatic vehicle and a source of generating additional income for Wong and many other film performers. This was television.

1950s

Anna May Wong was one of the few movie performers with the dexterity and agility to make the transition from silent films to talkies and then to the medium of television almost without any discernible difficulties. Certainly she was the only Asian American film star to transcend those styles of dramatic storytelling production. Although her next role was a small part as Su Lin in *Impact* (1949), she continued to extend her Hollywood persona as a genuine movie star in television.

In October 1951 Wong began working for Du Mont television (1946–1955)[58] as the star of *The Gallery of Mme. Liu Tsong,* in which she portrayed an amateur detective in the guise of an art dealer. It had been eight years since she had played a major role in any dramatic production. Conrad J. Doerr, a Santa Monica College student who rented two rooms at her San Vicente Boulevard Moongate Apartments in Santa Monica, claimed that Wong was "terrified not only returning to work, but over doing so in a new medium."[59] But the series, directed by William Marceau, showcased Wong as a mature, confident, and convincing Mme. Liu Tsong in eleven prime-time episodes airing between 9:00 and 9:30 P.M.[60]

More television was in store for Wong in the 1950s. But she also accepted the film role of Madame Liang in the first Asian American movie version of the novel and Broadway musical *Flower Drum Song,* earmarked for release in

1961. While anticipating rehearsals for this historic all-Asian American film, she worked for NBC's *Producer's Showcase* (1954–1957). She played the biracial Mrs. Hammond in "The Letter" by Somerset Maugham; the show aired on October 15, 1956. Since *Producer's Showcase* was live television, it was one of the most expensive shows made during the 1950s, with one episode aired every fourth Monday for three years. It was especially intended to broadcast color spectaculars just to sell new color television sets made by RCA. Wong also performed on CBS's *Climax Mystery Theater* (1954–1958) in an episode entitled "The Chinese Game." This aired on May 1, 1958.[61] She continued her television career on November 2, 1959, with a cameo in an ABC series, *Adventures in Paradise* (1959–1962).

THE JOURNEY ENDS HALFWAY, 1960s

During her long cinematic career, Anna May Wong played characters in comedies, musicals, mysteries, and gangster films. But it was television that would bring her to the most American of all genres, the western. On March 15, 1960, she portrayed an antiracist activist in one of 266 episodes of the popular ABC series *The Life and Legend of Wyatt Earp* (1955–1961). Her role was to aid Marshall Wyatt Earp, played by Hugh O'Brian (1930–), in upholding the rights of Chinese workers on the Western frontier. During this period she came out of film retirement at the urging of longtime friend Anthony Quinn (1915–2001) to play minor roles in *The Savage Innocents* (1959) as Hiko and in *Portrait in Black* (1960) as Tani.

In the winter of 1960 Wong played in two television series scheduled to be aired in early 1961. She completed production for the role as a housekeeper in NBC's *Barbara Stanwyck Show* (1960–1961) in early winter. During that period she also portrayed a Miss Lee in the British thriller series *Danger Man,* which was known as *Secret Agent* in the United States. "The Journey Ends Halfway" was the thirty-sixth episode in the first series of the long-running British show about global espionage, Cold War plots, and anticommunist intrigues. While completing the on-camera work for the *Barbara Stanwyck Show* and *Danger Ma*n, Wong was preparing in earnest for her role as Madam Liang in *Flower Drum Song.*

The Barbara Stanwyck Show aired on January 1961. But before she could screen the final production of "The Journey Ends Halfway," which was to air on April 30, 1961, the movie goddess from Chinese America who transcended racism, cinematic eras, foreign borders, familial doubts, and her own ambitions died of a heart attack. For six weeks, from December 1960 until she died on February 3, 1961, at the age of fifty-six, she was under intensive care at her home, 308 21st Place in Santa Monica, where she lived with her brother Richard after she sold the San Vicente house in 1956. Being a sufferer of Laennec's cirrhosis may have aggravated her heart problem.[62] At fifty-six her life was indeed a journey that ended halfway.

Although Anna May Wong died relatively young, she never had a problem with age. In June 1960 she told a reporter that she "would rather be 70 years young than 40 years old."[63] She also never had a problem with relocating from the United States when production or travel opportunities presented themselves. It was only fitting that Wong's final performance was in a British production, because her most satisfying work had been in Europe. There, this daughter of Los Angeles was respected and feted, and she probably would have remained in London, Paris, or Berlin if Europe had not been at war.

She also had thought about settling in Beijing, China. Following her triumphs in *Shanghai Express, A Study in Scarlet,* and *Chu Chin Chow* and especially her failure to land the part of O-lan in *The Good Earth,* China beckoned. Unlike many Asian American actresses then and now, Wong took on China with the enthusiasm that she always possessed when she tackled a cinematic role. But it was more than just traveling to China. She told Carolyn Anspacher that "I shall study the customs and language of China since they are so strange to me. I shall study the Chinese theater that I know as casually as you. Then I shall be able to tell whether I am really Anna May Wong or Wong Liu Tsong."[64]

NOTES

1. Maurice Yacower, "Elstree Calling," in *Hitchcock's British Films* (Hamden, Conn.: Archon Books, 1977), 114.

2. "Elstree Calling," *London Times,* 10 February 1930, 6.

3. "Elstree Calling," 6.

4. "Screen Star Has Her Homecoming After Much Delay," *Seattle Daily Times,* 6 September 1931, 14; James Robert Parish and William T. Leonard, eds., "Anna May Wong," in *Hollywood Players: The Thirties* (New Rochelle, N.Y.: Arlington House, 1976), 534, "Anna May Wong Is Dead at 56, Actress Won Fame in '24," *New York Times,* 4 February 1961, 7.

5. Wong, cited in Parish and Leonard, "Anna May Wong," 534.

6. *New York Times,* 12 October 1930, 3.

7. "Star at Hawaii: Anna May Wong Nearing Homeland," *San Francisco Chronicle,* 24 May 1936, 6; Felix Weiss, "Heads and Tales," *Christian Science Monitor Magazine* (18 September 1935), 4.

8. Cited in Parish and Leonard, "Anna May Wong," 534.

9. "Screen Star Has Her Homecoming," 14.

10. Wong, cited in John Scott, "European Bouquets Get Notice: Chinese Flapper Crashes Continent Before Finding Recognition Here," *Los Angeles Times,* 23 August 1931, 2.

11. Wong, cited in Scott, "European Bouquets Get Notice," 2.

12. "Screen Star Has Her Homecoming," 14.

13. "Anna May Wong, Homesick 'Returns,'" *New York Times,* 18 October 1930, 23; Parish and Leonard, "Anna May Wong," 534.

14. "Role for Anna May Wong: She Will Act As a Chinese Girl in Wallace's 'On the Spot,'" *New York Times,* 23 October 1930, 34.

15. "All for Mr. Wallace; A Chinese Actress Reaches Broadway, and If She Is Not Wong, Sue Her," *New York Times,* 16 November 1930, 3.

16. Brooks Atkinson, "Presenting Edgar Wallace," *New York Times,* 30 October 1930, 7.

17. Margaret Lane, *Edgar Wallace: The Biography of a Phenomenon* (London: Hamish Hamilton, 1964), 270.

18. John Baxter, *The Hollywood Exiles* (New York: Taplinger, 1976), 115; Lane, *Edgar Wallace,* 271.

19. Lane, *Edgar Wallace,* 271.

20. "All for Mr. Wallace," 3.

21. "Anna May Wong, Combination of East and West; Chinese Actress, Born in U.S., Won Fame in Films, Now Is in 'On the Spot,'" *New York Herald Tribune,* 9 November 1930, 15.

22. "Anna May Wong, Combination of East and West," 15.

23. Wong, cited in "All for Mr. Wallace," 3.

24. Parish and Leonard, "Anna May Wong," 534.

25. Parish and Leonard, "Anna May Wong," 534; "Role for Anna May Wong," *New York Times,* 23 October 1930, 34.

26. "Screen Star Has Her Homecoming," 14.

27. "Theatrical Notes," *New York Times,* 3 January 1931, 21.

28. "Curran Bills 'Precedent' for Monday," *San Francisco Chronicle,* 6 October 1931, 11.

29. "Injuries Fatal to Mrs. Wong: Mother of Oriental Film Actress Dies Following Auto Accident," *Los Angeles Times,* 12 November 1930, 5.

30. "Wong's Beauty Talk to Draw Record Crowd," *San Francisco Chronicle,* 2 October 1931, 13.

31. "Chinese Star Advises Care in Makeup," *San Francisco Chronicle,* 13 October 1931, 15.

32. "Chinese Star Advises Care in Makeup," 15.

33. Sarah Berry, *Screen Style: Fashion and Femininity in 1930s Hollywood* (Minneapolis: University of Minnesota Press, 2000), 95.

34. Berry, *Screen Style,* 95.

35. Parish and Leonard, "Anna May Wong," 535.

36. Charlotte Libov, "Hoping to Regain a Bygone Elegance," *New York Times,* 14 June 1987, 3.

37. Bland Johansen, "Hollywood on Parade," *The New York Mirror,* 15 July 1932, 2.

38. Philippa, "Almost in Confidence," *Hong Kong Sunday Herald,* 22 March 1936, 3.

39. Barrie Roberts, "Anna May Wong: Daughter of the Orient," *Classic Images* 270 (December 1997): 21; Parish and Leonard, "Anna May Wong," 533.

40. "Canada Stops Chinese Star," *San Francisco Chronicle,* 29 March 1932, 3; *Los Angeles Times,* 29 March 1932, 5.

41. Robert W. Pohle and Douglas C. Hart, *Sherlock Holmes on the Screen: The Motion Picture Adventures of the World's Most Popular Detective* (London: Thomas Yoseloff, 1977), 121.

42. The key figure in *Daughter of Shanghai* and *Dangerous to Know* was director Robert Florey. He was "presented with the challenge of revitalizing the career of Anna May Wong, who had been absent from the screen for two years and with whom he had previously been associated on *A Study in Scarlet* in 1932" as a screenwriter who adapted the film from the novel by Sir Arthur Conan Doyle. Brian Taves, *Robert Florey: The French Expressionist* (Metuchen, N.J.: Scarecrow Press, 1987), 44–45, 53, 206–11.

43. Read Kendall, "Around and About Hollywood," *Los Angeles Times,* 32 December 1934, 2.

44. Kendall, "Around and About Hollywood," 2.

45. John R. Newham, "Chinese Puzzle," *Film Weekly* (17 June 1939): 19; Helen Zia and Susan B. Gall, eds., *Notable Asian Americans* (Detroit: Gale Research, 1995), 415.

46. Margaret Kamm, "Anna May Wong Gives Views on Theater of East, West," *Honolulu Advertiser,* 30 January 1936, 4.

47. *Variety,* 2 June 1937, 4.

48. Warner Brothers to Anna May Wong, Letter and Contract, January 17, 1938, 1–3, in Karen Janis Leong, "The China Mystique: Mayling Soong Chiang, Pearl S. Buck and Anna May Wong in the American Imagination" (Ph.D. dissertation, University of California, Berkeley, spring 1999), 155.

49. "A Shocking Threat to Anna May Wong, Extortionist Also Perils Selznick," *San Francisco Chronicle,* 25 March 1937, A1.

50. "Extortionist Menaces Film Mogul, Player," *Seattle Daily Times,* 24 March 1937, 1.

51. "Extortionist Menaces Film Mogul," 1.

52. "Extortionist Menaces Film Mogul," 1; "Actress Menaced Again," *San Francisco Chronicle,* 3 April 1937, 4.

53. *White Plains Reporter,* 3 August 1937, 4.

54. "Wong's Anzac Dates," *Variety,* 26 April 1939, 7.

55. Parish and Leonard, "Anna May Wong," 536.

56. *San Francisco Chronicle,* 27 March 1942, 9.

57. "Signs New Contract," *New York Times,* 13 March 1942, 22.

58. For Du Mont's rise and fall, see Ted Bergmann, *The Du Mont Television Network: What Happened? A Significant Episode in the History of Broadcasting* (Lanham, Md.:

Scarecrow Press, 2002); R. D. Heldenfels, *Television's Greatest Year, 1954* (New York: Continuum, 1994), 187–99; see also Charles Strum, "Our Television Shows: An Alien Experience," *Seattle Times,* 26 August 2001, A11; Gary Hess, *An Historical Study of Du Mont Television Network* (New York: Arno Press, 1979); Donald E. Zimmerman, "The Portrayal of Women in Mass Media, 1949 to 1956: The Du Mont Television Network Versus Popular Films, Books, Magazines and Songs" (Ph.D. dissertation, Union Graduate School, Cincinnati, Ohio, 1979).

59. Conrad J. Doerr, "Anna May Wong," *Films in Review* 10 (December 1968): 661.

60. Bergmann, *Du Mont Television Network,* 95; Roberts, "Anna May Wong," 23; "Adventure Series," Associated Press Photo, 9 September 1951.

61. "Climax," Associated Press, 19 April 1958.

62. Roberts, "Anna May Wong," 23.

63. "Miss Wong Gave Films Exotic Flavor," *New York World Telegram,* 4 February 1961, 35.

64. Wong, cited in Carolyn Anspacher, "Star Goes 'Home,' Anna May Wong Leaves for China," *San Francisco Chronicle,* 24 January 1936, 17.

PART II

LIFE'S FUNDAMENTALS

SIX

CHINA

China! For many Chinese Americans, that country holds an irresistible allure. Its physical size, its enormous population, the longevity of its civilization and history, the succulent seductiveness of its many cuisines, and its ever-changing life philosophies and polities all contribute to a fascination that no Chinese outside of China can resist. The Chinese born in the United States are especially susceptible.

For some Chinese Americans, China, like its porcelain namesake, is merely a curiosity that a few weeks in a freezing Beijing storm or in the humidity of a Guangzhou summer can readily cure. These tourists often say that they have "done China" like they have "done Rome." Going to China is like paying off an obligation for looking Chinese. Once the debt is cleared, they then retreat to their cloistered American existence and a China represented by Pearl Buck, some silk scrolls, a bamboo *mah jong* set, and made-for-Hollywood movies about the Chinese. They become "Americans" again.

China holds no more fascination for these Chinese Americans than some whimsical look at a part of their forebears' lives, which they believe were primitive (even bordering on the savage), quaint, traditional, un-Christian, undemocratic, and definitely "un-American." No matter how many times they travel to China, the country and its people remain alien and strange.

For other Chinese Americans like Anna May Wong, China was certainly a curiosity; she thought the "people always sipped tea and philosophized about life."[1] But there was also a personal side to Wong's attraction to China. Before leaving for China on January 24, 1936, she already knew that she did not belong there. This China sojourn, which lasted for eleven months, was ostensibly to visit her father, Sam Sing Wong. Taking his youngest children—Mary, Frank, Roger, and Richard—he left America in November 1934 on the SS *President Wilson* to live with his first wife in a *Taishan* village near Guangzhou and to manage the family farm.[2]

From a professional perspective, Anna May Wong envisioned her China trip as a study leave during which she could learn from Chinese theater and improve her repertoire of acting skills. A consummate professional with a legendary penchant for adaptation, she also wanted to discover the "real" Chinese so that she could bring various authentic Chinese persona to American cinema. Perhaps feeling the sting of being rejected for roles in *The Good Earth,* she remarked in Honolulu that:

> It seems to me that our stage leaves too little to the imagination, except of course some of the Shakespearean productions. I believe this is one of the primary reasons why American audiences stay away from the theater in droves while Chinese audiences, I am told, attend in droves. There is little in current American drama to challenge the imagination.[3]

This was almost an evangelical mission for Wong, who detested her many demeaning and stereotypical film roles during the 1920s and believed that the American media needed a refreshing stab at a reality-based cinema. That meant portraying the Chinese genuinely as real people with human characteristics. She remarked that "for a year, I shall study the land of my fathers. Perhaps upon my arrival, I shall feel like an outsider. Perhaps instead, I shall find my past life assuming a dreamlike quality of unreality."[4]

In particular, Wong was curious about twentieth-century Chinese women in Beijing and Shanghai. She was anxious to learn about their habits and characteristics. To place this anthropological study into a greater comparative focus, she also wanted to learn about the "women who lived in China before the present Government."[5] As a vehicle to understanding Chinese women of the Qing Dynasty and those in the 1930s so that she could better portray them in American cinema and theater, Wong decided to embark on yet another language excursion. This time she wanted to take up the study of the *guoyu,* or Mandarin Chinese. Like the acquisition of British English, French, and German during her sojourn in Europe in the late 1920s, language became a means of grasping the true meaning of the world in which she lived. As a speaker of the southern dialect of Cantonese, she hoped that learning Mandarin was one way in which she could help the people of China to understand her.[6]

Wong knew that to understand a people's culture, a fluency in that language was essential. In the case of a southern dialect or Cantonese-speaking Anna May Wong from California, the challenge of a heavily accented immigrant Chinese daughter learning *guoyu* could have been insurmountable. She may have even been aware of a Qing Dynasty proverb that northern Chinese people fear neither the sky nor the earth. They fear Cantonese people speaking Mandarin. Perhaps there may have been a saying about Chinese Americans speaking Cantonese. Later in 1936 Wong encountered a mild disdain toward her California-accented southern dialect. At a party in Shanghai, she met "one of the ladies (who) spoke my dialect and so I began to chatter away merrily in Cantonese. After a few minutes, she said, 'Miss Wong, do you mind going back to English? You speak Chinese charmingly, but you have such a marked American accent.' I always said that only my family or people with ears of love could understand my Chinese, but I never really believed it until now."[7]

With clearly defined aims in China, Wong was a different type of overseas Chinese venturing for the first time to her grandparents' homeland. She was no mere tourist. Wong did not go to China to discover *it* and then retreat to the United States like Chinese American tourists before her to become "American" again. When she left the United States in 1936, she left behind her doubts about "being American" and about "being Chinese." What China gave her was a profound sense of self, of being empowered, and of finding her own individual agency that had no ethnicity, nationality, or race pinned to it. By living and traveling in China, Anna May Wong was no longer an "American." She was no longer even a "Chinese."

By being empowered and discovering her own agency, she liberated herself from ethnicity, nationality, and race. China was the culmination of a profound internal transformation that began with her films and stage performances in Britain, France, and Germany in the late 1920s. Although Wong mused just before embarking on her Asian voyage that "I am going to a strange country and yet, in a way, I am going home. I have never seen China, but somehow, I have always known it,"[8] China was not like going home because that Asian place had never been her physical home.

Once Anna May Wong returned to Los Angeles and could reflect on her China voyage to the journalist Louise Leung, she said "You know I had never been to China, but somehow it seemed that I had always been homesick for it."[9] Like many Chinese Americans, she understood this uncommon pull from her grandparents' country. Its four thousand years of human development, a vast reservoir of humankind, traditions of artistry and creativity, and many varied banquets were not some trinkets to be dismissed with a capricious flick of a wrist. But unlike the ordinary Chinese American tourist, she seized China on her own terms, never allowing it to submerge her. Still, she let the essence of China invade her spiritually and cerebrally until she came to terms with a country about which she had said, before encountering it: "I found it exciting to face that broad ocean and to realize that far to the westward lay China, the country I have known only in shadowy dreams."[10] Before this China sojourn, even her friends had remarked on her ambivalence about "being Chinese."

> I've been told by someone who knows me well that a constant conflict is going on in my mind. She says that I'm torn between my race, my own people and their inherited tastes and prejudices passed down for thousands of years and the social customs and ideas of my American homeland and western friends. All I knew of the Orient was what my father told me. I had supposed that I was American and nothing else.[11]

Once in China, those "shadowy dreams" disappeared. It was almost as if Anna May Wong welcomed her seduction by China. The country became simply a crystallization of all her life energies and experiences, first revealed in her American and European existence. By embracing completely her Chineseness in China, she became Anna May Wong, an individual who was beyond ethnicity, nationality, or race.

Being Chinese no longer burdened or even haunted her. It was as if once she knew who she was, it did not matter what she was or from where she came. She had faced being Chinese in China and now she could move on. China revealed the existential moment for the most famous actress from Chinese America.

Wong was always ahead of her generation. From the time of her first brush with Hollywood at the age of fourteen when she landed a part as an indistinguishable lantern holder among three hundred other extras in the Boxer Rebellion–inspired *The Red Lantern* (1919)[12] to her regeneration as a consummate existential world traveler in 1936, this Chinese American woman had already ventured into many time zones and cultures. By the age of thirty-one she had lived many lives. Her eleven-month period in China and Asia was just one of them.

In 1936 the Republic of China was seething with dramatic social change, military crossfire, and widespread political tensions. Intellectually gifted, Wong absorbed all these dynamics with the ease of a veteran actress learning difficult Shakespearean lines. In fact, these profound cataclysmic upheavals in China were to provide the catalyst for Wong's personal and spiritual awakening.

In contrast to China, the United States in 1936 was isolated intellectually, staid in its conservative thinking, and existed in a never-ending linear monotony that discriminated against, incarcerated, or ostracized anyone who did not look European and white. There was nothing to learn from such a place. China was dramatically different. It had panache and spirit. On the threshold of monumental social change, it was dangerous and volatile. Politically and militarily, it was split apart by bandit gangs, communists, nationalists, secret societies, and warlords.[13] Just over the eastern horizon and beyond the China seas, a more menacing and unforgiving specter was emerging. The Japanese were leering covetously at China as a delectable prey waiting to be devoured. On the sidelines, but certainly attempting to manipulate the situation, was the acquisitive cohort of imperialists from Britain, France, Germany, and the United States. This then was the China that the daughter of a laundryman from Los Angeles was to encounter.

ASIA PACIFIC IN 1936

With her sister, Lulu, Anna May Wong left San Francisco for China on January 24, 1936, aboard the SS *President Hoover.*[14] Auspiciously, that day was also Chinese New Year. For many Chinese, a new year meant a new beginning. In her first dispatch for the *New York Herald Tribune,* she wrote in a detached American manner:

> I sailed on Chinese New Year which our Oriental friends considered an excellent omen. Though the Chinese government has ordered that New Year be celebrated on January 1, the people have gone on glorifying their ancient day. That is the time when, my father has told me, the entire nation puts on its best clothes and pays calls and the air is heavy with the smoke of firecrackers. Every Chinese tries to pay off all his debts before the New Year. He who is unlucky enough to fail must carry a lighted lantern when he goes on the street, to indicate that for him New Year's Day has not yet dawned.[15]

Honolulu, Hawaii, was her first stop. She exclaimed, "I am looking forward with much joy to seeing the first outpost of the East."[16] At Honolulu, which was indeed the most Asian of all North American cities, the Chinese Consul General, K. C. Mui, met Wong aboard ship with "a great armful of flowers. He bought blossoms of every color, so as to be sure that some of them match my costume."[17] Upon receiving the flowers, she excitedly asked, "Do they make these every day? They must begin work very early. This one *(maunaloa),* if you were a bit tipsy, might begin to crawl. It looks something like what I imagine a Chinese dragon looks like. Oh! I love Honolulu."[18] In fact, Honolulu was so enchanting that Wong proclaimed:

> England has the tempo that suits me. I love it there, but Honolulu is dangerously taking me away from that love. It is wonderful here. Why, here I know exactly what I am eating, with whom I am eating. I don't have to rush according to the clock. Tell the people of Honolulu that I am coming back sometime for a real visit.[19]

For part of the next twelve hours on this Pacific island, Mui and Professor Ruth Yapp from the University of Hawaii drove her through Honolulu "streets hedged by hibiscus and shaded by flowering limes" to the "cliff known as the Pali where we stood in a rushing wind and peered over the parapet toward the distant sea."[20] Lunch in Honolulu was at Waikiki Lau Yee Chai, a "palatial Chinese restaurant where bird's nest soup was served."[21] Wong remarked that the American dish, chop suey, which "though usually delicious is a western adaptation of the Chinese cuisine," was mercifully not ordered. Later the Consul General took Wong to Waikiki Beach, where she cascaded along in an outrigger canoe. The next day was spent on ship heading toward Yokohama, the last stop before Shanghai and China.

Yokohama was a necessary stopover on anyone's trip to China even though Japan had already demonstrated its imperialistic designs on Asia. The key cause of the Japanese war in Asia was the Manchurian, or Mukden, Incident of September 18, 1931. On the pretext of quelling Chinese terrorism, demonstrated by a rather harmless bomb that exploded on the Southern Manchurian Railway tracks near the city of Mukden (Shenyang), Japanese soldiers had seized the northern Chinese province of Manchuria in 1931. On March 9, 1932, the province was renamed Manchukuo (Land of the Manchus), with the last emperor of China, twenty-five-year-old Henry Puyi, as its chief executive. The last Qing ruler had hoped to revive his family's lost prestige and wealth in Manchukuo, but the Land of the Manchus was now ruled and managed by Japanese thugs, bandits, smugglers, dope pushers, brothel keepers, and every conceivable riffraff.[22]

Chinese offices and functionaries were created to appear to be part of an efficient and productive structure serving the needs of the people of Manchuria. But the truth was closer to a grotesque squad of Japanese criminals and henchmen whose job was to overshadow, emasculate, and control. It was a bizarre world of Chinese theater *fantastique* ostensibly starring Henry Puyi as a half-emperor presiding over a half-Chinese territory. Actually, the major players came from Japan and dominated a stage populated by Chinese extras existing in a shell of reality. Images played an increasingly significant part in Manchukuo. In fact, "images constituted a new realm of 'hyper real' experience where images replace reality and the distinction between reality and irreality is blurred."[23]

Japan's terrorism in Manchukuo was no secret to the world, as their actions were well documented in the global press. Even the League of Nations and such leading powers of the day as Britain and France knew about Japan's treachery. But that international institution and those countries were not likely to punish a fellow imperialist country until Pearl Harbor. Meanwhile, the United States lamely protested by merely evoking the Kellogg-Briand Pact of 1928, which outlawed war.[24] With headlines about the situation in every major international newspaper, Wong knew that the Japanese had already begun their conquest of China. But there was nothing she could do to avoid Yokohama and Japan if she wanted to visit her father in Guangdong province.

IMPRESSIONS OF JAPAN, 1936

Wong's first glimpses of Japan were through the port of Yokohama. She exclaimed that there was a "veil of falling snow—a most unexpected view for a person who had always pictured Japan draped in wistaria and half hidden under a foam of cherry blossoms."[25] While Wong contemplated a serene and seemingly harmonious Japan, she and many Japanese were unaware of the development of ultranationalist plots in Tokyo that would crack any semblances of cohesiveness and stability that still existed in the Asian theater.

Even while traveling through Japan, Wong already possessed a profound dislike for the Japanese because they had invaded and occupied China in the early 1930s. In 1932 she expressed her indignation at the Manchurian Incident of 1931 with a strongly worded article entitled "Manchuria," in which she exhibited a growing individual nationalism about being Chinese, now articulated by the Chinese American communities in Los Angeles and throughout the urban areas of the United States. Wong compared the "ancient, patient wisdom of China" with the "brash and superior militancy of Japan," stating that "China has copied very little from other nations; she has adapted some innovations, but she has kept her distinct identity. There are qualities in Chinese civilization which are irresistible, yet having enough to hold it aloof."[26] In a strikingly hard-hitting, eloquent, and exceedingly passionate diatribe against the Japanese, Wong declared:

> Never has the world so felt the need of spiritual rejuvenation to relieve it of the weariness of the whirl and click of machines and the nerve-strain of

speed and of crushing size. Thus we are witnessing the greatest renaissance in history, which will culminate in a new interest and happiness in the philosophy of life. Just as fate destined the exquisite lotus to bloom high above the polluted torrents, thus despite the iron heel of Japan, will the endangered bud of Chinese culture bloom forth in its consummate moral purity and spiritual elegance above the mire of blood and destruction.[27]

Unlike many prominent Chinese Americans, Wong used her celebrity and fame to publicly express political views. She exhibited a profound sense of integrity and anger uncommon in Hollywood, where European American actresses were only interested in becoming rich and famous. With the article "Manchuria," the chances of Wong becoming wealthy were practically eliminated, because her progressive political views branded her as outspoken and defiant. That would alienate the rich, who usually prided themselves on more conservative perspectives. Moreover, Japan was still a member of the imperialist union, and there was hardly a whimper from Britain, France, or the United States when Japanese troops stormed into Manchuria. Wong's views were contrary to conservative and official government policy in Washington, D.C. She was blatantly criticizing one of the West's major Asian allies.

While Wong was being greeted warmly by Japanese journalists when she arrived in Japan on February 7 in the late evening,[28] young extremist officers advocating a more aggressive imperialistic campaign in China and Southeast Asia were plotting to murder members of the civilian government. Intrigues culminating in the political assassinations of the prime minister, Inukai Tsuyoshi, and other members of his cabinet on May 15, 1932, led ultimately to the February 26 Incident of 1936.

On February 26 these officers were successful in cutting down two former prime ministers, Takahashi Korekiyo and Admiral Saito Makoto. Although other cabinet members and military officials as well as the current prime minister, Admiral Okada Keisuke, escaped the assassins' weapons, these right-wing soldiers had forced the civilian government to capitulate to their designs and machinations. The imperialistic thrust of Japanese foreign policy was now under the manipulation and control of the military.[29]

Certainly neither Wong nor the effete Japanese press knew about the monumental turn of events being plotted in early February. The advance of the military in Japanese life would eventually lead to absolute warfare in Asia and Pearl Harbor in 1941, but now the Japanese journalists were content to scribble down any nonsense about the world's most famous actress from Chinese America.[30]

Wong observed that even with her views of Japan freshly imprinted in her mind with the 1932 article "Manchuria," she was circumspect. As she was to demonstrate often in her life, the most famous actress from Chinese America could always relate to the moment at hand. In Yokohama she enthused that "on the dock, I saw women in thin kimonos looking like half-frozen humming birds, stevedores in straw raincoats that made them resemble shredded wheat biscuits and *jinrikisha* lanterns bobbing in the snowy dusk." As she contemplated such a serene landscape, the stampede erupted. She exclaimed that "a wildly trampling cavalcade came galloping up the gangplank. In a moment I was so completely surrounded by pointing cameras that I felt like all of the Noble Six Hundred."[31]

One of Japan's major newspapers, *Asahi Shinbun,* reported that "she pulled her beautiful black hair up. Her jacket, skirt, shoes, hat and veil were all in black. Her shirt and tie were in white and her nails painted red. Her beauty is Asian beauty in absolutely every way."[32] After presenting their cards and bowing in politeness and respect, other journalists then badgered Wong about the purpose of her Asian voyage and her love life. Some also asked about whether she thought Asian women should perm their hair and what she liked about Japan.

To the question about traveling to Asia, Anna May Wong said that "I am also Asian like you Japanese. As all Asians are, I am also very eager to be filial to my father as much as I can and to spend some time with him."[33] As for her love life, she explained that "I was wedded to my art. A few minutes later the reporters smiled in unison, made four or five deep bows and clattered down the gangplank as hurriedly as they had come."

Wong toured Yokohama with a small party, visiting such high spots as the Sunshine Bar, a local dance hall where "little taxi dancers dressed in foreign clothes and high heeled shoes were huddled like forlorn sparrows around a charcoal brazier." When she returned to the SS *President Hoover,* a late edition of one of the local newspapers was thrust upon her. "It stated that I am engaged to a wealthy Cantonese named Art. Such are the hazards of interviews in the East."[34]

TOKYO, KOBE, AND OSAKA

While in Tokyo, which reminded her of Berlin with its gray, massive buildings, Anna May Wong was interested in the people. She watched the kimonoed women with "their stiff obis giving them the effect of being strangely round-shouldered. There were pale students in semi-military uniforms, businessmen in ordinary western suits, youths arrayed in kimonos and cowboy hats, and several workmen dressed in knitted sweaters and long woolen underwear."[35]

As a regular tourist, she visited a modern department store where the floor walkers wore morning coats. After seeing several Japanese women enter a Buddhist temple, she decided to follow. There she observed that "beside the altar stood the priest, a Japanese gentleman dressed in a very foreign frock coat. When he ended his talk, the women joined in singing something that seemed strangely familiar; in a moment or so I recognized it—it was 'Onward Christian Soldiers,' adapted to Japanese words."[36]

After arriving at the port of Kobe, Wong was able to visit Kyoto, with "its tiny thatched houses, the rural temples with their curling eaves and the stunted pines that stood out—lined against the sky made me feel that we were riding through a long series of Japanese prints." She heard the "booming of the great bells sounds in the streets" and witnessed "parties of pilgrims carrying their lunches and up-to-date thermos bottles, hurry from shrine to shrine." At a local Buddhist temple there were "no modern methods here." Besides observing worshipers at the "tranquil face of Kuanyin, the Goddess of Mercy," she also saw an "altar to Kannosubeno-Kami, the goddess of lovers. People suffering from unhappy love affairs were busily tying paper prayers to the lattice before the shrine. We were told that it is necessary to fasten them with the thumb and little finger of the right hand: if any other finger even touches the prayer while it is being fastened the effect is completely spoiled."

Wong noted that, almost as if it were a deliberate foil to the traditional and religious city of Kyoto, the industrial town of Osaka was "swatched in veils of smoke which had rightly been called the Pittsburgh of the East." In Osaka, she made a final comment on Japanese womanhood: "Osaka women are criticized for using more rouge and wearing brighter kimonos than their sisters elsewhere in Japan, but when one has seen the pall of soot that covers houses and trees, one cannot blame them for trying to lighten the prevailing gloom."

But Japan was not China, and while on that island empire she lamented that "all this time, however, I was conscious of a growing nostalgia for the East I had failed to find. Although I have reveled in the beauty of Japan and admired its modern achievements, I have not yet found the serene spiritual tempo I had hoped to discover in the East. With ever mounting anticipation, I look forward to China."

CHINA IN 1936

Following a voyage of eighteen days, Anna May and Lulu Wong finally arrived in Shanghai on February 11, 1936, at 2:00 P.M. At the dock they were not only met by their brother, James Norman, but also "literally besieged by admirers who were lucky enough to get the necessary Customs passes enabling them to board the tender that went down the river to meet the giant liner that moored at the buoys. Old ladies teetering precariously on bound feet, scholarly looking gentlemen in long silk robes, school girls in tight jackets and short skirts and returned students in western dress were pointing toward us and talking excitedly."[37]

As usual, Wong was dressed to fit the occasion, with a mink coat and a London-designed hat in the shape of a tiger. Resplendent in black, she met more than two hundred journalists from Chinese newspapers and the British-owned *North China Herald*. In *guoyu* and the Shanghai dialect, the reporters asked her why she was in China and what the state of American and British cinema was, as well as what she thought of Irving Thalberg's film, *The Good Earth*. While listening to these journalistic queries, Wong admitted that the questions in Chinese seemed "as strange to me as Gaelic. I thus had the strange experience of talking to my own people through an interpreter."[38]

After her first encounter with the Chinese press, six British soldiers marched aboard and accompanied Anna May Wong and her two siblings to the Park Hotel in the heart of the city. She exclaimed happily that "this tumultuous greeting from my own people touched me more than anything that ever has happened to me in my motion picture career. Incidentally I wonder how the idea got abroad that the Chinese are always without emotion."[39]

THE HINTERLAND

Although Wong looked forward to embracing her grandparents' country and culture, there were ominous signs that not all was as jubilant in China as her first day in Shanghai. Outside of Shanghai, the Nationalist *(Guomindang)* forces, led by Jiang Jieshi (Chiang Kai-shek, 1887–1975), were in a pitched battle for supremacy with the Chinese Communist Party *(Gongchandang)* led by Mao Zedong (1895–1976). Jiang's Fifth Extermination campaign, planned by his German advisers, especially General Alexander von Falkenhausen (1878–1966), had begun with an economic blockade in October 1933. For a year, 900,000 Nationalist troops engaged the Red Army in the Jiangsi-Fujian and Anhui-Henan-Hubei areas. *Guomindang* press releases boasted that "about 1,000,000 people were killed or starved to death in the process of recovering Soviet Jiangsi,"[40] where the *Gongchandang* headquarters were located.

On October 16, 1934, Mao and his Red Army of ninety thousand realized that they had to clear out of Jiangsi or face annihilation. Thus began the Long March to the northern province of Shaanxi and a new military and political base. Journalist Edgar Snow (1905–), who was the first American to witness the beginnings of the People's Republic of China in the 1930s, related:

> Besides the main strength of the army, thousands of red peasants began this march—old and young, men, women, children, Communists and non-Communists. The arsenal was stripped, the factories were dismantled, machinery was loaded onto mules and donkeys—everything that was portable and of value went with this strange cavalcade. As the march lengthened out, much of this burden had to be discarded, and the Reds told me that thousands of rifles and machine guns, much machinery, much ammunition, even much silver, lay buried on their long trail from the South. Some day in the future, they said, Red peasants, now surrounded by thousand of policing troops, would dig it up again. They awaited only the signal—amid the war with Japan might prove to be that beacon.[41]

By October 20, 1935, when it succeeded in reaching northern Shaanxi, slightly south of the Great Wall, the Red Army numbered only eight thousand. While the *Guomindang* and its allies harassed and engaged in daily skirmishes with the *Gongchandang,* Red losses, especially in Guizhou, Sichuan, and Sikang, resulted more from encounters with indigenous warriors, fatigue, sickness, and starvation than from actual conflicts with the *Guomindang* army and its allies.[42]

The Long March was one of humankind's most amazing military feats. The Red Army climbed eighteen mountain ranges (five of which were permanently covered with snow), crossed twenty-four rivers, foraged through twelve provinces, seized sixty-two cities and towns, and managed to evade or punish the armies of ten different provincial warlords on this journey of six thousand miles. Of the 368 days, 235 were devoted to daylight marching, while 18 days were spent moving at night. The rest of the days were spent resting, sleeping, cleaning and repairing their weapons, foraging for food, recruiting peasants, and negotiating with warlords and tribal bandits for passage through their territories. The average distance covered daily was almost twenty-four miles. The march can be compared to the Flight of the Torgut, Napoleon's retreat from Moscow, and even Hannibal's march over the Alps.[43]

While Mao Zedong and his Red Army established strategies to consolidate their resources after such a staggering undertaking, Jiang Jieshi prepared to mount yet another campaign against the communists. But during 1936 there was another plot brewing. In an effort to persuade Jiang to cease pursuing the communists and concentrate on the immediate task of fortifying defenses and coordinating offenses against the Japanese, one of Jiang Jieshi's northern allies, Zhang Xueliang

(1901–2001), decided to kidnap the *Guomindang* leader in hopes of persuading him to engage in an anti-Japanese campaign. This was the Xi'an (Sian) Incident of December 12, 1936. Jiang was eventually released, but he had promised to unite all forces against the Japanese. This meant uniting with his domestic enemy, the communists and the Red Army led by Mao Zedong. Civil war was put aside for the greater good of the country. Jiang Jieshi's advocacy of a united front elevated him to the status of a national hero with a new legitimacy to lead the nation.[44]

AN INTERNATIONAL STAR IN SHANGHAI

In Shanghai Wong began her own campaign to learn about China, its culture, and its people. The urban Chinese world in which she found herself was vastly different from that of the rustic headquarters of an unknown Mao Zedong in Baoan and later in Yen'an. Urbane, sophisticated Shanghai was also a contrast to the national capital of Nanjing, which was essentially a dull and pedestrian regional city that housed the center of Jiang Jieshi's political and military machines. Compared to the peasant Mao and warrior king Jiang, who were situated in a backward Asian country devastated by Western and Japanese imperialism and colonialism that brought only starvation and wretchedness to the Chinese people, Wong was an international celebrity who exuded glamour and the height of fashion. She was neither agrarian, plain, violent, desperate, nor uncultured. She was 1930s chic and the personification of a new and unique Asian American coolness. Her portrayal of Hui Fei in *Shanghai Express* (1932) only accentuated her hipness.

Wong's films with a Chinese motif and story line were widely circulated in the Republic of China. Her status as a Chinese American woman in a predominantly European American profession heightened her mystique and prominence in every Chinese locale. Although she was not always the lead in her films, these movies were often advertised in Shanghai and elsewhere. In 1925 she played Annabelle Wu, who moved the plot as the main protagonist in the theft of military fortification plans in the comedy *Forty Winks*.[45] Contained in a large billboard advertisement next to an equally gigantic display of Chesterfields that encouraged smoking "when three is company," that film was blatantly announced to travelers of Shanghai venturing along Nanjing Road.[46] In the United States it was Wong who seemed to tower over the male star, Raymond Griffith (1890–1957), in select advertisements, even though Viola Dana (1897–1987) was the leading female performer in *Forty Winks*.[47] At four foot eleven, Dana was dwarfed by Wong, who was five foot seven by the time she was twenty in 1925.

As a result of advertisements for films like *Forty Winks,* Chinese people everywhere, in Beijing, Singapore, Hong Kong, Kuala Lumpur, and the countless overseas Chinatowns in the West, who may not have heard of Mao Zedong or Jiang Jieshi, had heard of Anna May Wong. If they were lucky, they had even seen one of her films.

Here was a woman who looked Chinese, yet spoke American English and acted like a Westerner. She certainly did not gesture, stand, or walk like a Chinese from China. When she spoke Cantonese, it had a distinct California flavor. It was almost as if she had descended from the heavens with her patented bangs, stylish Western clothing, and ultra detached demeanor. Whether Wong died a thousand deaths in her portrayal of doomed characters in *The Toll of the Sea* (1922) and *Piccadilly* (1929) or played a "Whiteface" by impersonating a European American like Mrs. Pyke in *A Study in Scarlet* (1933), she gave the screen impression that she was an integral part of Western society even when her roles smacked of blatant racism. At least it was old-fashioned and indigenous European American racism.

Unlike most Chinese in the West, she was a player in an important European American industry. In the Asian world, where Europeans still held sway, that fact alone gave her enormous cachet, recognizable status, and instant credibility and legitimacy. In the eyes of the Chinese people especially, she epitomized success in the European American and white world.

REPRESENTING AMERICA AND HOLLYWOOD

The tumultuous greetings from scores of fans in Yokohama and Shanghai attested to Wong's popularity. Her films guaranteed her celebrity status in Asia; she was always *the* "must" guest at any Shanghai dinner party. In 1936 Hollywood represented the most powerful and influential mass medium in the world. Through its films, it was becoming the vehicle upon which European America based its claim to cultural dominance in the world. It personified the latest in film techniques, story ideas, cinematography, and marketing. In 1922 Anna May Wong was the female lead in the first Technicolor movie ever produced, *The Toll of the Sea,* which solidified the United States as the major initiator of dramatic innovations in the cinema. Thus it was not surprising that the first technically devised sound picture, *The Jazz Singer* (1927), would be a European American innovation.

By the 1930s Hollywood was the world's capital of filmmaking. European stars like Luise Rainer, Greta Garbo, and Marlene Dietrich flocked to that California city because that was the place to earn a good living. Anyone arriving in China from Hollywood was arriving from the hippest and most modern place on earth. Wong's American and Chinese cultural pedigree made her persona even more intriguing. She came from an advanced nation with one of the highest standards of living in the world. This contrasted her immediately and sharply with the Chinese in other parts of the world. Because she was the only major actress of Chinese origin from Hollywood, she represented to Chinese everywhere a sophistication matched only by her cool and hip demeanor. At thirty-one she also epitomized what a young woman from Chinese America could accomplish even under suffocating racial conditions. China only strengthened her enormous will to succeed.

NOTES

1. Wong, cited in Edward Sakamoto, "Anna May Wong and the Dragon Lady Syndrome," *Los Angeles Times,* 12 July 1987, 41.

2. Darrell Y. Hamamoto, *Monitored Peril: Asian Americans and the Politics of TV Representation* (Minneapolis: University of Minnesota Press, 1994), 250; "Wong Family Takes Vacation in Orient," *Seattle Daily Times,* 10 November 1934, 2.

3. P. T. Gialanella, "Anna May Wong Arrives All 'A-Dither' Over Trip," *Honolulu Star-Bulletin,* 29 January 1936, 1.

4. Wong, cited in Carolyn Anspacher, "Star Goes 'Home,'" *San Francisco Chronicle,* 24 January 1936, 17.

5. "Mob Meets Chinese Film Star: Miss Anna May Wong Given Warm Welcome," *North China Herald,* 19 February 1936, 310.

6. Anspacher, "Star Goes 'Home.'"

7. Anna May Wong, "Anna May Wong Recalls Shanghai's Enthusiastic Reception," *New York Herald Tribune,* 31 May 1936, 6.

8. Anna May Wong, "Anna May Wong Tells of Voyage on 1st Trip to China," *New York Herald Tribune,* 17 May 1936, 1; "Anna May Wong Writes of Journey 'Home,'" *San Francisco Chronicle,* 17 May 1936, 10.

9. Louise Leung, "East Meets West: Anna May Wong Back on the Screen After an Absence of Several Years, Discusses Her Native Land," *Hollywood* (n.d.): 40.

10. Wong, "Anna May Wong Tells of Voyage," 6.

11. Geraldine Sartain, "Tragic Real Love Story of Anna May Wong," *San Francisco Chronicle,* 4 July 1937, 16.

12. Geraldine Gan, *Lives of Notable Asian Americans* (New York: Chelsea House, 1996), 83–84.

13. For an in-depth discussion of these contending factions, see Anthony B. Chan, *Arming the Chinese: The Western Armaments Trade in Warlord China, 1920–1928* (Vancouver: University of British Columbia Press, 1982).

14. "64 Vessels Tied Up by Strikes in West," *New York Times,* 26 January 1936, 3; Barrie Roberts, "Anna May Wong: Daughter of the Orient," *Classic Images* 270 (December 1997): 22.

15. Wong, "Anna May Wong Tells of Voyage," 1.

16. Wong, "Anna May Wong Tells of Voyage," 6.

17. Anna May Wong, "Anna May Wong Relates Arrival in Japan, Her First Sight of the Orient," *New York Herald Tribune,* 24 May 1936, 1.

18. Wong, cited in Gialanella, "Anna May Wong Arrives," 1.

19. Wong, cited in Margaret Kamm, "Anna May Wong Gives Views of Theater of East, West," *Honolulu Advertiser,* 30 January 1936, 4.

20. Wong, "Anna May Wong Relates Arrival," 1.

21. Wong, "Anna May Wong Relates Arrival," 1; "Anna Scorns Minor Role," *Honolulu Advertiser,* 30 January 1936, 1,4.

22. For a concise analysis of the Japanese in Manchukuo, see Anthony B. Chan, *Li Ka-shing: Hong Kong's Elusive Billionaire* (Toronto: Macmillan, 1996), 19–23.

23. Jean Baudrillard, *Simulations: In the Shadows of the Silent Majority,* trans. Paul Foss et al. (New York: Semiotext(e), Inc., 1983).

24. Immanuel C. Y. Hsu, *The Rise of Modern China* (New York: Oxford University Press, 2000), 548–52.

25. Wong, "Anna May Wong Relates Arrival," 1.

26. Anna May Wong, "Manchuria," *Rob Wagner's Script* 5, no. 153 (16 January 1932): 6–7; Box 2, Rob Wagner Collection, 6, cited in Karen Janis Leong, "The China Mystique: Mayling Soong, Pearl S. Buck and Anna May Wong in the American Imagination" (Ph.D. dissertation, University of California, Berkeley, spring 1999), 381.

27. Wong, "Manchuria," 7.

28. "A Dutiful Daughter, Anna May Wong: A Welcome Guest to Yokohama" *(Anna May Wong Joyo Kikou), Asahi Shinbun,* 8 February 1936, 11.

29. Edwin O. Reischauer, *Japan: The Story of a Nation* (New York: Alfred A. Knopf, 1981), 196–98.

30. "Anna May Wong Will Come to Japan" *(Anna May Wong Jyo Toyo Homon), Asahi Shinbun,* 21 January 1936, 7.

31. Following quotes about Japan are from Wong, "Anna May Wong Relates Arrival," 1–2.

32. "A Dutiful Daughter," 11.

33. "A Dutiful Daughter," 11.

34. All quotes regarding Japanese reporters are from Wong, "Anna May Wong Relates Arrival," 1–2; Philip Leibfried, "Anna May Wong," *Films in Review* (n.d.): 150.

35. Wong, "Anna May Wong Recalls," 2.

36. Following quotes regarding Wong's trip to Japan are found in Wong, "Anna May Wong Recalls," 2, 6.

37. "Mob Meets Chinese Film Star," 310; Wong, "Anna May Wong Recalls," 6.

38. Wong, "Anna May Wong Recalls," 6.

39. Wong, "Anna May Wong Recalls," 6.

40. Edgar Snow, *Red Star Over China* (New York: Grove Press, 1938, 1968), 188.

41. Snow, *Red Star Over China,* 188–89.

42. Zhou Enlai's conversation with Edgar Snow cited in Snow, *Red Star Over China,* 432.

43. Snow, *Red Star Over China,* 204–5; see also Jerome Ch'en, *Mao and the Chinese Revolution* (New York: Oxford University Press, 1965), 185–200, for an interpretative analysis.

44. Hsu, *Rise of Modern China,* 565.

45. "Forty Winks," *Variety,* 4 February 1925, 39; "Forty Winks Compels Laughs," *Seattle Post-Intelligencer,* 29 March 1925, 17.

46. Billboard photo of *40 Winks* is contained in Lynn Pan, *Shanghai: A Century of Change in Photographs, 1843–1949* (Hong Kong: Hai Feng Publishing, 1993), 74.

47. "Mirth Merchants," *Seattle Post-Intelligencer,* 25 March 1925, 7.

SEVEN

SHANGHAI COOL

Shanghai has been described by Edgar Snow as the Sodom and Gomorrah of Asia. Travel writer John Gunther called it "a political ulcer on the face of China."[1] When Anna May Wong arrived in 1936, it was a metropolis of four million people of many nationalities. It was one of the three largest cities in the world. Just before the beginning of the Japanese invasion of China in 1937, 37,273 foreigners lived in Shanghai.[2] Those foreigners played a significant role in how the city was managed and how it presented itself to the world.

As a result of the Treaty of Nanjing of 1842, foreigners moved into China to extract as many riches as possible from the Chinese. Their utter contempt for the Chinese led them to establish racially segregated living quarters. Since Shanghai became their chief *entrepot,* it was automatically divided into the Chinese city and foreign areas. The main non-Chinese area was the International Settlement of about nine square miles. Established in 1845, it was managed jointly by the Americans, British, and Japanese. Another part of Shanghai City was the French Concession, set up in 1849. It was about half the size of the International Settlement. Because of the many contending factions in Shanghai, the city's foreign colonization was never complete. This led to a multitude of different political and cultural possibilities. As a result of this volatile environment, left-wing activities flourished in Shanghai; even the Chinese Communist Party was established there.

In 1921 the inaugural meeting of the party was held at the Bowen Middle School for Girls in the heart of the French Concession. No doubt the radical traditions of the French Revolution permeated even into its Shanghai concession. The contradiction was obvious. As the French argued about equality, fraternity, and independence from oppressive regimes, they operated with the same repressive tools as their monarchies to subjugate the Chinese in their own country.

If Shanghai lacked anything, it was restraint. Wealth could be made in the morning and lost before sundown. During the 1930s it was a wide open urban metropolis where all sorts of bankers, beggars, courtesans, drug dealers, entrepreneurs, gangsters, labor organizers, performers in film and the theater, pimps, revolutionaries, and students congregated to make a living or to advocate a cause. By 1932 it was recognized as the greatest city and port in Asia.[3] There were certainly other Asian cities, but the ambitious and adventurous never ventured to Bangkok, Beijing, Kuala Lumpur, Manila, Saigon, Singapore, or Tokyo if they could go to Shanghai.

With the Treaty of Nanjing, Shanghai, like all of China, had lost its independence. It was a semicolonial territory ruled by foreigners, especially the British, overseeing Chinese functionaries and underlings. Jiang Jieshi was the de facto leader of China, but his leadership always had to accommodate the foreigners and their avarice. For foreigners, the business of Shanghai was business. As the main port city in China, Shanghai not only attracted many diverse characters and rascals, but its foreign settlements introduced foreign culture to Shanghai and by extension to China.

SHANGHAI ENTERTAINERS: LIAISONS

The description of Shanghai as the Asian version of Sodom and Gomorrah was based on the fact that by 1935 more than 100,000 prostitutes roamed the streets or plied their trade in such brothels as dingy dives, love hotels, or comfortable apartments in the city's "flowery world." "Taxi dancers in the dance halls, masseuses in the massage parlors, waitresses in the vaudeville houses, guides in the tourist agencies, female vendors of newspapers, cigarettes and fruits, and itinerant menders of sailors' clothing all engaged in prostitution, either because their jobs required it or because their precarious incomes needed augmenting."[4] By far the largest number of Shanghai whores were the "pheasants" *(yeji* or *zhiji)* or solo streetwalkers.

Before 1910 brothels included the secretive, high-class, and expensive trysting houses that provided private liaisons between courtesans and wealthy patrons, usually from the merchant class. With the introduction of hotels, public whorehouses developed, especially in the French concession. These were known as "salt-pork" shops *(xianrou zhuang)*.[5] At the low end of the prostitution hierarchy were the "flower-smoke rooms" *(huayan jian)*, often situated in filthy quarters where johns could smoke a bit of opium to get in the mood. There were also "nail sheds" *(dingpeng)*, usually in makeshift shacks where ten cents to one yuan would be the going rate for those on a limited income like rickshaw drivers and construction workers yearning to "drive a nail."[6]

European whores in Shanghai numbered about ten thousand during the 1930s, with White Russians who had fled the October 1917 revolution forming the majority at eight thousand.[7] Many of the Russian prostitutes lived and worked in the French Concession, where regulations on drugs and solicitation were not as severe as in the pristine and evangelical International Settlement, where American and British missionaries and "soul converters" lurked. Until the arrival of the White Russians, most Chinese men avoided European prostitutes because of the expense and their frightful appearance. "Most of them have big teeth and tousled hair, as ugly as devils and as frightful as lionesses. They freeze the hearts of the beholders. The Spanish, however, are different— brilliantly beautiful, with tender soft skin, and with a warm and delicate body. The Russian invasion of the market had lowered the charges to somewhere between $30 and $3."[8]

By the late 1920s and early 1930s, even "legitimate" or nonprostitution-centered Chinese–European liaisons had become more frequent. The contact between Chinese and Westerners was less rigid, and Eurasian children from these engagements were the result. In 1929 the gossip in Shanghai centered around Zhang Xueliang's affair with Edda Ciano (1910–1995), daughter of Benito Mussolini (1883–1945) and the wife of Galeazzo Ciano (1903–1944), the Italian minister to China.[9] Edda Ciano epitomized foreign decadence with her craving for "dry martinis, poker games, fast cars, and Roman gallants"[10] as well as young warlords like Zhang Xueliang. Their liaison was not a scandal, because it was happening in Shanghai, where scandal was commonplace.

SHANGHAI CABARETS

While visiting Shanghai Anna May Wong caught a glimpse of its elite nightlife. At the heart of any party was Western dancing, which became almost an obsession with artists, film and theater performers, members of the wealthy class, scholars, students, and many characters of the underworld like gangsters, pimps, and prostitutes. Jazz, ballroom, fox-trot, and other Western forms of modern dance permeated Shanghai social life. Dancing in China gave rise to a new industry. The Chinese could exhibit their Westernization by participating in ballet, charity balls, dancing school, song and dance performances, and tea dances. Other popular dance gatherings and parties were put on by people in government departments, military units, and university student organizations.[11]

At the first official party given in her honor by Chinese diplomat Wellington Koo (1887–1985) and his Java-born Chinese wife, Oei Hui-lan (1899–1992), Wong met many of the key officials of the Republic of China. Wong had met the Koos in 1933 at a London party while he was the Chinese ambassador to Britain.[12] Before leaving for France, where Wellington Koo was to be an envoy for the *Guomindang* government in 1936, Oei Hui-lan invited the crème de la crème of Shanghai's social elite to meet the famous movie star from Chinese America.

Wong met many Chinese women who were "the leaders of local society, and thus, Shanghai being the Paris of the nation, they set the fashions for all China. Modern Chinese dresses are made very simply. They consist of a high-necked, short-sleeved coat, falling straight to the ankles. It is fortunate that nearly all Chinese women are slender, for there are no tucks or darts anywhere to help hide unsightly curves. The only trimmings are plain or jeweled buttons and pipings of contrasting colors."[13] At this and succeeding parties, Wong danced with virtually everyone who asked her. She was the Chinese American celebrity from the United States who looked Chinese but was not.

Through the numerous cabarets in the city, dancing was also readily available to the general public. Many were owned by Chinese entrepreneurs who operated outside of the international districts to avoid their laws. During the 1930s, fifty thousand dancing hostesses or taxi dancers became an integral part of the entertainment circuit.[14] These female entertainers replaced the traditional courtesans or "singsong girls" who had flourished in a more restrictive time that demanded these relationships be kept discreet and prudent, especially when they involved prominent figures of the government or literati.

By 1927 when the Nanjing era began with Jiang Jieshi's seizure of political power, southerners from Guangdong, Fujian, and Zhejiang provinces had begun moving northward. They brought a special brand of corruption and lawlessness in the form of the Green Gang that would pervade all aspects of *Guomindang* politics and commerce.[15] The southerners also brought liberal ideas about commerce and entertainment.[16] "Almost from the day the southerners came to town, Shanghai embarked upon an era of whoopee enough to send past emperors spinning in their marble tombs. The pace of the city's world-famed night life was stepped up out of recognition and the responsibility for this rested almost solely upon Chinese shoulders—youthful ones, for their owners were drawn mainly from the student classes. It wasn't long before they were crowding foreigners off their own dance-floors, and they were big spenders too."[17]

While the southern influence pervaded the Shanghai entertainment world, a northern impact also changed the landscape of the city's popular culture forever. After the Bolsheviks seized power in Russia, many refugees and émigrés arrived in Shanghai through Vladivostok and Harbin, a northern Chinese outpost. For these men and women escaping the Soviets, Shanghai was particularly inviting because travelers did not need a passport to enter. The city gave them a new start.

Unlike the average unskilled Chinese immigrant to Shanghai, the Russians were dancers, entertainers, musicians, and singers who all contributed to the cabaret scene. A 1930s guidebook recommended Ladow's Casanova, Venus Cafe, Vienna Ballroom, Palais Cafe, and the Ambassador as the city's best cabarets. At the Majestic Hotel, where many luminaries including Madame Wellington Koo and Zhang Xueliang stayed while in Shanghai, the Russian jazz orchestra Ermoll's played nightly. It also had a "First-Class Floor and Catering—(with) 100 Charming Dance Hostesses."[18] Two days after Wong arrived in Shanghai, she was taken to the Cathay Tower nightclub. Describing the city's diversity, she exclaimed that "this night club is managed by a German, who proudly produced autographs of Marlene Dietrich and Lillian Harvey. There was an American orchestra and the star entertainer was a Filipino. So, this is China!"[19]

By 1934 twenty-five thousand mostly Jewish or White Russians lived and worked in the International or French settlements. Many of the Russian shops and homes were located on Avenue Joffre, and the area was known as Little Russia or Nevsky Prospekt. A Russian bookstore on Avenue Joffre published more Russian books in Shanghai than in Berlin or Paris. Other shops included the famous Siberian Fur Store that serviced the wealthy. There was also the Viener Sausage factory, owned by A. Lang and N. Semin on Route Dollfus, as well as the Art Decoration Picture store on Avenue Joffre. Restaurants proliferated, specializing in beef stroganoff, chicken à la Kiev, and borscht, which appealed to an increasingly urbane and international Chinese clientele, many of whom had studied in Europe or the United States. In addition, a European sense of style in Shanghai fashions, cabarets, magazines, nightclubs, and cinema began to emerge with the establishment of dress salons and beauty parlors operated by Russians.[20]

SHANGHAI CINEMA

In 1936 when Wong arrived in Shanghai, it was a city that rocked and seemed never to sleep. She exclaimed:

> It seems strange that Chinese dread the speed and noise of American cities, for surely there are more of both in Shanghai than I've ever coped with anywhere else. For twenty-four hours a day one hears the blare of automobile horns, the shouts of *jinrikisha* coolies, the rattle of buses and the high-pitched, blood a curdling squeak of the wheelbarrows that bring farm produce into the city. The tempo of the social life is such a gallop that a person from quiet Hollywood can hardly keep up with it. And my former mental picture was of people sitting in walled courtyards and drinking tea all day long![21]

With such dynamic nightlife filled with the money scent of the "flowery world," the hard drinking and hard dancing cabarets, and a fashionable émigré community that influenced many aspects of the entertainment world, the urban mass medium that personified all that was Shanghai developed in China and Asia during the 1930s. This was the art of the cinema. For Westerners to understand Chinese cinema, they often rendered it within their own cultural lenses and biases. Thus Shanghai, as the preeminent locus of Chinese filmmaking, became the *haolaiwu* (Hollywood) of Asia. But for the people of Shanghai, it was not *haolaiwu* or any other attribution or illusion to the West.

The cinema of Shanghai that Wong discovered was already well developed in 1936. During the 1920s such actresses as Wang Hanlun (1903–1978) and Yang Naimei (1904–1949) had paved the way for the evolution of a cinema industry complete with movie stars, movie magazines, throngs of adoring fans, and production houses. In addition, unlike Hollywood performers, Wang and Yang were able to control their own creative processes. With their many film connections and money maximized from previous films, both had established production houses by the late 1920s, the Hanlun Film Company and the Naimei Film Company.[22] Their film studios were just two out of about one hundred fifty production houses in the city that produced some six hundred films during the 1920s.[23]

Before Wang Hanlun and Yang Naimei, actors and actresses had almost no esteem or prestige in Chinese society. Many theatrical and early film performers often had little schooling and came from the realm of prostitutes, dancers, and bandits. Before the 1920s, about twenty short films were produced. Almost all the performers were male, with the female roles played by men in drag.[24] Both Wang and Yang defied those negative characteristics of the actress with their educated and moderately prosperous backgrounds. That they were able to create their own destiny and empowerment attested not only to their street smarts and business acumen but also to the fact that cinema now provided a fast track to becoming rich and famous.

By the time Wong arrived in Shanghai, the four major film studios that produced first-run films for China and Asia were the *Lianhua* (United), *Mingxing* (Star), *Tianyi* (Unique), and *Yihua* (China Artist).[25] Situated in Shanghai, which was the key location for left-wing ideas and activities, directors like Tian Han, Wu Yinggang, and Bu Wangcang, who were sympathetic to the communist cause, made films that suited their political inclinations for *Mingxing* and *Lianhua*.[26]

By 1928 Wang Hanlun had retired from the movie industry. She married a French citizen and together they operated the Hanlun Beauty Salon in the French Concession. Yang Naimei also entered into a different phase, but her period of opium addiction in the late 1930s caused many studios to refrain from hiring her. Eventually a rich Cantonese merchant became enthralled with this fading actress and married her. She died in Taibei in 1949 after they fled China following the civil war (1945–1949) between the armies of Mao Zedong's *Gongchangdang* and Jiang Jieshi's *Guomindang*.

The Shanghai movie industry continued to churn out films. Between January 1928 and December 1931, four hundred films were produced by about fifty filmmakers. About 250 of those were based on swordplay and martial arts centered around an unsolved mystery. Other films involved costume drama and legendary tales of immortals and monsters. Picture books and the adventure serial from newspapers formed the basis of stories, sometimes as a series. The eighteen episodes of *The Burning of Red Lotus Temple* (1928–1931), the thirteen-episode *Lady Adventuress on Wild River,* the thirteen-part *Great Adventurer East of the Pass,* and the smaller four-part *Red Butterfly, Adventuress* were some of the silent films that captivated Shanghai audiences. Many of these films reflected the Chinese narrative tradition, in which the directors and storytellers relied on a classical worldview and a nonlinear and parallel development of events and characters.[27] A Chinese remake of *The Thief of Bagdad* appeared as *Flying Bandit.*[28]

Since Hollywood studios like Paramount were well represented in Shanghai, they were able to move their first-run American films into Western-style cinemas such as the Carleton *(Ka'erdeng)*, Empire *(Empaiya)*, Nanking *(Naning)*, Odeon *(Aodian)*, Palace *(Zhongyang)*, Paris *(Bali)*, and Victoria *(Xin zhongyang)*. There were also less deluxe Chinese theaters devoted to screening purely Chinese films. In 1932 there were eight movie houses in the Chinese section, twenty-four in the International Settlement, and twelve in the French Concession. By the beginning of the Japanese invasion in 1937, Shanghai's film audiences had a choice of close to thirty-six film theaters. There were open-air theaters and cinemas in amusement halls. Thousands of customers patronized these theaters every year.[29] Although the Shanghai movie industry was flourishing into the 1930s, it could not compete with Hollywood. In 1929, 90 percent of all films viewed in China were from the United States. Chinese audiences were particularly eager to screen the latest American "talkies." Shanghai filmmakers knew that if they were to compete with foreign films, they had to produce their own sound films.

In 1931 *Mingxing* produced China's first "talkie" with Hu Die (Hu Rui-hua, also known as Butterfly Wu, 1907–1989) in the leading role. In the three-hour film *Genu hongmudan (Singsong Girl, Red Peony)*, Hu Die was selected to play Red Peony because of her facility in *guoyu* and her popularity in knight-errant films during the 1920s. The film was an immediate hit in the Philippines and Indonesia, where the producers were able to recoup most of their production costs overseas. The success of *Singsong Girl, Red Peony* galvanized the Shanghai studios to make films with song and dance using performers with stage experience.[30]

Hu Die was the prototype "talkie" film star. She trained at the China Film Academy in 1924 and made close to twenty films between 1925 and 1927. Once Wang Hanlun and Yang Naimei had vacated the Chinese film industry, Butterfly Wu became one of its leading movie queens. The other was Ruan Lingyu (Ruan Fenggeng, also known as Lily Yuen, 1910–1935), whose acting and film performances have been compared to the subtleties and film performances of major Hollywood actresses. She "was one of the great actresses of film history, as perfectly and peculiarly adapted to the film as we recognize Greta Garbo to be. Most of her Chinese admirers explain her special place in their memories as somehow attached to her tragic early death in 1935."[31]

Like Anna May Wong, Hu Die and Ruan Lingyu started their film careers as teenagers and came from a Cantonese background. By the 1930s they were recognized by critics as having genuine talent and ability as creative artists and professional actresses rather than as decorative sexpots.[32] Wong, Hu, and Ruan performed in many films that were progressive in tone, patriotic in substance, and anti-Japanese in focus, as well as in the usual roles of femme fatales, seductresses, and prostitutes. During Wong's visit to Shanghai movie lots, she met Hu Die.[33]

As part of Hearst Metrotone news covering Wong in China, cinematographer Hai-sheng Wong shot footage of the historical meeting between Anna May Wong and Hu Die. Arriving at *Mingxing* studio, the camera captures Hu welcoming Wong. They converse and Wong signs an autograph book. Wong and Hu then enter one of the studio's sets while a film is being directed.[34] These photo opportunities of the reigning movie queen from Chinese America and the best known film star from China were reminiscent of Alfred Eisenstaedt's famous shot of Marlene Dietrich, Anna May Wong, and Leni Riefenstahl at the Berlin Press Ball in 1928.

Social commentary and social change conditioned the plots of several of Anna May Wong and Hu Die's movie projects in the 1930s and 1940s. During the war years, Wong would star in *Bombs Over Burma* (1942) and *The Lady from Chungking* (1942), two anti-Japanese films. In the 1930s, Hu was cast in left-wing-inspired films. She played the frustrated daughter in *Wild Torrent* (1933), the salt worker's daughter in *Salty Tide,* the saleswoman in *Rouge and Powder Market,* and the poor, honest carpenter's wife and the haughty number seven wife of a warlord in *Twin Sisters* (1934).[35]

Wild Torrent was especially significant because it was the first example of a Western-style film script based on Hollywood techniques of storytelling, production values, and cinematography. Before 1933, written documents resembling a "shooting script" were founded on storytelling elements from Beijing opera and urban drama, with rough outlines of main scenes that allowed for extensive improvisation by the performers.[36] Hu Die's *Twin Sisters* was also important for her career because it screened at the Moscow International Film Festival and the Berlin Film Festival in 1935.[37]

As for Ruan Lingyu, she played in such progressive films as *Three Modern Women* (1933), *Little Toys* (1933), and *Goddess* (1934), which emphasized serious class struggle and morality. In her last film, *New Woman* (1934), she played a woman writer who takes her own life. This film foreshadowed her suicide on March 8, 1935. Ruan's death revealed the extent to which Chinese audiences now identified with film stars. Three days after her suicide, more than ten thousand mourners viewing her casket stalled traffic throughout Shanghai. During her burial on March 14, two thousand people showed up to pay their last respects. Hu Die and Ruan were China's leading actresses. Their private lives were made public with every fan magazine and newspaper story about the film world.[38]

By the time Wong arrived in Shanghai in 1936, the cinema was already embedded in China's culture. When asked by journalists about Chinese cinema just after she arrived in Shanghai, Wong "confessed herself unconversant, but hoped that the Chinese would soon be able to take their place in the picture world as she knew that the Chinese cinema fan was an ardent one."[39] The reception to Ruan Lingyu's death certainly attested to Wong's belief that moviegoers in China were enthusiastic, and in Shanghai they were fanatical.

FILM CENSORSHIP

While in Shanghai Wong was invited by Jiang Jieshi's government in Nanjing to a special meeting with the film censors at the Department of Cinematography in the Shanghai Special District Film Censorship Committee.[40] Established on January 1, 1930, the committee's aim was to protect the character and morality of the nation. Politically, its aims were to screen left-wing activities that might lead to potential confrontation with the *Guomindang*. Culturally, the censors were especially interested in protecting China from salacious and morally corrupting foreign influences.

Shanghai Express was one such foreign film that the censors thought brought disfavor upon China. Its focus on Western and Chinese prostitution in the heart of China from Shanghai to Beijing angered nationalists, who were experiencing firsthand details of Japanese atrocities in the city on a daily basis. The idea of prostitution in a fictional Western film seemed to trivialize the real-life atrocities generated from the Japanese. From January 28 to March 5, 1932, the *Guomindang's* Nineteenth Army attempted to fend off the murderous advance of the Japanese army.[41] But the Chinese army could not contain this Japanese military thrust. In May a peace agreement stipulated that *Guomindang* soldiers could only be based outside the city within a radius of thirty kilometers.

Under these military and political circumstances, in which yet another foreign power was unabashedly humiliating China and murdering its citizens, the patriotic fervor of the Chinese people could not be contained. Immediately after Japan's first aggression in January, Paramount brought *Shanghai Express* to the city for its first showing. Although it was offered to patrons under the Chinese title *Not Afraid of Death*, opening night was abruptly interrupted in the middle of the screening when the writer Hong Shen (1894–1955) led a protest of students from Fudan University, where he was a professor of drama. This action also led to the banning of *Shanghai Express* by the *Guomindang* censors. They ordered that all prints of the film be destroyed. Paramount simply ignored the censors' demands. In retaliation, the censors refused to issue licenses for any future Paramount films that were earmarked for screening in Shanghai. Again, Paramount ignored them and showed its films without the proper license. The intervention of the American embassy helped intimidate the Chinese.[42] This was another example of the multitude of arrogant reactions from foreign institutions and individuals to Chinese rules and regulations that China had to endure before national liberation in 1949.

The fallout from the *Guomindang* censorship of *Shanghai Express* in 1932 affected Wong when she arrived in Nanjing in 1936. Little did she know that her invitation as the guest of honor at a *Guomindang* banquet would result in some negative responses because of her roles in American films. "They made speeches that lasted for four hours, but instead of the usual stereotyped 'welcome to our city' speeches, they all took turns berating me for the roles I played. Since I didn't speak Mandarin then, I had to answer in English. I told them that when a person is trying to get established in a profession, she can't choose parts. She has to take what is offered. I said I had come to China to learn, and that I hoped I would be able to interpret our country in a better light. It all ended with their apologizing to me!"[43]

While Wong was perturbed by such uncharitable responses during her stay in Nanjing, she also told the government officials and reporters who criticized her roles in demeaning parts that film performers hardly ever write the scripts for the characters and that her performances were often dictated by the directors. Deciding on what types of roles she could accept was completely out of her hands if she expected to work often.[44]

The hypocrisy of these criticisms was exposed when Swedish actor Warner Oland, who specialized in "Yellowface" roles, was praised by the Chinese press and government officials for his cinematic performances. Traveling to China at about the same time as Wong, Oland's most famous role was that of the fortune-cookie-spouting Hawaiian detective Charlie Chan, whose main objective in movie fantasy was to defend the European American status quo. Oland also played the Eurasian warlord Henry Chang, who raped Hui Fei and branded a German opium dealer with a hot iron in *Shanghai Express*.[45] But the Chinese press and officials conveniently overlooked this despicable role along with other parts such as his portrayal of the diabolical Fu Manchu.

They lauded Warner Oland, a European from Sweden, because they knew he was just an actor. His roles were also a depiction of men of power and authority. Since China was at one of its lowest social and political points in the 1930s, epitomized by the infamous warning in the Public Gardens, "Dogs and Chinese Not Allowed," this demonstration to the world of power and authority even by a Swede masquerading as a Chinese detective, general, and scientist seemed to be better than nothing.

Wong also portrayed characters of fiction like Hui Fei, Su Quan, Sada, Delamar, Loo Song, Oneta, Ohtai, Nan Lo, and Annabelle Wu. But these women characters had neither power, authority, nor agency. She was criticized because she always played courtesans, dancers, evil ladies, and fallen women with such conviction and authenticity that she was completely believable. It was as if her acting prowess pushed the audience from the edge of movie fantasy to the familiar place of stark reality. In *Fifth Avenue* (1926) and *Shanghai Express,* she transcended the fictional character of such hookers as Nan Lo and Hui Fei from the vivid imagination of Hollywood to the back streets of Shanghai where women plied their trade in "salt-pork shops," "flower-smoke rooms," and "nail sheds." This Chinese American performer's unflattering portrayal of Chinese women reminded China of its lack of value in global affairs. Her performances were just too real. That made some Chinese men cringe!

Wong could only laugh at this hypocrisy. But in her usual gracious manner, she clearly recognized the predicament of the *Guomindang* government: "I can understand why government officials are so earnest about the censorship idea—not because they are hypersensitive, but because they are self-conscious and want people to see their best side, not their worst."[46] Eventually the central government recognized her talents and even offered Wong the opportunity to manage one wing of its motion picture business.[47]

CHINESE ACTING PROFESSION

At the beginning of her sojourn in China, Wong told Shanghai reporters that she did not intend to perform in a Chinese film while in the country. Her general objective was to learn all she could about China as "she is intensely curious to see all that there is."[48] While in Shanghai she began to "learn all she could" by attending many social functions. One was a reception given in her honor by the city's mayor, Wu Tiecheng (1888–1953), in his house on Avenue Haig.[49] Like Wong, Wu was Cantonese. But because of his ties with Sun Wen (Sun Yat-sen), the father of the Chinese revolution, and Jiang Jieshi, the de facto leader of the central Chinese government, he wielded enormous power even in a northern city like Shanghai. That a Chinese American actress could receive an invitation from a powerful political figure like Wu attested to Wong's own power of celebrity.

Wong had established such a formidable reputation as a celebrity, movie star, and actress in the United States and Europe that she could not be dismissed simply as a "film performer." By the 1930s with the popular acclaim for Hu Die and Ruan Lingyu, Chinese audiences were more favorably disposed to stage and cinema actresses. In Shanghai Wong was courted and entertained by people of political and social prominence. Mayor Wu introduced her to many of the studio executives from *Lianhua, Mingxing, Tianyi,* and *Yihua.* At such gatherings, she must have become aware of the Chinese movie industry and the international exploits of such stars as Hu Die. She may have been privy even to the gossip surrounding the suicide of Ruan Lingyu.

The mayor's reception was also where Wong met the famous Chinese opera actor Mei Lanfang (1894–1961), who performed Beijing opera roles in selected films during the 1920s. Throughout his theatrical career he portrayed only female roles. When asked about his performances, Mei replied to Chinese America's most important actress that he knew "'Lady Precious Stream' so well that he could play it in his sleep."[50] Although she had previously encountered Mei Lanfang in London, Wong's impression of China's greatest stage performer remained of "a quiet, unobtrusive person with beautiful long hands and a dignified courteous manner."[51]

Chinese opera demanded years of serious apprenticeship and training. This was plainly exhibited when Wong was invited to an acting school. She concluded that "there is no glamor [sic] about acting in China. It's all hard work. I visited a school of Chinese drama where anyone who wishes to act must go in training from the ages of fourteen to twenty. A two-month trial is given and if the candidate shows ability, he is allowed to remain. Perhaps if there was such a training school in Hollywood, we wouldn't have so many actors!"[52] With such knowledge of China's stage performers, Wong later admitted: "I am convinced that I could never play in the Chinese theater. I have no feeling for it. It's a pretty sad situation to be rejected by the Chinese because I am too American."[53]

She may have been convinced that the Chinese had rejected her because of her American ancestry, but Wong surrounded herself with all that was Chinese in China. By totally embracing her Chineseness, she transcended her American past, which smacked of overt racism and the constant reference to the superiority of European "whiteness"[54] while always extolling individualism and freedom. To be a legitimate and credible American was to be European and racially "white." She was Chinese and racially "yellow."

In European America, being Chinese and racially "yellow" meant little. She was always a "Chinese" because she looked Chinese even when she sought to be and act American, with her flapper slang and costume during the early 1920s. She was, in fact, truly American in being and action. She even walked and stood like a European American. But she was neither European American nor "white."

While in London she had hired an Oxford tutor to help her develop an English accent after her performance in *The Circle of Chalk,* which garnered mostly negative reviews about her speech. By accepting the superiority of British English, she attempted to be European in voice. In doing so, Wong reached out to "Europe" and the ancestral idea that being "American" was to be European first. But even with a quite convincing English accent and the acquisition of French and German for her films on the continent, she could not change the fact that she would always look Chinese.

In China she was beginning to discover herself. Finally, it did not matter what she was or from where she came. It did not matter if European America accepted her as an American. By being in China, she accepted herself as Anna May Wong, who had many parts to her persona: woman, thinker, writer, actress, traveler, risk taker, and agent. The flaccid ideas of ethnicity, nationality, and race no longer had any relevance. But to travel beyond these labels, she knew that she had to extend her thinking, widen her perspective, and open her mind.

CHINESE WOMEN

One of Wong's aims before leaving Shanghai was to learn all about Chinese women so that she could play them more authentically in European American movies. She also wanted to examine herself as a Chinese woman. In Shanghai she was pleasantly surprised by what she observed about the place of women in Chinese society:

> One phase of local social life that surprises and pleases me very much is the freedom enjoyed by the women. Japanese wives, trudging meekly after their lords, seem far more repressed and dependent than the women of China. Unlike the old-fashioned Chinese gentleman, a modern Shanghai husband does not refer to his invisible wife as "the mean one of the inner compartments." Instead, he takes her out to dances, restaurants and night clubs and expects her to serve as hostess in his home. The women in Shanghai actually have more freedom than many Europeans.[55]

The astonishment in Wong's recognition that Chinese women were in fact women of substance was even more revealing when placed in the context of her own ideas and ideals of women in Chinese America, including her mother, Gon Toy Lee. In her 1926 memoir, "The True Life Story of a Chinese Girl," she reflected on traditional Chinese marriages:

> My father has two wives, this first one who has always remained in China with her son, and the second one, my mother, whom he married later. That's where the Chinese men have it all over the rest of us. They can marry as many times as they choose, though the first wife seems to be considered

the most important, if she has a son. In fact, father's wife writes to us and tries to direct our affairs, and so does her son, my half-brother. You can see that the Chinese woman's life is not a particularly enviable one. She is considered far beneath the male members of her household, and is a servant to them. I just see myself being let in for anything like that![56]

From an essentially stereotypical and negative view of the Chinese woman that was conceived and nurtured by her own confined experience and observations of her family in Los Angeles and Chinese America, Wong's perceptions had evolved and matured just as she was to embark on her first European experience in 1928. At the age of twenty-three, she said enthusiastically that "Chinese men are quite wonderful to their women. They do not show their affection as Americans do by rushing into the house, grabbing their wives and kissing them madly, but their love is true and deep."[57] By the time she encountered China and Chinese women in Shanghai in 1936, her ideas about Chinese women and men had crystallized.

GOODBYE SHANGHAI

Anna May Wong was in Shanghai during two periods. The first was spent enjoying her status as a movie star from the United States. Besides being feted by Shanghai social and political elites with banquets, dancing, and receptions and being invited to participate in games of chance like *paigu, mah jong,* and *chai moy,* she was invited by Mayor Wu Tiecheng to witness the first public mass wedding at the new civic center in the city. Mass weddings would become part of the *Guomindang's* New Life Movement, which was started in 1934 to rejuvenate the moral fiber of the nation in hopes of galvanizing a spiritual reawakening, especially in a city as decadent as Shanghai. It was an attempt to uplift the morale of the Chinese people, now under heavy attack from the Japanese.

The mass weddings encouraged simplicity through uniform dress and costumes, thus reducing the cost of individual ceremonies. These were *wenmin jiehun* or civilized wedding ceremonies that allowed Western and Chinese bridal gowns and traditional male dress. But the wedding costumes seemed incongruent, "neither new nor old, neither Chinese nor western, neither a horse nor a donkey."[58] Wong noted that "the brides' costumes were a strange medley of eastern and western styles. As a rule, white outfits appear only at funerals, but some of the brides compromised by wearing a pink jacket and trousers, combined with a long white veil of mosquito netting."[59]

The mingling of Western and Asian styles was practiced not only by the New Life Movement's newlyweds. Wong also sought a healthy integration of American and Chinese in her own wardrobe. But her emphasis was on the Chinese. Madame Wellington Koo introduced her to a silk shop known as Laou Kai Fook's. Wong celebrated this discovery by exclaiming that "it proved to be an enormous place, heaped to the roof with shimmering bolts. I was dazzled by the richness of the colors. It seemed as if the aurora borealis had been broken into bits and distributed through the shop."[60] Taking advantage of Koo's personal tailor, Wong ordered several pieces of one-hundred-year-old silk to be made into Chinese gowns. "I used him so much, and recommended him to so many of my friends who liked what he had done for me, that Mrs. Koo had to find herself another tailor. A Chinese gown with its simple lines, looks quite easy to make, but it takes an expert to keep it from hanging like a Mother Hubbard."[61] These dresses and many more "slit high on the sides to reveal lace of pleated pantalettes" were "inventions of her own combining the old with the new in Chinese fashions."

These Chinese gowns would be a mainstay in her new wardrobe when she returned to the United States. They were displayed in many of Wong's post-China films. Once described as one of the best dressed with her stylish European haute couture fashions inspired by her life in London and travels on the continent, Wong now entered her most relaxed and self-confident period. In 1938 *Look* magazine featured her (holding a dagger) on its March 1 cover and named her the world's most beautiful Chinese woman.[62] During this period she transcended her angst about Hollywood and European America and gained a new meaning as an enriched human being whose persona was beyond race and ethnicity; her humanity was able to develop completely. She was certainly Chinese in look with her new Beijing and Shanghai inspired garments, but now her sensitivity toward the whole possibility of existing and living became part of a new attitude and thinking. She explained that "a rhythm in the life there [China] harmonized with something in me that had been out of tune. I was no longer restless."[63]

RECLAIMING ROOTS

After her first visit to Shanghai, Wong left for Hong Kong, where she would join her father and siblings for an extended stay in the ancestral home in *Taishan*, a district outside of Guangzhou, the "only real Chinese city that she had seen and ... it was a revelation to her."[64] In Hong Kong, Wong was reported to be "an elegant, sophisticated young woman dressed in the latest creations from

Hollywood with the Chinese background."[65] Before venturing to *Taishan,* she also spent some time in the Philippines in April to escape the spring chill in Hong Kong, where she had caught the flu. In the Philippines she dined with President Manuel Quezon (1878–1944) and met young members of the social elite like Conchita Sunico, Miss Philippines of 1935; Nicasio Osmena, son of future president Sergio Osmena (1878–1954); and Pacita Roxas, daughter of Manuel Roxas (1882–1948), also a future president.[66] Once recovered from her illness, Wong returned to Hong Kong and the family reunion in China.

Wong had not seen her father and siblings for more than two years. Her entry into *Taishan* was a cause for celebration. Because many *huayi* or overseas Chinese in the United States and Canada emigrated from *Taishan,* the sight of yet another Chinese American bearing gifts was commonplace. In fact, there was an old southern Chinese saying that you can always tell if a well-dressed and prosperous Chinese expatriate is returning to *Taishan* by the column of sleek, new automobiles heading out of Guangzhou to *Taishan.*

Wong's first trip to *Taishan* was no different from that of a prodigal child returning to her maternal home and birthplace. As a famous film star from Hollywood, she was already known in China and *Taishan.* Her initial welcome from almost everyone in her father's village was an exhibition of exaltation fit for an Empress Dowager and awe reserved only for celestial beings. Homespun banquets and official receptions from village elders were the norm. Considered a goddess from heaven, Wong was amused by the response to her being there. She said that "many women could not believe I really existed. They had seen me on the screen but they thought I was simply a picture invented by a machine. I'll never forget the banquet they gave me. There were 43 courses, and to be polite, I had to eat liberally of all of them."[67]

After her visit to *Taishan,* Wong returned to Shanghai on the SS *President Coolidge.* This time she pursued her third aim in China, learning *guoyu.* Now that she had visited with her father and had made notes about Chinese women, she decided to hire a tutor who spoke neither English nor Cantonese in an attempt to expedite her learning of Mandarin. During this second period in Shanghai, "after that first round of parties that were disappointingly just like parties in Paris or London or Hollywood, I felt tranquil and at peace."[68] Three years later, at age thirty-four, she was all partied out. Wong explained:

> I know that when I used to go to many big parties, I found that I was talking too much. There is an atmosphere at many big affairs that is almost malicious. Light, gay but malicious gossip is the spice of the evening. Someone says something, usually about someone who isn't present or someone who is far enough away not to hear, and the rest laugh and join in. You think of

something smart, something witty, something not quite kind about a figure in the public eye or a mutual acquaintance or someone connected with pictures, if you are in pictures.

At the moment, you are amusing, gay: you make people laugh and they look at you admiringly for the time being, or they seem to do so. I have done things like that, and afterward I have suffered terribly because of what I had said. I've wished the words unsaid, but I couldn't say them.

So, I do not go to many big parties now.[69]

After Shanghai, Wong spent some time in the dynastic capital of Beijing. Here she visited the Forbidden City and the many museums where she discovered that her fondness for Chinese art was real and personal. She reflected that "I always had a weakness for Chinese art, but I thought it was exaggerated. I found that it wasn't. The trees look like they do in a Chinese painting. Even the ruins are alive in Beijing, not dead like the ruins in Rome. If I could ever leave my work, I'd choose Beijing for my home."[70] Even in 1934 when she was working on *Chu Chin Chow* in London, Wong had contemplated making China her home. She remarked to Vivien North that "I want to leave China till the last. Because I have always felt that, if I liked it half as much as I think I will, that I should settle down there and I don't want to do that until I've been around a bit!"[71]

While in Shanghai and Beijing in 1936 her sojourn was recorded for public consumption by Hearst Metrotone news for obvious publicity reasons as well as for personal home viewing. The film was later shown on the ABC travel program *Bold Journey* in 1956.[72] This twenty-year-old footage was remarkable in that it was one of the first documentaries in the history of European American cinema on which commentary was made by a Chinese American who spoke "uninterrupted in complete, intelligent, syntactically correct English sentences."[73] In this episode no longer were viewers treated to European Americans providing their commentary on China and the Chinese in their patronizing, fortune cookie clichés. Wong could interpret China to European America in a sophisticated and sagacious manner. The dragon lady cliché and courtesan image that were revealed in many of her films were no longer relevant. At a mature fifty-one, she had reached a certain destination in her life, and she was able to impart opinions about China with worldly verve and long-standing experience.

Like many Chinese Americans seeking their roots, Anna May Wong's China odyssey was encapsulated into her persona. Before 1936 her only knowledge of China was from books written by the likes of Pearl Buck and more vividly from stereotypical European American films that depicted untruths about the Chinese. She had lived without a real knowledge of China and traveled the earth to places like Britain, France, and Germany unfulfilled. Her thoughts of China in 1934 were of trepidation and misconceptions. She admitted that:

> I've a faint feeling of fright about going to China. You see, although all my early teaching has been Chinese, although I speak and write Chinese, I think I should probably need an interpreter. There are so many dialects.
>
> Another thing too, that makes me want to wait is the thought of the poverty in China. There's poverty everywhere. Now I know and I feel bad enough when I see those poor little things wrapped up with newspapers in the parks. But somehow I could not bear to look on the poverty of my own people.[74]

However, once in China, she exclaimed that "so many of my preconceived ideas have been upset that I feel like a Chinese Alice who has wandered through a very strange looking-glass."[75]

BACK TO THE PLACE OF BIRTH

Anna May Wong returned to San Francisco via the Matson–Oceanic liner *Monterey* on November 28, 1936, after a few days spent in Honolulu. She was forced to linger in the tropical United States because of a shipping strike in Hawaii.[76] After eleven months in China and Asia, she was no longer simply an American. In fact, she was no longer a Chinese or even a movie star. At thirty-one she not only transcended the constraints of ethnicity, race, and nationality but also was finally free from them. She had learned to be Anna May Wong. "During the time she was away, she studied, she traveled, she learned to live. She forgot acting other people's lives for a while—she took time to find herself."[77] Her films during the post-China period showed a self-contained and self-confident Chinese American woman who no longer craved attention, adulation, or respect from European America. Her personally developed Daoist philosophy reflected a special new way of looking at life. China was a spiritual reawakening from a life of cinematic artificiality, false praise, and material acquisition. She explained to journalist Louis Leung that after China she was finally "in harmony with heaven and earth."[78] By discovering her own empowerment, she created her own inner hipness. It was the ultimate existential coolness. Anna May Wong had found her own personal agency, and she reveled in it.

The sojourn in China was a defining moment for Wong. After two periods in Europe, where she became an international star and, more important, developed a mature and cosmopolitan worldview, she was ready for China. It was almost as if she were embracing China as a potential suitor. That she never returned again to the country may not have been as important as internalizing the essence of the Chinese way of thought so that her life's philosophy would sustain her for the next twenty-three years. It was only after this profound encounter with China that Anna May Wong understood the purpose of living and what her role in life was really all about.

NOTES

1. Gunther, cited in Jerome Ch'en, *China and the West* (London: Hutchinson, 1979), 208–9.

2. Ch'en, *China and the West,* 207.

3. Betty Peh-T'i Wei, *Shanghai: Crucible of Modern China* (Hong Kong: Oxford University Press, 1987), 64.

4. Gail Hershatter, *Dangerous Pleasures: Prostitution and Modernity in Twentieth Century Shanghai* (Berkeley: University of California Press, 1997), 39.

5. Hershatter, *Dangerous Pleasures,* 45.

6. Wei, *Shanghai,* 134; Hershatter, *Dangerous Pleasures,* 49–50.

7. Henry Champly, *The Road to Shanghai: White Slave Traffic in Asia,* trans. Warren B. Wells (London: John Long, 1934), 188–89.

8. Ch'en, *China and the West,* 217.

9. Madame Wellington Koo, *No Feast Lasts Forever* (New York: Quadrangle, 1975), 180.

10. Piers Brendon, *The Dark Valley* (New York: Alfred A. Knopf, 2000), 560.

11. Andrew D. Field, "Selling Souls in Sin City: Shanghai Singing and Dancing Hostesses in Print, Film and Politics, 1920–49," in *Cinema and Urban Culture in Shanghai, 1922–1943,* ed. Zhang Yingjin (Stanford, Calif.: Stanford University Press, 1999), 99–100.

12. James Robert Parish and William T. Leonard, eds., "Anna May Wong," in *Hollywood Players: The Thirties* (New Rochelle, N.Y.: Arlington House, 1986), 535.

13. Anna May Wong, "Anna May Wong Recalls Shanghai's Enthusiastic Reception," *New York Herald Tribune,* 31 May 1936, 6.

14. Edna Lee Booker, *News Is My Job: A Correspondent in War-torn China* (New York: Macmillan, 1940), 238.

15. For more on the Green Gang, see Brian Martin, "The Green Gang and the *Guomindang* State: Du Yuesheng and the Politics of Shanghai, 1927–37," *Journal of Asian Studies,* 54, no. 1 (February 1995): 64–92; Frederick Wakeman, *Policing Shanghai, 1927–1937* (Berkeley: University of California Press, 1995), 244–76.

16. Field, "Selling Souls in Sin City," 101.

17. John Pal, *Shanghai Saga* (London: Jarrolds, 1963), 112.

18. Lynn Pan, *Shanghai: A Century in Photographs, 1843–1949* (Hong Kong: Hai Fei Publishing, 1993), 91.

19. Wong, "Anna May Wong Recalls," 6.

20. Pan, *Shanghai*, 92, 118–19.

21. Anna May Wong, "Anna May Wong Finds Shanghai Life Glamorous," *New York Herald Tribune*, 14 June 1936, 2.

22. For a profile of Wang Hanlun and Yang Naimei, see Michael G. Chang, "The Good, the Bad and the Beautiful: Movie Actresses and Public Discourses in Shanghai, 1920s and 1930s," in Zhang, *Cinema and Urban Culture in Shanghai*, 132–42, 293, n. 41.

23. Joshua Shi, "Film Stars Light Way for Future Women," *Shanghai Star*, 27 June 2000, n.p.; Chang, "The Good, the Bad and the Beautiful," 142.

24. Shi, "Film Stars," n.p.

25. For a concise description of the major Shanghai film studios, see Jay Leyda, *Dianying: An Account of Films and the Film Audience in China* (Cambridge: MIT Press, 1972), 60–113. For photos of the *Mingxing, Tianyi,* and *Lianhua* studios, see Tang Zhenchang, *Shanghai's Journey to Prosperity, 1842–1949* (Hong Kong: Commercial Press, 1976), 56.

26. Chang, "The Good, the Bad and the Beautiful," 144.

27. Dazheng Hao, "Chinese Visual Representations: Painting and Cinema," in *Cinematic Landscapes: Observations on the Visual Arts and Cinema of China and Japan*, ed. Linda C. Ehrlich and David Desser, trans. Douglas Wilkerson (Austin: University of Texas Press, 1994), 60.

28. Leyda, *Dianying*, 61–63; Yingjin Zhang, "Introduction," in Zhang, *Cinema and Urban Culture in Republican Shanghai*, 5.

29. Leo Ou-fan Lee, "The Urban Milieu of Shanghai Cinema, 1930–40: Some Explorations of Film Audience, Film Culture, and Narrative Conventions," in Zhang, *Cinema and Urban Culture in Shanghai*, 75 270, nn. 6–7. For the playbill of Johnny Weissmuller in *Tarzan and His Mate* at the Nanking, see Pan, *Shanghai*, 123.

30. Chang, "The Good, the Bad and the Beautiful," 143.

31. Leyda, *Dianying*, 87; Pan, *Shanghai*, 125.

32. Chang, "The Good, The Bad and the Beautiful," 149.

33. Geraldine Sartain, "Tragic Real Love Story of Anna May Wong," *San Francisco Chronicle*, 4 July 1937, 5.

34. "Anna May Wong Visits Shanghai," Hearst vault material, HVMc520r1, 11289, 1936, University of California, Los Angeles.

35. Leyda, *Dianying*, 87.

36. Zhen Zhang, "Teahouse, Shadow Play, Bricolage: 'Laborer's Love' and the Question of Early Chinese Cinema," in Zhang, *Cinema and Urban Culture in Shanghai*, 267, n. 1.

37. Chang, "The Good, the Bad and the Beautiful," 143.

38. Chang, "The Good, the Bad and the Beautiful," 296–97, n. 88.

39. "Mob Meets Chinese Film Star: Miss Anna May Wong Given Warm Welcome," *North China Herald*, 19 February 1936, 310.

40. Anna May Wong, "Anna May Wong 'Amazed' at Chinese Appetite," *New York Herald Tribune,* 7 June 1936, 2.

41. For an in-depth description of Japan's aggression in Shanghai in 1932, see Christian Henriot, *Shanghai, 1927–1937: Municipal Power, Locality and Modernization* (Berkeley: University of California Press, 1993), 85–94.

42. Leyda, *Dianying,* 82; Ruth Vasey, *The World According to Hollywood, 1918–1939* (Madison: University of Wisconsin Press, 1997), 153–55; Zhang Yinjin, "Prostitution and Urban Imagination: Negotiating the Public and Private in Chinese Films of the 1930s," in Zhang, *Cinema and Urban Culture in Shanghai,* 170, 301, n. 44.

43. Wong, cited in Louise Leung, "East Meets West: Anna May Wong Back on Screen After an Absence of Several Years, Discusses Her Native Land," *Hollywood* (n.d.): 55; Buddy Barnett, "Anna May Wong: Hollywood's Orient Express," *Cult Movies* (1996): 21.

44. Edward Sakamoto, "Anna May Wong and the Dragon Lady Syndrome," *Los Angeles Times,* 12 July 1987, 41; Neil Okrent, "Right Place, Wong Time," *Los Angeles Magazine* (May 1990): 94–95.

45. For an informed analysis of *Shanghai Express* and Warner Oland's role in it, see Gina Marchetti, *Romance and the "Yellow Peril": Race, Sex, and Discursive Strategies in Hollywood Fiction* (Berkeley: University of California Press, 1993), 57–59, 64–65.

46. Wong, cited in Leung, "East Meets West," 55.

47. "Anna May Wong Comes Home," *San Francisco Chronicle,* 29 November 1936, 7.

48. "Mob Meets Chinese Film Star," 310.

49. For a profile of Wu Tiecheng as mayor, see Henriot, *Shanghai, 1927–1937,* 80–102; Wong, "Anna May Wong 'Amazed' at Chinese Appetite," 2.

50. Wong, "Anna May Wong 'Amazed' at Chinese Appetite," 2; Pan, *Shanghai,* 122.

51. Wong, "Anna May Wong 'Amazed' at Chinese Appetite," 2.

52. Wong, cited in Leung, "East Meets West," 55.

53. Sakamoto, "Anna May Wong and the Dragon Lady Syndrome," 41.

54. For a provocative discussion of "whiteness," see the essays in *Critical White Studies: Looking Beyond the Mirror,* ed. Richard Delgado and Jean Stefancic (Philadelphia: Temple University Press, 1997).

55. Wong, "Anna May Wong Finds Shanghai Life Glamorous," 2.

56. Anna May Wong, "The True Life Story of a Chinese Girl," *Pictures* (August 1926, September 1926), at http://www.mdle.com/Classic Films/Feature Star/star49e2.htm (accessed 31 July 1998).

57. Wong, cited in Alice L. Tildesley, "I Am Lucky That I Am Chinese," *San Francisco Chronicle,* 3 June 1928, 3.

58. Pan, *Shanghai,* 112.

59. Wong, "Anna May Wong 'Amazed' at Chinese Appetite," 2.

60. Wong, "Anna May Wong Recalls," 6.

61. Wong, cited in Leung, "East Meets West," 55.

62. "The World's Most Beautiful Chinese Girl," *Look* (1 March 1938): cover, 36–37; Leung, "East Meets West," 55.

63. Wong, cited in Leung, "East Meets West," 40.

64. "Miss Anna May Wong Back," *North China Herald,* 1 April 1936, 9.

65. "Anna May Wong Off Screen," *Hong Kong Sunday Herald,* 22 March 1936, 2.

66. "Miss Anna May Wong Back," 19; for the Associated Press photo of Wong, Sunico, Osmena, and Roxas, see Associated Press Photo, 6 April 1936.

67. Wong, cited in Leung, "East Meets West," 40, 55.

68. Wong, cited in Leung, "East Meets West," 40.

69. Wong, cited in Alice L. Tildesley, "Why Waste Your Time?" *Seattle Daily Times,* 9 April 1939, 9.

70. Wong, cited in Leung, "East Meets West," 40.

71. Wong, "There's a Secret Anna May Wong," *Picturegoer Weekly* (8 September 1934): 8.

72. Hearst Newsreel, Hearst Newsreel collection, UCLA, 1936; *Bold Journey,* Julian Lesser, producer, John Stephenson, host, "Native Land," ABC *Primetime,* 1956.

73. Darrell Y. Hamamoto, *Monitored Peril: Asian Americans and the Politics of TV Representation* (Minneapolis: University of Minnesota Press, 1994), 251.

74. Wong, "Anna May Wong 'Amazed' at Chinese Appetite," 2.

75. Wong, "Anna May Wong 'Amazed' at Chinese Appetite," 2.

76. "Anna May Wong Comes Home", "Anna May Wong Enjoys 'Vacation,'" *Seattle Daily Times,* 29 November 1936, 9.

77. Leung, "East Meets West," 40.

78. Wong, cited in Leung, "East Meets West," 40.

EIGHT

LIFE'S VALUES

From those early days in Los Angeles when she gawked at such film stars as Ruth Roland, Pearl White, and Mae Murray to her later triumphs in Hollywood, Berlin, and London, Anna May Wong was a constant practitioner of living. There were no countries or boundaries that prevented her from seeking out the existential vicissitudes of her persona. Once she discovered her own spiritual fulfillment, personal agency, and professional empowerment following her journey in China, she began to understand the meaning of life and her role in the universe.

After 1936 she was no longer restless. Although she toured Australia with a vaudeville troupe in 1938, this travel was a manifestation of her China War Relief efforts to raise money for her grandparents' homeland, not a longing to seek out the unusual or to acquire yet another foreign experience. This was the political side of Chinese America's most famous actress, which lasted until Hiroshima and Nagasaki in 1945.

A NONLINEAR SETTING

Anna May Wong had always perceived the world as a global entity that possessed many centers and no boundaries or borders. She was never confined by the shackles of the Judeo-Christian worldview that envisioned life as an either/or proposition in the United States. In this European American world, human existence was constrained and compelled to act within a good or evil mode, a black or white state, or in the case of a Chinese American, a white or yellow motif. It was an environment that proclaimed and institutionalized the superiority of European Americans and "whiteness" over all others, especially Chinese Americans and their "yellowness." This was decidedly uninviting to Wong, who sought a wider perspective. While Wong was forced to endure the racism of European America, she was neither interested in nor willing to continue being a victim of its grotesque economic facets.

When Europe welcomed her Chinese American celebrity and consummate acting abilities, she rushed into its arms with joy. No doubt if Europe had not been in the midst of war at the end of the 1930s she would have lived there as long as she could, like such expatriates as Josephine Baker (1906–1975) and Paul Robeson (1898–1976). In many ways, because of her cosmopolitanism, language abilities, sophistication, and cool demeanor, she was suited to the expatriate life. Europeans understood her multidimensional persona and welcomed it. She believed that most of Europe with its cultural richness, founded on an eclectic tradition of welcoming artists and performers, cared more about talent and creating and less about race and ethnicity. Later in the 1930s this welcoming attitude of Europeans would be put to the test with the emergence of the most racist nation in modern history, Nazi Germany.

Wong was part of the exodus of Hollywood stars like Louise Brooks (1906–1985) who also felt constrained in the United States. "They had restless souls, like Chekhov's heroines who sit on the wide-open steppes and moan all day long: 'God! I'm stifling here! I can't breathe! When, oh when, do we go to Moscow?' So, in the end, they pack their grips and lit out for their spiritual home. Hollywood saw them no more—for a time, at least."[1]

For Wong the world was never just Hollywood, a one-dimensional, linear town glorifying the creepy, exotic, erotic, and violent, encased in a veneer of respectability but always concealed beneath a layer of seedy prejudice based on race, ethnicity, and citizenship. While toiling in pre-1928 American roles that demeaned, disfigured, subordinated, and stunted the Asian American persona, Wong's "hidden tiger" was to expand her repertoire of acting skills and techniques. Her work in *The Toll of the Sea* and *The Thief of Bagdad* no doubt caught the eye of several European producers. But who had the courage to take a chance on this Chinese American actress who could pull in the paying customers with her sensitive, human performances?

Paul Leni directed Wong as the "Nautch dancer" in *The Chinese Parrot* (1927). As a German director who was once an avant-garde painter and set designer, he knew many of his own country's filmmakers and may have raved to Richard Eichberg about the ease with which she took direction on a film set. It was not only her extraordinary performances in *The Toll of the Sea* and *The Thief of Bagdad* but also her professional reputation as a no-nonsense, punctual, and always prepared actress that prompted Eichberg to sign Wong to a contract for two German films, *Song* (1928) and *Pavement Butterfly* (1929) for the studio *Universum Film Aktien Gesellschaft* (UFA) in collaboration with British International Pictures (BIP). Through BIP and Elstree Productions, she was also cast in the leading role as Hai Tang in *The Flame of Love* (1930), the German version, *Hai Tang* (1930), and the French remake, *L'amour maitre des choses* (1930). Richard Eichberg was the principal director of these movies. *Piccadilly* (1929), directed by E. A. Dupont for BIP and World Wide, was probably her most famous film during Wong's first European period. This film solidified her celebrity in Britain.

Without her particular global perspective and thirst for adventure, Anna May Wong never would have embarked on a personal and professional odyssey in Europe. If she had accepted Hollywood's attempt to continually typecast her as a "sweet china doll" or a "sexy, saucy slave," she would have stayed in Tinseltown and endured until she could no longer. In fact, if she had accepted Hollywood's determination to hire her only in secondary casting, she would never have prospered. It was either work as a supporting actress or nothing. This was a black or white proposition that she declined. That gloomy situation was her only future in the European American film industry in 1928 when she made the decision to leave the United States for Europe.

Wong was never a Milquetoast who would bend to the whims of her studio bosses. Before her first German film, *Song,* in 1928, she worked in three films for First National, Universal, Paramount, and MGM and two each for United Artists, Pathe, and Warner Bros. At the studios of Robertson Cole, Metro, Producers Releasing Corporation, Fairmont Pictures/Hi-Mark Productions, Chadwick, and Tiffany, this Chinese American actress was hired for one film only. Working for so many and such varied film studios was a common road that many aspiring film performers traveled. At this point in her career she took what roles were available. Except for *The Toll of the Sea,* these films neither challenged her enough nor represented positive characters. Rather than continuing this transient studio life, she went into exile.

With almost no cinematic opportunities to appear in European American starring roles, Anna May Wong enthusiastically seized the invitation to work for Richard Eichberg as his main female lead in five European films. By accepting Eichberg's contract, she dismissed Hollywood's linear, one-dimensional, and dichotomous interpretation of her talents and abilities. In doing so, she was denying European America its smug, arrogant definition of itself as the sole agent in determining the fate of at least one Chinese American woman. This was her first taste of empowerment. She now knew that if she was to have a future as a film actress, her destiny must remain enveloped within her own personal agency.

FAMILY

That Wong at the age of twenty-three could simply leave the United States for Europe with the confidence of a mature and fearless international star did not just happen overnight. Certainly the companionship of her oldest sister, Lulu,[2] helped relieve much of her initial anxiety and trepidation about traveling to a foreign continent. These two young Chinese American women in their twenties gave each other the moral courage and comradeship to deal with adversities and to excel. But what gave Wong that inner strength to move beyond the constraints and restrictions that a Chinese American woman with her unique ambitions would inevitably encounter was simply "being Chinese." She could draw on the power and guidance of her immediate family and the positive, nurturing attributes gleaned from Chinese culture and its ways of thinking.

As a member of a large working-class Chinese American family, Wong was the second child of Sam Sing Wong and Gon Toy Lee. Because her parents were born in the United States, the Wong children were third-generation Americans. The oldest was Lulu, with James, Mary (Liu Hueng), Frank, Roger, and Richard born respectively after Anna. Another daughter was born in either 1919 or 1920, but she died at an early age.[3] Wong also had a half brother who was the son of her father's first wife in China. The size of the family was typical of immigrant Chinese families with roots in the Chinese countryside. Like peasant families in China that needed many hands to work the land, large families in Chinese America were imperative because of such labor-intensive occupations as laundry or restaurant work that many were forced to accept. Living in a hostile and foreign European America that had enacted the Chinese Exclusion Act of 1882 and countless other acts discriminatory toward the Chinese,[4] survival demanded unpaid and trustworthy labor, usually found among family members. Survival also required a carefully chosen set of principles that could help the family face obstacles and provide nourishment for growth.

The large size of Anna May Wong's family, nestled outside of Los Angeles Chinatown in a laundry with two-room living quarters on North Figueroa Street, meant that there had to be order and structure for the Wongs to survive.

Regardless of gender, that meant every able-bodied member of the family had to work. Her parents treated all the children equally when it came to work at the laundry. No one was spared. As early as ten years old, Anna May often labored with Lulu or James, hustling large mounds of dirty laundry to be deposited on the back porch of the shop. They would also "pack the bundles up in Arroyo Seco while their father waited at the bottom of the hill."[5] Thus Wong knew the value of hard work at an early age. Throughout her life she never took the notion of work or the money that came from work for granted. She also knew that a life of toil in the back of a laundry was not for her. But the laundry proved to be prosperous for the Wong family, as Sam Sing Wong eventually bought a home on Flower Street while still making a living at the Figueroa shop.

THE RECTIFICATION OF NAMES

At the heart of a relatively stable home life at the Wong household was a simple hierarchical structure. This was the idealized Chinese notion of the rectification of names that was first revealed by Kong Qiu (551–479 B.C.E.), also known in the West as Confucius. Living during a period of tremendous social upheaval and political uncertainty at the conclusion of the Spring and Autumn period (771–256 B.C.E.), his philosophical principles were influenced by an era of continuing danger, intense hostility, perpetual violence, and abject poverty. This was a world without order. For people to endure and prosper, there had to be a clear guide for them in their behavior. This could only be accomplished when everyone knew and implemented the content of their roles in society. The name "ruler," for example, possessed a content of a person who was "morally worthy" and "politically effective" to be a ruler.[6] Once the ruler no longer followed these tenets, chaos ensued. Consequently, for a society or a family to survive and enjoy stability and harmony, the people must know and follow the content of specific roles assigned to them. In the *Confucian Analects:*

> The prince Jing of Qi asked Confucius about government. Confucius replied, *"There is government,* when the prince is a prince, and the minister is a minister; when the father is a father, and the son is a son." "Good!" said the prince, "If, indeed, the prince be not the prince, the minister not minister, the father not father, and the son not son, although I have my revenue, can I enjoy it?"[7]

While the Wong family was not living in the era of widespread war and violence that shook what was to be known later as the Spring and Autumn period, the fact that they were living among European Americans who sometimes perpetrated violence on the lives of Chinese Americans either through physical force or the enactment of legislation dictated a need for effective principles of behavior to survive and prosper. The rectification of names was one such principle that endured in the Wong household.

Although Chinese families hardly spoke of the "rectification of names" in strictly Confucian terms as expounded by the sage in the *Confucian Analects,* it reverberated in many Chinese and Chinese American households. Sam Sing Wong accepted his role as "father" and proceeded to adhere to the content of "father" by creating an occupation enabling his wife and children to survive and prosper. His wife, Gon Toy Lee, accepted her role as "mother" and proceeded to raise her children as a Chinese or Chinese American mother ought to raise them. The seven children all recognized their roles as "children" and acted accordingly with obedience and loyalty. The three daughters, Lulu, Anna May, and Mary, all possessed their own roles as "daughters" and acted accordingly. As female members of the family it was expected that they would marry and move out of the house. But it was apparent that Sam Sing Wong was a pragmatic father. He recognized that in an increasingly hostile and dangerous Los Angeles, daughters could also work and contribute to the family well-being. While he adhered to many of the Chinese principles and values, he was not bound by them if that meant destitution and misery for his family. His *Taishan* peasant background encouraged adaptation and improvisation.

Treated as laborers and potential wage earners like children of peasant families in China, Anna May Wong and her sisters were accorded almost son-like status. In particular, Wong simply behaved as if she were a son with her manifestation of daily toil in the laundry and later as an independent wage earner in the film industry that helped finance her father's and siblings' travel to China and residence in *Taishan* for two years. Despite their peasant roots and working-class background, the Wongs were an upwardly mobile family. Having escaped the poverty of southern China, this was one Chinese American family determined to prosper in a new land in spite of its racial pitfalls. As a typical *huayi* (overseas) family in Chinese America, there was nothing special about their existence, which was full of hard work, long days, and a penchant for education. Sam Sing Wong in particular set a high standard of work for himself and his family. He used to exclaim during the hectic hours of toil in his prosperous laundry that "I have time to die, but I haven't time to lie down!"[8] What set the Wong family apart from every other industrious Chinese American household in the country was its movie star daughter, Anna May Wong.

THE FIVE RELATIONSHIPS

While the Wong family followed the tenets of observing the roles assigned to them by virtue of rectifying names, they also adhered to the duties of the five relationships. Propounded by Mengzi or Meng Ke (390–305 B.C.E.), also known in the West as Mencius, the idealized notion of the Five Relationships formed the basis of Chinese human interaction within universal obligations. Mengzi proclaimed that:

> If men (*ren*= humans) have satisfied their hunger, have clothes to wear, and live at ease but lack good teaching, they are close to the birds and beasts. This was a subject of anxious solicitude to the sage. *Shun* (a legendary sage-ruler) was distressed about this and he appointed Xie to be the minister of instruction, to teach the basic relationships of life; how, between father and son, there should be affection; between sovereign and minister (and subject), righteousness; between husband and wife, attention to their respective spheres; between old and young, a proper order; and between friends, fidelity.[9]

Of the five types of human interaction, the key relationship for Anna May Wong in her family was father and daughter. Sam Sing Wong was the patriarch who dispensed rewards, praise, punishment, and protection. He was the one who cast judgment on Wong's cinematic ambitions. He was a major influence in her early success as a Hollywood actress. Since Wong's sisters Lulu and Mary were also stage and film performers, the father, moreover, had a say in their artistic development. Lulu was praised by Anna May for her performance in the film *Eskimo,* while Mary was Anna May's understudy in the Broadway play *On the Spot.*[10]

After Wong's debut as an extra in *The Red Lantern* (1919), her parents were adamantly opposed to their second daughter's choice of a cinematic profession.[11] No doubt they had little knowledge of what a film career entailed. In 1919 there were absolutely no Asian American female role models in Hollywood for them to even consider. That their daughter was contemplating acting as an occupation in European America was not only an innovative idea but also a revolutionary notion. The vague impression that uneducated Chinese Americans with peasant backgrounds would have about the people in the theatrical business bordered on the fantastic and stereotypical. The prevailing opinion transported across the Pacific was that theatrical performers in China came from a class of prostitutes, dancers, and thieves. Female roles were almost always played by male actors in drag. Certainly no daughter of any upstanding Chinese or Chinese American family would be allowed to perform onstage.

But in the United States, acting and performing in films were totally different than in China. There was also the added attraction of a bigger paycheck.

The fact that Hollywood paid more per picture than a small shopkeeper like Sam Sing Wong could make in a year convinced him that insisting that his daughters, especially Anna May, ought to marry, leave home, and produce a family was counterproductive. Certainly he knew that being in the movies would pay much more than Anna May's job at the Ville de Paris department store, where she was working when she heard that Metro studio was looking for three hundred extras in Alla Nazimova's *The Red Lantern*.[12] As a Chinese American living in European America, he understood the necessity of adaptability, seizing every opportunity and moving with the flow. His daughter was one such opportunity that could help the family prosper. She worked in the laundry, at a department store, and now in the movies. At least she was an industrious and ambitious daughter whose life went beyond her immediate family and the back rooms of a laundry.

After her first role as an extra, Wong appeared unbilled as an extra in *Dinty* (1920), *The First Born* (1921), and *Mother O'Mine* (1921). In her immediate family, only her siblings knew that she was working in still more pictures; her parts were unheralded and sometimes unseen among a cast of many. To keep her from prowling the Hollywood studios looking for work, her father often locked her in her room at the laundry.[13] Little did he know his daughter was attracting the attention of important directors.

One of those directors was Marshall Neilan who, after casting her in *Dinty,* created especially for her the credited role as Toy Sing in *Bits of Life*. After this film Wong could no longer expect anonymity. That meant that her father had to be told about her good fortune. In her memoir Wong remembered that, "Of course my parents had to know, presently that I was doing screen work occasionally. Marshall Neilan offered me a part in *Dinty* and I had it out then and there with my father. He said I was disgracing his family and all that sort of things, but I told him that I was determined to be independent some day, that I just couldn't be like the girls who live in China and it was no use trying to make me over."[14]

Although Wong's father was initially opposed to his daughter's involvement in the picture business, he warmed to the idea if he could have a hand in her career. Here was the manifestation of his role as a father and his interaction with his daughter based on the Chinese principles of human relationships. His affection for his daughter demonstrated a genuine caring that went as far as making sure that an escort or chaperone accompanied her to the studios. It was often Sam Sing Wong himself who drove her to the studios.

At first Wong saw her father's interest in her career as simple parental meddling. She lamented: "My father was still opposed to my career. When I was to work in a picture, he always went out to the big touring bus that called for the extras and looked to see if other women—respectable women were there. Unless plenty of Chinese women were in the bus, I could not go. One day a boy from the studio told me of an opportunity for work at Culver City and offered to call for me in his car, but when he came my father would not let me go. 'No other girl going?' he asked and when I said 'No,' he forbade me leaving the house."[15]

Eventually Wong resented her father's interference in her life and choice of career so much that she moved out of the family home and into a chic Hollywood apartment. At the age of nineteen she continued learning about the various aspects of performing and living freely. She proclaimed to reporter Alice Tildesley that "I am proud to say that everything I own in my name, every educational advance I have made—dancing lessons, piano, voice—I have paid for with my earnings. The little car out there is the car *Peter Pan* (1924) paid for: I was the Indian maid in that picture."[16]

For about three years the most famous Chinese American actress in the world lived the life of a 1920s flapper, with the clothes and slang to match. Journalists marveled at her "tiptilted hat, pure Parisian heels, sheer silk stockings and a Persian lamp wrap."[17] Her "pert shop-girl slang" was the envy of many young Asian and European American twenty-year-olds in its fluency and hipness.[18] When Wong was late for an interview with *Photoplay's* Mary Winship, she apologized by exclaiming, "I bet I've kept you waiting—I'm the limit. A friend brought me down. I couldn't find a taxi and I haven't got a car myself. I ruined the last one. I had been trying to beat a motor cop to a bridge. I beat him all right, but I missed the bridge."[19]

By 1925 the American flapper image and apartment living had begun to wear thin. There was something missing in simply being like all the other young European American women who blended in with the latest fad. She could be a flapper, but she was always a Chinese American woman imitating a European American flapper. It seemed incongruous. By the age of twenty-one Wong realized that if she were to succeed in Hollywood, blending in with the current, mundane atmosphere that all the other European American movie hopefuls had embraced was just not enough. She had to create her own atmosphere and define her own idea of what was chic. In fact, she had to *be* her own atmosphere.

While Wong was on the threshold of creating and being her own unique atmosphere and hipness, Sam Sing Wong invited her back to the family home with an offer of her own living quarters independent from the rest of the family. Anna May Wong accepted, and she transformed herself from an ordinary actress living a forced rendition of a European American flapper into a celebrity

with a Chinese style and grace. Other celebrities sought her out. Hollywood reporter Helen Carlisle remarked: "Not only do they visit her, but in return, she is
invited to social affairs where most of Hollywood is excluded. When Harrison
Fisher, the New York artist, is at his Ambassador bungalow, he would hardly consider a party complete unless Anna May Wong was there. Emil Jannings turns an
indifferent shoulder to many of our film stars, but when he entertains, you'll find
Anna May Wong among his guests."[20]

The change came about because of Sam Sing Wong's intervention in his
daughter's career, which by 1927 included more than twenty films. In 1927
alone she had appeared in eight films. But none of these had star billing. By
this time her father thoroughly supported her career in the film industry. His
new attitude was evident in his evolving and constant devotion to his daughter. Wong remarked that "sometimes when I have not been working for a week
or two, my father will come to me and say: 'Are you sure you have plenty of
money. You know that I can always give you anything. Do not borrow from
anyone, but come to me.'"[21] Wong also saw the changed demeanor that her father had toward her. She proclaimed that "he is proud of me now though. He
is always telling people that today all the nicest girls in China are on stage. I
was lucky too because unlike most of the extra girls, who struggled along on
five to seven-fifty a day when they worked, I had no worry over money. My
father was willing to take care of me."[22]

With support from her family, Anna May Wong could concentrate on
creating her own persona, which became so original that "men and women
from the world of arts and letters seek her out. Many a celebrity has visited her
little house where she serves tea in a truly ceremonious manner. If they request
it, she displays her Chinese costumes which included her warrior's robe of
heavy white brocade, studded with silver."[23] As part of the film social elite,
Wong had arrived. At twenty-one she was a Hollywood movie star and a
celebrity. But she was not a leading actress. Although she would leave for Europe in 1928 seeking to fulfill that ambition in Richard Eichberg's films, she
never forgot her family.[24]

FILIAL PIETY (*XIAO*)

One of the key principles that joined members of Chinese or Chinese American families together was filial piety or *xiao*. This was essential to the well-
being and cohesiveness of a family, especially in environments that fostered
danger and hostility. In the *Confucian Analects:*

Now filial piety is seen in the skillful carrying out of the wishes of our fore-fathers, and the skillful carrying out of their undertakings.

The Master said, "A youth, when at home, should be filial, and abroad, respectful to the elders. He should be earnest and truthful. He should over-flow in love to all, and cultivate the friendship of the good. When he has time and opportunity after the performance of these things, he should employ them in polite studies."[25]

In the Wong family, Sam Sing Wong and Lee Gon Toy expected all their children to show them proper respect and obedience. Although Anna May was disrespectful and did not show proper obedience to her parents when she decided on a film career, her return to the family home in 1926 demonstrated that she could, in fact, exhibit proper filial piety to her parents. She explained that "Chinese children are brought up with a great deal of discipline, a sense of responsibility and a tremendous loyalty to each other. They may not be demonstrative and kiss each other, but a Chinese family will stick together through fire. White people often kiss each other a good deal, but desert each other in any kind of trouble."[26]

Despite some reports that father and daughter were estranged later in Wong's career, she often demonstrated her filial piety[27] to him and her loyalty to the rest of the family. When her father sold the laundry in 1934 and returned to China with his younger children, Wong financed the trip and much of their residency in *Taishan*. Just after she returned from her first European sojourn, she proclaimed that "it's wonderful my success, because now I feel I can help my family—there are so many of them. When I went away, my brothers were little boys. I couldn't believe it when I saw them—all grown up, with long trousers and deep voices."[28]

She helped finance James's master of arts degree from the University of Southern California, which he received two days after Wong returned from Europe. She also provided some financial assistance to Roger, who wanted to study engineering, and to Richard, who studied photography.[29] Because she felt that she had "provided for them during my lifetime sufficiently to make them self sustained," she purposely omitted James, Frank, and Roger from her final will in 1958.[30]

By the time Anna May made her final will, her parents had already passed away. Her father died of natural causes in 1949 at the age of ninety-one. Her forty-three-year-old mother, Gon Toy Lee, had been struck down by a car driven by Joe Rondoni in front of the North Figueroa Street home on November 11, 1930.[31] The only other unpredictable death in Wong's life was her sister Mary's untimely demise at her own residence. Los Angeles police detective R. H. Halsell reported that Mary Liu Heung Wong hung herself in her garage on July 25,

1940.[32] The beneficiaries of Wong's estate were her oldest sister, Lulu, and her youngest brother, Richard. Throughout her successful film career, her parents and siblings benefited from Wong's loyalty and benevolence to her family.

EDUCATION: PRACTICAL LEARNING

At the center of human progress in Chinese and Chinese American societies was the Confucian emphasis on study. Since the days of Confucius, who was considered China's first private teacher, the educator and the literati class have always been revered. Learning remained at the cornerstone of Chinese life and civilization. Through the provincial and central government examination systems, impoverished Chinese youths from peasant and merchant classes could rise up into the scholar gentry class and into a system of power and privilege. This was the ideal that many attempted to attain. Education and learning could help further a person's ambition and career. In the Sam Sing Wong household, education and learning were always revered. The oldest son, James, went on to complete a graduate degree. Roger studied engineering, and Richard learned the intricacies of photography.

As for Anna May Wong herself, she was the consummate lifelong learner, beginning with her prodding of camera crews and studio hands for more knowledge about film techniques and acting during her early days roaming the studio lots in 1917. When she realized that acting in European films demanded facility in German, British English, and French, she embarked on language study with a view toward their usefulness in future work. Her appetite for learning about the art, culture, foods, people, politics, social conditions, and theater of China was voracious when she embarked on an eleven-month sojourn in her ancestral homeland and Asia. Even though she never completed high school, her education was continuous and spanned several continents; she avidly learned about different cultures and languages. Returning from China, she continued her study of Chinese philosophy and fashioned a practical sense of life that was reflected in her lifestyle and many of her comments.

NOTES

1. Cedric Belfrage, cited in Hans J. Wollstein, *Vixens, Floozies and Molls: 28 Actresses of Late 1920s and 1930s Hollywood* (Jefferson, N.C.: McFarland, 1999), 258.

Family Trio, L-R, Liu Ying Wong (Lulu), mother Gon Toy Lee, Liu Tsong Wong (Anna May), 1908. Courtesy of the Academy of Motion Picture Arts and Sciences.

Magnificent Perspective 1926.

Strolling in Limehouse, London 1929. Courtesy of the Academy of Motion Picture Arts and Sciences.

Contemplation 1935.

Modeling 1938.

Daoist Mood 1945.

Portrait 1960. Courtesy of the Academy of Motion Picture Arts and Sciences.

Performing in German in her Viennese operetta, *Springtime (Tschuin Tschi)* 1930. Courtesy of the Academy of Motion Picture Arts and Sciences.

Playing Lotus Flower in Hollywood's first Technicolor film, *The Toll of the Sea* 1922. Courtesy of the Academy of Motion Picture Arts and Sciences.

Playing the Mongol spy and infiltrator in *The Thief of Bagdad* 1924.
Courtesy of the Academy of Motion Picture Arts and Sciences.

Playing the Mongol spy and infiltrator in *The Thief of Bagdad* 1924. Courtesy of the Academy of Motion Picture Arts and Sciences.

Playing Princess Ling Moy in *Daughter of the Dragon* 1931. Courtesy of the Academy of Motion Picture Arts and Sciences.

Playing Hui Fei with Marlene Dietrich in *Shanghai Express* 1932.

Playing Dr. Mary Ling with Akim Tamiroff in *King of Chinatown* 1939.

As Lin Ying in *Bombs Over Burma* 1942. Courtesy of the Academy of Motion Picture Arts and Sciences.

Anna May Wong's last role as Tani in *Portrait in Black* 1960. Courtesy of the Academy of Motion Picture Arts and Sciences.

2. "Screen Star Has Her Homecoming After Much Delay," *Seattle Daily News,* 6 September 1931, 14.

3. *Fourteenth Census of the United States, 1920 Population, Los Angeles County, CA, January 19, 1920,* United States Department of Commerce and Labor, cited in Karen Janis Leong, "The China Mystique: Mayling Soong, Pearl S. Buck and Anna May Wong in the American Imagination" (Ph.D. dissertation, University of California, Berkeley, spring 1999), 117, n. 6.

4. For the literature surveying European American racial discrimination against Chinese Americans and Asian Americans, see Sucheng Chan, "Asian American Historiography," *Pacific Historical Review* 65, no. 3 (August 1996): 363–99.

5. Rob Wagner, "Two Chinese Girls . . . by Rob Wagner, Stenographic Notes of a Recent Broadcast, *Script* 16, no. 390 (November 21, 1936): 4, 28, cited in Leong, "The China Mystique," 350.

6. Frederick W. Mote, *Intellectual Foundation of China* (New York: Alfred A. Knopf, 1989), 44.

7. *Confucian Analects,* Book 12, no. 11, cited in Zhong Shuhe, *The Four Books* (Changsha, Republic of China: Hunan Publishing House, 1994), 171.

8. Sam Sing Wong, cited in Alice E. Tildesley, "I Am Lucky That I Am Chinese," *San Francisco Chronicle,* 3 June 1928, 3; Geraldine Gan, *Lives of Notable Asian Americans* (New York: Chelsea House, 1995), 83.

9. Mengzi, Book 5, 5, cited in Zhong, *The Four Books,* 359; aFeng Yu-lan, *A Short History of Chinese Philosophy* (New York: Macmillan, 1964), 73; *The Doctrine of the Mean,* cited in Zhong, *The Four Books,* 4.

10. "Anna May Wong Off the Screen," *Hong Kong Sunday Herald,* 22 March 1936, 1; "Screen Star Has Her Homecoming," 14.

11. Dan Thomas, "British Gold Lures Hollywood Stars," *Seattle Daily Times,* 6 January 1935, 1.

12. Wollstein, *Vixens,* 248.

13. Barrie Roberts, "Anna May Wong: Daughter of the Orient," *Classic Images* 270 (December 1997): 20.

14. Anna May Wong, "The True Life Story of a Chinese Girl," *Pictures* (August 1926, September 1926), at http://www.mdle.com/Classic Films/Feature Star/star49e2.htm (accessed 31 July 1998).

15. Wong, cited in Tildesley, "I Am Lucky That I Am Chinese," 23.

16. Wong, cited in Tildesley, "I Am Lucky That I Am Chinese," 23.

17. Mary Winship, "The China Doll," *Photoplay Magazine* 24, no. 1 (June 1923): 35.

18. Helen Carlisle, "Velly Muchee Lonely," *Motion Picture Magazine* 35, no. 2 (March 1928): 41.

19. Wong, cited in Winship, "The China Doll," 35.

20. Wong, cited in Carlisle, "Velly Muchee Lonely," 41.

21. Wong, cited in Tildesley, "I Am Lucky That I Am Chinese," 3.

22. Wong, cited in Tildesley, "I Am Lucky That I Am Chinese," 3.

23. Carlisle, "Velly Muchee Lonely," 41.

24. Carlisle, "Velly Muchee Lonely," 41.

25. "The Doctrine of the Mean" and "The Confucian Analects," cited in Zhong, *The Four Books,* 39, 67; For an in-depth study of *xiao* and Chinese Americans, see Wei Djao, *Being Chinese: Voices from the Diaspora,* (Tucson: University of Arizona Press, 2003).

26. Wong, cited in Betty Willis, "Famous Oriental Stars Return to the Screen," *Motion Picture Magazine* 43, no. 3 (October 1931): 44.

27. Roberts, "Anna May Wong," 20.

28. Wong, cited in Willis, "Famous Oriental Stars Return," 45.

29. "Screen Star Has Her Homecoming," 14.

30. Last Will and Testament of Anna May Wong, Harold J. Ostly, Santa Monica County Clerk, February 28, 1961, #439787, Book 1457, 276.

31. "Injuries Fatal to Mrs. Wong," *Los Angeles Times,* 12 November 1930, 5.

32. "Anna May Wong's Sister's Suicide," *New York Herald Tribune,* 26 July 1940, 26.

NINE

DAOIST BUTTERFLY

Anna May Wong adhered to many of the Confucian principles that helped shape her family life and provide a clear rationale and structure for her Chinese American family to survive and prosper in a dangerous and hostile environment predominantly occupied by European Americans. While these principles based on Confucian notions governing human interaction influenced her relationships, she also investigated other Chinese concepts to help focus her own personal view of the world and her place in it. One of her major influences was Daoism.[1]

Unlike Confucian principles, which dealt specifically with human relationships, Daoism was philosophically more concerned with the "concept of Non-being which is the *Dao (Tao)* or Way and its concentration in the individual as the natural virtue of man which is *De (te),* translated as 'virtue' but better rendered as the 'power' that inheres in any individual thing."[2] As a philosophy, it taught the doctrine of following nature. Like the Confucianists, Daoists were especially perplexed by the intricacies of living in the contemporary world.

The Daoist emphasis on human beings living in harmony with nature, cut off, if necessary, from other people, exalted the primacy of nature. The "naturalistic" contrasted sharply with Confucian principles, which stressed human relationships or "humanistic" aspects.[3] Within the idea of "naturalism," some concrete themes emerged that influenced Wong's philosophical attitudes toward life.

One of the early Chinese thinkers who influenced many ideas of Daoism was Yang Zhu (circa 395–335 B.C.E.). He advocated the idea of "preserving the self" while simultaneously rejecting the notion of "conquering things."[4] The "preservation of self" did not mean embarking on a path of hedonism or sensuality. It simply meant "preserving life and maintaining what is genuine in it, not allowing things to entangle one's person."[5] He explained that "it is out of the human passions that the ear desires variegated sounds, the eye variegated colors and the mouth variegated flavors. The ear, the eye, the nose and the mouth are in the service for life; though the ear desires the sound, the eye the color, the nose the fragrance, the mouth the flavor, if they are harmful to life, they should be discarded."[6]

The concept of "despising things and valuing life" was also contained in Lu Buwei's commissioned work, *Lu's Spring and Autumn Annals,*[7] which came after Lao Zi[8] and Zhuang Zi (369–286 B.C.E.), two of Daoism's greatest thinkers. This was a remarkable work because it preserved the doctrines of many schools and writings and stories that were thought to have been lost during the pre–Qin Dynasty (221–207 B.C.E.) era.[9] In the chapter "The Importance of Self," people "despising things and valuing life" was illustrated in the following memorable lines:

> Our life is our own possession and its benefit to us is very great. Regarding its dignity, even the honor of being Emperor could not compare with it. Regarding its importance, even the wealth of possessing the world would not be exchanged for it. Regarding its safety, were we to lose it for one morning, we could never again bring it back.[10]

Lao Zi, the reputed founder of Daoism, also stated this emphasis on life over acquisitions. He proclaimed that "he who in his conduct values his body more than he does the world, may be given the world. He who in his conduct loves himself more than he does the world, may be entrusted with the world."[11] This concept of "despising things and valuing life" was also the focus of Anna May Wong's philosophy.

SWELLING TORRENTS

One of the clearest and best examples of Wong's attitude of "despising things" and repelling negative constraints and "destructive world thought" was during her exchange with a furniture salesman:

A young man came out to see me about some item in the furnishing of my house and I rode into town with him to examine the further pieces he had described to me. He was a Jew. As we rode, we discussed the appalling state of the world and the persecution both our races are undergoing across the different oceans.

Then he said: "I think it is wrong for us to let our minds dwell on the injustice and evils that are being done to our people. That is not a constructive thing to do. The way to change this condition is not to say: 'I hate the Japanese!' Or 'I hate Hitler!' See what they are doing to a defenseless and helpless people. See how cruel and bestial they are to young children and old women!'

"No, the way to change these conditions is to change our own thoughts. We must think only good so that good will spread around us and others will begin to think good thoughts, too, so that at length the good will go out and wrap itself around the figures we now believe to be evil and turn them to goodness. Then and only then, peace will come."[12]

After reflecting on these comments, she said that "the fault is in all of us, of course. I haven't managed it yet, but I hope to get rid of useless thoughts of hate too."[13]

Although Wong concentrated on the Daoist concept of "despising things," and in this case, eliminating "useless thought" or "things," the fact that she concurred with the attitude of extricating oneself from the danger and violence of the global "warring states" was in accordance with the early Daoists. Like these individuals, who were also living in a "warring state" period, Wong was simply attempting to answer the question posed in the *Confucian Analects,* "Disorder, like a swelling flood, spreads over the whole empire, and who is he that will change it *for you?*"[14] In this case, the magnitude of the problem of international conflict had no individual solution except to change one's mental attitude, withdraw from the world, and remain relatively inactive. This was the famous Daoist concept of *wuwei:* "conquering the world is invariably due to doing nothing; by doing something one cannot conquer the world."[15] The precise meaning of this passage and "doing nothing" emphasized engaging in lesser activity or doing less or not overdoing it. It did not mean being lazy or remaining immobile. Therefore, Wong did not simply remove herself from the "swelling flood" of global warfare engulfing the world in 1939, but rather had a thoughtful answer to the specific terror in China based on Daoist principles.

POLITICAL THOUGHTS AND ACTIONS

After 1936 China became an integral part of Wong's life. It clearly defined her notions about her place in the world. Her opinions about Japan's invasion of

China were succinctly articulated in her 1932 article, "Manchuria," in which she condemned the Japanese act of military and political aggression. When *Los Angeles Times* columnist Harry Carr ventured to China from the United States in 1933 via a Japanese ocean liner, *Chichibu Maru,* he was reprimanded by Wong, who gave him "a pair of chopsticks as a sarcastic editorial footnote." Carr explained that "the significance of the silver tips is that they turn black if the food is poisoned."[16]

When Alice Tildesley interviewed Wong about her philosophical views in 1938, Chinese America's most famous actress was already preparing for an extensive vaudeville tour of Australia, with much of her earnings to be donated to the China War Relief Fund. Before leaving for Australia she auctioned off many of her movie costumes for the relief fund.[17] A New England newspaper even reported that she paid only $60 per month for a small Santa Monica apartment while finding ways to raise money like selling her artifacts, jewels, and Chinese dresses.[18] She went fund-raising in Arizona, Massachusetts, Michigan, Oregon, and Wisconsin, drawing on the scattered and regional Chinese American community for assistance. Public events like the Los Angeles Moon Festival, parades, pageants, and radio appearances were also part of her China War Relief efforts.

After she returned from Australia in 1940, Wong chaired the Motion Picture Actors' Division of the Bowl of Rice yearly fund campaign for medical supplies and assistance to China. She endorsed the statement made by the national chair, Colonel Theodore Roosevelt Jr., who said that "China's need for medical aid is so great that it is hard for the imagination to grasp it. For three long years she had endured the same sort of war from the air that England is experiencing now; her cities have been laid waste and her people driven from one place to another in a pitiful search for safety where no safety can exist. These mass migrations and the hardships which the migrants have had to endure have resulted in untold suffering and sickness and widespread epidemics of dread diseases."[19]

In 1941 Wong was assisted by performers from a Broadway musical as she sold Hollywood costumes and artifacts at the Actors Thrift Shop on West Forty-Eighth Street in New York.[20] In December 1942 she began her work as an air raid warden in Santa Monica, proclaiming that "as an American-born Chinese, I feel it is a privilege to be able to do my little bit in return for the many advantages bestowed upon me by a free democracy."[21]

Wong's political agenda concerning the war in China was never more evident than in her performances in *Bombs Over Burma* (1942) and *The Lady from Chungking* (1942). Financed and produced by Producers Releasing Corporation (PRC), the films were programmers or second features of the double bill in theaters across the United States. Shot and edited in two weeks, which was rather languid for this Poverty Row studio, because it often completed a picture in five days,[22] *Bombs Over Burma* highlighted Wong as Lin Ying, "a school teacher pressed into service for the Chinese government (who) rises above the importance of her part and the thin plot."[23] In *The Lady from Chungking,* Wong was Madam Kwan Mei, a Chinese guerrilla leader intent on blowing up a Japanese deployment of troops outside Chongqing (Chungking) and eliminating the nasty Japanese general in charge of the battalion.

Neither *Bombs Over Burma* nor *The Lady from Chungking* were film vehicles that enhanced Wong's career. But professional considerations were clearly not uppermost in her mind. Far from it; in fact, both films were public expressions of her political conviction, beginning in 1932, that the Japanese simply had to leave China, and if they did not, they would pay a price even though that cost was only on celluloid. Wong wanted to bring the Japanese atrocities into the theaters across the United States so that even middle America could understand the extent of the Asian war zone. These two films were made primarily to gain the sympathy of all Americans who might donate money to the China War Relief Fund.

Bombs Over Burma and *The Lady from Chungking* provided Wong with the opportunity to express her political sentiments in the most forceful manner possible and to go from simply mouthing the scripts of European American writers and directors with their built-in prejudices and stereotypes about Asia and Asians throughout her career to delivering patriotic lines and gestures. As a movie star, using film for political purposes was an obvious modus vivendi. In an industry that constantly glorified the bottom line, Wong's ultimate monetary sacrifice was giving up her paycheck of $4,000 for both films to the China War Relief Fund.[24] This amount might not have seemed significant, but the fact that she did further emphasized the Daoist admonition to "despise things and value life." These films placed her priorities firmly within the reality of her Hollywood persona and her place in the larger world. By 1942 eliminating useless things and valuing life, especially Chinese lives in Asia, were uppermost in her political convictions.

Useless Things

In the Tildesley interview, Wong had already succinctly illustrated her post-China view of life. On acquisitions and the retention of "things," she proclaimed:

> Lately as I looked over my possessions, I've thought: "Why do we cling to useless things?" Wouldn't it be a good idea if all of us cleaned house twice a year and got rid of everything not being used? In our short lifetime we can only wear so much, eat so much and make use of so much. Why keep on hand what we don't use, when others lack essentials?

I have heard women say that every house should have an attic, and that attics should be storerooms as they were in the past, where a householder could go to find anything he needed. Perhaps that was once true, when people lived in isolated places where shops were few and distant. But today it is more economical to buy what we need as we go along than to use storerooms for additions.

Even if we might need some object three or four years hence, who knows that we will live so long? In the meantime, why shouldn't some person benefit from it now?[25]

Useless People

While useless things merely clutter a physical space, people who no longer matter not only hinder a person's mental health but also depreciate precious time in a life span that is too short. On useless people, Wong was even more adamant:

I know, but isn't it true? We outgrow people, or they outgrow us; we are useless to one another. Others may not find them useless, but we do—they mean nothing to us, they waste our time. As we grow up, we all accumulate acquaintances who have attracted us at certain periods of our immaturity, or who have become known to us because we went to school together or worked in an office or a studio or because we were introduced by friends. Today we have no real use for each other and we only clutter up each other's lives.

Each of us has very few real friends. Perhaps we can count them on the fingers of one hand and the acquaintances who interest us and from whom we receive stimulation are not too many. But all of us know a great many extraneous people who take up far too much of our time. These people should be shed. Firmly shed. I am lucky in having one defense against time wasters now. I'm on a 10-cent telephone service and those who have nothing to do seldom care to waste the money calling me. The ones who really matter don't mind spending the dime.[26]

On the issue of useless people, Wong's experience in Hollywood with a vast number of vacuous characters she encountered daily seemed to manifest itself in her comments about human relationships.

Evil and Sweetly Smiling People

Anna May Wong further delineated specific types of people to avoid. The most terrifying were the evil ones who set out to impart great harm and suffering. Wong was of course adamantly against these people:

We are likely to avoid people whom we think of as evil influences. Not many of us are attracted to wickedness, so it isn't necessary to be on the lookout for definitely evil acquaintances so much as for dull ones, for those who contribute little, who merely take our time and strength. It's not unkind to shed such people, because they are easily content with someone else, but if we let them consume our time, we lose and they gain nothing.[27]

Evil and dull people may be readily discerned. But the worst are those who are neither evil nor dull. There are the harmless fools who contribute little to a person's meaningful existence. Wong explained that "there are innocuous people who should be dispensed with also. They are passively sweet, smiling persons who add nothing to our happiness or entertainment. We may amuse them briefly, but why should we give so much of ourselves to someone who doesn't matter when they are those who need us."[28]

Avoiding people with "sweet smiles" and those who were purposeful in their negative intent was foremost in Wong's attitude toward humankind. After twenty years of dealing with characters from Hollywood and European studios, she understood why and how certain performers were cast in specific roles. She knew that her inability to land the O-lan role in *The Good Earth* (1937) was not because of her acting abilities but a result of a European American tradition of "Yellowface" and the narrow and prejudicial views of studio bosses. These racist attitudes not only hindered expression of her talent but also prevented her from starring in roles with substance. This could have warped and damaged her psyche, but Wong never allowed those external, negative constraints to savage her life and retained an attitude of purging useless thoughts.

Useless Thoughts: Regrets

For Anna May Wong, eliminating useless people also meant eliminating useless thoughts, especially those thoughts of regret that did nothing to enhance a person's life. In this instance, she might have been referring to being overlooked for the part of O-lan in *The Good Earth*. After returning from her reflective stay and spiritual travel in China in November 1936, not landing that role became trivial and irrelevant. Since the notion of regret meant desiring an object (role of O-lan) and not obtaining it, Wong simply abandoned this idea of old desires. It was as if she had read and internalized Lao Zi's admonition on desire and happiness. He stated:

> The five colors blind the eyes. The five notes dull the ear. The five tastes fatigue the mouth. Riding and hunting madden the mind. Rare treasures hinder right conduct.

There is no disaster greater than not knowing contentment with what one has; no greater sin than having desire for acquisition.[29]

In Wong's case, regret as desire ought to be purged from a person's psyche because it served no useful purposes. She remarked:

We clutter our minds with thoughts that crowd out those that would advance us, either in some material way—which doesn't matter so much—or in some spiritual fashion.

We fill our minds with thoughts of regret, for example. We think: 'Why did I do this? Why didn't I do that? Now, I have made a dreadful mistake and it is too late to undo it. Oh, why can't I go back and do it differently? I should be so much wiser then.'

We can't go back and live things over or correct mistakes already made, so let's forget the regrets.[30]

Past Lives

On the history of a person's life and the accomplishments gathered in the past, Wong explained:

Again we let our thoughts wander over the past, living in past glories, smiling over the honors we once had, or in past happiness, reliving the sweetness of old days or dwelling on cruelties or injustices that have been visited on us or ours when such thoughts are of no use.

We can recall pleasant things at times, if we don't make a habit of it to the detriment of the good thoughts that might occupy our minds and produce good results now. But none of us wishes to deteriorate into the sort of pathetic person who bores everyone with accounts of how many curtains he used to take thirty years ago; how many distinguished guests he once entertained; how beautiful his home was in the good old days; how many different kinds of food he had upon the table.[31]

The lesson that Wong attempted to impart in her notion of useless thoughts is reminiscent of Zhuang Zi's "sitting in forgetfulness." The Daoist sage declared: "I have abandoned my body and discarded my knowledge, and so have become one with the Infinite. This is what I mean by sitting in forgetfulness."[32] Wong illustrated this further: "The European nobility who [were] turned out of their estates during various revolutionary upheavals seemed to have been of two kinds: those who immediately set to work to build up new lives forgetting the glamorous past, and those who cling to former glory and now live in mournful squalor, not attempting to rise because their eyes are now turned backward."[33]

Useful Thoughts

If many thoughts and people are useless, what then were "useful thoughts" for Anna May Wong? She suggested that thoughts must be cultivated. In fact, "thoughts should stay in the mind until they mature. Then they will blossom and do good. As it is, half-grown, we pop them out into the world and they wither away, uselessly, because they haven't the strength of maturity. A thought is like a flower; if it is forced too early, it soon dies."[34] To avoid thoughts or flowers dying prematurely because they were not equipped to encounter the world, Wong reasoned that proper care, astute sensitivity, and continuing attention were the major contributors to their healthy existence.

Death

As for people, Anna May Wong also explained that care, sensitivity, and attention ought to be given to good friends when they are alive. But she lamented:

> When we pick up a newspaper and discover that someone whom we cared for and whom we haven't seen for some time is dead, it is a dreadful blow. We cry out 'Oh, why didn't I pay more attention to him while he was here?' He would have loved to have gone to the theater when I had those tickets and took that duty guest. Or he would have enjoyed hearing about my trip to China or telling me about his experience on the magazine, but I was too busy seeing people I don't like.
>
> We can't go back. We look at that item in the paper and realize that we've been wasting our lives on those we care nothing about instead of those we love. We can do nothing about it, but we vow not to repeat a mistake to devote ourselves to the ones who matter to us.[35]

In this case, Wong was not at a stage where she could follow the *Dao* of avoiding the useless and embracing the useful. But after this reflection on friendship and death, she could understand Lao Zi's admonition: "Name or person, which is more dear? Person or fortune, which is more important?"[36] For Daoists, the essence of this passage was to accentuate the idea of "despising things and valuing life." To Wong's detriment, she was caught initially in the vortex of the mundane and could not transcend the social pressures of dealing with people whom she disliked at the expense of people whom she liked. But she was able to "practice enlightenment" through the Daoist method of starting with the opposite to achieve anything and to understand the opposite to retain anything. In this situation, she associated with undesirable people whom she disliked to understand the opposite of not associating with desirable people whom she liked. Only when she associated with the undesirables did she know the fruitfulness of associating with the people whom she liked.

CONTEMPLATION

Discovering the positive dynamics of useful thoughts and useful people was part of Wong's philosophical journey, which included a sense of contemplation that embraced the present only. She explained that "contemplation is almost a forgotten thing. Yet, it will do much for us. What we all need is more solitude, less excitement. We should all try to be by ourselves for certain periods. We all talk too much, so we should put a curb on our tongues and put in more time thinking."[37] Thus, with contemplation and reflection, Wong hoped to attain "the peace of the soul."[38] After her sojourn in China and extensive contemplation and reflection about the nature of existence and nonexistence, which culminated in her provocative interview with Alice Tildesley, she could enjoy such a state of being.

CONTRADICTIONS

The Daoist concept of *wuwei* was also related to the elimination of anything that was contrary or opposite. Through this process, contradictions were summarily canceled out. By not engaging in the contradiction of "hating" the Japanese or Germans, thereby negating the opposites of love and hate, Wong transcended the either/or dichotomy so prevalent in Western society. She followed the contention of Zhuang Zi that the "true sage judged not the rights and wrongs of mankind and thus lived quietly in his generation."[39] This then was Wong's continuation of a thought process that began with assessing a world with many centers and no borders or boundaries. The nonlinear approach to life began when she left the United States for Europe in 1928.

Like most Chinese Americans, one of the most profound contradictions that Anna May Wong faced in her lifetime was the either/or proposition of being "either Chinese or American." Some expressed this contradiction by simply ignoring it. Others believed that they are half Chinese and half American. Zhuang Zi would argue that these opposites had to be eliminated before a true philosophy of life could emerge.

Before 1936, when Wong finally went to China, this opposite of "either Chinese or American" was truly perplexing for her. Her European American flapper period during the early 1920s certainly complemented the European period during the late 1920s and early 1930s, but neither addressed the issue of "being Chinese" except to negate its existence. She always seemed to be dangling between cultures and psyches. Even on board the SS *President Hoover* on January 24, 1936, waiting to leave for China, she anxiously concluded that "it is difficult to believe, as I sit in my stateroom, surrounded by books, candy and other going-away presents, that I am actually on my way to the East. Already the farewells of yesterday seem remote; a link with the past has been broken and I feel that I am suspended between two worlds."[40]

Those two worlds resonated when she remarked:

> I am very proud of being American; for years, when people have asked me to describe "my" native country, I've surprised them by saying that it is a democracy composed of forty-eight states.
>
> But I've always been aware of another country, in the background of my mind, just as I have never forgotten that my real name is Wong Liu Tsong, which means "Frosted Yellow Willow."[41]

The two worlds in Wong's mind were contradictions. As she lived and traveled in China, she began to internalize facets about the Chinese people, their actions, and their thoughts. While "becoming Chinese" in Asia, she discovered that she was not negating her European American side. In fact, she was following the "axis of the *Dao* upon which one could rotate freely so as to accommodate various possible circumstances—that is, an attitude of escaping from the reality of life."[42] According to Zhuang Zi, "the true sage, while regarding contraries as identical, adopts himself to the law of Heaven. This is called following two courses at once."[43]

After China, Wong learned to follow "two courses at once." These were the European American "way" and the Chinese American "way." By doing so she created another path that empowered her to follow neither the European American "way" nor the Chinese American "way" because they no longer existed as separate entities. Thus, by embracing China and eliminating opposites, she was able to transcend her race as a Chinese, her ethnicity as a Chinese American, and her nationality as a European American. By living and traveling in China, she was no longer an "American." She was no longer even a "Chinese." By following the *Dao,* or way, accentuated by her life and travels in China, she discovered a profound sense of self-being, of being empowered, and of finding her own individual agency that had no race, ethnicity, or nationality attached to her evolving human persona as Anna May Wong.

Her initial suspension between European America and Chinese America was reminiscent of Zhuang Zi's own contradiction between ego and reality. In a famous Daoist allegory, he confirmed:

> Once upon a time, I, Zhuang Zi, dreamed I was a butterfly, fluttering hither and thither, to all intents and purposes a butterfly. I was conscious of only following my fancies as a butterfly, and was conscious of my individuality as a man. Suddenly, I awoke, and there I lay, myself again. Now I do not know whether then I was a man dreaming I was a butterfly, or whether I am now a butterfly, dreaming I am a man.[44]

For many Chinese Americans, Zhuang Zi's butterfly dream resonated in reality. Were they Chinese Americans dreaming about being European Americans, or were they European Americans dreaming about being Chinese Americans? By eliminating opposites, these existential concepts of race, ethnicity, and nationality became irrelevant.

Anna May Wong's existence paralleled that of the short life span of a butterfly. She only lived to the age of fifty-six. It was almost as if she knew in 1934 that her life would be short. She confessed that "this is such a short life that nothing can matter very much either one way or another. I have learned not to struggle but to flow with the tide. If I am to be rich and famous, that will be fine. If not, what do riches and fame count in the long run?"[45] At the age of twenty-nine, during her second sojourn in Europe, she could reflect on her immature period as a Hollywood flapper:

> Time adjusts all things. We can't hurry the slowly grinding mills of the gods; and we do not wish to. I—that flustered, worried, defensive little Hollywood flapper—found happiness when I ceased to worry about time. No one can give me what belongs to someone else; and no one can take away that which is mine.[46]

No one ever gave Anna May Wong a free ride in her life. Although Hollywood attempted to diminish her talents, abilities, and focused ambitions by casting her in "Orientalist" roles that demeaned and emasculated Asians and their images in the eyes of the world, thus causing her to move to Europe, no one could take away what she possessed. Her extraordinary will to succeed, a passion for acting, and a creative philosophical mind that helped her understand the world were always hers. Wong's struggle to survive in Hollywood reflected that of many Chinese Americans living in European America. But the life she led and her accomplishments for a Chinese American woman of the 1920s and the 1930s under the exacting dimensions of primitive European American racism were incomparable.

She studied and learned about the true meaning of life, putting things in order so that unnecessary desires would not interfere with how she lived. What was remarkable about her life was that she was the first Chinese American woman to leave a substantial body of work that included not only films, stage, and nightclub acts but also written reflections on life and death that transcended her narrow existence in the United States and embraced her many lives in Europe and China.

While she traveled through life as a celebrity, her films were her most important works. Yet in life as in her career, prejudicial attitudes precluded Wong from playing some of Hollywood's choicest roles. One major roadblock was the racist notion of "Yellowface," a theatrical device designed to exclude Asian American performers from playing Asian or Asian American roles. Its insidiousness was defined by its longevity, extent, and impact.

NOTES

1. Barrie Roberts, "Anna May Wong: Daughter of the Orient," *Classic Images* 270 (December 1997): 20.

2. Fung Yu-lan, *A Short History of Chinese Philosophy* (New York: Macmillan, 1964), 31.

3. Fung Yu-lan, *Chuang-Tzu* (Beijing: Foreign Language Press, 1931, 1989, 1991), 8. For a concise analysis of early Daoism, see Frederick W. Mote, *Intellectual Foundation of China* (New York: Alfred A. Knopf, 1989), 59–76.

4. He Zhaowu et al., *An Intellectual History of China* (Beijing: Foreign Language Press, 1991), 43. He and his colleagues argued that Yang Zhu and the Daoists were similar in that they preached "completeness of living and preservation of what is genuine" (47). But there were so many differences separating them that Yang ought not to be placed in the Daoist school.

5. Fung, *Short History of Chinese Philosophy,* 61.

6. Yang Zhu, *Lushi Chunqiu,* cited in He, *Intellectual History of China,* 45–46.

7. Lu Buwei (290–235 B.C.E.) was a prime minister in the Qin state during the Warring States period (403–221 B.C.E.) and before the unification of China under Qin-shi Huangdi. He commissioned three thousand scholars to write *The Spring and Autumns Records of Lu (Lushi Chunqiu).* See Li Yingquan, *Luoyang: Famous Capital of the Nine Dynasty (Luoyang: jiuchao mingdu)* (Wuhan, Republic of China: Chinese Geological University Press, 1997), 180.

8. The dates of Lao Zi, reputed founder of Daoism, are shrouded in mystery. According to Sima Qian's *Records of the Historian,* he was a contemporary of Confucius and served as a functionary in the house of Zhou. See He, *Intellectual History of China,* 86ff. Mote, *Intellectual Foundation of China,* 63–67.

9. He, *Intellectual History of China,* 119–23.

10. *Lushi Chunqiu,* Book 1, no. 3, cited in Fung, *Short History of Chinese Philosophy,* 63.

11. Lao Zi, chapter 13, cited in Fung, *Short History of Chinese Philosophy,* 64.

12. Wong, cited in Alice L. Tildesley, "Why Waste Your Time?" *Seattle Daily Times,* 9 April 1939, 9.

13. Wong, cited in Tildesley, "Why Waste Your Time?" 9.

14. *Confucian Analects,* Book 18, no. 6, cited in Zhong Shule, *The Four Books* (Changsha, Republic of China: Hunan Publishing House, 1994), 241.

15. *Laozi,* chapter 48, cited in Fung, *Short History of Chinese Philosophy,* 100.

16. Harry Carr, "The Lancer," *Los Angeles Times,* 15 December 1933, 1.

17. "Actress to Aid China War Fund," *New York Times,* 22 June 1938, 6.

18. Cited in Karen Janis Leong, "The China Mystique: Mayling Soong, Pearl S. Buck and Anna May Wong in the American Imagination" (Ph.D. dissertation, University of California, Berkeley, spring 1999), 400.

19. "Bowl of Rice Drive Launched by Mayor," *New York Times,* 17 September 1940, 2.

20. "Anna May Wong at Thrift Shop," *New York Times,* 2 December 1941, 3.

21. Wong, cited in Ronald Takaki, *Strangers from a Different Shore* (Boston: Little, Brown, 1989), 373; *San Francisco Chronicle,* 13 December 1942, 10.

22. Wheeler Dixon, *Producers Releasing Corporation* (Jefferson, N.C.: McFarland, 1986), viii. According to Dixon, "many of the westerners were shot in two or three days." The fourteen days allotted for *Bombs Over Burma* may have been the result of the presence of Anna May Wong, a star vehicle.

23. *Variety,* 12 August 1942, 22.

24. Anna May Wong was contracted to appear in four films for Producers Releasing Corporation, the first being *The Devil's Sister.* Apparently only *Bombs Over Burma* and *The Lady from Chungking* were ever made or at least released to the viewing public. "Signs New Contract," *New York Times,* 13 March 1942, 22.

25. Wong, cited in Tildesley, "Why Waste Your Time?" 9.

26. Wong, cited in Tildesley, "Why Waste Your Time?" 9.

27. Wong, cited in Tildesley, "Why Waste Your Time?" 9.

28. Wong, cited in Tildesley, "Why Waste Your Time?" 9.

29. Lao Zi, chapters 5, 46; Fung, *Short History of Chinese Philosophy,* 101.

30. Wong, cited in Tildesley, "Why Waste Your Time?" 9.

31. Wong, cited in Tildesley, "Why Waste Your Time?" 9.

32. Zhuang Zi, *The Book of Zhuang Zi,* cited in He, *Intellectual History of China,* 102.

33. Wong, cited in Tildesley, "Why Waste Your Time?" 9.

34. Wong, cited in Tildesley, "Why Waste Your Time?" 9.

35. Wong, cited in Tildesley, "Why Waste Your Time?" 9.

36. Lao Zi, chapter 44, cited in Fung, *Short History of Chinese Philosophy,* 64.

37. Wong, cited in Tildesley, "Why Waste Your Time," 9.

38. Fung, *Short History of Chinese Philosophy,* 109.

39. Zhuang Zi, cited in He, *Intellectual History of China,* 102.

40. Anna May Wong, "Anna May Wong Tells of Voyage on 1st Trip to China," *New York Herald Tribune,* 17 May 1936, 1.

41. Wong, "Anna May Wong Tells of Voyage," 1.

42. He, *Intellectual History of China,* 102.

43. Zhuang Zi, cited in He, *Intellectual History of China,* 102.

44. Zhuang Zi, cited in He, *Intellectual History of China,* 101.

45. Wong, cited in Harry Carr, "I Am Growing More Chinese—Each Passing Year!" *Los Angeles Times,* 9 September 1934, 3.

46. Wong, cited in Carr, "I Am Growing More Chinese," 3.

PART III

LIFE IS CINEMA

TEN

"YELLOWFACE," MASKS,
AND STEREOTYPES

As a theatrical device, "Yellowface" was the European and European American penchant for insisting that white performers portray Asians in film and on stage. It was almost as if, in their distorted makeup of slanted eyes, high cheekbones, yellow skin, and monkeylike walk, actors painted a grotesque mask covering their own selves. By portraying Asians in "Yellowface," they were telling the audience that they alone had the authority to speak for Asians. This seemed to give them license to depict Asians as they saw fit, often in racial stereotypes. Europeans and European Americans also performed in roles calling for Africans, Arabs, Hispanics, South Asians, and Natives in "Blackface," "Brownface," or "Redface."

During her sojourn in Europe, Anna May Wong never personally encountered the racist notion of "Yellowface" that hampered her career in the United States. Except for F. Viguier, who played Wang Ho in "Yellowface" in *L'amour maitre des choses,* authentic Asians played the roles in her films, such as Ley On as Wang Ho in *Weg zur schande der* and the English version, *The Flame of Love.* In *Pavement Butterfly,* Nien Song (Soen) Ling was the other Asian. Director Richard Eichberg strove for as much authenticity as possible. The search for reality was also apparent in the British International Pictures's production of *Piccadilly* (1929), in which Shosho's friend, Jim, was played by a cafe owner turned actor,

King Ho-chang, in an authentic atmosphere of London's Chinatown. However, in Wong's inaugural London stage play, *The Circle of Chalk,* "Yellowface" was prominent, with Laurence Olivier as Po.

In Wong's first cinematic experience, *The Red Lantern* (1919), Yalta-born Alla Nazimova played two roles, a biracial Mahlee and a European Blanche Sackville, in Hollywood's most expensive blockbuster of that year at a cost of $250,000.[1] Except for eight hundred Asian extras, which included a fourteen-year-old Anna May Wong, only one Asian actor, Yukio Aoyamo, was cast to portray an Asian role, Sing. The rest of the Asian roles went to the likes of Virginia Ross as Lung Ma, Noah Beery (1882–1946) as Dr. Sam Wang, Edward Connelly (1859–1928) as General Jung-Lu, and Henry Mann as Chung.[2]

In her succeeding films in the United States before living in Europe in 1928, Wong would encounter widespread "Yellowface," with Helen Jerome Eddy (1899–1990) playing Loey Tsing in *The First Born* (1921), George Siegmann (1882–1928) as Foo Chang in *Shame* (1921), Lon Chaney (1883–1930) as Chin Chow in *Bits of Life* (1921), Frank Lanning portraying Chang Wang in *Drifting* (1923), and Lon Chaney as Mr. Wu and Renee Adoree (1898–1933) as Wu Nang Ping in *Mr. Wu* (1927). Wong would also work in films with the diminutive Angelo Rossitto (1908–1991) as Chang Loo in *Old San Francisco* (1927), Jason Robards Sr. (1892–1963) playing Eugene Fong in *Streets of Shanghai* (1927), and Myrna Loy (1905–1993) as Isobel and State Street Sadie in *The Crimson City* (1928).

European Americans and European performers portraying Asian characters were endemic in Hollywood and in European studios. After her tour de force performance in *Shanghai Express* (1932), Anna May Wong felt that her stardom could uplift her beyond the racist concept of "Yellowface." The role that she coveted was O-lan in the film version of *The Good Earth,* a best-seller written by Pearl S. Buck (1892–1973) in 1931. But this role went to a German-born, Oscar-winning actress named Luise Rainer (1910–),[3] who was selected to star opposite Austrian–Hungarian-born performer Paul Muni (Meshilem Meier Weisenfreund, 1895–1967), who played Wang Lung, the confused Chinese peasant husband. Rainer and Muni were the biggest box office stars to perform in "Yellowface" during the 1930s.

"Yellowface" was so ingrained in Hollywood's psyche that Wong had little chance to capture one of the most sought after roles in Tinseltown. After seventeen years of acting in films and stage plays, Wong no doubt figured that she had arrived at a time when she could command lead roles that reflected positively on her as an internationally known actress and on the Chinese people. Metro-Goldwyn-Mayer's reluctance to cast Wong as either O-lan or the concubine Lotus was "one of the most notorious cases of casting discrimination in the 1930s."[4]

If Pearl Buck had had her way, someone like Anna May Wong would have been cast in the title role. In an authorized biography, she "hoped they would use Chinese actors in the leading parts."[5] As for the stage adaptation of *The Good Earth,* written by Owen Davis and his son, Donald, Buck was "discouraged because the American actors were so un-Chinese, even in the abrupt, ungraceful fashion in which they walked. I was used to the graceful movements of the Chinese."[6] Even Pearl Buck was therefore displeased when she discovered that Europeans like Luise Rainer and Paul Muni had been hired to play the lead roles. In fact, she saw the film version two days after it opened because she did not want to be pestered by the media for a reaction. She saw it again on television but "found it so painful, so that I have never looked at it again."[7]

"YELLOWFACE" AND HOLLYWOOD

By asking MGM to cast Asian performers to play Asian parts, Buck was not aware that she was asking the European American producers to abandon century-old, pervasive ideas and impressions about China and the Chinese. This was not simply the notion that Hollywood had a star system, which excluded any Asian performers as major box office attractions. It was far more than just the European American preference for determining who starred in what film. In fact, in her desire to play O-lan, Anna May Wong was also challenging Hollywood to overthrow its notion of how European Americans depicted China and the Chinese. This was the European American cultural tradition called "Yellowface," which had a racist life of its own and thus influenced the thinking, for more than 170 years, of casting agents, directors, producers, and studio heads in their selection of performers to play Chinese and Asian parts in plays and films.

"Yellowface" branded and characterized the Chinese as the Other: the foreign and the alien. What Wong was attacking was the way in which European Americans, since the eighteenth century, had arrived at their perspective and thoughts of China and the Chinese. Both Pearl Buck and Wong ran smack into Hollywood's version of "Yellowface."

Like most North Americans curious about China during the 1930s, Anna May Wong, as a third-generation American, became familiar with the country and its inhabitants by reading fictional accounts by such sinophile writers as Pearl S. Buck.[8] In the novels, the Chinese were depicted as simple, idol-fearing animists full of superstitions with a reliance on the wisdom of ancient sages and a defeated but stoic view of life. With these European American cultural attitudes toward China and characteristics of the Chinese ingrained in the populace of the United States, Wong mused that the country was "a place where the people always sipped tea and philosophized about life."[9] Anna May Wong's view of China and its people was a decidedly European American notion tinged with the flavor of a California Chinatown. It smacked more of Los Angeles or New York than Beijing or Guangzhou.

That Pearl Buck would have a profound influence on how Wong and countless other Americans perceived China was a given in the United States, because only American writers of European descent had any credibility in the perception of things foreign, especially of a place as alien, bizarre, and "inscrutable" as China and its people. What Buck and her ilk produced were memory pieces[10] that would endure in the classrooms of middle America, the New York boardrooms of corporate finance, and the countless universities that embraced "Oriental" rather than Asian studies. China and the Chinese, in particular, became the Other. This Asian country and its Asian people became the foreign adversaries of the United States and its citizens because they were of national security concern to European American academics and policy makers in Washington, D.C., and across the country.[11]

THE *ORPHAN OF CHINA*

Before Pearl Buck's fictional ruminations on China and its people during the twentieth century and especially the cinematic production of her novel, *The Good Earth,* in 1937, the European American public had had its first theatrical taste of China in the *Orphan of China (L'Orphelin de la Maison de Tschao),* first performed with European actors at the Southwark Theatre in colonial Philadelphia on January 16, 1767. This was even before the first sighting of an actual Chinese person in the United States.[12] In 1768 it played in New York at the John Street Theatre. Even after the founding of the republic in 1776, the play continued to be staged at the John Street Theatre, by performers from the British army, in 1779 and 1787.[13] The fact that it remained popular with European actors playing Chinese parts demonstrated that its central theme remained important for citizens of the republic and the British monarchy.[14]

The *Orphan of China* was the first public exhibition of "Yellowface" in the history of the United States. It began an American tradition of localizing the idea of China and its people within a European perspective. This created hegemony whereby Americans of European heritage decided how China and the Chinese people ought to be characterized, described, discussed, illustrated, and presented without any input from the Chinese themselves. As a public attraction, the portrayal of the Chinese in the *Orphan of China* was the beginning of a European American system that depicted the Chinese as odd and outlandish and later cruel, cunning, debauched, drug-addicted, effeminate, filthy, heathen, un-Christian, enslaved, and wise, but emasculated in a fortune cookie, robotlike manner. These characteristics eventually became "common sense" through films, folk wisdom, religions, schooling, television, theater, and any public vehicle that portrayed the Chinese.[15] They formed the distinctive Chinese part of the national identity of European America. Yet the original aim of the *Orphan of China* was to depict the Chinese within the intrigues of dynastic politics, not to establish "Yellowface."

Written by Ji Junxiang as *Zhaoshiguer (Sole Heir of the Zhao Clan)* in 1330,[16] the *Orphan of China* arrived in Europe in 1735[17] via a circuitous route much like the journey of *The Circle of Chalk (Le Cercle de Craie).* Like *The Circle of Chalk,* the *Orphan of China* was one of a hundred plays grouped in an original Yuan dramatic repertory called *A Hundred Pieces,* and it was also one of four plays from the collection that was translated into French and thus made its way into the theaters of Europe.

Like *The Circle of Chalk,* the *Orphan of China* was translated from the Chinese into French. A Jesuit priest, Joseph Premare (1666–1736), rendered *Zhaoshiguer* into *L'Orphelin de la Maison de Tschao (The Orphan of the House of Zhao).*[18] Later Voltaire Francois Marie Arouet (1694–1778) adapted it as *Orphelin de Chine,* a "dramatization of the morals of Confucius" to demonstrate the ascension of morality over politics to rebuke the assertion of Jean Jacques Rousseau (1712–1778) that moral corruption was always victorious over art and science.[19] Voltaire's version played in Paris on August 20, 1755.[20] The English-language adaptation by Arthur Murphy (1727–1805) appeared as the *Orphan of China* on April 21, 1759, at the Theatre Royal on Drury Lane in London.[21]

A minor operetta, the *Orphan of China* was the first Chinese drama ever translated into a European language. Consequently, European playwrights who envisioned a Chinese ambience for their writings sought direction initially from Premare's French translation, which later inspired not only Murphy's English version but also adaptations in German and Italian.[22] There was also another English translation by Thomas Percy in his *Miscellaneous Pieces Relating to the Chinese,* published in 1762.[23]

The *Orphan of China* centered around the treachery of a military leader during the middle of the seventh century B.C.E. After seizing territories of the Zhao family, this officer sends his soldiers to annihilate all of the family members, especially the lone male heir. But a retainer, loyal to the Zhao household, shields the male heir and brings him up as his own son. Eventually the boy grows up and exacts revenge on the military leader for his duplicity.

The *Orphan of China* played in Britain and the United States during much of the eighteenth century. Its greatest critic was Oliver Goldsmith (1730–1774), famous for *The Vicar of Wakefield* (1766). In the *Critical Review* he stated:

> Of all the nations that ever felt the influence of the inspiring goddess, perhaps the Chinese are to be placed in the lowest class: their productions are most phlegmatic that can be imagined. In those pieces of poetry, or novel translations, . . . there is not a single attempt to address the imagination, or influence the passions.[24]

Although Goldsmith called Chinese plays uninspiring and essentially unrewarding while referring to the *Orphan of China,* the play itself evoked treachery, disloyalty, dishonor, and revenge as well as faithfulness and honesty, with the characters played by such leading British actors as David Garrick (1717–1779). The American adaptation in Philadelphia and New York was constructed exotically, with the European players in Middle Eastern dress surrounded by an "oriental" motif. Thus, "Yellowface" phenomenon was first delivered to European American audiences via a minor Yuan tragedy that had gone through several translations and adaptations.

"Yellowface" was given credibility by none other than one of Europe's most influential literary geniuses, Voltaire. With such a pedigree, the distorted and essentially negative portrayal of China and the Chinese gained recognition, especially among European American intellectuals, literary figures, merchants, military officers, and politicians, who were the only ones who could afford to attend the theater. Even before European Americans actually met their first flesh and blood Chinese or visited China, they already had an idea of the Chinese and China because "Chineseness first appeared in America within the displacing structure of the variety stage."[25]

The *Orphan of China* was the first overt theatrical performance that helped determine how European Americans envisioned and imagined China and the Chinese from a perspective of racial superiority. It was in fact the beginning of racial branding or formation, a process of "historically situated *projects* in which human bodies and social structures (were) represented and organized."[26] As a racial project, the *Orphan of China* began an odyssey of institutional racism in the media portrayal of China and the Chinese as inferior, subordinate, and Other that endures today.[27] They were not part of the civilized Western world known as Europe and the United States and never could be. "Yellowface" was the visual and linguistic expression of the racial branding of the Chinese in European American theater and later in cinema and television. These mass media would have a profound impact on the national cultural life of the United States during the twentieth century. In fact, "Yellowface" would be an integral part of the widespread media permeation that would determine how European Americans viewed China and the Chinese in the twenty-first century.

KIM-KA!

The popularity of the *Orphan of China* in Britain and the United States helped perpetuate the idea that images of China and the Chinese could be interpreted by Europeans without any input from the Chinese themselves. One of the earliest surviving theatrical productions conceived in the United States was *Kim-Ka!*, written in 1852 by the Ravel family, a French itinerant troupe that eventually settled in New York during the 1840s. *Kim-Ka!* was the second major racial project that would expand the racial branding of China and the Chinese in the United States. It played to packed houses in New York City between 1852 and 1870. [28]

Kim-Ka! is the story of a love relation between Lei, a Chinese emperor's daughter, and Ventillateur, a French aeronaut. During a grand festival in honor of the emperor set in the imperial gardens, Ventillateur's helium balloon is blown off course from Paris toward Beijing. "The storm drives him across the spot where Keying and Pwan-Tin-Qua are making their observations. Ventillateur in his flight knocks them down and upsets them and their instruments. At last, the bold Aeronaut succeeds in landing in safety, but afraid of the damage he has caused, he seeks for a hiding place." [29]

Eventually Ventillateur enters the women's quarters of the imperial palace and they "are astonished by the manly beauty of the adventurer. They turn him round and admire his fine proportions, but they are soon interrupted by the footsteps of his pursuers. The ladies immediately push the adventurer behind them and form a screen to hide him from his enemies." [30] In the annals of "Yellowface," this scene began the European American male writers' fantasy of Asian women lusting after European American men.

In his escape, Ventillateur falls backward into a pavilion where Lei is "absorbed in reflection. Hearing a noise, she turns her eyes and perceives the bold aeronaut. For the first time, she sees before her the man whose image has haunted her maidenly dreams." [31] It is love at first sight for both.

But the emperor's soldiers are still in pursuit and finally corner the Frenchman in a garden, where he begs for his life. Lei and her attendants plead with Kim-Ka to spare this foreigner's life. "The Emperor refuses, but his daughter tells him that she loves the stranger, and that she will put an end to her existence if the Emperor does not give his consent to her union with him. Kim-Ka will consent on the condition that Ventillateur becomes a Chinese subject and has his head shaved."[32]

The Frenchman tells the emperor that he does not mind renouncing his French citizenship for a Chinese one. But he does mind losing his hair. The emperor then orders Ventillateur to be confined in a tub of punishment. Only his head and hands can be seen in this Ravel version of Chinese water tub torture. For the Frenchman, it is only a joke, and he announces that "it is more pleasant to marry a princess even if she be a Chinese one than to take a cold bath shut up in a tub."[33] They marry.

While this Ravelian tale is a preposterous one, especially the absurd love between a Chinese princess and a French airman, it demonstrated the Chinese daughter's total lack of intelligence in announcing her love for a "stranger" and her ignorance of Chinese marriage customs and traditions. It showed the father's simplemindedness in accepting a foreigner for a son-in-law simply because he consented to having his head shaved. In the development of racial representations, both the Chinese daughter and father were depicted as Chinese ninnies. Yet what was even more compelling was the total ineptitude of the Ravel family in its understanding of actual Chinese customs and history.

Representing the real China and the Chinese, however, was never on the minds of these French performers. The tale engrossed European American audiences in New York, and for almost twenty years this theatrical performance portrayed the Chinese as childlike, gullible, mesmerized by things foreign, and fundamentally stupid. It illustrated the backwardness, ties to ancient traditions, and overt inferiority of the Chinese while European Americans and Europeans were depicted as highly intelligent, forward looking, adventurous, innovative, and superior. The Chinese were not like Europeans and never could be. Thus, they were the Other because they were beyond the pale of civilization. This racial representation of the Chinese as intellectually and culturally inferior established Europeans and by extension Americans of European heritage as evolving to a higher racial order based on the Darwinian theory of the day. In fact, "the early use of the 'Orient' is in keeping with what could be called an Anglo-American desire to define (European) Americanness by noting difference, especially racial. This theatricalization of difference emerged out of necessity, out of the need to justify the extermination of native Americans and the institution of slavery."[34]

Demeaning the Chinese as the Other, as different from European Americans, was just part of European America's need to categorize the people who counted and those who did not. The attribute of "whiteness" was at the very core of this process. European Americans, because of their "whiteness," counted in the definition of Americanness, while Americans of African, Asian, and Native heritage did not because they were not white.

The "Yellowface" phenomenon branded and exemplified the Chinese as the Other, as foreign, as alien. It demonstrated that Americans of European heritage were the only ones qualified to classify China and the Chinese. "Yellowface" was an example of European American hegemony in that Americans of European heritage selected themselves to determine the essence of being Chinese in the United States. They chose the visual and linguistic branding iron that ultimately conditioned a century-long negative perspective of China and the Chinese in the eyes of non-Chinese, especially those of European American ancestry. The principal Chinese characters in *Kim-Ka!* were played by members of the Ravel family. They were Francois as Kim-Ka, Antoine as the Mandarin Pwan-Tin-Qua, and Jerome as the prime minister, Keying. Flora Lehman portrayed the princess, Lei. Here, French Americans decided how the Chinese in *Kim-Ka!* behaved, spoke, and thought.

While *Kim-Ka!,* in its fantastic characterization of China and the Chinese, enjoyed a sustained popularity in the theaters of New York between 1852 and the 1870s, the real flesh and blood Chinese people who began arriving in California were met with violent opposition and racist laws that sought to exclude their participation in American life. One year after *Kim-Ka!* opened in New York City, California enacted the Foreign Miner's License Tax Act. No doubt this law was aimed at the many Chinese who arrived in California seeking their fortune in gold mines. In 1854 the supreme court of California passed a law that prohibited any Chinese from testifying against people of the white race.[35]

Once Chinese immigrants began to work in other occupations, special taxes were established especially for them. Chinese engaged in fishing had to pay a monthly tax of $4.00 beginning in 1860. In 1862 a monthly Chinese police tax of $2.50 was imposed on all Chinese of both genders who worked in occupations other than those that specialized in coffee, rice, sugar, and tea. In 1870 a law stipulated that Chinese or Mongolian immigrants had to prove they were people of "correct habits and good character" before being allowed to enter California. In the same year the state supreme court provided segregated schools for Chinese and non-Chinese children. There was also a law in San Francisco that required any rooming house to "provide at least 500 cubic feet of clear atmosphere" for all adult persons in their rooms. But the law was only used against Chinese housing. In 1876, moreover, there was a "queue ordinance" that required every male prisoner to have his "hair cut to within one inch of his scalp."[36]

NEW BROOMS SWEEP CLEAN

These racist laws were just some of the many passed against the Chinese in California during the time of the *Kim-Ka!* performances in New York. While one section of the United States engaged in legally denying the Chinese any rights and privileges, another part perpetuated a distorted image of China and the Chinese in character, morals, intelligence, and dress. In 1871 the linguistic branding of how the Chinese spoke English through theatrical performances began with *New Brooms Sweep Clean*. It was a distortion that would eventually permeate many of Anna May Wong's films, the Fu Manchu and Charlie Chan movies, the television series *Bonanza* (1959–1973), and such contemporary films as *Chinatown* (1974), the *Year of the Dragon* (1985), and *Big Trouble in Little China* (1986). As a significant element in the racial branding of the Chinese in the eyes of European Americans, this always demeaning and equally offensive language of "Yellowface" ensnared and crippled every Asian American performer who ever acted on stage or in the movies.

As a play, George M. Baker's *New Brooms Sweep Clean* was not specifically earmarked for the professional stage. Written as an amateur production, it was more of a reflection of the current attitudes of European Americans toward the Chinese than a creation of them. In the play there is a European American, Pat Regan, disguised in "Yellowface" as a Chinese named Jing Jimalong. In contrast to the non-Chinese roles, Jing Jimalong is clearly demeaned and subordinate to the European Americans. Jing Jimalong continued the European American idea that the Chinese dined on dog meat:

> Jing Jimalong: *Faith, I'd jist like to know what a Chinese dish is, onyhow, afore I'd cook it. Bedad! I must scrub up my jeography, shure. Faith, thim fellars cook rats and mice and puppies! That's it. Where will I find a puppy?*
> *. . . Vhat shall I say. Me try cookee bow-wow; bow-wow no likee cookee him. Bow-wow muchee Ki I! Me muchee Ki-I too—bow-wow muchee run into closet: muchee crockery—bang,—bang,—bang, muchee pieces all breakee. Muchee ,—muchee,— muchee, —and be jabers!*[37]

Baker's coining of a nonsense name, Jing Jimalong, to refer to all Chinese was an obvious reference to the many tones in Cantonese. It was also one of the first examples of the growing tendency of American writers of European descent to ridicule the Chinese. In fact, Jing Jimalong was an integral part of the European American tradition of mockery and disdain that befell Americans of color. In this tradition, Charles A. Loder's *Hilarity Songster* and the well-known "Yellowface" singer, Luke Schoolcraft, infanticized the Chinese with nonsense words and pidgin English that concretely branded the Chinese as the Other.[38] Loder's rendition crackled with delight:

> Ki, Ki, Ki, Ching, Ching, Ching,
> Hung a rung, a chickel neckey
> Suppe, fatte hung
> Eno Posa keno Posey, keno John,
> Chinese manee goode manee from Hong Kong.[39]

Schoolcraft used the same introduction of Ching, Ching, Ching that was familiar to Baker's Jing Jimalong. He cackled:

> Hi! Hi! Hi! Ching! Ching! Ching!
> Chow, chow, wellie good, me likie him.
> Makie plentie sing song, savie byh and bye.
> China man a willie man, laugh hi! hi![40]

The European American mockery of how the Chinese spoke English undermined the actual commercial language that was spoken by Chinese merchants and traders in nineteenth-century California. Originally established as a legitimate linguistic vehicle that helped grease the commercial transactions between Chinese and European entrepreneurs in the late seventeenth century, Canton English had its own codes, grammatical rules, and vocabulary. But the fact that it existed threatened European America's cultural superiority. Therefore, American writers of European heritage attempted to reinforce the hegemonic power of standard English by mocking the spoken English of others. By doing so, they were able to set the linguistic standard for participation in citizenship. They argued that if people of color, especially the Chinese, could not speak standard and "proper" English, how could they ever fit into the social fabric of the United States? Ridiculing the Chinese with their pidgin English laced with nonsense words illustrated that these "heathens" could never be part of America. This linguistic branding was at the center of the racism practiced against the Chinese by European Americans. It was an integral part of the "Yellowface" tradition.

AH SIN

The linguistic branding of the Chinese even found its way into the writings of such well-known authors as Bret Harte (1836–1902) and Mark Twain (Samuel L. Clemens, 1835–1910). In 1876 they wrote *Ah Sin* (Ah Sin = "I Sin").[41] On

July 27, 1877, the play opened in New York at Daly's Fifth Avenue Theatre. Before that it played a preview performance in Washington, D.C.[42] Since such celebrity writers as Harte and Twain overtly engaged in the "Yellowface" phenomenon, *Ah Sin* played a major part in its evolution.

The play was originally the focus of a narrative poem, "Plain Language from Truthful James" or "The Heathen Chinee" (1870).[43] Centered in the "Yellowface" tradition, Ah Sin was portrayed by the European American actor C. T. Parsoe, as the "Heathen Chinee." As a character in the play, Ah Sin merely moved the story along. As a plot-advancing or a window dressing device, Ah Sin relegated the concept of the Chinese to a subordinate role.

Like the movie roles of the Chinese and Asians played by Anna May Wong during the 1920s and 1930s, the "Yellowface" portrayal of Ah Sin represented the Chinese as diseased, moral degenerates who were politically detrimental to the European American population. One of the major characters, Broderick, introduces Ah Sin with "Here, you slant-eyed son of the yellow jaunders (referring to jaundice), what have you been up to. You here yet—you moral cancer, you unsolvable political problem—what's up now?"[44]

Ah Sin is portrayed as a harmless, less than human, and childlike ninny. While he is setting a table, the character Mrs. Tempest remarks:

> Mrs. Tempest: *Poor afflicted creature, when he shakes his head it makes me nervous to hear the dried faculties rattle. Wait please, let me show you. Well, upon my word, this mental vacuum is a Chinaman to the marrow in one thing, the monkey faculty of imitating. Now spread your tablecloth.*
>
> *Do it this way, next time—Set your plates now. Oh you innocent, is that all! You provoking—But I won't scold you. Here poor neglected thing. This the way to set. Oh, is there nothing to you but imitation?*
>
> *Poor dumb animal, with his tail on top of his head instead of where it ought to be.*[45]

Mrs. Tempest proclaims that "Poor Ah Sin is harmless—only a little ignorant and awkward."[46]

To further enhance his inferiority and that of the Chinese people, Ah Sin continues the "Yellowface" linguistic branding of the Chinese in his response to the European Americans in the play and to the mass theater audience of European America. He remarks on the morality of marriage and his own uncivilized and pagan ways:

> Ah Sin: *Mellican man no likee Chinaman hab two wifee—Chinaman no likee wifee, sell wifee—poor wifee got no home—Mellican man no likee wifee, lun away, let poor wifee starve—Mellican man too mucheee—civilized.*[47]

THE CHINESE MUST GO

Unlike the Harte and Twain production, *Ah Sin,* which set the Chinese as a textual bystander in the imagination of European Americans, Henry Grimm's play, *The Chinese Must Go* (1879), introduced the Chinese as the frontispiece of the anti-Chinese harangue that seized the innermost essence of European America's fear and hatred of the Chinese.[48] This was the first prominent theatrical introduction of the European American concept of the "Yellow Peril."

The Chinese Must Go helped create images of the Chinese as a threat to the white European America that endures to this day. It provided the popular text that introduced the Chinese as the "sojourner," as the Other. It was the first sighting of the inanimate Chinese as the Confucian-spouting person of wisdom who would eventually leap forward onto the Hollywood screen as Charlie Chan. Even more compelling, *The Chinese Must Go* introduced Slim Chunk Pin, the diabolical and evil pimp, who, unlike the regular Chinese men, spoke perfect English. He was the theatrical precursor to the twentieth-century movie version of that diabolical, evil white slaver and global conqueror, Dr. Fu Manchu.

The opening scene of Grimm's farce set a tone of fear and dread among the European American audience with a dialogue between two opium smoking Chinese characters:

> Ah Coy. *I tellee you, white man big fools; eaty too muchee, drinkee too muchee, and talkee too muchee.*
> Sam Gin. *White man catchee plenty money; Chinaman catchee little money.*
> Ah Coy. *By and by white man catchee no money; Chinaman catchee heap money; Chinaman workee cheap, plenty work; white man workee dear, no work—sabee?*
> Sam Gin. *Me heap sabee.*
> Ah Coy. *White man damn fools; keep wifee and children—cost plenty money; Chinaman no wife, no children, save plenty money. By and by, no more white workingman in California; all Chinaman—sabee?*[49]

The European American concept of the Chinese as the "sojourner," as the Other, was an attempt to demonstrate that these people from China only desired to milk European America of its wealth and then scurry back to their Asian motherland. It suggested that the Chinese never wanted to be citizens of the United States, because they were always without family. They were the consummate bachelors.

European Americans argued that the aims of the Chinese sojourner were greed and opportunism.[50] If the Chinese were sojourners, interested only in a temporary stay in the United States, then whatever racist laws or comments were directed toward them were of little consequence. The argument went that they were asking to be abused because they had no loyalty to the country and would eventually leave the United States. In reality, this was simply a myth so that European Americans could rid the country of the Chinese without remorse or regret. Grimm's tale placed the Chinese firmly in the sojourner context. In the words of Ah Coy, "Sam Gin been here many years; white people plenty money then. White people no money now. Chinaman take too muchee money to China."[51]

As for the Charlie Chan image, Grimm introduced the Mandarin, the wise priest and sage of China. Remarkably, this Chinese spoke fluent American English with a ten-commandment inflection:

> The Mandarin: *Thou whose order the fire obeyest, I humble pray thee to protect this house, and all its inmates against conflagration. Thou who commandest the water, I humbly pray thee to guard this house, and all its inmates, against inundation. Thou who rulest the wind, I humbly pray thee to defend the fate of all creatures in the hollow of thy hand, I humbly pray thee to look with a pleasant eye on this house, and all its inmates, that they may prosper and be happy forever and ever.* (Then addressing the Chinamen.) *Now, children, arise and feed the idols with the choicest of the season. If you wish to retain their favor they must be pleased.*[52]

In Hollywood movies, the Hawaiian detective, Charlie Chan, like Grimm's Mandarin priest, evoked the image of the Chinese man who dispensed wisdom and knowledge like a Qing Dynasty scholar. For European Americans, the Mandarin priest and Charlie Chan represented the essentially harmless attributes of an ancient and dying China.

In contrast, the diabolical and evil Fu Manchu and Slim Chung Pin evoked the worst fears in the European American world. This was world domination personified by a global traffic in prostitution perpetrated by Chinese men who spoke English like European Americans. As an agent of the Six Companies, an actual Chinese American organization in San Francisco, Slim Chunk Pin was the thug who collected for this agency and enforced its rules. As the enforcer, he put fear in the hearts of both European Americans and Chinese workers. In a stern reply to a European American woman who owed money, Slim Chunk Pin shouts "I herewith order you to pay this Chinaman for his washing, and this Chinaman for his services; and mark you, if you don't, your life won't be safe a minute."[53]

Brutal and without remorse, Slim Chunk Pin is also stern with his Chinese charges. Sarcastically, he mimics Ah Coy's pidgin English:

> Ah Coy: *Dry up, will you? You are too muchee smart, too muchee sassy. This is the sixth time in eight months we have finished you with a situation, and now you are on our hands again. If we had all such chickens as you, the importation of coolies would be bad speculation. You have not half paid your passage money yet.*[54]

Finally, Slim Chung Pin loses his composure and threatens Ah Coy:

> Slim Chung Pin: *Shut up, you rat-smasher. Mind, now, if you don't improve you will get your wind cut off one of these days. We didn't import you to lose money; we can have that easier by gambling in stocks* (To Ah Coy.) *Look at Sam. He fulfills his contracts with the Company like a man, and saves money besides.*[55]

With characters that predated the Chinese as sojourner (as the Other), Charlie Chan, and Fu Manchu, Henry Grimm's *The Chinese Must Go* played a pivotal part in the evolution of the "Yellowface" phenomenon in American theater. Since theater and cinema eventually became entwined because of such common threads as storytelling, acting and performing, narrating, staging, and lighting, the discovery of Chineseness and things Chinese by European American audiences and storytellers revolved around the Chinese as the Other. As "Yellowface" traveled through the theaters of European America and into the minds of their audiences, it provided the basic racist foundations of how Hollywood would depict China and the Chinese in movies. It branded the Chinese as evil and treacherous, foolish and simpleminded, ninnies and docile, and incomprehensible and quaint. The Chinese were also seen as wise and harmless.

Since they had no knowledge of China and the Chinese from a Chinese point of view, European Americans were convinced that the Chinese were a race of people like Slim Chung Pin and Fu Manchu who spoke standard American English to conceal their real objective of seizing and dominating the Western world. If the Chinese spoke in Confucian or fortune cookie aphorisms like the Mandarin priest or Charlie Chan, they revealed their stark adherence to Chinese ways that were so anachronistic with the prevailing "modern and innovative" concepts of the Western world that they were inoffensive in their actions and words. They were emasculated beyond redemption and, therefore, did not constitute a threat to Western civilization. As men without their manhood, the Mandarin priest and Charlie Chan could exist in the European American world as quaint, benign, and laughable figures.

The Legacy of The Chinese Must Go

Henry Grimm's *The Chinese Must Go* spawned a generation of American writers of European heritage who perpetuated the racial branding of the Chinese in the theaters and movie houses of European America. While it also demonstrated that the Chinese was the "Yellow Peril" out to conquer European America, the theatrical denigration of the Chinese continued to be personified in Emma E. Brewster's *A Bunch of Buttercups* (1881) and T. S. Denison's *Patsy O'Wang: An Irish Farce with a Chinese Mix-Up* (1895). These plays continued the linguistic branding of Chinese workers as ignorant, pidgin-speaking dolts.[56]

In 1899 the racial branding of Chinatown as the location of the "Yellow Peril," with its attendant evil, opium dens, and white slavery, came aggressively into America's theater through Joseph Jarrow's *The Queen of Chinatown*. This play crystallized the negative images of the Chinese. Chinatown as their geographical location was depicted by European Americans as doubly terrifying. Any European American daring to venture into Chinatown would be met with mystery, violence, and debauchery. Chinatown was particularly perilous for European American women.

In the play, Hop Lee abducts Beezie Garrity, who becomes the "Queen of Chinatown." But it was Garrity's curiosity about the "mysteries" of Chinatown that pushed her into the opium dens of Hop Lee. She whimpers:

> Beezie Garrity: *A slumming expedition to Chinatown; a trial of the pipe for sport. I became fascinated; came again and again. Gradually, I lost lover, friends, family, all. Society turned its back upon me and now I have no other world.*[57]

Of course, as in all the plays before *The Queen of Chinatown,* European American performers played the Chinese protagonists.

In 1903 the American Mutoscope and Biograph Company launched its own "Yellow Peril" theme, with the first European American movie depicting the Chinese as villains and labor threats to the country, *The Chinese Rubbernecks*. A year later it produced the *Chinese Laundry: At Work* and the *Heathen Chinese and the Sunday School Teachers.* In 1908 the ultimate depiction of Asia (Japan) and Asians (Japanese) as direct competitors for world domination was crystallized in *The Yellow Peril*. This film internalized in the minds of European America that the threat of Asia and the Asians to Western civilization was real and substantial.

In the film, a Chinese servant, personifying China and indirectly Japan, creates chaos for his employers, who represent the West. Retaliating against their undisciplined and disloyal underling, the European Americans toss the

Chinese out a window. A police officer catches and beats him. Finally the Chinese is set on fire.[58]

In 1913 the "Yellow Peril" theme became more terrifying for European Americans and Europeans with the publication of *The Insidious Dr. Fu Manchu* by Sax Rohmer (Arthur Sarsfield Ward, 1883–1959). Eventually Rohmer's thirteen novels, four short stories, and a novelette, written between 1913 and 1959, captured the essence of Chinese villainy on such a scale that movie versions were certain to follow.[59]

The Cheat (1915), directed by Cecil B. DeMille (1881–1959), and *Broken Blossoms* (1919), by D. W. Griffith (1875–1948), predated the films of Fu Manchu. They were some of the first films to place the Asian male in the context of the "Yellow Peril."[60] In these movies, an Asian man strives to capture, seduce, and debauch the flower of European American womanhood. In *The Cheat,* the Japanese actor Sessue Hayakawa (1889–1973) played a sadistic Japanese villain in the original production. This was followed by his portrayal of a Burmese villain in the reissue. In both productions, his quest is to possess a European American woman by branding her on the shoulder as a symbol of his conquest.[61] For this sexual transgression, he is nearly lynched.

In *Broken Blossoms,* originally entitled *The Chink and the Child* in the original story, Richard Barthelmess (1895–1963) in "Yellowface" portrayed an alienated, love-starved Chinese pedophile named Cheng Huan who lusts after a twelve-year-old white orphan girl played by Lillian Gish (1893–1993). Although Cheng Huan is scripted as a kind and sensitive individual, he is still out to possess a European American female, and a child at that![62]

Miscegenation, or the mixing of the races, with its horror of potential sexual relations between "yellow" Asian men and "white" European American women, threatened the masculinity of European American men so much so that the basis of Chinese–European American conflict became a contest of securing scarce resources, which in this specific case were European American women. The threat of the "Yellow Peril" in the eyes of European American men perpetuated the status of European American women as chattel, as product. To ensure that "yellow" men would be totally unattractive to European American women in theaters and films, Asian men were racially branded as thoroughly emasculated, without any sexuality or manhood. They were depicted as effeminate individuals speaking in nonsensical jabber, reeking of ginger and opium and working in traditional women's occupations such as washing clothes or cleaning house. If the Chinese language was actually spoken, it was usually by a minor but real Chinese character. The language of the Chinese (often Cantonese) was incomprehensible to European Americans, who likened it to "a bunch of phonograph records playing backwards."[63]

Actual Chinese performers speaking the Chinese language in European American movies was strange enough. But a Chinese American or a Chinese performer playing a heroic Chinese male who was aggressive, fully confident, and powerful not only would have been out of place in European American theater and films, it would have been incomprehensible, both then and now. Thus, as the Other, the Chinese male represented by Cheng Huan was "what a pencil sketch was to painting; it lacked that variety, that amplitude, that abundance of life which was the condition of perfectibility. Like those individuals who possessed so little fecundity that, after a gracious childhood, they attained only the most mediocre virility."[64] Despite his sexual appetite, however, Chuan Heng was "sensitive and fragile, slender and pale, with his tilted head, his withdrawn, curved body, and his dreamy countenance."[65] Eunuch-like and sexually grotesque, the Asian male in the guise of Cheng Huan was consummately unappealing. He was socially castrated. In *Broken Blossoms*, therefore, D. W. Griffith "didn't give the Chink any balls."[66]

MARCO MILLIONS

By 1927 "Yellowface" was an integral part of the theatrical tradition of European America. Along with the idea of the "Yellow Peril," it pervaded American films; European American moviemakers could not resist the temptation of casting European American performers in Chinese roles. More important, these movies portrayed Asians and Asian Americans in thoroughly negative and subordinate roles. They were always a threat to Western civilization.

From the release of *Broken Blossoms* in 1919 to 1927, Anna May Wong appeared in twenty films. This was even more remarkable because she began in a bit part in *The Red Lantern* (1919) when she was only fourteen. When she was nineteen, Wong played the Mongol spy and infiltrator in *The Thief of Bagdad* (1924). This picture catapulted her to international fame. However, she continued to play negative and demeaning roles in Hollywood. She portrayed Zira in *The Fortieth Door* (1924); Keok, an Inuit, in *The Alaskan* (1924); Tiger Lily in Peter Pan (1924); Annabelle Wu, an adventuress and vampire, in *Forty Winks* (1925); Nan Lo, a prostitute, in *Fifth Avenue* (1926); the Dragon Horse in *The Silk Bouquet / The Dragon Horse* (1926); Ohtai in *A Trip to Chinatown* (1926); and Oneta in *The Desert's Toll* (1926). Wong also played herself in *Mary of the Movies* (1923) and in *Screen Snap Shots No. 3* (1925).

While Anna May Wong was advancing from a mere bit part in her screen debut in 1919 to more substantial roles by 1927, one of European America's best-known playwrights began "reading and taking millions of notes"[67] about China and the Chinese as motifs for his new work on the travels of Marco Polo. Eugene O'Neill (1888–1953) had had an idea previously about China and the Chinese "in the 1918–1920 notebook: 'The Play of Andrew,' which was originally to have been a sequel to *Beyond the Horizon.*"[68] By the summer of 1923, Eugene O'Neill had begun to write his version of China and the Chinese in *Marco Millions*.

Despite O'Neill's genius, he could not overcome the European American traditions of "Yellowface" and the "Yellow Peril." All of his Chinese and non-Western characters were performed by European Americans. These characters themselves were separately listed under the heading "Heathen" (in the order in which they appeared). The "Heathens" were the "Yellow Peril's" usual suspects: A Magian Traveler, A Buddhist Traveler, A Mohometan Captain of Ghazan's Army, The Ali Brothers (Mahometan merchants), A Prostitute, A Dervish, Two Buddhist Merchants, Two Tartar Merchants, A Mongol Priest, Emissary from Kublai, Kublai (the Great Kaan), Princess Kukachin (his granddaughter), Chu-Yin (a Cathayan sage), General Bayan, A Messenger from Persia, Ghazan (Khan of Persia), A Buddhist Priest, A Taoist Priest, A Confucian Priest, A Moslem Priest, and A Tartar Chronicler.[69]

In 1928 *Marco Millions* came "to a generous and abundant production at the hands of the Theater Guild."[70] The story revolved around Marco Polo and his father, whose only interests in life were "getting ahead" and "becoming rich." For O'Neill, the Polos represented the values of the European American bourgeoisie and the businessmen who were the true children "of the will to live, the true expression of meaningless striving."[71]

In the hands of Eugene O'Neill, Marco Polo personified the flower of European American avarice, expansionism, and Christian missionizing. He was

the traveler, the heralded ideal specimen of western civilization, a youth of average intelligence, with little worldly experience but possessing a secret touch of the poet, whose journey is not a pilgrim's progress—even though he was the pope's ambassador—to convert idolaters and to discover the spiritual treasures of the East but an extensive business trip to exploit its material wealth.[72]

As a full-length satire of bourgeois values, *Marco Millions* was a direct attack on European American greed and acquisitiveness seen through the adventures of Marco Polo in China, but despite his good intentions, Eugene O'Neill, like Marco Polo, was unable to see beyond his own European American prejudices and stereotypes about non-Westerners. Throughout his play he was thorough in his denigration of non-Europeans. The Arabs, for example, were characterized in Magian's words as follows:

> Magian: *And I, for my sins, am hawking a novelty, a block-printed book, for an Arab house. It contains one thousand Arabian lies, with one over for good measure, all full of lechery—at least so they instructed me to tell people to get them to buy.*[73]

As if to illustrate that he had seen and internalized the script of the Arabs in Douglas Fairbanks and Anna May Wong's *The Thief of Bagdad*, O'Neill targeted the Mahometan Captain of Ghazan's Army with these well-known offerings: "By all the demons, you startled me! But you traders are like fleas, one finds you everywhere!" and "Allah forbid I touch what belongs to a corpse." He is even more animated with "But Allah afflicted me! When I reached the last village with my camel floundering, I found the accursed villagers had driven off their beasts to escape requisition." Finally, the captain's curse included the popular "Pig of an infidel!"[74]

While O'Neill linguistically branded his Arabs in stereotypical ways, he invested his Chinese characters with fully formed English words. Although he did not resort to pidgin English, he could not resist illustrating the wisdom of the East in the figure of Chu-Yin, "a Cathayan sage." But even this representation was couched in a way that smacked of the Mandarin priest in *The Chinese Must Go* and that Hawaiian detective, Charlie Chan. In fact, Chu-Yin, like the Mandarin priest and Chan, could not help but spout this fortune-cookie aphorism: "Love is to wisdom what wisdom seems to love—a folly. I reasoned, love comes like the breath of wind on water and is gone leaving calm and reflection."[75]

Since O'Neill's carefully crafted China and the "East" smacked of "Oriental wisdom and intuitiveness," he measured the "Eastern philosophy of calm intuition and mysticism" in contrast to "Western assertive action and rational practicality."[76] Chinese wisdom and knowledge proved to be no match for the materialism and greed for power and authority personified in the acquisitive Marco Polo.[77] China and the Chinese were never discovered. Rather they were represented by European American actors, Balliol Holloway (1883–1967), Dudley Digges (1879–1947), and Margalo Gilmore (1897–1986), playing their "Yellowface" roles as Kublai Kaan, Chu-Yin, and Princess Kukachin, respectively, in a quasi-Chinese setting constructed by Lee Simonson that was reminiscent of a summer camp for adolescents or a summer holiday for their parents.[78]

From Arthur Murphy's Philadelphia opening of the *Orphan of China* in 1767 to Eugene O'Neill's New York opening in 1927 of *Marco Millions*, China and the Chinese were fixed and described within a definite European American perspective and without any input from the Chinese. To accentuate the

European American hegemony over the formation of the meaning and significance of China, the Chinese, and Chinese Americans, the racial formation and
branding of "Yellowface" were invented, nurtured, and transmitted throughout
European American theater and films.

The most startling and violent expressions of "Yellowface" in Hollywood
films were the films of the evil and diabolical Dr. Fu Manchu, who exemplified an attempt to extinguish Western civilization. The Fu Manchu movies also
represented the "Yellow Peril." European actors such as the Swede Warner
Oland (1880–1938), Boris Karloff (1887–1969) from England, the German
Harry Brandon (1912–1990), and Christopher Lee (1922–) from England
played the lead role.

As a contrast to Fu Manchu, Earl Derr Biggers (1884–1943) invented the
effete, eunuch-like Charlie Chan after reading about Chang Apana, a Chinese
detective in Honolulu in 1919. Mumbling the wisdom of the "Oriental" like
the Mandarin priest and Chu-Yin, Charlie Chan, unlike the menacing Fu
Manchu, was a servant of the West. Always accommodating and never menacing, he sought to root out murderers, thieves, and corrupt officials in European
America so that the Western world could thrive. In fact, "Chan's passive persona, rendered affectedly quaint by an 'abundance of aphorism' often prefaced
by a 'Confucius says,' was as remotely threatening to white Americans as the
continuing fear of an Asian immigration deluge was at last superfluous."[79] His
aphorisms, supposedly quoted from Confucius, were hilarious in their inven-
tiveness and pithy in their pidgin English:

> Theory, like mist on eyeglasses, obscures fact.
> Hasty conclusion easy to make, like hole in water.
> Man who fears death dies a thousand times.
> Man without name like dog without fleas.
> Caution sometimes Mother of suspicion.
> Guilty conscience like dog in circus—many tricks.
> Sharp wit sometimes better than deadly weapon.
> Only a very brave mouse will make its nest in a cat's ear.[80]

These "gems of wisdom" from the "inscrutable Orient" mocked the
Chinese inability to speak standard American English. They relegated the
Chinese, through the character of Charlie Chan in forty-eight films
(1926–1950), to the position of the Other, so foreign and alien that they were
unworthy of citizenship.

During the completion and performance onstage of Eugene O'Neill's
Marco Millions in 1927, the American film audience received a taste of China

and the Chinese in the first three Charlie Chan movies, *The House Without a Key* (1926), *Behind That Curtain* (1927), and *The Chinese Parrot* (1927). As a minor character in these films, Charlie Chan, the island sleuth, was played respectively by George Kuwa (1885–1931), E. L. Park, and Kamiyama Sojin (1884–1954). None of these were actors from Chinese America. In subsequent years only such European and European American performers as Warner Oland, Sidney Toler (1874–1947), and Roland Winters (1904–1989) played the Charlie Chan character in the lead role.

As the "Yellowface" tradition in European America reached new heights with the Fu Manchu and Charlie Chan movies, a strange new industry was also revealed. Like the racial formation of "Yellowface" and the "Yellow Peril" that gave rise to linguistic branding and the Asian threat, body branding also became common. This racial cosmetology centered around the epicanthic fold or eyefold of Asians.

In an attempt to re-create the Asian look in European American performers, a jelly mold of Asian eyes was made by a cosmetologist. The mold was then remolded into clay and then into rubber, which was glued with spirit gum onto the eyes of a European American performer. To give the eyes a further slant, the makeup artist glued translucent, flesh-colored plastics tabs to the skin near each of the temples. Rubber bands laced to the tabs and hidden under a wig could then be stretched to provide whatever degree of "Oriental" slant of the eyes the director wanted.[81] This was the body branding of "Yellowface."

From the theatrical performances of the *Orphan of China* in 1767 and *The Chinese Must Go* in 1879 to the films of Fu Manchu and Charlie Chan in the twentieth century, the linguistic and body branding of "Yellowface" was located firmly in European America's culture and tradition. "Yellowface" reaffirmed whiteness as the supreme attainment in any dramatic production. "Yellowface" and "Yellow Peril" formed the distinctive facets of the Chinese and Chinese American place in the national identity of European America.

As a creation of European Americans, "Yellowface" and "Yellow Peril" eventually became "common sense" through films, folk wisdom, religions, schooling, television, theater, and any public vehicle that portrayed the Chinese. "Yellowface" and "Yellow Peril" were racial projects that branded the Chinese as the Other; foreign and alien. No Asian performer, then or now, can escape the sinister influences of "Yellowface" and "Yellow Peril." These two cultural aspects of European America, however, were not just about race.

By substantiating the supremacy of whiteness through "Yellowface" especially, European Americans reassured themselves what they were not: not yellow, not foreign, not effeminate (not eunuch-like), and therefore not gay.[82] "Yellowface" performers like David Garrick in the *Orphan of China,* the Ravel family in *Kim-Ka!*, Pat Regan in *New Brooms Sweep Clean*, C. T. Parsoe in *Ah Sin*, Richard Barthelmess in *Broken Blossoms*, Balliol Holloway in *Marco Millions*, Warner Oland as Dr. Fu Manchu, and Sidney Toler as Charlie Chan did not express themselves simply in Chinese roles. Rather, their "unannounced object of attention was *white* (European) America."[83] Thus "Yellowface" went beyond the simple performance of European American actors in Chinese roles. "Yellowface" gave European American males the opportunity to "appropriate and use elements" of Chinese American life to express their own perceptions of China and the Chinese and in turn present their own identities of Europeanness (whiteness), gender (male), and sexuality (straight).[84]

As the scenario of *The Good Earth* played out from casting to the film's release in 1937, the tradition of "Yellowface" and its companion, "Yellow Peril," shunted Anna May Wong aside as she reached for more positive Asian roles. Yet "Yellowface" and "Yellow Peril" were so ingrained in European American theater and film that Wong could never have overcome their constraints. Although she was born and raised in Los Angeles, she was always portrayed as the "daughter of the dragon" and "the child of China," with choice Asian roles given to European American performers in "Yellowface." Thus, she became a constant reminder to Asian America of the "Yellowface" phenomenon that has dogged every Asian American performer in the twentieth century. As racial branding, "Yellowface" in Hollywood lives on. The portrayal of manicurist Miss Swan by Alex Borstein (b. 1980) on Fox Television's *MAD TV* (2000) showed the European American actor in slant-eyed makeup with a clipped accent. In May 2000, Susan Sarandon (b. 1946) also appeared as Miss Swan in "Yellowface" in one of *MAD TV*'s episodes.[85]

Despite the power of "Yellowface," Anna May Wong was not crushed by its insidious impact. Certainly she was not cast in some of the more lucrative roles like O-lan in *The Good Earth*. She was even hired by Paramount to coach Dorothy Lamour (1914–1996) on how to act "Asian." But her career was remarkable because of its variation in roles and languages. While most of her films were financed by European or European American producers, her starring role in *The Silk Bouquet* (1926) was financed by the Chinese Six Companies, located in San Francisco. Set in fifteenth-century Ming China (1368–1644), the picture cast about two hundred performers, including James B. Leong and Chew Chin Chon. Although it was not totally an all-Asian cast, with such film stars as Anna Nuttley and William Veigh playing the Western parts, the story was one of the first ever produced by Chinese backers.[86]

In the vast scheme of Hollywood productions, *The Silk Bouquet* was a negligible contribution. But it was an Asian American production for an Asian American market. It depicted Asians and Asian Americans in genuine roles with strong, resourceful characters. For Wong, this was less reassuring, because her career was firmly founded in European America, not in Asian America. To succeed, she accepted roles that would help fortify her celebrity. If that meant working as an exotic or an erotic, she would do it. But she would play the exotic or erotic Asian woman on her terms even in her first major starring role, as rape victim Lotus Flower in *The Toll of the Sea* (1922).

NOTES

1. Epes W. Sargent and Walter K. Hill, "The Red Lantern Stars Nazimova," *The Moving Picture World* (10 May 1919): 920.

2. "Special Service Section on Nazimova in '*The Red Lantern*,'" *Motion Picture News* (10 May 1919): 3059–63; "*The Red Lantern*," *Motion Picture News* (10 May 1919): 3039.

3. Luise Rainer won consecutive Oscars for *The Great Ziegfeld* (1936) and *The Good Earth* (1937). In *The Good Earth* she refused to make up as a Chinese for her role as O-lan. She said that "the makeup man wanted to make a complete mask," but she insisted on playing the part without any makeup. She continued: "I came one day when they tested people for mass scenes. There were many Chinese people—cooks, waiters, servants. . . . And my pocketbook under my arm fell. As I bent down, one of the little Chinese women also bent down. Our heads hit, and she looked at me. . . . She was O-lan." Cited in Marie Brenner, *Great Dames: What I Learned from Older Women* (New York: Crown, 2000), 187.

4. Sarah Berry, *Screen Style: Fashion and Femininity in 1930s Hollywood* (Minneapolis: University of Minnesota Press, 2000), 111.

5. Pearl S. Buck, cited in Theodore F. Harris, *Pearl S. Buck: A Biography* (New York: John Day, 1933), 148.

6. Buck, cited in Harris, *Pearl S. Buck,* 148.

7. Buck, cited in Harris, *Pearl S. Buck,* 150.

8. Edward Sakamoto, "Anna May Wong and the Dragon Lady Syndrome," *Los Angeles Times,* 12 July 1987, 41.

9. Wong, cited in Sakamoto, "Anna May Wong," 41.

10. For a provocative concept of the "memory piece," see Neil Harris, *Cultural Excursions: Marketing Appetites and Cultural Tastes in Modern America* (Chicago: University of Chicago Press, 1990), 307–8.

11. The chief academic architect of the concept of China and the Chinese as the "Other" in opposition to the United States and Americans of European heritage was Harvard University professor John K. Fairbank, whose career helped shaped China studies in the state departments of the United States and Canada. See Paul M. Evans, *John Fairbank and the American Understanding of Modern China* (New York: Basil Blackwell, 1988).

12. James S. Moy, *Marginal Sights: Staging the Chinese in America* (Iowa City: University of Iowa Press, 1993), 9; Dave Williams, ed., *The Chinese Other, 1850–1925: An Anthology of Plays* (Lanham, Md.: University Press of America, 1997), ix–x.

13. A. Owen Aldridge, *The Dragon and the Eagle: The Presence of China in the American Enlightenment* (Detroit: Wayne State University Press, 1993), 21.

14. John Kuo Wei Tchen, *New York Before Chinatown: Orientalism and the Shaping of American Culture, 1776–1882* (Baltimore: Johns Hopkins University Press, 1999), 18–19.

15. The concepts of hegemony and "common sense" follow the thoughts of Antonio Gramsci. See Antonio Gramsci, *Selections from the Prison Notebooks,* ed. and trans. Quentin Hoare and Geoffrey Nowell Smith (New York: International Publishers, 1971), 182.

16. The original Yuan play, *Sole Heir of the Zhao Clan,* was performed by some of the best actors in Chinese theater. It was so popular that it lasted into the Ming Dynasty. See William Dolby, *A History of Chinese Drama* (New York: Harper & Row, 1976), 10, for Yan Rong's approach to playing the part of the elderly former minister who protects the orphan baby.

17. Chen Shou-yi, "The Chinese Orphan: A Yuan Play," *T'ien Hsia Monthly* 3, no. 2 (September 1936): 90.

18. Joseph Premare, *"L'Orphelin de la Maison de Tschao,"* *Description, geographique, historique, chronologue, politique, et physique de l'empire de la Chine et la tartarie chinoise.* (Paris: n.p., 1735).

19. Dawn Jacobson, *Chinoiserie* (London: Phaidon Press, 1993), 79; Tchen, *New York Before Chinatown,* 20.

20. Tchen, *New York Before Chinatown,* 20.

21. Chen, "The Chinese Orphan," 109.

22. Chen, "The Chinese Orphan," 89.

23. Chen, "The Chinese Orphan," 91.

24. Oliver Goldsmith, cited in Chen, "The Chinese Orphan," 113.

25. Moy, *Marginal Sights,* 9.

26. Michael Omi and Howard Winant, *Racial Formation in the United States,* 2d ed. (New York: Routledge, 1994), 55.

27. The classic work on Orientalism as a systematic body of knowledge portraying non-Europeans, especially Arabs and by extension Asians as the "Others" or "Orientals," is still Edward Said, *Orientalism* (New York: Vintage, 1979).

28. Williams, *Chinese Other,* 1.

29. *Kim-Ka!,* in Williams, *Chinese Other,* 3.

30. *Kim-Ka!,* in Williams, *Chinese Other,* 4.

31. *Kim-Ka!,* in Williams, *Chinese Other,* 5.

32. *Kim-Ka!,* in Williams, *Chinese Other,* 6.

33. *Kim-Ka!,* in Williams, *Chinese Other,* 7.

34. Moy, *Marginal Sights,* 11. (My quotation marks and parentheses.)

35. For the full text of the Foreign Miner's License Tax Act of 1853, called *An Act to Provide for the Protection of Foreigners, and to Define their Liabilities and Privileges* [Approved

30 March 1853] and Chinese May Not Testify Against White Men in Court, 1854, in *Reports of Cases Argued and Determined in the Supreme Court of the State of California, 1854,* see Cheng-Tsu Wu, ed., *CHINK: Anti-Chinese Prejudice in America* (New York: World Publishers, 1972), 21–25, 36–43.

36. For Further Restrictions on Chinese Immigrants, 1870, or *An Act to Prevent the Importation of Chinese Criminals and to Prevent the Establishment of Coolie Slavery* [Approved 18 March 1870], the "Cubic Air" Ordinance, 1870, *Regulating Lodging Houses* [Approved 29 July 1870], and *Removing the Chinese Pigtail: The Queue Ordinance, 1876,* see Wu, *CHINK,* 35–36, 65, 66.

37. George M. Baker, *New Brooms Sweep Clean,* in Williams, *Chinese Other,* 9–23.

38. Robert G. Lee, *Orientals: Asian Americans in Popular Culture* (Philadelphia: Temple University Press, 1999), 37.

39. Charles A. Loder, "Chinese Song," in *Chas. A. Loder's Hilarity Songster: Containing a Collection of the Favorite Songs As Sung by This Great German Comedian* (New York: New York Popular Publishing Company, 1885), cited in Lee, *Orientals,* 37.

40. Luke Schoolcraft, "The Heathen Chinee," in *Shine On: Rembrances of the South* (Boston: Louis P. Goullaud, 1874), cited in Lee, *Orientals,* 37.

41. Williams, *Chinese Other,* 27.

42. Moy, *Marginal Sights,* 24–25.

43. William F. Wu, *The Yellow Peril: Chinese Americans in American Fiction, 1850–1940* (Hamden, Conn.: Archon Books, 1982), 22–23.

44. *Ah Sin,* in Williams, *Chinese Other,* 45, 46.

45. Williams, *Chinese Other,* 71, 72.

46. Williams, *Chinese Other,* 81.

47. Williams, *Chinese Other,* 63.

48. Moy, *Marginal Sights,* 40.

49. *The Chinese Must Go,* in Williams, *Chinese Other,* 99.

50. For an examination of the sojourner myth, see Anthony B. Chan, *Gold Mountain: The Chinese in the New World* (Vancouver, B.C.: New Star Books, 1983), 127–30.

51. *The Chinese Must Go,* in Williams, *Chinese Other,* 102.

52. *The Chinese Must Go,* in Williams, *Chinese Other,* 118.

53. *The Chinese Must Go,* in Williams, *Chinese Other,* 102.

54. *The Chinese Must Go,* in Williams, *Chinese Other,* 102.

55. *The Chinese Must Go,* in Williams, *Chinese Other,* 102.

56. *A Bunch of Buttercups,* in Williams, *Chinese Other,* 122–24. For an analysis of *Patsy O'Wang: An Irish Farce with a Chinese Mix-Up,* see Lee, *Orientals,* 78–81.

57. Beezie Garrity, *The Queen of Chinatown,* in Williams, *Chinese Other,* 191–92.

58. Thomas W. Bohn and Richard L. Stromgren, *Light and Shadows* (Port Washington, N.Y.: Alfred Publishing, 1975), 192–93; Raymond Durgnay, "The 'Yellow Peril' Rides Again," *Film Society Review* 5 (2 October 1969): 36.

59. For an exacting analysis of the Fu Manchu character, see Lee, *Orientals,* 113–17.

60. For a complete and in-depth analysis of *The Cheat* and *Broken Blossoms,* see Lee, *Orientals,* 120–32. For other views, see Marshall Deutelbaum, "*The Cheat,*" in *The Ri-*

vals of D. W. Griffith: Alternate Auteurs, 1913–1918, ed. Richard Koszarski (Minneapolis, Minn.: Walker Art Center, 1976), 44; Sumiko Higashi, "Ethnicity, Class and Gender in Film: DeMille's *The Cheat,"* in *Unspeakable Images: Ethnicity and the American Cinema,* ed. Lester D. Friedman (Urbana: University of Illinois Press, 1991), 130; DeWitt Bodeen, "Sessue Hayakawa," *Films in Review* (April 1976): 193; Vance Kepley, "Griffith's *Broken Blossoms* and the Problem of Historical Specificity," *Quarterly Review of Film Studies* 6, no. 1 (winter 1978): 37–47; Dudley Andrew, *"Broken Blossoms:* The Art. and Eros of a Perverse Text," *Quarterly Review of Film Studies* 6, no. 1 (winter 1981): 81–90. Sandwiched in between *The Cheat* and *Broken Blossoms* was a thoroughly "Yellow Peril" film called *The Yellow Menace* (1916).

61. Grace Kingsley, "The Splash of Saffron," *Photoplay* 9, no. 4 (March 1916): 139.

62. John Kuo Wei Tchen, "Modernizing White Patriarchy: Re-viewing D. W. Griffith's *Broken Blossoms,"* in *Moving the Image: Independent Asian Pacific American Media Arts,* ed. Russell Leong (Los Angeles: UCLA Asian American Studies Center, 1991), 133–43.

63. Eugene Franklin Wong, *On Visual Media Racism: Asian in American Motion Pictures* (New York: Arno Press, 1978), 126.

64. Ernest Renan, cited in Said, *Orientalism,* 149. Rendered in the past tense.

65. Lewis Jacobs, *The Rise of the American Film* (New York: Columbia University Press, 1969), 388.

66. Rodger Larson, "An Innocence, An Originality, A Clear Eye: A Retrospective Look at the Films of D. W. Griffith and Andy Warhol," *The Film Journal* 1, nos. 3–4 (fall–winter 1972): 85.

67. Virginia Floyd, ed., *Eugene O'Neill at Work: Newly Released Ideas for Plays* (New York: Frederick Ungar, 1981), 57.

68. Floyd, *Eugene O'Neill,* 57.

69. Eugene O'Neill, *A Play: Marco Millions* (New York: Boni & Liverright, 1927), ii–viii.

70. John Mason Brown, "Marco Millions," *Theater Arts* (March 1928): 34, in *O'Neill and His Plays: Four Decades of Criticism,* ed. Oscar Cargill, N. Bryllion Fagin, and William J. Fisher (New York: New York University Press, 1961), 25.

71. John H. Houchin, ed., *The Critical Response to Eugene O'Neill* (Westport, Conn.: Greenwood Press, 1993), 110.

72. Floyd, *Eugene O'Neill,* 57.

73. O'Neill, *Marco Millions,* 15.

74. O'Neill, *Marco Millions,* 19, 20, 23.

75. O'Neill, *Marco Millions,* 91–92.

76. An Min Hsia, "Cycle of Return: O'Neill and the Tao," in *Eugene O'Neill's Critics: Voices from Abroad,* ed. Horst Frenz and Susan Tuck (Carbondale: Southern Illinois University Press, 1984), 170–71.

77. Moy, *Marginal Sights,* 101.

78. Moy, *Marginal Sights,* 102.

79. Wong, *On Visual Media Racism,* 108; James Robert Parish, ed., *The Great Movie Series* (New York: A. S. Barnes, 1971), 90; Dorothy B. Jones, *The Portrayal of China and*

India on the American Screen, 1896–1955 (Cambridge: Massachusetts Institute of Technology Press, 1955), 34.

80. These "gems of wisdom" were found in *Charlie Chan in Egypt* (1935) and *Castle in the Desert* (1942), cited in Jones, *The Portrayal of China and India,* 34.

81. For an exacting description of how Wally Westmore "orientalized" Shirley Maclaine in *My Geisha,* see Frank Westmore and Muriel Davidson, *The Westmores of Hollywood* (New York: J. B. Lippincott, 1976), 208–9.

82. This section on "whiteness" has been conceptually influenced by David Wellman, "Minstrel Shows, Affirmative Action Talk, and Angry White Men: Marking Racial Otherness in the 1990s," in *Displacing Whiteness: Essays in Social and Cultural Criticism,* ed. Ruth Frankenberg (Durham, N.C.: Duke University Press, 1997), 312.

83. Wellman, "Minstrel Shows," 312.

84. Wellman, "Minstrel Shows," 312–13.

85. Yaoyi Lena Winfrey, "Yellowface: Asians on White Screens," *IMDiversity* (2003), at http://www.imdiversity.com/villages/asian/article_detail.asp?Article_ID=6349 (accessed 17 May 2003); Guy Aoki, "Asian Americans in a 'Bamboozled' World," *Los Angeles Times,* 23 October 2000, at http://www.madtvcentral.com/alexarticle.html (accessed 17 May 2003).

86. "Tale of Orient Told in Picture Form," *San Francisco Chronicle,* 12 February 1926, 11.

ELEVEN

THE TOLL OF THE SEA (1922)

L ooking decidedly different from European American women in complexion, height, style, and demeanor, Anna May Wong electrified audiences with scenes punctuated with a raw sexuality that beckoned the camera to capture her every movement, from a quick flick of a cigarette to the slow London–Los Angeles drawl as she massaged her lines. These nuances characterized many of the films in which she played a prominent role. That she was radiantly Asian, especially with her trademark bangs immaculately and prominently etched on her forehead, gave her the panache to score acting points against her European American female cinematic counterparts, many of whom were shorter than Wong.[1] With a riveting profile that constantly attracted the audience's gaze, she stood out in every scene.

Endowed with flawless skin and a lean, narrow-hipped Cantonese body, she wore her costumes as if they were a second skin. Unlike European American women, her center of gravity was her erect posture (so evident in *Shanghai Express*), accentuated by her five feet, seven inch height[2] and a low torsoed, southern Chinese female figure. When she dressed in a classic *cheong sam,* Wong wore it as if her body perfected it as no other Chinese or Chinese American woman ever could. When European American women actually deigned to wear the *cheong sam,* as Myrna Loy did in her "Yellowface" role in

The Crimson City, it became apparent how hideous, grotesque, and laughable "whiteness" could be when it attempted to assume the "yellowness" of an Anna May Wong in a Chinese gown.

In a *cheong sam,* the European American woman with her wider and heavier body type appeared distorted, mismatched, and comic. The *cheong sam* was never made for a Western body. On the other hand, Anna May Wong could always wear European clothing with a style that showed an explicitly detached demeanor and coolness. That she was hip in her persona was always evident in how she stood; the way she spoke; how she responded to others on camera, in interviews, at parties, and in nightclubs; and even how she played solitaire. During her party days in Berlin, London, Los Angeles, and Paris, she was often a "must" invite because her hipness complemented her witty banter and legendary humor. In the European American elite film colony, she was a "savvy Hollywood actress" who was "silk sheath-skirt chic."[3]

In a 1939 interview with the *New York Post,* Wong exchanged quips with the reporter, Michel Mok, after telling him about her half brother in *Taishan* wanting the dollar watch advertised in a Los Angeles newspaper rather than being impressed by the photo of his half sister dressed in a gorgeous mink coat on the flip side of the page. She also revealed this family tidbit to Mok:

> I can see that you like Chinese stories and I can also see that you are a little surprised that we have a sense of humor. You don't know that the Chinese are the most humorous, the most fun loving people on earth.
>
> They have survived all these years of suffering because they know how to laugh. Laughter is the essence of Chinese life—it makes their days more fragrant. We in America rush about with long stern faces—and for what?
>
> I will tell you some more Chinese stories. In 1934, my father, my three brothers and two sisters were on a trip to China. On a day they sailed, a friend of mine, a Los Angeles newspaper woman (Louise Leung) was running about the ship, trying to get them all together for a picture. She found them all except my father, who was on the prowl, inspecting the boat. She burst into what she thought was his cabin. There sat a dignified old Chinese gentleman.
>
> "Oh excuse me," she stammered. "Have you seen Mr. Wong?" He said: "I do not know your face." She continued her frantic search and, after a while, in her confusion, again opened the door of the old gentleman's cabin. Before she had recognized the occupant, she repeated her question: "Have you seen Mr. Wong?" He said: "You are two who have asked for the same."[4]

Besides her playful manner, especially with journalists, Anna May Wong's cool, hip demeanor revealed her jocular attitude to life's unpredictability. This contrasted sharply with Hollywood's creation of her fictitious characters in film. Wong's cinematic roles in a sea of European Americans were designed to reveal an exotic, stern, and mysterious Asian being rather than a matter-of-fact person who relished the art of repartee. Her films served to create an aura of aloofness that seemed to encourage a sexual encounter but at the same time pushed aside the possibility of touching and intimacy. Since she hardly ever kissed the European-looking men in her films, she became the ultimate cinematic tease who drove European and European American male audiences wild, with their erotic expectations and illusions of what an Asian or Asian American woman could do for them and to them in the right circumstances. Anna May Wong was the classic Hollywood fantasy and every European American male's consummate wet dream, which Tinseltown nurtured and bet money on.

The exoticism of an Asian woman so alien to European America brought Wong notice, especially in *The Toll of the Sea*. She was certainly the Other in the emptiness of a world personified by standards of European Americans. When unbridled eroticism was expected from this Chinese American woman, it was in the form of a sexual passion that always remained foreign and thus forbidden to a European America conditioned by notions of miscegenation and racist ideas of the superiority of whiteness. For the most famous actress from Chinese America, if there was eroticism, it was always accompanied by an explicit exoticism, especially in *The Thief of Bagdad, Piccadilly, Shanghai Express*, and *Chu Chin Chow*.

EXOTICISM

In European American Hollywood, to be foreign was to be exotic. In many cases, to be foreign was to be un-European American. If the skin were light enough, however, a Rita Cansino could transform into Rita Hayworth (1918–1987). But a Dolores del Rio (1905–1983) was always Dolores del Rio and not Dolly Rivers because she could never exorcise her skin tone or her Latina aura. Likewise, Anna May Wong could never be Anna May Wright or White because her Asian essence always resonated sharply and unyieldingly. She was portrayed as the Other with an obvious sexuality attached to her roles even in many of her smaller parts. Yet within these restrictive confines of how European Americans in Hollywood perceived Chinese America's most famous performer, some of her major roles evoked an agency, empowerment, and heroism that were reminiscent of Chinese heroines.

THE HEROINE IN CHINESE FOLKLIFE

It is a truism in China that without female protagonists, women of agency, and female warrior generals, Chinese history would simply be half-cooked rice. The Chinese heroine has always resonated in the minds and folklife of the common people, if not in the writings of Chinese male scholars and historians. There have been many periods in Chinese history when patriarchy proved to have only diminishing returns, during which Chinese women were able to move events and influence power. Some of these women may have died a martyr's death. But the fact that they lived and flourished demonstrates that the image of Chinese females as docile, deferring, and weak or seductive, licentious, murderous, and cruel, found in many European American and European film and plays, was merely a result of the stereotypical and racist musings of male writers and directors.

What many Hollywood male writers could not understand was that the heroic tradition in China evoked the qualities of conviction, courage, loyalty, honor, and generosity. As a knight-errant, the heroine or hero lived up to the ideals and values of selflessness in the protection of the disenfranchised, weak, and oppressed. This might be manifested in open rebellion against tyrannical overlords. Besides demonstrating bravery, honor, and loyalty, these warrior were also honest and upright with absolutely no regard for monetary gain.

Even Confucian scholars like Mencius were sensitive to oppressive ruler who terrorized the populace. Mencius called for the "right of rebellion." He contended that the common people have the right to kill the tyrants who rule them.[5] In Chinese literary tradition, the novel *Water Margin,* also known as *All Men Are Brothers,* involved a bandit who lived in 1121. Written during the Ming Dynasty (1368–1644), it was an inspiration to such famous rebels and revolutionaries as Hong Xiuquan, Sun Wen, and Mao Zedong. Scholars, writers, and countergovernment warriors were integral parts of Chinese history. This meant that heroism played a key role in Chinese society, with heroes and heroines the lifeblood of this ideal.

In China the most famous heroine was Hua Mulan. Living during the Sui Dynasty (581–618), Hua entered into battle at the age of twenty against the Turks disguised as a male warrior. During the twelve years in which she led wave after wave of battalions against the barbarians, Hua became one of the empire's most respected generals. It was only when she retired that Hua Mulan's gender was made public.[6]

During the Tang Dynasty (618–907), Chen Shuozhen from Zhejiang province led a people's rebellion against the Tang emperors in 653. Their expansionist military policy in Tibet and Korea placed a huge burden on the common people because of heavy conscription and taxation. With several thousand soldiers, she succeeded in taking over key cities and counties and proclaimed herself the Wen Jia emperor. The people who supported her looked upon Chen as a deity. Eventually the Tang forces quashed the rebellion, and this woman warrior was executed.[7] Although she died a martyr, Chen exhibited bravery and selflessness in the fight against imperial oppression.

In succeeding dynasties there were many Chinese heroines, including She Saihua, Mu Guiying, Qin Liangyu, and Hong Xuanjiao. The Song Dynasty (960–1279) was the backdrop to some of the most powerful female leaders, whose fortitude and military prowess far surpassed that of many male warriors. The women of the Yang family especially raised the bar of heroism in courage, generosity, honor, integrity, loyalty, military skills, and selflessness.

The Song heroines were She Saihua and her daughter-in-law, Mu Guiying. She Saihua, also known as Lady She, was a non-Han who rose to prominence on the battlefield. Her entry into the Yang family as the military companion and wife of General Yang Yanzhao centered around two quick hand-to-hand battles in which the general was soundly defeated. Her military prowess proclaimed, she offered Yang not only his life but also herself in matrimony. Although Yang initially could not bear the humiliation of marrying his conqueror, who was a "mountain barbarian," and chose death instead, he relented when he heard She's voice of reason. Since the Liao tribes were enemies of both She Saihua and Yang Yanzhao, her marriage proposal was based on combining their forces against a common enemy. She also proclaimed her great respect for Yang. They married and produced a family of seven sons and two daughters; many of their offspring entered the military profession.[8]

She Saihua was certainly proactive and clear in her goals, much like Anna May Wong as she navigated her cinematic career. But She's exploits were overshadowed by Mu Guiying, who married She's son, Yang Zongbao. Like She Saihua, Mu selected her husband on the battlefield. However, unlike her mother-in-law, who defeated her prospective bridegroom in combat, Mu was more compliant and merely taught Zongbao the limits of his mortality, not once but three times. She epitomized the heroine in Chinese history, and there are many stories of her heroism and military exploits. These tales of female wonder, empowerment, and agency were captured in such stories as "Mu Guiying Assumes Command," "Mu Guiying Goes into Battle," "Mu

Guiying Sets a Trap," and "Mu Guiying Destroys the Tianmen Army," which were handed down orally from generation to generation in the local folklore during the Song Dynasty.[9]

In the Ming period, Qin Liangyu of Shu (Sichuan province) gained a reputation for defending China against rebel insurgents and Manchu invaders. Along with her husband, Ma Qiansheng of the county of Shizhu, she commanded an army called the White Lance soldiers, who fought off rebel forces in Bozhou and Yongning and Manchu invaders in the northeast. When Ma was killed in battle, she became the sole leader of the Shizhu forces and was known as the "first queen of an aboriginal tribe" in Ming history. She later ascended to the rank of general by imperial edict, which stated: "Wherever Qin Liangyu travels, whether conferring with a border official or a great military or civil statesmen, she will be treated with the utmost courtesy."[10] From 1630 to 1644 she commanded troops that fought off Manchu barbarians from China's Central Plains, Liaodong, and key passes along the Great Wall. Even when the Manchus were on the verge of victory, Qin Liangyu's Shizhu county was the last defiant Chinese military holdout.[11]

The Manchu invaders were to rule China as the Qing Dynasty from 1644 to 1911. During that period sporadic rebellions by the indigenous population finally erupted into the *Taiping Tianguo* (Taiping Heavenly Kingdom). A Hakka woman, Hong Xuanjiao was the sister of Hong Xiuchuan, the leader of the Taiping rebellion that attempted to overthrow the Qing from 1850 to 1864. She led a women's army against the Qing and was such a dangerous sharpshooter that she could bring down Qing officers at a distance, earning her the nickname "Consort Xia, the Expert Sharpshooter." Accurate and deadly with rifles and side arms, she was also fearless in her leadership. Once she stormed the city walls of Zhenjiang alone and implored her troops to follow, which they did, to the consternation of the city's militia. When Hong Xiuchuan's Taiping rebellion was defeated in 1864, Hong Xuanjiao escaped into obscurity with her son, Xiao Youhe.[12]

Anna May Wong's film characters embodied many of the heroic traits these women possessed. In her role as Toy Sing, the wife of Chin Chow (played by Lon Chaney) in *Bits of Life* (1921), Anna May Wong kills her sleeping husband with a crucifix that penetrates his skull after she bangs it through the wall next to his bunk in the adjoining room. That Chin Chow was abusive and constantly beating Toy Sing, especially after she gave birth to a girl, sanctified the "right of rebellion" or the right to challenge authority on the part of the wife. It was, in fact, a heroic deed.

In such later films as *Piccadilly, The Flame of Love, Shanghai Express, Chu Chin Chow, Daughter of Shanghai, Dangerous to Know, King of Chinatown, Bombs*

Over Burma, and *The Lady from Chungking,* Wong would portray Chinese heroines. Her first leading role as a courageous, generous, honorable, loyal, and selfless heroine was in *The Toll of the Sea* as Lotus Flower.

THE TOLL OF THE SEA (1922)

Between her inaugural film as one of the three hundred lantern holders in *The
Red Lantern* (1919) and the female lead as Lotus Flower in *The Toll of the Sea,*
Wong performed in only four other movies. In *Dinty* and *The First Born,* she
continued her work as an extra without notice or credit. In *Shame* and *Bits of Life*
she was billed as Lotus Blossom and Toy Sing, respectively. Her rapid ascension
to a starring role in just three years was remarkable in a European America that
had an ingrained "Yellowface" theatrical and cinematic cultural tradition.

Although she made no impression on the *New York Times* and *Variety* film
reviewers of *Shame* and *Bits of Life,*[13] Wong's performances certainly impressed
Chester M. Franklin (1890–1954), who was scouting for a Chinese lead for the
female role of Lotus Flower in *The Toll of the Sea.* Since a tightly knit fraternity
of movie directors controlled Hollywood, no doubt Marshall Neilan
(1891–1958), the director of *Dinty* and *Bits of Life,* had praised Wong's performance in both films to Franklin. The role of Toy Sing in *Bits of Life* had
been especially written by Neilan with Wong in mind. At seventeen years old,
just one year removed from a life as a tenth grader at Los Angeles High School,
the world seemed to be at Wong's feet, with a contract to play Lotus Flower
in Frances Marion's (1888–1973) screenplay of *The Toll of the Sea.* Although
Marion was excited about working in the new medium of color, she admitted
that this story "was practically the stepdaughter of Madame Butterfly."[14]

With an extensive operatic, theatrical, literary, and cinematic pedigree de-
scending from the likes of Gilbert and Sullivan's production of *The Mikado*
(1885), John Luther Long's *Madame Butterfly* (1896), Pierre Loti's novel entitled
Madame Chrysantheme (1887), Andre Messager's opera also called *Madame
Chrysantheme* (1893), Giacomo Puccini's opera *Madame Butterfly* (1904), and
Paramount's *Madame Butterfly* (1915), Chester Franklin's *The Toll of the Sea*
could have taken the usual way out and cast a "Yellowface" actress to play the
lead female role of Lotus Flower.[15] But bucking tradition was one of Franklin's
traits, and he placed a decidedly Chinese spin on the film when he not only
substituted China for Japan but also hired actual Chinese performers to play
the Chinese roles. Even the two Gossips, played by Etta Lee and Ming Young,
were clearly Asian or Asian American. That *The Toll of the Sea* was also in color

played a crucial part in casting real Chinese actors. Frances Marion, in fact, wrote the story with Anna May Wong in mind.[16]

While "Faraday" China was juxtaposed against the emerging power of European America over Asia in *The Toll of the Sea,* the setting was specifically in Hong Kong. Under the photographic direction of J. A. Ball, cinematographer Ray Rennahan (1896–1980) shot a variety of red and green visuals in the oceanside city of Santa Monica, California. The opening sequence of thundering ocean waves, unfortunately, was more evocative of west coast California and even west coast Vancouver Island than of the deep-water harbor port of Hong Kong, where crashing waves would have disrupted the fleet of cargo ships entering that southern Chinese city.

Despite the differences between the California and Hong Kong exterior locales, the story in *The Toll of the Sea* closely paralleled that of *Madame Butterfly.* In Paramount's version, B. F. Pinkerton (played by Marshall Neilan), of the gunboat *Abraham Lincoln,* exuded the maximum brutality and power of a superior, masculine military European America over Madame Butterfly, played by "America's sweetheart," Mary Pickford (1892–1979), who represented a totally feminine and racially inferior Japan. In the 1922 Chinese version of *Madame Butterfly,* Wong's Lotus Flower in *The Toll of the Sea* personifies a thoroughly emasculated, inferior, and debased feminine China that had been raped, possessed, exploited, and abandoned by Allen Carver, played by Kenneth Harlan (1895–1967). He represents the absolute power of a male European America that plundered with impunity and without remorse. In 1922 *The Toll of the Sea* was the ultimate political allegory, pitting a China attempting to regroup and survive with its abundant natural wealth and massive labor resources against a United States expressing its Manifest Destiny to acquire all that it could on a global scale. China was its first significant prey.

With the end of World War I and the resulting devastation in Europe, the United States had taken its first leap into the exalted stratosphere of world-class imperial power. Coming into the war late in 1917, European America sustained minimal commercial loss and in fact was able to maximize its global economic ascendancy. While at war the British, French, and German film industries had given way to the European military effort. Their cinemas collapsed under the weight of wartime exigencies. Consequently, European America's film industry prospered enormously while the overseas competition either lay dormant or withered away.[17]

When *The Toll of the Sea* was being shot in 1922, in China warlords with names like the Christian General (Feng Yuxiang), the dog meat general (Zhang Zongchang), and the Model Governor (Yan Xishan) were like locusts spreading, devouring, and suffocating all the many human facets of the nation that stood in their path to power.[18] The country's instability and powerlessness began with the defeat of the Qing Dynasty by Western imperialists in 1842. Its downfall was later exacerbated by rebellions and revolutions fueled by overseas Chinese money. Foreign armies, merchants, and missionaries eventually became ensconced in all of the major institutions, especially banking and transportation. China was indeed a semicolonial nation. This contrasted poignantly with a European America that was ready to assume a powerful presence in the world and to demonstrate that it was a fast-emerging nation to be reckoned with. Its arrogance and capriciousness were especially evident in the character of Allen Carver in the movie. He embodied the legitimization of a European American rule abroad that exulted maleness, whiteness, and consumer capitalism.

The Story

The Toll of the Sea is ostensibly a one-sided tale of the rape of Lotus Flower, an innocent, naive Chinese girl, by Allen Carver, a mature European American merchant. In 1922 Anna May Wong was seventeen years old, but she looked much younger in the film, perhaps fourteen. Even in the United States during the 1920s, sexual intercourse between a mature male and a girl as young as fourteen or even seventeen would be considered statutory rape in many American states. This would have been punishable by a lengthy jail term.

Compared to Cecil B. DeMille's *The Cheat* (1915), in which Asian men personified in Sessue Hayakawa's (1889–1973) character were depicted as depraved and sexually corrupted monsters who attempted to rape European American women,[19] Allen Carver was more diabolical and heartless. He not only raped the virginal Lotus Flower but produced a biracial male heir, Little Allen, played by Baby Moran. In the conventional Orientalist history of exoticism in the United States, the "rape narratives pose the danger that the 'pure' but hopelessly fragile and childlike white woman will be 'ruined' by contact with the dark villain."[20] Here the debauchery of "yellowness" prevailed. In *The Toll of the Sea,* the "pure but hopelessly fragile and childlike" female was a "little girl" of Chinese origin who was "ruined by contact with the *light* villain." In this case, the debauchery of "whiteness" took center stage.

The sadism (represented by Allen Carver) inflicted by European America on the politically fragmented and socially dysfunctional China (exemplified by Lotus Flower), however, did not end with Carver's rape and impregnation of Lotus Flower. Without divorcing or even attempting to annul his marriage to his Chinese wife, Carver audaciously introduces his second wife, Elsie Carver,[21] played by Beatrice Bentley, to Lotus Flower. By marrying a second time without divorce, he had certainly committed bigamy. But Elsie did not seem to mind, and in fact knew exactly what the situation was. In this scene, the titles stated that "In China—Allen's wife had heard the true story of the little girl who was waiting—and she felt that it was his duty to tell Lotus Flower why he could never return to her." This sense of "duty and honor" was condescending and disturbingly pathological. It could not hide the fact that Lotus Flower had been raped and impregnated. Now she was to be abandoned. Upon hearing that Allen Carver had married for a second time, Lotus Flower replies ironically: "You mean—you're not my honorable husband!" The words of abandonment echoed those pronounced earlier by one of the Gossips, played by Honolulu-born Etta Lee (1906–1956). After Allen Carver has departed to San Francisco, she sarcastically warns Lotus Flower that "Tis true! I have already been forgotten by four faithful American husbands."

What may have been even more compelling for Wong about Carver's introduction of his "second" wife was the fact that in Chinese America, when *The Toll of the Sea* premiered on November 26, 1922, at the Rialto Theater in New York, there were many "second" wives such as Wong's mother, Gon Toy Lee, whose husband's first wife remained in China. *The Toll of the Sea* was merely a cinematic portrayal of a very real situation for Chinese American women.

Realizing that her European American husband is simply abandoning her for his "second" wife in the new world, Lotus Flower is obviously despondent. However, according to the narration written by Frances Marion, women understand the failings of the wayward male: "The sympathy and understanding between good women the world over, brought Elsie back to the garden and led Lotus Flower to tell all." On meeting Elsie Carver, Lotus Blossom sarcastically states: "I'm very happy that honorable Mr. Allen brings his sweet wife to see me." As a Chinese woman, saving face now became Lotus Flower's raison d'être in light of Allen Carver's betrayal, treachery, and abandonment.

But the sadistic coup de grace inflicted by the Carvers is Elsie's intention to deprive Lotus Flower of her male child. Understanding the sanctity of the family, Lotus Flower gives up her boy so that he can live with a family containing a mother and a father. She pitifully remarks: "I have blessed my son with the name of Honorable Allen Carver. You will take him please, and keep him for always." This heroic gesture no doubt was accentuated by Lotus Flower's shame in admitting a European American into her extended family and being the mother of a biracial child. The physical and emotional liaison with Allen Carver also disrupted an otherwise stable and harmonious Chinese family unit.

The heroism, martyrdom, and self-sacrifice of Lotus Flower were finalized when she cries out: "Oh Sea, now that life has been emptied, I come to pay my great debt to you." In the wake of a sordid relationship that could only lead nowhere, Lotus Flower took her own life. In contrast to Allen and Elsie Carvers' sadism, amorality, and pathological inclinations, her suicide was less an admission of failure (as was the case of Madame Butterfly in a Japan that condoned *seppuku*) than a selfless act that personified self-actualization and a conscious act of empowerment that gave Lotus Flower control over her own destiny. Her death was not simply a reaction to Allen Carver's debauchery and treachery but a vivid realization of her familial obligations as a mother and a Chinese woman. It was indeed a powerful statement of nobility and agency, even if it meant death, because Lotus Flower was willing to accept the consequences of her misdeeds with a foreigner. Her heroism included not only her courage in defying convention and her generosity and selflessness in giving up Baby Allen but also her honor in remaining loyal to Allen Carver even in the face of his betrayal and abandonment.

Technicolor Movie

In addition to scoring her first starring role in *The Toll of the Sea,* Wong was in a project with a two-color additive system that produced Hollywood's first Technicolor film.[22] This was the "Technicolor Process Number Two" invented by Herbert Kalmus (1881–1963). Supervised by Kalmus's former student, Dr. Leonard J. Troland, this technique was based on the film being

> photographed by the substractive process, which uses a beam splitter prism camera, making red and green exposures on two frames of film simultaneously, with one frame being inverted. The film moved through the camera, two frames at a time, using twice as much film as would be needed for a regular black and white feature. Two prints were made from the negative—one for each color—utilizing stock of half normal thickness. These two pieces of film were then cemented together and dyed complementary colors.[23]

The fact that Kalmus's firm, Technicolor, produced *The Toll of the Sea* rather than a Hollywood production house demonstrated that private industry was willing to move the boundaries of scientific discovery and innovation at its own expense.

With a general release by Metro in many theaters across the United States only in 1923 because of the paucity of prints when the picture was completed, *The Toll of the Sea,* the first Technicolor film manufactured with the "Technicolor Process Number Two," was a resounding success, grossing more than $250,000, with Kalmus's company receiving a net of $165,000.[24] Film critics were as enthusiastic as the general public. Some hailed its innovation. The *Film Daily* raved that "the tones are clear, unconfused and the colors do not jump. They have shown good judgement in the selection of colors and there is no harsh mixing."[25] The *New York Times* remarked:

> Here are settings just waiting for reproduction in colors, and in them are Chinese people whose costumes of elaborate and finely embroidered silks and severely plain cotton permit richness and the effective variety of contrast. Also, the story has been photographed outdoors. Even its few interior scenes seem to have been made in the best results with the color camera.[26]

Variety's review stressed the color of the performers:

> So, it was a color process Technicolor gave to the filming that seemed to run quite short of the regulation five reels. Nothing in a moving picture can rise superior to the story. Coloring never will, never has, and doesn't here. The coloring runs without streaks, the camera catching the natural colors apparently, although what seemed something of a freak in this process is that the pallid color given to the complexion of the Chinese extended to the faces of the Americans as well. Perhaps white cannot be taken by this camera with its pallid shade enveloping all faces, white being open to question as a color or for coloring in specific connection. But it was a noticeable defect in the coloring scheme.[27]

Thus "the expensive use of color processes to differentiate nonwhite people from Anglo-Saxon actors was hardly coincidental."[28] Bankrolled by Herbert Kalmus and produced by Russian-born Joseph M. Schenck (1878–1961), *The Toll of the Sea,* with its emphasis on color, needed performers of color to contrast with performers of "noncolor." There was an obvious need to contrast "whiteness" with "yellowness" and not have a European American performer in "Yellowface" trying to contrast with "whiteness." Because *The Toll of the Sea* was Technicolor's major experiment in the production of a color film, Kalmus had conservatively budgeted for a short feature. But cinematographer Ray Rennahan had shot enough footage for a five-reel film, so Kalmus decided to edit it into a longer full-length feature. At silent speed, the film would run for more than one hour.

Reviews

That many Americans of all races saw *The Toll of the Sea* meant that Anna May Wong's star power was developing even though she had landed the lead because the movie was filmed in Technicolor. Film critics were especially upbeat about Wong's performance. The *Film Daily* declared that "the theme is really a very sympathetic one made doubly interesting and sincere by the splendid work of Anna May Wong. She is a clever little actress and displays fine emotional ability."[29] *Variety's* review began by castigating the film for "watering the stock of others" by copying the story of *Madame Butterfly.* It continued:

> Here it is, no different, other than in the locale, the nationality and a baby boy with the Chinese girl-wife rescuing her husband from the sea as he floated in at the opening of the picture, to win and lose him as he forgets his chink wife, the baby to come and the sea.
>
> Someone recognized this story needed something else, even beyond the extraordinary fine playing of Anna May Wong, who is an exquisite crier without glycerine.[30]

The *New York Times* was laudatory, exclaiming:

> Anna May Wong [is] naturally Chinese and exactly easily natural, even in her most tortured scenes. As the trusting child of a carelessly considered race whose roving American husband, like the Captain of "Mme. Butterfly" returns to his home for a "real" wife, Miss Wong stirs in the spectator all the sympathy her part calls for, and she never repels one by an excess of theatrical "feeling." She has a difficult role, a role that is botched nine times out of ten, but here hers is the tenth performance. Completely unconscious of the camera, with able pantomimic accuracy, she makes the deserted little Lotus Flower a genuinely appealing, understandable figure. She should be seen again and often on the screen.[31]

Thousands did see Anna May Wong again and often in her starring role in *The Toll of the Sea.* But in 1923 they were treated to her performances only in supporting roles. She played Rose Li in *Drifting* and the honky tonk girl in *Thundering Dawn.* While deciding what her next move would be after her triumph in *The Toll of the Sea,* Wong received an offer she could not refuse.

NOTES

1. At five feet, seven inches, Anna May Wong was a formidable contrast in height to a number of European American actresses at that time: Dolores Costello (five feet, four inches) in *Old San Francisco* (1927), Joan Crawford (five feet, four inches) in *Across to Singapore* (1928), Myrna Loy (five feet, six inches) in *The Crimson City* (1928), Mar-

lene Dietrich (five feet, two inches) in *Shanghai Express* (1932), and June Clyde (five feet, four inches) in A *Study in Scarlet* (1933).

2. Neil Okrent, "Right Place, Wong Time," *Los Angeles Magazine* (May 1990): 88; Geraldine Gan, *Lives of Notable Asian Americans* (New York: Chelsea House, 1996), 86; Helen Zia and Susan B. Gall, eds., *Notable Asian Americans* (Detroit: Gale Research, 1995), 414.

3. John Springer and Jack Hamilton, *Faces Then: Stars and Starlets of the 1930s* (Secaucus, N.J.: Citadel Press, 1974), 338.

4. Wong, cited in Michel Mok, "Anna May Wong, with Chinese Courtesy Makes a Newspaper Photographer Blush," *New York Post,* 26 April 1939, 15.

5. Frederick W. Mote, *Intellectual Foundations of China* (New York: McGraw-Hill, 1989), 50–51.

6. *Lady in the Picture: Folklore* (Beijing: Chinese Literature Press, 1993), 221–27. Although Hua Mulan was generally known to have lived during the Sui Dynasty, she was referred to as early as the Northern Dynasties (386–581). Li Nianpei, *Old Tales of China* (Singapore: Graham Brash, 1981).

7. Xiao Li et al., eds., *Yingxiang zhongguo lishi de nuren (A Hundred Women Who Influenced the History of China)* (Guangzhou: [Guangdong renmin chuban she] Guangdong People's Press, 1995), 164; John K. Fairbank, *China: Tradition and Transformation* (Boston: Houghton Mifflin, 1978), 97–99.

8. Cai Zhuozhi, *100 Celebrated Chinese Women,* trans. Kate Foster (Singapore: Asiapac Books, 1994), 166.

9. Cai, *100 Celebrated Chinese Women,* 167.

10. Imperial edict, cited in Cai, *100 Celebrated Chinese Women,* 167.

11. Cai, *100 Celebrated Chinese Women,* 167.

12. Cai, *100 Celebrated Chinese Women,* 167.

13. For *Shame,* see the *New York Times,* 1 August 1921, 6, and *Variety,* 5 August 1921, 25. For *Bits of Life,* see the *New York Times,* 17 October 1921, and *Variety,* 21 October 1921, 35. Although Anna May Wong was billed in these films, there was no mention of her performance.

14. Frances Marion, cited in Cari Beauchamp, *Without Lying Down: Frances Marion and the Powerful Women of Early Hollywood* (New York: Scribner, 1997), 143.

15. Nick Browne, "The Undoing of the Other Woman: Madame Butterfly in the Discourse of American Orientalism," in *The Birth of Whiteness: Race and the Emergence of U.S. Cinema,* ed. Daniel Bernardi (New Brunswick, N.J.: Rutgers University Press, 1996), 227–28. Other versions of Madame Butterfly, located in Vietnam, were *The Lady from Yesterday* (1985), David Henry Hwang's *M. Butterfly* (1988), and Claude Michel Schonberg's *Miss Saigon* (1991). For critical analyses of these performances, see Renee E. Tajima, "Lotus Blossoms Don't Bleed: Images of Asian Woman," in *Making Waves, An Anthology of Writings By and About Asian American Women,* ed. Diane Yen-Mei Wong (Boston: Beacon Press, 1989), 311; Marina Heung, "The Family Romance of Orientalism: From Madame Butterfly to Indochine," in *Visions of the East: Orientalism in Film,* ed. Matthew Bernstein and Gaylyn Studlar (New Brunswick, N.J.: Rutgers University Press), 158–83.

16. Beauchamp, *Without Lying Down,* 143.

17. Gina Marchetti, "Tragic and Transcendent Love in the Forbidden City," in Bernardi, *Birth of Whiteness,* 268–70; Deniz Gokturk, "How Modern Is It? Moving Images of America in Early German Cinema," in *Hollywood in Europe: Experiences of a Cultural Hegemony,* ed. David W. Ellwood and Rob Kroes (Amsterdam: VU University Press, 1994), 50; David W. Ellwood, "Introduction: Historical Methods and Approaches," in Ellwood and Kroes, *Hollywood in Europe,* 2.

18. For warlord history, see Anthony B. Chan, *The Western Armaments Trade in Warlord China, 1920–1928* (Vancouver: University of British Columbia Press, 1982).

19. Diane Carson, "Cultural Screens: Teaching Asian and Asian American Images," in *Shared Differences: Multicultural Media and Practical Pedagogy,* ed. Diane Carson and Lester D. Freidman (Urbana: University of Illinois Press, 1995), 169.

20. Gina Marchetti, *Romance and the "Yellow Peril": Race, Sex, and Discursive Strategies in Hollywood Fiction* (Berkeley: University of California Press, 1993), 8.

21. In the *Variety* review of *The Toll of the Sea* (1 December 1922, 35), the wife was named Barbara Carver. In the film, she was called Elsie.

22. *The Gulf Between* (1917) was actually the first Technicolor film with the "additive color." The color was "added" by tinted filters on the projectors. This was not a success. Richard W. Haines, *Technicolor Movies: The History of Dye Transfer Printing* (Jefferson, N.C.: McFarland, 1993), 2–3. The origin of the color film can be traced to the Pathe Company, which used stencil coloring rendered by hand as early as 1896. Anthony Slide, "*The Toll of the Sea,*" in *Magill's Survey of Cinema, Silent Films,* vol. 2, ed. Frank N. Magill (Englewood Cliffs, N.J.: Salem Press, 1982), 1145.

23. Slide, "*Toll of the Sea,*" 1143; *1920s,* at http://www. technicolor.com/about us/ his1920.html (accessed 31 July 2000); Haines, *Technicolor Movies,* 41–42.

24. Haines, *Technicolor Movies,* 6.

25. "Decidedly the Best Thing That Has Been Accomplished in Colors," *The Film Daily,* 3 December 1922, 7.

26. "*The Toll of the Sea,*" *New York Times,* 27 November 1922, 18.

27. "*The Toll of the Sea,*" *Variety,* 1 December 1922, 35.

28. Sumiko Higashi, "Touring the Orient with Lafcadio Hearn and Cecil B. DeMille: Highbrow versus Lowbrow in a Consumer Culture," in Bernardi, *Birth of Whiteness,* 342; Sumiko Higashi, *Cecil B. DeMille and American Culture: The Silent Era* (Berkeley: University of California Press, 1994), 184.

29. *Film Daily,* 3 December 1922, 7.

30. "*The Toll of the Sea,*" *Variety,* 35.

31. "*The Toll of the Sea,*" *New York Times,* 18.

TWELVE

THE THIEF OF BAGDAD (1924)

A t the age of eighteen, Anna May Wong received the first cinematic offer that was to profoundly influence her film career. It came from Douglas Fairbanks (1893–1939), one of Hollywood's hottest box office properties. Although it was not the lead female role, being in a film with a Hollywood megastar and a blockbuster budget guaranteed global exposure for the woman who would become the most famous actress in Chinese America.

By 1923 when Douglas Fairbanks first began his production of *The Thief of Bagdad,* he had reached superstardom along with his Toronto-born wife, Mary Pickford. In 1921 they were earning $19,230.77 per week.[1] Their celebrity was so entrenched in Hollywood that their every movement was chronicled in fan magazines and newspapers. Even their house, Pickfair in Beverly Hills, was a major tourist attraction. Weekends were especially congested, with concession stands and hawkers of hot dogs calling out to the onlookers outside the gate of their residence.[2] People strained to "catch another glimpse of the golden-haired movie queen and her d'Artagnan-like husband."[3] By 1924 Fairbanks epitomized adventure and swashbuckling action in such blockbusters as *The Mark of Zorro* (1920), *The Three Musketeers* (1921), and *Robin Hood* (1922).

Bankrolled by his own studio, United Artists, Douglas Fairbanks spent fourteen months producing *The Thief of Bagdad.* Designed by William

Cameron Menzies (1896–1957), the sets were so elaborate that audiences marveled at the "palace and city completed with shiny cupolas and towers, surreal bridges and staircases. The floors were glazed and the buildings were reflected on them. Walls were painted silver to make the city seem to float like a balloon, literally to drift off the ground among the clouds."[4] With a budget of close to $2 million, Fairbanks's "Orientalist" epic was *the* extravaganza film in which any aspiring movie star desired to be seen. Luckily for Fairbanks, his director, Raoul Walsh (1887–1980), was an affable collaborator. Walsh remembered that Fairbanks "liked everything. I'd go through it and say, 'Douglas, how do you feel about doing it this way or that way and doing it over here?' He'd say, 'That's great, let's go.'"[5]

Fortunately for Wong, her Lotus Flower had been such a sensation that Hollywood movers and shakers, including Douglas Fairbanks, took notice. But the new deal was not a straightforward sign and play contract; Fairbanks had to write a letter to Sam Sing Wong for permission to hire his daughter. Despite the publicity suggesting that Sam Sing Wong was opposed to Anna May's movie career, he was not opposed to Fairbanks casting his daughter as the Mongol spy and infiltrator draped in a bikini-like costume.[6]

During the early negotiations between her father and Fairbanks, Wong, at eighteen years old, was conscious of her emerging star image. More significantly, she was also very confident and willing to protest any slipups regarding her publicity or even the meaning of her Chinese name.

The initial advertisement by *The Thief of Bagdad* publicist stated that Liu Tsong meant "Two Yellow Widows" rather than "Frosted Willows." Of course, the full Chinese name of Anna May Wong was Wong Liu Tsong, with the surname Wong (or Huang) meaning "Yellow." Thus, the formal translation of Wong Liu Tsong was "Yellow Frosted Willow." Because of the publicist's inattentiveness, Fairbanks had to intervene to correct this misunderstanding.[7] But the fact that Wong protested immediately to such a megastar as Douglas Fairbanks was an indication that she was willing to put up with neither insults nor begging and unwilling to fit into the stereotype of Asian women as docile and deferring imposed by European American males.

ANNA MAY WONG'S ROLE

Contrary to the conventional view that Wong, as *The Thief of Bagdad's* Mongol spy and infiltrator, "unwittingly popularized a common Dragon Lady social type: treacherous women who are partners in crime with men of their own kind,"[8] her role as a slave to an Arabic princess portrayed strength, power, and intelligence. This was abundantly clear even though her two-piece scanty attire was exotic in its foreignness and her role was erotic in its gesture and body language to a predominantly European American audience. She stood out in contrast to the other characters in *The Thief of Bagdad,* an Orientalist epic full of outlandish and racist stereotypes like Muslims as agile thieves, fat, lazy, and spineless princes, or superstitious princesses; Africans as sword carriers; and Asians (Mongols) as diabolical, amoral, and cunning criminals.

Wong's self-confidence radiates in all of her scenes. This is especially the case in the scenes with the princess, played in a languid and contrived manner by the European American actor Julanne Johnston (1900–1988). Wong's role is performed with an intensity that is hard, robust, and alert, whereas Johnston's princess is soft, weak, and seemingly always in a daze. While Wong's vitality sizzles in every scene, Johnston's princess is demure and docile, waiting to be rescued.

In contrast to the other handmaidens of the princess, Wong's mannerisms and attire present the Asian woman as alluring and erotic. Her sexuality is transmitted through her body movements. Her large, penetrating eyes are certainly vivid and direct when set against those of the lethargic princess. But in comparison to the other two women in the film—the Slave of the Sand Board, performed by the Asian American Etta Lee, who was one of the Gossips in *The Toll of the Sea,* and the Slave of the Lute, played by another Asian American, Winter Blossom—Wong's Mongol spy glows in her uncompromising sexual intensity and dynamism. It was almost as if Wong's role was a stark repudiation of her as the naive and innocent Lotus Flower in *The Toll of the Sea.* Wong's part embodies such a streetwise and consummate survivor that her characterization in *The Thief of Bagdad* seems to be almost an apprenticeship and a dress rehearsal for Hui Fei in *Shanghai Express,* one of the most memorable and sophisticated parts in her career.

In creating the most compelling female role in *The Thief of Bagdad,* Wong brought to her character an absolute toughness and power that transcends her servile position as the Mongol spy and infiltrator, especially in the film's major defining scene, where she poisons the princess. At the forefront of a potential conquest of Bagdad by the Mongol prince, played by the leading Shakespearean actor in Japan, Kamiyama Sojin,[9] Wong's Mongol slave is actually a fearless, loyal, proactive, and self-directed spy in the employ of the Mongol empire.

Since the Mongol prince's magic apple would revive the princess from a permanent death, Wong's character has successfully infiltrated the palace walls and by her actions proves to be a highly successful spy. The poisoning of the princess is part of a deliberate and elaborate plot. Its purpose is not to bring about immediate death but to postpone the final departure from life. Since spies or intelligence officers are usually sent on missions because of their courage, ruthlessness, intellectual dexterity, and training in espionage, Wong's skimpy costume is merely a clever Mongol disguise for the real character. Even her overt eroticism as the Mongol slave is not meant to seduce but rather to camouflage. Moreover, the intention of Wong's character to control her slave owner through poison is an overt attempt at gaining her freedom. The fact that this mini-revolt against Arabic slavery is eventually foiled by the thief, with the princess and the thief living happily ever after, reinforces the system of slavery and its imposition by a monarchical ruling elite. Wong's actions against slavery are heroic acts against an oppressive system of human deprivation.

Although the Mongol prince's machinations, seizing Bagdad and marrying the princess, are eventually thwarted by Douglas Fairbanks's clever thief, the fate of Wong's Mongol spy and infiltrator remains in limbo. Just before the thief and the princess fly off on the magic carpet, Sojin's Mongol prince and his Counselor, played by Tokyo-born K. Nambu (b. 1890), are captured and strung up by their hair. Wong's Mongol slave, however, remains at large. Whether or not Douglas Fairbanks was planning a sequel to *The Thief of Bagdad,* with Wong's Mongol slave reappearing, only Hollywood's major male superstar would have known.

What *was* well known at the time of *The Thief of Bagdad*'s world premiere on March 17, 1924, at New York's Liberty Theater was that Douglas Fairbanks paid Morris Gest $3,000 per week as the impresario for *The Thief of Bagdad.*[10] His job was to turn the film into a theatrical extravaganza, a moneymaking live event. He was to provide a memorable "Arabian" atmosphere that along with the film itself would captivate and mesmerize the audience.

By 8:20 P.M. the Liberty Theater was already sold out, with hordes of moviegoers pushing their way into the theater's lobby. The audience was met not only by the city's police, who were hired to assist people to their seats, but also by the "beating of drums, the droning of voices in dirge like songs, and the odor of incense that emanated from the theater."[11] During the intermission, "ushers in Arabian attire made a brave effort to bear cups of Turkish coffee to the women in the audience."[12]

This stunning reception for Douglas Fairbanks's *The Thief of Bagdad* was everything Morris Gest had hoped for. After New York, the impresario extraordinaire declared:

> Later it will be given in other cities and in cases where it is impossible to find a theater large enough to accommodate the crowds I plan to present it in a tent, capable of holding 15,000 persons for a single presentation, the whole production going forth by special train. I will thereby reach great crowds which an ordinary theater cannot hold.

This is especially true in Russia where they have hardly any theaters, and where I will present the Fairbanks film in an American tent in Moscow and other big cities. These presentations will follow those in London and Paris.[13]

In addition to its screenings in Moscow, London, and Paris, *The Thief of Bagdad* was the longest running American film in Berlin. By January 23, 1926, it was playing in forty-five theaters across Germany, with an exclusive one-month engagement at Berlin's Capital Theater.[14] Germany's filmmakers and stars flocked to the movie. While Douglas Fairbanks's acrobatics and extravagant sets dazzled an international audience, German directors like Paul Leni (1885–1929) and Richard Eichberg (1888–1953) took particular notice of the woman who played the Mongol spy.

The Thief of Bagdad was such an extravaganza that even British royalty demanded and received a private showing just after its New York debut. In June 1924 the European premiere was screened at a private showing in Lord and Lady Mountbatten's London Brock House. As cousins of the king and queen, they invited the Prince of Wales, the Duke and Duchess of York, Prince Henry, and Prince George from the royal family. Others at this festive film evening included the Greek princesses Margarita and Theodore, Prince Serge Obolensky, Earl and Countess of Carnarvon, Lord Ivor Spencer Churchill, Lady Alexandra Curzon, Sir Robert Horne, Lord Younger, Sir Felix and Lady Helen Cassel, Brigadier General Trotter, a Major Metcalfe, Mrs. Alice Astor, and Mrs. Cornelius Vanderbilt and her daughter.[15]

REVIEWS

Despite its budget of close to $2 million, *The Thief of Bagdad* was unable to outdraw Douglas Fairbanks's equally popular *Robin Hood*. "Its played and earned figures were less than other Fairbanks films that cost half as much. The star was overwhelmed by his own production."[16] Raoul Walsh was also overwhelmed, especially after the picture was released. Not only did *The Thief of Bagdad* resurrect Walsh's flagging career as a director, but his work earned him a five-picture contract at Paramount.[17] While Walsh and Fairbanks in fact may have been delighted and even mesmerized by their own handiwork, film critics were uniformly enthralled.

Effusive in its praise, *Variety* wondered "why someone else did not think of it before is one of those things that lend to motion pictures that unknown quality—what they will develop. Doubtless others have prognosticated the production of a work of such caliber upon realizing the maze of detail, effort and executive brilliance."[18] In *Motion Picture World, C. S. Sewell* was almost speechless. He wrote that "words are weak, pitiful things when it comes to attempting to give any idea of the wondrous beauty, the spectacular magnificence of the marvelous mechanical effects in the new Douglas Fairbanks picture, *The Thief of Bagdad*. Nothing like it has been attempted before. It is an absolute departure in screen entertainment, a journey into untrodden fields."[19]

The *New York Times* was also wildly enthusiastic, especially about the visuals and innovations. Calling the film an "Arabian Nights Satire," its reviewer announced:

> It is a picture which reminds one of Barrie, of Kipling, of Hans Andersen, and for the time that one is beholding the miraculous feats of the photographer, the remarkable sets and costumes that are a feast for the eye, one forgets all about the humming, buzzing, brilliantly lighted Broadway, and for the time being, if you will, becomes a child again.
>
> It is an entrancing picture, wholesome and beautiful, deliberate but compelling, a feat of motion picture art which has never been equaled and one which itself will enthrall persons time and again. You can see this film and look forward to seeing it a second time.[20]

The *Film Daily* critic was equally enamored of *The Thief of Bagdad,* calling it "probably the most magnificent production of this kind ever made." But he did warn readers that even though Fairbanks was in most of the scenes, he and the cast were backed by a "very thin story." As for the cast itself, the reviewer abruptly wrote: "Doug, practically the whole show. Little for others to do. Snitz Edwards pleasing as his evil associate. Julanne Johnston pretty as unimportant heroine. Anna May Wong good. Others don't matter."[21]

REVIEWS OF ANNA MAY WONG

While the *Film Daily* called Wong's portrayal simply "good," *Variety* stated that "Anna May Wong as the little slave girl who is a spy for the Mongol Prince, proved herself a fine actress."[22] If Wong, at five feet, seven inches was "little," then Douglas Fairbanks, at five feet, six inches, could be described as "diminutive." The *New York Times* merely mentioned that "Anna May Wong impersonated the Mongol slave."[23]

Despite the reviewers' lack of notice of Anna May Wong's performance, *The Thief of Bagdad* brought Chinese America's first major movie star to the attention of a global audience. It was the first far-reaching, defining event of her cinematic career. Certainly her starring role as Lotus Flower in *The Toll of the Sea* was innovative, if only for its Technicolor technique. However, the fact that *The Thief of Bagdad* had not only a mammoth budget that brought talented builders, cinematographers, designers, impresario, and publicists together but also one of Hollywood's most popular and charismatic male superstars, who already had a box office string of commercial successes, meant that Wong was playing in one of Hollywood's most glamorous productions. She could not help but be noticed as a creative performer with her own unique interpretation. She was always ready to envelop herself in her roles and able to "counterfeit various emotions"[24] not her own.

After the release of *The Thief of Bagdad,* Wong signed for three minor roles, as Zira in the *Fortieth Door* (1924), as Keok in *The Alaskan* (1924), and as Tiger Lily in *Peter Pan* (1924). The following year was spent fending off unscrupulous promoters and developing her "speaking roles," dancing techniques, and singing style at such venues as the Orpheum Theater in San Francisco and with the Cosmic Production Company as it traveled across the Midwest in Kansas, Nebraska, and Iowa.[25] The year 1925 was a vast learning experience for Wong as she began to plot her career along the lines of acting, dancing, and singing in both theater and film. It was becoming apparent to Chinese America's first major film actress that her career was her sole business and that whatever it took to make it successful, she would do it. Working in legitimate theaters and on the vaudeville circuit gave her the experience and confidence to take on innovative developments in the film industry. If it meant working in "talkies," she would do that, too.

BACK TO HOLLYWOOD

With the 1925 vaudeville experience behind her, Anna May Wong returned to screen work in 1926 in small "Orientalist" parts like Nan Lo in *Fifth Avenue,* Ohtai in *A Trip to Chinatown,* Oneta in *The Desert's Toll,* and a lead role in *The Silk Bouquet,* also known as *The Dragon Horse.* In 1927 she appeared in seven nonstarring roles, and she was in three Hollywood films in 1928. When her last 1928 film, *Chinatown Charlie,* was being released by First National, Wong was already in Europe with a solid five-picture contract with Richard Eichberg. These would all be starring roles. But the film that caused a sensation in the English-speaking world was *Piccadilly* (1929).

NOTES

1. Booton Herndon, *Mary Pickford and Douglas Fairbanks* (New York: W. W. Norton, 1977), 216.

2. Jeffrey Charles and Jill Watts, "(Un)Real Estate: Marketing Hollywood in the 1910s and 1920s," in *Hollywood Goes Shopping*, ed. David Desser and Garth S. Jowett (Minneapolis: University of Minnesota Press, 2000), 263.

3. "Police Clear Jam at Movie Premiere," *New York Times,* 19 March 1924, 19.

4. Rob Edelman, *The Thief of Bagdad,* in *Magill's Survey of Cinema, Silent Films,* vol. 13, ed. Frank N. Magill (Englewood Cliffs, N.J.: Salem Press, 1982), 1109–10.

5. Raoul Walsh, cited in Peter Bogdanovich, *Who the Devil Made It* (New York: Alfred A. Knopf, 1997), 164.

6. "Troubles of a Bagdad Thief," *New York Times,* 19 March 1924, 19.

7. "Troubles of a Bagdad Thief," 19.

8. Yen Le Espiritu, *Asian American Women and Men: Labor, Laws, and Love* (Thousand Oaks, Calif.: Sage Publications, 1997), 94.

9. "'Thief of Bagdad' Is Great Film Drama," *Seattle Post Intelligencer,* 8 February 1925, 8; Sojin's versatility was never more evident than in the *Seven Samurai* (1954), directed by Kurosawa Akira. Sojin played the Minstrel. It was his last film before he died that same year.

10. "Fairbanks and Gest," *New York Times,* 13 April 1924, 5.

11. "Police Clear Jam at Movie Premiere," *New York Times,* 19 March 1924, 19.

12. "Police Clear Jam at Movie Premiere," 19.

13. "Gest Will Present New Fairbanks Film," *New York Times,* 13 April 1924, 5.

14. "Fairbanks Wins Berlin," *New York Times,* 23 January 1926, 19.

15. "Royal Party Enjoys 'The Thief of Bagdad,'" *Seattle Post-Intelligencer,* 8 June 1924, 4.

16. Herndon, *Mary Pickford and Douglas Fairbanks,* 243.

17. Kingsley Canham, *Michael Curtiz, Raoul Walsh, Henry Hathaway* (London: Tantivy Press, 1973), 88.

18. "*The Thief of Bagdad,*" *Variety,* 26 March 1924, 26.

19. C. S. Sewell, "*The Thief of Bagdad,*" *Moving Picture World* (29 March 1924): 397.

20. "*The Thief of Bagdad,*" *New York Times,* 1 March 1924, 13.

21. "*The Thief of Bagdad,*" *Film Daily,* 23 March 1924, 3.

22. "*The Thief of Bagdad,*" *Variety,* 26 March 1924, 26.

23. "*The Thief of Bagdad,*" *New York Times,* 13.

24. To "counterfeit various emotions" comes from a description of Mifune Toshiro and Shimura Takashi, two of Kurosawa Akira's major stars. Donald Richie, *The Films of Akira Kurosawa* (Berkeley: University of California Press, 1984), 221.

25. George C. Warren, "Anna May Is Pure Delight," *San Francisco Chronicle,* 22 January 1924, 11; Hans J. Wollstein, *Vixens, Floozies and Molls* (Jefferson, N.C.: McFarland, 1999), 250; "Picture Actors Jailed in Omaha Board Bill Dispute May Sue Hotel for $70,000," *San Francisco Chronicle,* 6 March 1925, 3.

THIRTEEN

PICCADILLY (1929)

Anna May Wong's portrayal of Shosho in *Piccadilly* was pure eroticism. Gilda Gray, born Marianna Michalsha (1901–1959) in Krakow, Poland, was cast as the lead in this British-financed film directed by Eward-Andre Dupont (1891–1956). But Wong's star presence relegated the "shimmy girl" to a distant second in persona, acting, charm, charisma, sexuality, and of course, exoticism. Even though Shosho would die in the end at the hands of Jim, her jealous Chinese suitor, portrayed by King Ho-Chang[1]—while Mabel Greenfield, played by Gray, eventually recovered her wayward mate, Valentine Wilmot, played by Jameson Thomas (1888–1939)—*Piccadilly* is quintessentially Anna May Wong. The story of jealousy, treachery, and death was secondary to the fiery and potent performance of Wong, whose various talents were now on display for a wider and more circumspect British audience, accustomed to quality stage acting in its long tradition of theater.

As Wong's last silent film, *Piccadilly* is also a smoking crescendo in the first part of her long career that would eventually take her to more legitimate stage work and then to an eleven-part television series entitled *The Gallery of Mme. Liu Tsong* in 1951. Of all her silent films, this British International production is Wong in her most erotic and exotic role. It is obvious that the camera loves her. It is almost as if this is her final audition as a smothering femme fatale who would later reveal herself as the complete Asian woman of agency and power, especially in her acts of selflessness, courage, humor, and heroism in the role of Hui Fei in *Shanghai Express* (1932).

THE EROTICISM OF ANNA MAY WONG: THE SCULLERY

In all of the major scenes in which Wong appeared, eroticism is the centerpiece. This conspicuous eroticism is first revealed in the scullery scene. Nightclub owner Valentine Wilmot has just emerged from an unpleasant experience with a drunken patron, played by Charles Laughton (1899–1962) in his third film. Billed as a "Night Club Hawk" in a small part, Laughton's vigorous protests about dirt on his plate, accentuated by pounding on the table, disrupt Mabel Greenfield's dancing. After escaping from the Laughton character, Wilmot enters the scullery with the dirty plate.

From a long shot with a vivid perspective of Shosho among her coworkers, Wilmot sees her dancing on a table. The camera then caresses Shosho's body with a slow tilt down, starting from a waist shot of a braless figure that meanders to a ragged apron and then to nylons streaming with runs. She is thrusting her hips forward and backward with a casual circular swinging motion. This tilt down shot ends with a visual of Shosho's working-class Mary Jane shoes. The eroticism evoked in this tilt down is reinforced by a slow tilt up shot of Shosho's body swaying, from the Mary Jane shoes and ripped nylons to her crotch and finally her waist. Wilmot, the scullery maids, and the audience see Wong's character with both nipples protruding through her sweater.

THE SPIRAL STAIRCASE

In the first encounter between Shosho and Wilmot following the scullery scene, a tilt up shot of Anna May Wong's character walking down a spiral staircase is more suggestive than revealing of her body. As she arrives at the bottom of the staircase, Shosho is dressed in a keyhole sweater with horizonal stripes reminiscent of a Parisian apache dancer. The sweater is matched with a pleated skirt well above the knees, but the nylons are still ripped. The contrast between a working-class and yellow Shosho and the elegant, upper-class, nightclub-owning, and white Valentine Wilmot is apparent. The most revealing contrast, however, is between the vibrant but cool sexuality of Shosho and the banal and emasculated Wilmot. While Wong's character sizzles, electrifies, and is alive, the

Jameson Thomas character, like Julanne Johnston's princess in *The Thief of Bagdad,* dampens, freezes, and is moribund. Valentine Wilmot is almost cadaverlike, not only during Mabel Greenfield's dancing as he peers down from the glistening staircase of his Piccadilly nightclub but also during Shosho's sexual beckoning in flat 12 as he waits for his deliverance.

PROPOSITIONED IN THE BOSS'S OFFICE

After the encounter with Wilmot, Shosho later goes to her boss's office. She is still wearing the same hot, apache-style clothing. The camera again tilts up from her Mary Jane shoes and tattered nylons. But this time it envelops a seated Shosho with legs apart. Here Wong exhibits her knowledge and wisdom from more than thirty films and live performances with a variety of expressions and gestures. The conversation revolves around her willingness to dance at the Piccadilly nightclub. Shosho exhibits a wide-eyed delight when Wilmot proposes that she perform an Asian dance. She replies, "I don't mind trying sir, if you want me to." With some surprise, she goes on to say that "Oh no, sir—I'm sure I shouldn't be frightened."

Even the way Shosho answers Wilmot reveals an eroticism that moves from willingness and deference to fearlessness and power. She is a woman of substance and strength, unlike Mabel Greenfield, who seems to pander to Wilmot. This undisguised courage becomes even more apparent when Shosho volunteers, "I did dance once in public in Limehouse. I live down there."

But the coup de grace in this conversational eroticism is the overt air of imminent peril. Shosho closes the dialogue with Wilmot by revealing that, "They wouldn't let me dance again, sir—there was trouble between two men along of me—knives—policemen." Thus, Shosho as Piccadilly's newest dancing sensation evokes not only a certain sexual passion but also a raw eroticism tinged with a threatening climax.

Like Marlon Brando (1924–) as Johnny Stabler in *The Wild One* (1954), Wong as Shosho exudes a sexuality that evokes an unbridled danger, a precarious life on the edge, a potential flirtation with violent death, and an invitation to enter the closed world of the radical chic. Both Brando as the alien rebel and Wong as the alien outcast in these films play illegitimate characters beyond the pale of conservative, respectable bourgeois society. Yet the people they encounter in *The Wild One* and *Piccadilly* simply want an intimate piece of their persona. They desire to be just as hip and cool as Marlon Brando and Anna May Wong. The Western audiences were just as enamored.

Like Brando, Wong was young, vibrant, beautiful, licentious, and dangerous. She pushed the boundaries of the erotic as heroic as she sought to navigate around a class system personified by Valentine Wilmot and his elegant
nightclub patrons. As a heroine, Shosho is an obvious working-class woman of
a certain ethnic origin attempting to survive in an increasingly hostile bourgeois environment, with the upper class and the court system weighted decidedly against her.

THE SEDUCTION SCENE IN FLAT 12

Following the success of Shosho's Chinese dance with Indonesian and Thai
overtones, accentuated by a scanty two-piece costume reminiscent of the Mongol spy in *The Thief of Bagdad,* she evolves from being a dishwasher with tattered
nylons into an elegant fashion piece. The inevitable seduction scene between
Shosho and Valentine Wilmot follows. The preliminary to the sexual scenario
created by German director Dupont is situated in Shosho's narrowly confined
and intimate dressing room, where after working her nails to a sharp perfection
as if she is ready for a kill, Shosho reveals the extraordinary ability to wear a tight
silklike black dress as if it were a second skin. Here Wong, the fashion model of
Los Angeles days, exhibits her natural flair for wearing London fashions.

From the room with no view except for Wilmot's visual coveting of
Shosho as he buttons her sleeves, the couple moves out into the night. To ward
off London's cold, damp weather, Wong's character is dressed in an elegant coat
with a wide fur collar and fur hem. The courtship begins with a medium shot
of Wilmot's left hand grasping Shosho's right hand in a rough Limehouse sa-
loon frequented by working-class drinkers and women slipping pound notes
into their nylons. It is almost an amusement park atmosphere, with one sign
over a scale offering to "ges-yur-wate." After witnessing a rowdy female drunk
being ousted from the establishment, they retreat to Shosho's flat, number 12.

Upon entering her flat, Shosho remarks to Wilmot that "you are the first
visitor to my new rooms." Now that she is the star dancer at the Piccadilly
nightclub, her new attire is matched by the splendor of her flat, with its gold-
fish, pagoda-type lanterns, and a portrait of the Buddha. This is "Orientalism"
at its most stereotypical and racist. As the yellow vampire, Shosho is portrayed
as a purveyor of licentious sex with an "emotional carelessness" and an un-
bound sexuality trapping the more than willing white male in her web.[2]

At her flat Shosho somehow has the time to change her clothes to reveal
yet another fashion ensemble. She is outfitted in a braless, low-backed, low-

neckline, sequined dress held up by two thin straps. The matching embroidered wrap later proves to be a veil that Shosho uses to entice Wilmot into her grasp.

After acting in more than thirty films since her days as an extra, Wong was finally to actually have her first on-screen kiss. However, as Shosho and Wilmot move in for the inevitable wet embrace, the moment of intimate touching ends on the editor's cutting room floor. This aborted kissing scene was a hot topic in the film, with Jameson Thomas remarking that "in England, we have less prejudice against scenes of interracial romance than in America. In France, there is still less, and in Germany, there is none at all. But we are careful to handle such scenes tactfully."[3] Apparently even Wong agreed to cut the scene.

The nature of the racial divide in Britain and the United States meant that the on-screen liaison between a yellow Shosho and a white Wilmot could never be consummated because of antimiscegenation laws prohibiting "inferior" yellows from mating legitimately with "superior" whites. But flouting these laws makes this biracial mating even more inviting. It was almost as if with Shosho as an illegitimate sexual possibility, Wong was the fulfillment of every European male's wet dream.

Valentine Wilmot pursues his own lustful desires, reveling in what Gustave Flaubert described in *l'Education sentimentale.* In that book, upon encountering the Oriental Other, the hero remarked:

> As for me, I scarcely shut my eyes. Watching that beautiful creature asleep (she snored, her head against my arm: I had slipped my forefinger under her necklace), my night was one long, infinitely intense reverie—that was why I stayed. I thought of my nights in Paris brothels—a whole series of old memories came back—and I thought of her, of her dance, of her voice as she sang songs that for me were without meaning and even without distinguishable words.[4]

This quotation perfectly epitomizes Wilmot's lust for Shosho as an example of European men lusting after Asian women while regarding them as the Other.

After Wilmot leaves the reclining Shosho in her apartment, Mabel Greenfield, who is anxiously pacing the street outside the flat, enters the room. On seeing Greenfield, who is in high heels but is still shorter than her, Shosho taunts her, in this witty repartee scripted by Arnold Bennett (1867–1931):

Shosho: *What is it?*
Greenfield: *It's this. I want you to leave Valentine alone.*
Shosho: *Oh, you want me to give you back what you couldn't keep.*

The two shot here reveals Anna May Wong's height and slimness as she hovers over over the substantial Mabel Greenfield.

Greenfield: *I'm desperate! I love him—you don't and he doesn't really love you. He's too old for you.*

The two shot here shows Greenfield on the left facing Shosho, whose left profile is prominent.

Shosho: *He isn't too old for me—but you're too old for him.*

At forty-one years old, Jameson Thomas, who played Valentine Wilmot, was sixteen years older than Wong, who played Shosho. Gilda Gray, who played Mabel Greenfield, was twenty-eight in 1929. After this cutting remark about age, Greenfield turns away, realizing that what Shosho has said is true.

Shosho: *I want him and I shall keep him.*

Mabel then pulls a small handgun out of her purse and faints. Shosho is later found dead by Bessie (played by Hannah Jones), the old woman in the scullery and Shosho's surrogate mother. After the initial court scene where murder charges have been laid against Mabel Greenfield, Jim confesses to the murder. With no rational reason given for Jim's actions, Wilmot and Greenfield are exonerated.

The murder of Shosho in *Piccadilly* was, in fact, a huge problem. It was as if "Orientals were rarely seen or looked at; they were seen through, analyzed not as citizens, or even people, but as problems to be solved or confined or—as the colonial powers openly coveted their territory—taken over."[5] The political parody in *Piccadilly*, like that in *The Toll of the Sea*, revealed Europe or European America as the sole arbiter of justice. Criminal acts by non-Europeans were to be "solved or confined." The solution to Shosho's death was simple. Pin the murder on Jim and perpetuate the "Orientalist" notion that Asian males are simply "love-struck losers."[6] That was exactly what the writer Arnold Bennett did. Thus, "Easterners are best dealt with when intimidated and what better instrument of intimidation than a sovereign Western ego."[7]

The impudence of this yellow woman's licentious liaison with a white European male, causing a fracture in his relationship with a white European woman, results inevitably in the death of Shosho. But death comes at the hands of the obvious agent of death, the Chinese male, although in *Piccadilly* Jim is constantly referred to as the "Chinese boy." Here dangerous and illegitimate sexuality is eliminated by a member of the same yellow race as Shosho so that the victims of "Oriental debauchery" are absolved from Shosho's murder. It is as if Valentine Wilmot and Mabel Greenfield remained pure and untouched even after their exciting encounter with Shosho.

The death scene was classic Anna May Wong; she often complained that she "died a thousand deaths." She was, in fact, one of the best Hollywood actresses at dying a convincing death, which was no easy feat. In an interview with London reporter Vivien North of *Picturegoer Weekly,* Wong's classic humor was revealed when she talked about her many "screen deaths":

> Because on the screen, it's very necessary to do something conclusive with any personality that's at all glamorous or exotic. One cannot leave them just floating around. They are *too* definite.[8]

In *Piccadilly,* Wong's character is indeed not left "just floating around." Immediately before she expires, Shosho has a look of profound horror when Jim picks up the gun from the floor and shoots. She expresses obvious pain as the bullet enters her body and then keels over. Years as a successful silent film actress perfected her expressions, body language, and gestures so that she could "counterfeit various emotions" not her own.

Anna May Wong as Shosho, the dancer and femme fatale, outplays both Gilda Gray and Jameson Thomas. While Gray's Mabel Greenfield is weak, chubby, reactive, and prone to fainting when events prove too much for her, Wong's Shosho is always strong, attractively slender, proactive, assertive, rational, virile, and all business. The camera loves Wong, and it shows in her performance. These characteristics of Shosho also contrast sharply with the Valentine Wilmot character, who is reactive, emasculated, muddle headed, and emotional, especially when he dismisses Greenfield's dancing partner, Victor Smiles, played by the Australian Cyril Ritchard (1899–1977), because Mabel does not like Smiles making passes at her. Since it is Smiles who brings in the crowd, not Mabel Greenfield, this is a bad business decision. Wilmot of course attempts to rectify this irrational decision by hiring Shosho, with her Asian dance, as the nightclub's major attraction. His courtship of Shosho results in her death and the loss of an attractive and exotic moneymaker at the cabaret.

REVIEWS

Even though *Piccadilly* was written by Arnold Bennett with Gilda Gray in mind, the picture was dominated by Wong's virtuoso performance. In *Variety,* the reviewer exclaimed that "In present silent houses, *Piccadilly* is okay for a week or a day, this due to Miss Gray's name, the story and Anna May Wong who outshines the star."[9] Later the reviewer encapsulates the plot with this less-than-inspired piece of prose: "Then the owner falls for the chink. She likes the idea, despite her Chinese lover who would correspond to the piano player over here, as he's the chink's uke player."[10]

Whereas the *New York Times*[11] had little to say about Wong's performance, Marjory Collier in *The Picturegoer* gave her this backhanded compliment:

> In *Piccadilly*, she played the vamp—very successfully. A. E. Dupont's production, if it sometimes repels, is always arresting.
>
> He allows no milk and water effects. Whether as a slattern of the scullery, or with ivory skin showing through transparencies and black lace sleeves or engirdled by her dancing apparel, Anna, under his direction, dominated the singularly drab and uninspiring plot.
>
> By her immobility, her reposeful body movements that are certainly her Oriental heritage, she gave a touch of dignity to the siren she portrayed. Nevertheless she remained a siren—nothing more.[12]

Although reviewers continued to portray Wong as a siren or femme fatale, the fact that she was able to capture such an enriched role as Shosho in *Piccadilly* provided her with the opportunity to develop her persona as one of the world's foremost female film stars. With this leading role and other major performances in film and theater behind her, the European producers, directors, and audiences raised Wong to the status of an icon who understood the bottom line and worked toward achieving profitability for her backers. Europeans recognized that her exoticism and eroticism sold tickets. Wong knew that sexuality and being Chinese "could be used to ensure continued interest in her career, and that continued interest could in turn be leveraged against studio politics regarding the development of worthwhile projects for the actor."[13]

With the release of *Piccadilly* in 1929, Anna May Wong was ready to fulfill the rest of her five-picture contract with Richard Eichberg. Of all the directors in Wong's career, he gave her the chance to thrive as a leading female performer. Following the completion of the Eichberg trilogy of *The Flame of Love* in 1930, she returned to the United States to perform in *On the Spot*. In the following year she portrayed Ling Moy, daughter of Fu Manchu, played by Swedish actor Warner Oland (1879–1938) in the *Daughter of the Dragon*, which was the first of the Fu Manchu series. In 1932 she would work again with Oland in one of Hollywood's all-time blockbusters. This time Oland would die at the hands of Anna May Wong's character, Hui Fei. That film was *Shanghai Express*.

NOTES

1. Since King Ho-Chang owned restaurants, this may explain why there were two specific restaurant scenes where Jim and Shosho and other diners were devouring fried chicken and mashed potatoes with knives and forks. The second scene, with a series of footage depicting Chinese customers eating with chopsticks, is rich in content. "A British Picture: *Piccadilly*," *New York Times*, 15 July 1929, 25.

2. Edward Said's brilliant study of Orientalism informs this analysis of *Piccadilly*. Edward Said, *Orientalism* (New York: Vintage Books, 1979). See especially the section on Gustave Flaubert and the "Oriental" woman, 6, 180, 186–87, 207.

3. Jameson Thomas, cited in Audrey Rivers, "Anna May Wong Sorry She Cannot Be Kissed," *Movie Classics* (November 1939): 39.

4. Gustave Flaubert, *l'Education sentimentale, Flaubert in Egypt*, cited in Said, *Orientalism*, 187.

5. Said, *Orientalism*, 207.

6. Renee E. Tajima, "Lotus Blossoms Don't Bleed: Images of Asian Women," in *Making Waves, An Anthology of Writings By and About Asian American Women*, ed. Diane Yen-Mei Wong (Boston: Beacon Press, 1989), 312.

7. Said, *Orientalism*, 193.

8. Wong, cited in Vivien North, "There's a Secret Anna May Wong," *Picturegoer Weekly* (8 September 1934): 8.

9. "*Piccadilly*," *Variety*, 24 July 1929, 35.

10. "*Piccadilly*," *Variety*, 35.

11. "A British Picture: *Piccadilly*," *New York Times*, 25.

12. Marjory Collier, "The Chinese Girl: East Meets West in Anna May Wong," *The Picturegoer* (May 1930): 26–27.

13. Cynthia W. Liu, "When Dragon Ladies Die, Do They Come Back As Butterflies? Re-Imagining Anna May Wong," in *Countervisions: Asian American Film Criticism*, ed. Darrell Y. Hamamoto and Sandra Liu (Philadelphia: Temple University Press, 2000), 30.

FOURTEEN

SHANGHAI EXPRESS (1932)

From the beginning of the rehearsals in 1927 in Berlin for *Song* (1928), Anna May Wong's first European film directed by Richard Eichberg moved her from merely playing bit parts opposite lesser and forgettable female performers like Estelle Taylor (1894–1958) in *The Alaskan,* Viola Dana (1897–1987) in *Forty Winks*, Marguerite De La Motte (1902–1950) in *Fifth Avenue,* and Pauline Starke (1901–1977) in *Streets of Shanghai* to leading roles with complicated characterizations in German, British, and French films. Now Wong was no longer pitted against European American actresses. There were no foils to compare or contrast her to. She was on her own as the principal female lead. This was what she had always wanted. That European directors would take a chance on a Chinese American actress revealed more about their recognition and understanding of cinematic talent as opposed to the narrow notions of racial superiority in the minds and psyche of many European American producers, who relegated her to cinematic window dressing.

It was only when Wong became a film celebrity in Europe that Broadway and Hollywood took serious notice of this daughter of Los Angeles. This was achieved both through her acting abilities and her uncanny knack of creating publicity. With her well-chosen words about being Chinese, projecting an aura of mystery to non-Asians, and the capacity to exude a cool sense of elegant fashion in her dress, style, and demeanor, she captured the imagination of the European entertainment world. Creating an almost always accessible persona that was decidedly hip and on the cutting edge of the exotic and erotic, she became an essential attraction at the best parties in Berlin, Paris London, and Vienna. She was one of the hottest numbers in those European capitals. This type of networking proved to be essential in landing key roles She went to Europe to be seen and heard. Even such a colossal and bankable writer as Edgar Wallace took notice of her. Because of her European success the offer from Lee Ephraim, with the blessing of Wallace, to play Minn Lee in *On the Spot* was no accident.

Landing a two-contract film deal with a major studio like Paramount wa also no accident. After four years in Europe and a successful stint in a New York play, Wong had earned her ticket back to Hollywood. It was now nine years af ter her first European American starring role as Lotus Flower in *The Toll of th Sea*. As Ling Moy, the daughter of Fu Manchu in *Daughter of the Dragon*, the role appeared to be a repeat of all the other negative Hollywood characters she had played between 1922 and 1927. But that role was merely a warm-up to Wong best-remembered performance. When she was cast as the courtesan Hui Fei in *Shanghai Express* (1932), the script at first glance seemed to be a mere regurgi tation of her characterizations of Keok, Annabelle Wu, Nan Lo, Ohtai, Oneta Loo Song, Delamar, Sada, Su Quan, and Su in her pre-European films.

THE MAKING OF *SHANGHAI EXPRESS*

With Vienna-born Josef von Sternberg (1894–1969) as director and longtime Berlin friend Marlene Dietrich (1901–1992) in the female lead, Wong would be working with consummate professionals. The film promised excellence and excitement even though the part of Hui Fei smacked of her previous roles a adventuresses, hookers, and ladies of "dubious morals." With such diverse star as Dietrich, Clive Brook (1887–1974), Warner Oland (1880–1938), Eugen Pallette (1889–1954), and James Leong (Leong But-Jung, 1889–1967), Wong was in good company. Set during China's civil war between the Nationalist and Communists, *Shanghai Express* had the makings of a genuine blockbuster

In the political backdrop to the film, there appeared a menacing Japan with its incessant invasion of China, its takeover of Manchuria, and the "specter" of the "rising tide" of communism in the early 1930s. In its politica dimension, *Shanghai Express* was timely. While Wong was preparing for he role, she was growing increasingly sensitive to the brutality of Japanese impe rialism. She was so outraged that she would pen a polemical diatribe against Japanese aggression called "Manchuria."[1]

To lend authenticity to the sets of *Shanghai Express*, Josef von Sternberg constructed the Beijing (Peiping or Peking) railway station, replete with real Chinese extras. He explained:

> Having survived *An American Tragedy* (1931), I continued to "gloat lovingly" on the next theme "repugnant to the normal mind." This repulsive subject concerned the journey of a train from Peking to Shanghai. A China was built of papier-mâché and into it we placed slant-eyed men, women, and children, who seemed to relish being part of it. We borrowed a train from the Sante Fe, painted it white, and added an armored car to carry Chinese soldiers with fixed bayonets.[2]

Built in San Bernardino, California,[3] the railway set provided a relaxed introduction to the main characters. Wong's Hui Fei sets the tone of the story as the first of two protagonists. She enters the introductory railway scene with a detached demeanor, stepping down effortlessly from a palanquin as if this were simply part of her daily routine. Whereas the five foot, seven inch Hui Fei, in a loosely fitting *cheong sam* makes her entrance with a casual presence, the veiled and feathered Shanghai Lily, played by the five foot, two inch Marlene Dietrich enters the train station with a flourish and purposefully after alighting from a motorized taxi.

The contrast between the two women is startling. Shanghai Lily is the intense, modernized, and motorized Western woman. She is the female foil to Hui Fei, who represents China in all its backwardness and traditional decadence, made even more primitive by her reliance on a human-powered vehicle.

After leaving the palanquin, Hui Fei hesitates on the steps of the first-class car. She glances to her left, revealing Wong's much-photographed left profile. Then she turns completely to the camera as if she has spotted someone spying on her or she is searching for signs of imminent danger, thus evoking an aura of mystery. Hui Fei is composed among a "multiplicity of objects and figures" with a frame that "never becomes unobstructed."[4] With this profile shot in particular, the cinematographer Lee Garmes (1898–1978) captures that special side of Wong's beauty.

Even though the extras are all Chinese or Asians, thus providing a definite authenticity to the scenes, the inability of the casting agents and von Sternberg to distinguish the northern (*guoyu* or Mandarin) dialect from the southern speech (*Guangdong hua* or Cantonese), especially in the Beijing and bandit scenes, reveals a surrealism that only Western filmmakers could have conjured up. In the heart of the Beijing railway station, the tobacco chewing train engineer argues in Cantonese with a peasant over his cow blocking the train's path. Likewise, when Wong's *Taishan* dialect riffs with the Cantonese dialect of the military police inspector, it not only seems out of place but ludicrous. In addition, with Warner Oland in "Yellowface" playing the communist rebel Henry Chang, his Chinese utterances, especially when he propositions Hui Fei, border on the hilarious and bizarre.

Although some speakers of the southern dialect were certainly in Beijing and in the areas between Beijing and Shanghai, they were a rarity. Ordinary citizens like the engineers, peasants, and soldiers on the train were more apt to speak *guoyu* in northern China. Nevertheless, the Chinese clock revealed not only genuine simplified characters from three to seven but also complicated characters from one to two and eight to twelve that were usually reserved for numerals written on bank checks to avoid illegal tampering. Whereas the dialects may have been imposed arbitrarily and subject to the availability of Chinese-speaking extras, the design of the clock suggests an obsession with detail.

Strict authenticity was not Josef von Sternberg's main interest. Although he had never visited China, he proclaimed that "though my performers could not respond to my instructions with the same speed as the train which contained them, I thought the canvas of China, as evoked by my imagination, quite effective."[5] Evoking China in his own cultural image was how von Sternberg conceptualized *Shanghai Express.*[6]

Von Sternberg was an imperious director who sometimes made unrealistic demands, causing some consternation among the actors. His direction, with a view toward "stylizing performances,"[7] may have been too difficult for a performer like Warner Oland. Von Sternberg remarked:

> I had an actor who said to me when he was engaged, "They call me One-take Warner." It took me hours in one of the scenes of *Shanghai Express* to get Mr. Oland to say no more than "Good Morning"—and this with the aid of a blackboard. But worse than that sort of thing can be a scene where an actor believes that every time he opens his mouth the audience will be staggered with delight. The swiftest way to make an enemy of an actor is to dare point out that placing words in proper order and breathing with relief after each comma and period is not sufficient to invest them with the intended meaning.[8]

Warner Oland's inability to please von Sternberg may have caused the Swedish actor some sleepless nights. He never worked for von Sternberg again.

But his portrayal of the revolutionary Henry Chang brought him much acclaim. In fact, one of the one thousand Chinese extras was so impressed by Oland's Asian looks that the aged gentleman engaged the actor in a simple Cantonese conversation. Oland was later told by the film's interpreter, Tom Gubbins of the Asiatic Costume Company in Los Angeles, that "this old man has never worked in a picture before and he really thinks you're Chinese. He wants to know if you are from Canton. He says you look like a boy he used to know there."[9]

While von Sternberg was highly critical of Oland's work ethics, he lavished attention on making his star, Marlene Dietrich, appear extraordinarily good. She was not only lit well by Lee Garmes, but "some shots were almost like engravings."[10] Since mise-en-scène and well-composed camera shots were the key components in von Sternberg's directorial signature in *Shanghai Express,* almost all of the interaction among the protagonists, especially between Wong's Hui Fei and Dietrich's Shanghai Lily, were explored through the use of such facets as body language, clothing, a flick of a hand, stylized hair, poses, and posture, all contained within contrived camera angles, framing, and astute top lighting.[11]

Shanghai Lily as the symbol of the Western world is costumed in black to accentuate and contrast her whiteness and blondness. She is almost always shot full frame as if to establish that she has little to conceal. On the other hand, Hui Fei as the personification of an alien nonwhite world is always attired in light clothing to magnify and differentiate her yellowness and dark hair. She is often shot in profile, not only to stress her fully angular features but also to suggest that she has something to hide, thus portraying a certain inscrutability. This juxtaposition is initially to set them apart, but as the story unfolds, the suffocating confinement and political and sexual machinations in the moving train bring them together to strategize their way out of a seemingly untenable situation. The results are unexpected.

The cool, detached, and seemingly debauched Hui Fei assumes a heroic posture by killing her captor and rapist, Henry Chang, in a hot fury of revenge, thus saving the entire contingent of hypocritical Anglo-Saxon Westerners from the Chinese menace. These men and women from the West appear to be upright and civilized people, but in the end they are not what they seemed to be. They represent disgrace, drug dealing, fanaticism, obsessive gambling, and pettiness. Hui Fei inadvertently saves these despicable humans from the Asian menace in the form of the sadistic communist general Henry Chang. It is as if the yellow woman had extricated the "white Christian civilization represented by the group on this journey. In their encounter with the savage (Henry Chang and the Chinese), this microcosm of Western culture cleanses itself of any excessive, forbidden desires or moral trespasses to survive."[12] By rescuing this group, von Sternberg places Hui Fei contextually as the moral compass between white bourgeois patriarchy and yellow revolutionary patriarchy, in fact between white evil and yellow evil.

Hui Fei as a proactive, reality-based heroine emerges from the same Chinese tradition as Hua Mulan and She Saihua. The intense and seemingly imperturbable and emasculating Shanghai Lily eventually evokes a Christian god to save Captain Donald Harvey, played by Clive Brook, from the menacing evil of the biracial Henry Chang. As the product of a white father and a yellow mother, Warner Oland's rebel is the result of miscegenation, a Western taboo that inevitably ends in his demise. Hui Fei's heroic elimination of Chang saves Shanghai Lily from having to comply with the general's proposition to live with him. The general's death is also the moral extrication of the scandalous union of a white–yellow sexuality that could only have resulted in a grotesque and morally stunted Asian–European "savage" like Henry Chang. In European American Hollywood, the offspring of miscegenation could only meet with a horrible death. When Will Hays (1879–1954) became president of the Motion Picture Producers and Distributors of America in 1922, he banned specific romances in European American filmmaking. One of these prohibitions was miscegenation, which was classified as "race suicide." Biracial pairings could only result in tragedy and inevitable death either for the "offending" nonwhite protagonists or the children of such a union.[13]

Both Wong's and Dietrich's characters emerge from this ordeal vastly different from their initial entrance into the confinement of the Shanghai Express. As the train finally lurches into the railway station at Shanghai, a throng of Western journalists and photographers welcomes Chinese heroine Hui Fei, who also receives a monetary reward. Even in a fictional account of Shanghai, Wong's character has achieved celebrity status. On the other hand, Shanghai Lily, the vamp, presumably lives happily ever after with army physician Donald Harvey and becomes Shanghai Lily, the housewife.

The Wong–Dietrich liaison in *Shanghai Express* was not the first time the two had partnered up. Wong encountered Dietrich at the Berlin Press Ball in 1928. Along with actress and director Leni Riefenstahl, they were photographed by Alfred Eisenstaedt in a series of famous stills.[14] The commentary on these pictures in *Film Museum Berlin* is especially scorching:

> The Hollywood star Anna May Wong stands between them, wearing a tight strapless black dress. The pearl necklace, centered on her upper body, emphasizes her central position in the photograph. She has an arm around the back of each of the Berliners, who, tellingly, are not touching each other.

Few today remember this Asian American star. Yet as a representative of Hollywood, she symbolically stands for both the demarcation line separating the two German women through their lifetimes, as well as the point of intersection of these two careers whose development was so divergent till the end.

Marlene Dietrich—an icon of seduction—was one of the few Hollywood stars to don the U.S. army uniform in order to speak out against the Nazis. Leni Riefenstahl—an icon of the seduced—was, according to Goebbels, the only one who understood the National Socialist politico-cultural project so perfectly that she could be entrusted, without misgivings, with the job of documenting the Reich Party Convention in Nuremberg in 1934 (*Triumph des Willens,* 1935), as well as the Olympic Games in Berlin in 1936 (*Olympia, Teil I, Fest der Volker, Teil II, Fest der Schonheit,* 1938).[15]

For the modern German commentator, Anna May Wong, as a symbol of Hollywood, is revealed as the sectional crossover defining Dietrich's career as legitimate and upright as she sought to entertain and Riefenstahl's work as debauched and depraved as she apologized for the Nazi terror. The irony, of course, is that this European writer considered Wong, a movie star from Chinese America, to be the representative of European American Hollywood. This places Wong contextually as the political division between good and evil. When Alfred Eisenstaedt snapped his shutters closed at the Press Ball, Wong had just arrived in Berlin in the spring of 1928[16] to work for Richard Eichberg in *Song* (1928). In fact, Wong, Dietrich, and Riefenstahl were merely three young aspiring actresses in their twenties all looking for that crucial break in their emerging careers. It was only natural that they socialize and exchange information about future prospects.

The Wong–Dietrich connection was expanded in *Shanghai Express.* When shooting began in 1931, Anna May Wong and Marlene Dietrich had already developed a theatrical repertoire of the erotic and the seductive, performed cinematically with energy, subtlety, and elegance. As friends they projected a familiarity in all of their scenes in *Shanghai Express,* as if their early Berlin days were being replayed.

Although there is a romantic plot between Shanghai Lily and Captain Donald Harvey, with the couple eventually reunited in Shanghai, it is a mundane human interlude played out in countless other films. The real action and soul of the film are with Wong and Dietrich. Their cosiness was even sustained off the set.

As a megastar, Dietrich demanded and received a grand dressing room, where she stashed her large collection of Richard Tauber (1891–1948) records. Anna May Wong and Marlene Dietrich spent their nonworking hours amusing themselves listening to the vast array of Tauber's operas and popular tunes.[17]

Wong's close relationship with Dietrich off the set of *Shanghai Express* was accentuated by her sizzling erotic portrayal of Hui Fei, which exploded in all of her scenes with Dietrich. Whether there was any sexual relationship between Wong and Dietrich has always been a matter of conjecture because of Dietrich's open interest in both women and men. Although Hollywood rumors always tied Wong with Dietrich in a lesbian relationship, Wong was also linked with Dolores del Rio. In a review of George Hadley Garcia's *Hispanic Hollywood*, Michael Blowen of the *Boston Globe* wrote that "Dolores del Rio numbered among her lovers Henry Fonda, Orson Welles, and Anna May Wong."[18]

REPARTEE ON THE *SHANGHAI EXPRESS*

Whether Wong was truly a lesbian, bisexual, or pretended to be for the Hollywood gossip mill, she was a genuinely convincing performer who had the ability to "counterfeit various emotions" not her own. Her portayal of the exotic and erotic courtesan, Hui Fei, had already been exhibited in her many previous roles and disguises, beginning with the Mongol spy in *The Thief of Bagdad*. Certainly Josef von Sternberg was not asking for a replay of Lotus Flower in *The Toll of the Sea*. In fact, Wong's roles following *The Toll of the Sea* appeared to be a repudiation of this naive, innocent, self-sacrificing, preadolescent figure.

Hui Fei is an amalgamation of Keok, Annabelle Wu, Nan Lo, Ohtai, Oneta, Loo Song, Delamar, Sada, Su Quan, Su, Shosho, Hai-tang, and Ling Moy. If there is any Lotus Flower in Hui Fei, it is ostensibly in her self-sacrifice, which emancipates the train's psychological derelicts, Donald Harvey and Shanghai Lily, from Henry Chang's clutches. But this collective value in Chang's death is quickly dispelled:

> Lily: *I don't know if I ought to be grateful to you or not.*
> Hui Fei: *It's of no consequence. I didn't do it for you. Death canceled his debt to me.*[19]

With that pronouncement, Hui Fei establishes her own personal agency. She is no longer to be used, abused, and dismissed as some inconsequential yellow harlot searching for victims. Her empowerment comes at the expense of the death of another Asian character, as if yellows were battling to liberate the contingent of European misfits, but this is also the struggle of a Chinese female being sexually harassed and abused by a biracial Asian–European male while minding her own business.

Hui Fei could have either walked into the sea, like Lotus Flower, or simply sought retribution. Screenwriter Jules Furthman (1888–1966) called for Hui Fei to choose the latter course, thus ensuring her survival in a hostile patriarchal environment. While not as overt, she was like Masago, played by Kyo Machiko (1924–) in Kurosawa Akira's *Rashomon* (1950). They both pour scorn on their attackers and prove to be the catalyst that moves the stories to their conclusion.

Death gives Hui Fei ultimate power and also a cash nexus of $20,000. As she walks away alone from the annoying journalists and photographers at the Shanghai railway station, she is the sole winner in the human lottery on the Shanghai Express. With her own agency, she needs no one. Her identity as a powerful heroine is consolidated and intact. On the other hand, Shanghai Lily becomes merely another sacrifice in a patriarchal romance that has no room for a strong woman. She goes willingly into the arms of the respectable and bourgeois British physician, Donald Harvey, as if he is her sole savior from a life of decadence and debauchery as a "'coaster' who lives by her wits along the China coast."[20] Shanghai Lily assumes Harvey's identity. She becomes dispossessed and powerless in Harvey's presence.

THE STANDARD OF RESPECTABILITY

The key determinant of social class is apparent in the repartee among three women: Mrs. Haggerty, played by Louise Closser Hale (1872–1933), Shanghai Lily, and Hui Fei. On hearing a loud blast of big band jazz from Shanghai Lily's Victrola phonograph, Mrs. Haggerty "entering into the vestibule, sticks her head into the compartment, nodding affably to Lily, who is preening herself, and Hui Fei, who remained seated."[21] Hui Fei continues to play solitaire.

> Mrs. Haggerty: *I heard your gramophone, ladies, and thought I'd come in and get acquainted, if you don't mind.*
> Shanghai Lily: *Not at all. Come in.*
> Mrs. Haggerty: *It's a bit lonely on a train, isn't it? I'm used to having people around. They put my dog in the luggage car.*

During this exchange, Hui Fei stops dropping cards on the small table and looks up. She laughs softly at Mrs. Haggerty's concern about her dog as if this was the most important consideration in the old woman's life.

Mrs. Haggerty: *That's why I dropped in on you. I've been visiting my niece in Peking. She married a seafaring man. He hasn't been home in four years and she ain't been very cheerful. I have a boarding house in Shanghai. Yorkshire pudding is my specialty. . . .*

Mrs. Haggerty pauses to take calling cards out of her purse and hands them to Shanghai Lily and Hui Fei. They both take the cards with a cool detachment. While Shanghai Lily inspects her card, Hui Fei casually drops the card onto the table without looking at it.

Mrs. Haggerty: *. . . and I only take the most respectable people.*
Shanghai Lily: *Don't you find respectable people terribly dull?*
Mrs. Haggerty: *You're joking, aren't you. I've only known the most respectable people. You see. I keep a boarding house.*
Shanghai Lily: *What kind of house did you say?*
Mrs. Haggerty: *A boarding house!*
Shanghai Lily: *Oh!*

In this scene, Marlene Dietrich's Shanghai Lily has two roles. She portrays the comedienne to the serious and straightlaced Mrs. Haggerty with her "rigid morality." In fact, Haggerty is actually a stand-in for Brook's rigid Captain Harvey in this scene.[22] Then Dietrich's character abruptly changes to a setup or straight role to Wong's Hui Fei, who delivers the punch line as the closer in this repartee. Finding Shanghai Lily disrespectful with her mocking tone, Mrs. Haggerty turns to Hui Fei for some positive stroking.

Mrs. Haggerty: *I'm sure you're very respectable, Madam.*

Although she continues her diatribe on respectability to Hui Fei, Mrs. Haggerty's "rising inflection indicates a faint doubt" that what she has just said might not receive a welcoming response. With her left hand holding a cigarette and in mid-sentence before she acknowledges Mrs. Haggerty's presence, Hui Fei with her hair tied behind her back glances slightly at the card in her hand before turning to face the boarding house owner. Her answer, in excellent English, is in direct contrast to Mrs. Haggerty's Cockney accented, nonstandard English.

Hui Fei: *I must confess I don't quite know the standard of respectability that you demand in your boarding house, . . . Mrs. Haggerty.*
Mrs. Haggerty: *I've made a terrible mistake! I better look after me dog!*[23]

Wong's Hui Fei, in an elegant, long-sleeved, cotton-buttoned, traditional silk *cheong sam,* is in contrast to both Shanghai Lily and Mrs. Haggerty. While she is an accomplice with Shanghai Lily in their put-down of working-class Mrs. Haggerty's pomposity, Hui Fei sets herself apart from Shanghai Lily by her erudite and witty questioning of Mrs. Haggerty. She seems more annoyed by Mrs. Haggerty's charade as an upright Westerner living in China than by Shanghai Lily's obvious toying with the old lady and her pretensions.

In this scene, Hui Fei matches Shanghai Lily's cool demeanor with her own subtle hipness. Both women as truth tellers expose what people appear to be and what they really are. In sharp contrast to Shanghai Lily and Mrs. Haggerty, Hui Fei not only speaks her double-edged sentence in polished English but also with an air of sophistication. Wong's English diction and enunciation are made more pronounced by her well-publicized lessons with an Oxford graduate in London in 1929. She is one Chinese American who speaks English without any "Asian" accent because she was born and raised in the United States of America. The tone of her voice also implies that Hui Fei knows what "the standard of respectability" is, and it certainly is not Mrs. Haggerty's notion. If respectability means authenticity or genuineness rather than haughtiness and pretense, then the courtesan Hui Fei is respectable.

THE EROTICISM OF HUI FEI

Beside the sultry, almost masculine voice of Wong's Hui Fei, her words in English resonated with a deep, mature eroticism that was much more poignant than the almost baby-faced innocence of Marlene Dietrich's Shanghai Lily. Both certainly exuded a sexuality that attracts both men and women. But Wong's mastery of the erotic, as exhibited in Hui Fei, was the result of ten years of playing in the backlots of Hollywood studios as a secondary performer and in Europe as a female lead, where she listened and learned. On the other hand, Dietrich was almost always cast as a leading female performer. She was also fortunate to have a director like Josef von Sternberg, who served as an advocate for her talents and abilities to Hollywood producers. Unfortunately for Wong, no Hollywood director ever came forth as a mentor or advocate. The closest to a von Sternberg that she had was Richard Eichberg, who did not leave Nazi Germany for the United States until 1938.[24] By that time, Wong had moved on to other pursuits.

When *Shanghai Express* was released in February 1932, Anna May Wong had just turned twenty-seven. But she was a mature twenty-seven, with the look, stance, and voice of a woman who had traveled the world and experienced life. What she brought to the role of Hui Fei was just that worldliness that could only be obtained by dealing with the hard knocks of life in European America and surviving the blows. She knew about life, and this showed in her portrayal of Hui Fei, who demonstrated genuine suffering after her confrontation with Henry Chang.

Even in the immediate encounter with a common soldier, "On the landing upstairs, Hui Fei is being pushed along through a group of soldiers on guard duty there. One of them gets a hold of her, leering and tweaking her cheek,"[25] she is able to "counterfeit various emotions" and is passionately defiant.

The height of Wong's eroticism as depicted in Hui Fei occurs when Shanghai Lily sees her take out a "heavily bejewelled dagger" from her bag. She clutches Hui Fei's wrists from behind. Shanghai Lily then pulls the wrists back, thereby expanding Hui Fei's chest and revealing protruding nipples through her silk *cheong sam*. With great concern, she warns Hui Fei:

Shanghai Lily: *Don't do anything foolish!*

Shanghai Lily's embrace from behind evokes a mutual eroticism between the two women. It is almost as if their touching has been exhibited before in moments outside the studio. Certainly there is a familiarity gained from their Berlin days and in their private moments listening to music. This passionate embrace contrasts sharply with the flaccid encounter between Shanghai Lily and Donald Harvey in the scene on the back platform of the train. The script calls for an embrace and a kiss between Dietrich and Brook, but the result is a frigid meeting without fire or zeal. They seem to "walk through" this scene, stiff and upright as though duty-bound. Likewise, the final kiss and embrace at the end of the story are more perfunctory than passionate, joyless and emotionless.

While Shanghai Lily warns Hui Fei not to do anything foolish, the fury in the courtesan's face and the aggression that surge through her body suggest real rage against Henry Chang. With disheveled black hair falling over the right side of her face, Hui Fei in her braless traditional Chinese dress with the silk buttons on the right side of the garment takes the tip of the dagger casually between her thumb and index finger and drops the weapon hard on the table. This is a compelling scene in which Dietrich again sets up Wong's punch line:

Hui Fei: *When are we leaving?*
Shanghai Lily: *I wish I knew. I suppose as soon as Captain Harvey comes down.*
Hui Fei: *If he's up there, he may never come down.*

With that final statement, Wong's Hui Fei moves the story to its ultimate conclusion.

She is later seen advancing toward Henry Chang in his darkened warlord headquarters and, in an instant, stabs him twice. Chang's death is a mere anticlimax to the intimate relationship between Hui Fei and Shanghai Lily, which is passionate, meaningful, and rewarding. Real emotions are demonstrated between the two women. This was because of a friendship that involved familiarity with each other's speech, thoughts, and body movements rather than any lesbian proclivities. Even if there were lesbian tendencies in the Hui Fei–Shanghai Lily relationship, it mattered little to the final story.[26] Whereas Wong played a fictional part as a seasoned actress, Dietrich was merely playing a cinematic image of herself. Wong became Hui Fei in *Shanghai Express;* Dietrich was always Dietrich.

REVIEWS

Some critics lavishly lauded Josef von Sternberg's virtuoso direction. Mordaunt Hall of the *New York Times* exclaimed that "it is by odds the best picture Josef von Sternberg has directed, even though he had a kind of pattern in the Russian film, *Chinese Express,* which exhibited at the Cameo a year or so ago."[27] Robert E. Sherwood concurred:

> *Shanghai Express* is a technological triumph for the principal protagonist of this drama is the railroad train, a perfect vehicle for the express of von Sternberg's peculiar intelligence. He has recorded the progress of this vehicle with such remarkable expertness that one is given no opportunity to worry about the insufficiency of its human cargo.
>
> He can make his camera talk and his microphone listens in a positively human manner. Thus, he establishes communion with the physical senses of this audience and he exploits this communion with remarkable skill.[28]

Variety was not as kind:

> Von Sternberg, the director, has made this effort interesting through a definite command of the lens. As to plot structure and dialog, *Shanghai Express* runs much too long close to old meller and serial themes to command real attention. Hence, the finished product is an example of what can be done with a personality and photographic face such as Miss Dietrich possesses and the ways to circumvent a trashy story.[29]

When the film was released in France, the Paris periodical *L'humanite* praised the technical expertise of Josef von Sternberg. But the reviewer Leon

Moussinac asserted that the film "expresses beyond its poorly melodramatic and bourgeois exotic theme, some thing simply low, a false poetry, an artificial reality if one can say, a decadent and doctored 'artistic' taste. *Shanghai Express* is 'successful' but is a decadent product of the bourgeois camera."[30]

The Academy of Motion Picture Arts and Sciences nominated *Shanghai Express* for Best Photographer (Lee Garmes), Best Picture, and Best Director, with Garmes taking home the only Oscar for the film. Of the seven pictures that von Sternberg directed with Marlene Dietrich as his female lead, *Shanghai Express* was the most successful, especially at the box office.

The *New York Times* called Marlene Dietrich's performance "impressive. She is languorous but fearless as Lily. She glides through her scenes with heavy eyelids and puffing on her cigarettes. She measures every word and yet she is not too slow in her foreign accented speech."[31] On the other hand, *Variety* stated that *Shanghai Express* "is not a film which will help Miss Dietrich to any extent. Indeed, film-goers seeing the German girl for the first time will be disappointed in view of what other fans have probably told them. However 'Express' shouldn't do her any harm either. It therefore sums as Miss Dietrich being on a treadmill until her next comes along."[32]

Of all the reviews, only the *London Times* intelligently mentioned the Wong–Dietrich connection: "Nothing in an admirable film is better than the first meeting between Lily and Hui Fei (Anna May Wong). They look at each other, neither intently nor curiously, but in that look, the attitude each takes to life finds its perfect and complete expression."[33]

Wong's fully formed Hui Fei in *Shanghai Express* was never appreciated by critics and producers in Hollywood. At twenty-seven years old, she was still referred to by Mordaunt Hall as "the Chinese girl, who arrays herself in silks bought by ill-gotten money."[34] Hall previously had declared that "Anna May Wong makes the most of the role of the brave Chinese girl."[35]

Following the release of *Shanghai Express* in February 1932, Marlene Dietrich would star in *Blond Venus* (1932) with Cary Grant (1904–1986). Anna May Wong, however, was not so fortunate. Paramount declined to renew her contract. Then World Wide Pictures offered her a role as Mrs. Pyke in a Sherlock Holmes thriller called *A Study in Scarlet* (1933).[36]

NOTES

1. Anna May Wong, "Manchuria," in Rob Wagner, *Script* 6, no. 153 (16 January 1932): 6–7, Box 2, Rob Wagner Collection, 6, cited in Karen Janis Leong, "The China

Mystique: Mayling Soong, Pearl S. Buck and Anna May Wong in the American Imagination" (Ph.D. dissertation, University of California, Berkeley, spring 1999), 381.

2. Josef von Sternberg, *Fun in a Chinese Laundry* (New York: Macmillan, 1965), 262.

3. "Even Chinese Think Oland Is Oriental," *Seattle Post Intelligencer,* 10 February 1932, 5.

4. Carole Zucker, *The Idea of the Image: Josef von Sternberg's Dietrich Films* (Cranbury, N.J.: Associated University Presses, 1988), 22.

5. Von Sternberg, *Fun in a Chinese Laundry,* 263.

6. Herman G. Weinberg, *Josef von Sternberg: A Critical Study* (New York: E. P. Dutton, 1967), 60–61.

7. Andrew Sarris, "Introduction," in *Morocco and Shanghai Express: Two Films by Josef von Sternberg* (New York: Simon & Schuster, 1973), 9.

8. Von Sternberg, *Fun in a Chinese Laundry,* 106.

9. Tom Gubbins, cited in "Even Chinese Think Oland Is Oriental," 5.

10. Thierry de Navacelle, *Sublime Marlene* (New York: St. Martin's Press, 1982), 51.

11. Gina Marchetti, *Romance and the "Yellow Peril": Race, Sex, and Discursive Strategies in Hollywood Fiction* (Berkeley: University of California Press, 1993), 62–63.

12. Marchetti, *Romance and the "Yellow Peril,"* 61.

13. Thomas Cripps, *Slow Fade to Black: The Negro in American Film, 1900–1942* (New York: Oxford University Press, 1977), 94.

14. Wolfgang Jacobson, ed., *Film Museum Berlin* (Berlin: Filmmuseum, 2000), 170.

15. Jacobson, *Film Museum Berlin,* 170.

16. Tim Bergfelder, "Negotiating Exoticism: Hollywood, Film Europe and the Cultural Reception of Anna May Wong," in *"Film Europe" and "Film America": Cinema, Commerce and Cultural Exchange, 1920–1939,* ed. Andrew Higson and Richard Maltby (Exeter, England: University of Exeter Press, 1999), 307.

17. Hans J. Wollstein, *Vixens, Floozies and Molls: 28 Actresses of Late 1920s and 1930s Hollywood* (Jefferson, N.C.: McFarland, 1999), 253. When Richard Tauber died in 1948, he left 735 records to be enjoyed by the listening public.

18. Michael Blowen, "Hollywood Hotline," *Boston Globe,* 28 September 1990, 46.

19. Sarris, *Morocco and Shanghai Express,* 126.

20. Sarris, *Morocco and Shanghai Express,* 64.

21. Sarris, *Morocco and Shanghai Express,* 70.

22. Zucker, *Idea of the Image,* 106.

23. This entire dialogue is found in Zucker, *Idea of the Image,* 70–72.

24. Corinna Muller, "Richard Eichberg," in *Cinegraph, Lexikon zum deutschsprachigen Film,* ed. Hans-Michael Bock (Munich: Edition Text + Kritik, 1985), D1–6, cited in Bergfelder, "Negotiating Exoticism," 314.

25. Bergfelder, "Negotiating Exoticism," 109.

26. For a different view of the Wong–Dietrich lesbianism rumors, see Marchetti, *Romance and the "Yellow Peril,"* 66.

27. Mordaunt Hall, "Marlene Dietrich in a Brilliantly Directed Melodrama Set Aboard a Train Running from Peiping to Shanghai," *New York Times,* 18 February 1932, 25.

28. Sherwood, cited in Weinberg, *Josef von Sternberg,* 60–61.

29. *Variety,* 23 February 1932, 13.

30. Leon Moussinac, "From Mongol Train to *Shanghai Express," L'humanite* (20 May 1932): 5.

31. Hall, "Marlene Dietrich in a Brilliantly Directed Melodrama," 25.

32. *Variety,* 23 February 1932, 13.

33. "Carlton Theater, Shanghai Express," *London Times,* 18 March 1932, 2.

34. Mordaunt Hall, "Marlene Dietrich Travels in China," *New York Times,* 28 February 1932, 4.

35. Hall, "Marlene Dietrich in a Brilliantly Directed Melodrama," 25.

36. Chris Steinbrunner and Norman Michaels, *The Films of Sherlock Holmes* (Secaucus, N.J.: Citadel Press, 1978), 42.

FIFTEEN

A STUDY IN SCARLET (1933)

During the final production of *Shanghai Express,* Anna May Wong signed a one-picture deal with a small Hollywood studio called World Wide Pictures to play the female lead in a Sherlock Holmes adaptation entitled *A Study in Scarlet* (1933). World Wide Pictures reasoned that any film involving Sherlock Holmes was a surefire moneymaker. What inspired this studio was the popularity of the stories by Sir Arthur Conan Doyle (1859–1930) and the enthusiastic response of audiences to the film versions of the stories about the London detective.

Ever since publication of Doyle's first story about Britain's most famous fictional sleuth in 1900, the adventures of Sherlock Holmes had always had a strong following. In an English-speaking world racked by a global depression, his stories and those made into films were a welcome respite from reality. For many British-trained actors, the part of Sherlock Holmes guaranteed a large audience. Clive Brook of *Shanghai Express* fame was one such performer, who knew that this coveted role would add luster to his cinematic resume.

Before playing Captain Donald Harvey in *Shanghai Express,* Clive Brook acted in the first talking Sherlock Holmes picture, entitled *The Return of Sherlock Holmes* (1929), directed by Wong's theatrical mentor, Basil Dean. In the same year *The Return of Sherlock Holmes* was released, Wong performed in the London play *The Circle of Chalk,* opposite Laurence Olivier and directed by Dean. Once

Shanghai Express was completed, Brook's subsequent picture was his second and final starring role as the British investigator in *Sherlock Holmes* (1932).

Coming off his success as Shanghai Lily's lover, Clive Brook's theatrical career had reached a pinnacle of acclaim and recognition. With his stardom clearly at its zenith, studio bosses at Paramount decided that they had to capitalize on Brook's cinematic momentum. Following the colossal triumph of *Shanghai Express,* they reasoned that producing another rendition of the ever-popular Sherlock Holmes with the equally popular Clive Brook as the clever Baker Street detective was a license to print money. This resulted in *Sherlock Holmes* (1932).

Like Paramount, World Wide Pictures also wanted to capitalize on the success of both *Shanghai Express* and the Sherlock Holmes series. Since it could not sign Clive Brook, who was already tied contractually to Paramount, and a film involving Sherlock Holmes simply did not fit in well with the sophisticated and erotic style of the German-accented Marlene Dietrich, World Wide Pictures turned to *Shanghai Express's* third lead, Anna May Wong. Wong was an obvious signing.[1] That she was also versatile and not averse to playing different characters made her a natural choice for Mrs. Pyke.

In *A Study in Scarlet,* Wong's Mrs. Pyke was center stage. Her sparkling performance was even more apparent when contrasted with the solid but uninspired characterization of Sherlock Holmes by Reginald Owen (1887–1972), who earlier had played Watson to Clive Brook's Holmes in *The Return of Sherlock Holmes.* Like the heroines in *The Toll of the Sea* and *Shanghai Express,* Wong portrayed Mrs. Pyke as a strong, proactive, and confident woman. Certainly she outperformed the only other female in the film, June Clyde (1909–1987), who portrayed the innocent and naive Eileen Forrester. After working under the mature direction of Josef von Sternberg in the *Shanghai Express,* Wong now encountered Edwin L. Marin (1899–1951) as the director of *A Study in Scarlet.* Since this was only his second picture as a solo director, a veteran star like Wong no doubt had more to contribute to the making of this movie than he did.

Sophisticated and mature, Mrs. Pyke, like Shosho in *Piccadilly,* wore the latest London fashions. It was almost as if *A Study in Scarlet,* produced at the California Tiffany Studios, was merely a showcase for Anna May Wong's modeling talents and acting abilities. In her first encounter with Reginald Owen's Sherlock Holmes, Wong's Mrs. Pyke wore a soft round hat slouched to her right and a double-breasted tweed coat enclosing a dark turtleneck sweater.

In a pivotal scene when Mrs. Pyke invites Eileen Forrester and Jabez Wilson to visit her, Wong's mannerisms and style exude confidence and purpose in her character, especially as she saunters from the living room, where she towers over June Clyde in height and maturity, to the front door to accept a telegram. Dressed in a low-cut black dress with shear sleeves, she gives every appearance that she is in control. Later, dressed in an evening pantsuit ensemble with three conspicuous cloth buttons holding the top together in an obvious attempt to evoke a Shanghai motif, she strolls haughtily and casually along a corridor to the bedroom door of her guest, Jabez Wilson, as if she is modeling a mink coat on a Milan runway. After many years in Hollywood and European studios, Wong could hold and manipulate a scene as long as she wanted with little effort.

That Wong was able to steal every scene in which she performed in *A Study in Scarlet* was an understatement. She drew on her large repertoire of gestures and body language, so familiar in her silent films. When she is about to exit an elevator, Sherlock Holmes appears. On meeting the London sleuth, her eyes dart from one side to the other as if she is evoking a typical silent expression of caution and anxiety. Her deep, resonating voice, always on the cusp of masculinity and so evident in *Shanghai Express,* is used to effect in this mystery as she confronts Holmes or dazzles a smitten Jabez Wilson, played by Dublin-born actor Joseph M. Kerrigan (1884–1964), whose delight at spending a night in the same house as Mrs. Pyke overshadows his nervousness.

In the scene at the Savoy Hotel, Mrs. Pyke is dressed in a satin gown with wide sleeves and holds a black cigarette. This is quintessentially Anna May Wong, exhibiting her famous cool and detached demeanor. Framed by a sparkling foreground of a blazing fireplace, which evokes warmth and intimacy, Mrs. Pyke deftly controls the scene with her casual delivery of lines that almost border on insolence, reminiscent of the famous Hui Fei's dissection of Mrs. Haggerty's pretense and pomposity in *Shanghai Express.* The scene opens from a fade of the Savoy Hotel sign to Mrs. Pyke pouring tea for Jabez Wilson.

Mrs. Pyke: *It's so kind of you to come. Knowing my late husband as intimately as you did, I felt that I could turn to no better person to help me through this trying time.*
Jabez Wilson: *Well, you know, anything I can do.*
Mrs. Pyke: *You are very nervous today.*

Wilson takes the cup of tea from Mrs. Pyke.

Jabez Wilson: *Well, I can't help it. You know. Look at my hands. I'm trembling all over.*

Wilson puts the cup of tea down on the closest table.

Jabez Wilson: *There, that will stop the racket at any rate.*
Mrs. Pyke: *My late husband always spoke of you in the warmest terms. And you know the high regard in which I always held you.*
Jabez Wilson: *Oh, have you?*

Mrs. Pyke: *Can you doubt it? You are the only one who knows of my husband's affairs. Everything has been left in the most terrible disorder. My house in the country will be sold. I wonder if you could spare the time.*
Jabez Wilson: *Yes?*
Mrs. Pyke: *You could be my guest over the weekend and we can go over his papers together.*
Jabez Wilson: *Really now with pleasure. I could do with a bit of a change.*
Mrs. Pyke: *We could drive down . . . would tonight be possible?*
Jabez Wilson: *Tonight? No, you see. I've got an important meeting tonight.*
Mrs. Pyke: *Then tomorrow!*
Jabez Wilson: *Tomorrow. May I make a little confession? You know, Mrs. Pyke, I've always admired you tremendously.*

Cast against the working-class Cockney dialect of white Europeans on the Beijing to Shanghai express train and in London, the elite and polished London—Los Angeles English of Wong's yellow and Asian characters propelled her beyond the demeaning stereotypes of the little China doll in *The Toll of the Sea* and the conniving Asian types in many of her films during the late 1920s. Her Mongol spy in *The Thief of Bagdad* was of course the ultimate exhibition of Asian cunning and intelligence. The role of the sophisticated and fashionably dressed Mrs. Pyke gave Wong a distinctly different look.

Despite speaking in a British-accented voice complemented by London fashions, Wong's Mrs. Pyke, as a Chinese, was still the Other in this drama. Even the working-class maid in her palatial mansion speaks of her in a condescending manner to Sherlock Holmes, disguised as a prospective house buyer. Referring to a photo of Mrs. Pyke, the maid says:

The Maid: *That's mistress. Such a good looker. Such eyes. She walks like a cat. Such a figure. Such a fine bit of goods. An English lady makes her look like nothing.*

The only other Asian in *A Study in Scarlet* was Mrs. Pyke's manservant, Ah Yet, who is also a member of the criminal gang, Scarlet Ring, led by Thaddeus Merrydew. Played by veteran Japanese American actor Tetsu Komai (1894–1970), Ah Yet has no speaking lines, but his presence provokes derision and scorn from Jabez Wilson and William Baker, performed by Cecil Reynolds in his first acting role.

Komai had already worked with Wong as Lao in *Daughter of the Dragon* (1931) and was to work in more than fifty pictures. On the other hand, Reynolds was Charlie Chaplin's (1889–1977) personal Hollywood physician, who also consulted on films that required medical advice. In his second and final role, he played a minister in Chaplin's *Modern Times* (1936).

Even though *A Study in Scarlet* was Reynolds's inaugural film, Edwin L. Marin, the director, gave him a multitude of scenes and lines. As a member of the Scarlet Ring, he is prominent in the meetings and intrigues. The meeting that Jabez Wilson was referring to during his fireside chat with Mrs. Pyke at the Savoy Hotel was the Limehouse rendezvous with the rest of the Scarlet Ring's criminal gang. As the Limehouse scene opens, Jabez Wilson and William Baker express their fury at a London newspaper's classified:

ANYONE SUPPLYING
INFORMATION
concerning the
"SCARLET RING"
will be rewarded. Apply
SHERLOCK HOLMES
221A Baker Street.

Seeing this help wanted advertisement, Wilson and Baker realize that one of their members in the Scarlet Ring has broken its code and given it to Sherlock Holmes. In a low whisper, Baker exclaims, "It's one of us, that's certain. You can leave the girl out. Can't be the dumb Chinaman," referring to the smoking Ah Yet, seated a table away. Although Wilson admired Mrs. Pyke, an Asian, Baker and Wilson had little to say that was positive about the other Asian character in the film.

A Study in Scarlet took only the title and main characters from one of Sir Arthur Conan Doyle's stories, but it exhibits the prerequisite intrigue, murder, extortion, and terror so often found in a typical Sherlock Holmes melodrama. The plot involves murder by shooting, poison, and knifing as well as a real estate land grab concocted by the Scarlet Ring, which specializes in snatching jewels. It is also reminiscent of an Edgar Wallace plot twister, with "screams in the night, secret panels,"[2] flashing knives, sinister killers, and midnight fog. Yet without Wong in the lead female role, the film would have been simply another routine and forgettable crime drama ground out within a two-week deadline by Tinseltown's relentless movie machine.

REVIEWS

The Kinematograph on August 10, 1933, called *A Study in Scarlet's* adaptation "artless" and "free yet entertaining"; the characterizations were "artificial."[3]

The reviewer found Anna May Wong's Mrs. Pyke "nothing to quarrel with."[4] Likewise, in the *New York Times,* Mordaunt Hall proclaimed:

> Anna May Wong does well in her part. The atmosphere of London thoroughfares, including of course Baker Street, is quite well reproduced. And there are also some glimpses in a tap room (pub) that may make some sigh with regret that only a 3.2 is, so far, here.[5]

In *Variety,* the reviewer wrote that Anna May Wong as Mrs. Pyke, Alan Dinehart (1889–1944) as the murderous Thaddeus Merrydew, and Warburton Gamble (1883–1945) as the genteel Dr. Watson were "particularly up to their assignments."[6]

After completing *A Study in Scarlet* in 1932, Wong returned to Europe, where her stardom was never questioned and her talents were celebrated by audiences and the media. Europe was home to the most famous actress from Chinese America, with London as her welcoming base. For the next two years she lived the life of a noted movie star and Hollywood celebrity in Great Britain.

NOTES

1. Chris Steinbrunner and Norman Michaels, *The Films of Sherlock Holmes* (Secaucus, N.J.: Citadel Press, 1978), 42.

2. Steinbrunner and Michaels, *Films of Sherlock Holmes,* 44.

3. *The Kinematograph,* 10 August 1933, cited in Robert W. Pohle and Douglas C. Hart, *Sherlock Holmes on the Screen: The Motion Picture Adventures of the World's Most Popular Detective* (New York: A. S. Barnes, 1977), 121.

4. *The Kinematograph,* 121.

5. Mordaunt Hall, "Sherlock Holmes and the Murderers Turn Up in a New Guise in Old-Time Thriller," *New York Times,* 1 June 1933, 15.

6. *Variety,* 6 June 1933, 14.

SIXTEEN

CHU CHIN CHOW (1934)

While in London Anna May Wong starred in *Tiger Bay* (1933), *Chu Chin Chow* (1934), and *Java Head* (1934). Of the three films, *Chu Chin Chow* received the most acclaim, not only from European audiences but also from American movie fans. Even his White House handlers allowed President Franklin D. Roosevelt (1882–1945) and his family to screen the film privately in honor of his mother's birthday during its initial Broadway showing in September 1934.[1] They were thrilled with the performance, which seemed to confirm the *London Times* observation that *Chu Chin Chow* "is easily the biggest thing in its class that has ever come from England" and "marks a definite challenge by Great Britain to American producers."[2]

Adapted from a collection known as *The Arabian Nights* or *The Thousand and One Nights (Alf Laylah wa Laylah),* this series of writings began to be formed by al-Jahshitari into a collection in Iraq during the tenth century. A collection of completely non-European narratives with many of the plots originating in India, *The Arabian Nights* was a ploy by Scheherazade to save herself from being murdered by her jealous husband, King Shahrayar. Having no faith in any of his previous wives, this deranged ruler would wed them one day and then have them executed on the next day. To save the king and the social chaos issuing from his misogynistic psychosis, Scheherazade offered herself as a wife. But to save herself from death the next morning, she began reciting stories from the Persian *Hazar Afsana* (a thousand tales) for a thousand and one nights, beginning on her wedding night, thus beguiling the king into forgetting about her execution.

The stories from *The Arabian Nights* eventually caught the imagination of Europeans. Like the stories and plays from the Yuan Dynasty, these Arabic narratives were transmitted to the West via translations by Christian priests. The first to attempt a European edition of *The Arabian Nights* was Abbe Antoine Galland (1646–1715), who published his French translations from 1704 to 1717. English translations came from a sixteen-volume tome published by Sir Richard Burton (1821–1890) and John Payne, with nine volumes being issued from 1882 to 1884. There are also a 1937 translation from the French edition of J. C. Mardrus by E. Powys Mathers (1892–1939) and the recent work of Husain Haddawy, two volumes published in 1990 and 1995.

The Arabian Nights became so popular in the European imagination and perception of the Arab and Indian worlds that some Europeans even began to question the authenticity of the work. Without a smattering of any Arabic, Indian, or "Oriental" language, nineteenth-century British traveler and raconteur Alexander W. Kinglake (1809–1891) began popularizing the notion among Westerners that the energy and innovation of the tales in *The Arabian Nights* were so considerable that they could have been conceived and written only by Europeans. He based this idea on the perception that a "mere Oriental, . . . for creative purposes, is a thing dead and dry—a mental mummy."[3]

In the vast repertoire of *The Arabian Nights,* such stories as *Aladdin, Ali Baba and the Forty Thieves,* and *Sinbad the Sailor* were the major crowd pleasers. Inspired by *Ali Baba and the Forty Thieves,* an Australian, Oscar Asche (1871–1936), adapted this tale into a comic operetta, entitled *Chu Chin Chow.* During the grim days of World War I it entertained London audiences with 2,238 consecutive performances from August 31, 1916, to July 22, 1921. Between 1917 and 1918, Morris Gest, who later collaborated with Douglas Fairbanks on *The Thief of Bagdad* (1924), produced the play in New York for 105 performances.[4] In 1923 Jameson Thomas, who would later star opposite Anna May Wong in *Piccadilly* (1929), played Omar, the young male lover in the first film version of *Chu Chin Chow.* His female love interest was named Zahrat.

THE MAKING OF THE 1934 *CHU CHIN CHOW*

With a track record of sustained longevity and box office success, it was inevitable that *Chu Chin Chow* would debut as a talking picture. Realizing that the London stage play of *Chu Chin Chow* was a huge hit during wartime, the producers at Gainsborough Pictures reckoned that a talking *Chu Chin Chow* during the opening curtains of the second European civil war might prove just as profitable.

Filmed at the Gainsborough studio lots in Islington and Shephard's Bush with a budget of $500,000, *Chu Chin Chow* was destined to be a true musical extravaganza, directed by a former music hall comedian, Walter Forde (1896–1954), who was one of the best British directors of entertainment features.[5] Directing such famous British music hall performers as George Robey (the Prime Minister of Mirth, 1869–1954) playing Ali Baba and such unknowns as Thelma Tuson as Alcolom, wife of Kasim Baba and radio performer, Malcolm MacEachern (Jetsam) as Abdullah, Forde endeavored to provide *Chu Chin Chow* not only with comedic flavor but also with inspired singing and dancing. Other notable cast members were singer John Garrick (1902–1966) as Nur-al-din Baba, Ali Baba's son, and Pearl Argyle (1910–1988), one of Britain's premier ballerinas, as Marjanah, the love interest of Nur-al-din.

Playing opposite Wong as Zahrat, the forty thieves' slave spy in Kasim Baba's household, was German character actor Fritz Kortner (1892–1970) in the role of Abu Hasan. After murdering the Chinese merchant, Chu Chin Chow, Abu Hasan impersonates him in "Yellowface" at Kasim Baba's feast. Throughout the film Kortner is Abu Hassan in "Brownface" and during the final scene plays a slave in "Blackface."

Since she was a major bankable asset with extensive experience in American and European films, Wong was the key to success for the film. But unlike the 1923 silent film of *Chu Chin Chow*, in which Zahrat was matched with Omar, in the 1934 talking version the Zahrat role was rescripted as a conspirator in the pay of Abu Hasan and later as a heroine who saves the Ali Baba family, rather than being only a lover of the young son of Ali Baba. Of course even in Britain love interests between yellows and whites were forbidden, although a crack did appear in Wong's next picture under the direction of Basil Dean. In *Java Head* (1934), Wong as the yellow woman Princess Taou Yuen actually has one of her first on-screen kisses with the white man Gerrit Ammidon, played by John Loder (1898–1988). Dean wrote that Loder and Ralph Richardson (1902–1983), who played his elder brother, William Ammidon, in the film "spent most of their time standing on the sidelines, drooling at the celestial beauty of Anna May."[6]

German Hungarian art director Erno Metzner (1892-1953) elaborately designed the desert caves and Arabic palace sets of *Chu Chin Chow*. They were classic examples of "Orientalism." As European Jews, Metzner and Kortner worked in London after escaping Hilter's pogroms in Austria and Germany.[7] Metzner's pseudo-Arabic set designs were created to include Anna May Wong's Zahrat "as their chief piece of dressing," thus evoking the idea of the

"Oriental" as the Other.[8] The entire production was redolent with "Yellow-face," "Brownface," and "Blackface," with numerous Europeans grotesquely playing Chu Chin Chow's retainers and underlings, Arabic merchants, princes, princesses, slaves, dancers, cooks, pastry chefs, cadaver menders, and the forty thieves. The only authentic performers were Wong as the Asian slave spy and Kyoshi Takase as an Asian entertainer.

The film even had a singing part for Wong, although it is obvious that her serenade of Abu Hasan is sung by an uncredited female singer. But her dance at the conclusion of the film is vintage Wong, reminiscent of Shosho's pan-Asian choreography in *Piccadilly*. Her performance as Zahrat is also quintessentially Wong, with her characteristic use of the raised eyebrow, the all-knowing smile, and the body language learned from years as a silent film actress. Compared to one-dimensional female characters like Thelma Tuson's giggling and silly Alcolom or Pearl Argyle's earnest and always correct Marjanah, Wong's Zahrat exhibits a wide range of emotions and gestures. Her anger is natural when Abu Hasan chains her to the wheel of death in the cave. She is playful and naughty when manicuring Alcolom's feet. Just as she is about to beautify the right foot of Kasim Baba's wife, Wong's character stabs her with a pedicure instrument. Alcolom gasps:

> Alcolom: *Ana, what are you doing, you hen head?*
> Zahrat: *Oh, my mistress, I ask your apology of a thousand pardons.*
> Alcolom: *You've ruined my foot forever, you left-handed cow.*
> Zahrat: *I'll soon cure it. I have some morsus of Egypt that will soothe any wound.*

This scene illustrates Wong's comedic presence. In the final dancing scene, where Zahrat flings a dagger at a "Blackface" Abu Hasan, Wong reveals herself once again as a consummate actress as she exhibits utmost hatred and contempt for Abu Hasan:

> Zahrat: *Lift up your head so that I can see your face and taste my vengeance to the full.*

Yet once Abu Hasan rolls to his death after clinging to a huge gong, Zahrat is able to demonstrate genuine compassion and remorse at his demise.

THE HEROINE

Zahrat's strategy of rolling the forty oil urns filled with thieves into a large well, dancing in place of Pearl Argyle's Marjanah, and knifing the master thief and murderer, Abu Hasan, supplemented by an arrow from Nur-al-din Baba, saves the Ali Baba family from destruction. Like the heroine, Hui Fei, who kills Henry Chang in *Shanghai Express*, Zahrat performs the heroic deed of vengeance by knifing her abuser, Abu Hasan. In doing so, Hui Fei and Zahrat were both heroines in the Chinese tradition of Hua Mulan, Chen Shuozhen, She Saihua, Mu Guiying, Qin Liangyu, and Hong Xuanjiao. Here, Zahrat exhibits the traits of courage, astute strategy, and selflessness, although this was tempered by vengeance. But this is evidently a sacrifice because of her love for Abu Hasan. This affection is clearly noticed by Marjanah when Zahrat pours wine for Abu Hasan at the Kasim Baba's feast, where Abu Hasan was impersonating Chu Chin Chow. But she rejects this love because of his witless abuse and her inner strength as a woman of power in an arena of patriarchy.

In *Shanghai Express* and *Chu Chin Chow,* Wong's characters are powerful women who will not tolerate the behavior of vile, rapacious, and murderous men. By saving herself as an individual in a collective whole, she also saves the people inhabiting the collective whole. Although Zahrat has a moment of weakness at Abu Hasan's death, both Hui Fei and Zahrat walk away from their deeds as heroines. In the 1930s Wong's film characters continued to have distinctly different looks. Her charismatic style of performance showed the Asian American woman as an individual of agency who could assume empowerment as a dynamic force to be reckoned with when the time and place dictated it. Her characters were truly women of substance.

REVIEWS

Film reviewers were unanimously enthusiastic about *Chu Chin Chow.* The *New York Times* reviewer exclaimed that there was "no fault with the cast," calling Fritz Kortner's Abu Hasan "brilliant" and praising George Robey as the "lovable and laughable Ali Baba."[9] He continued with the comment that the

> film is pretty much what it was meant to be—a comic operetta. And, for the color and excitement, those who remember the fairy tale will find a convincing model of the mountain retreat with its "Open Sesame" password, a few red blooded battles with scimitar and arrow, and always the picturesque costume and language of a picturesque period.[10]

The *London Times,* reviewing a Tivoli Theater screening, revealed:

> With the help of expert advice the Eastern settings of this film have been constructed with unusual accuracy and would provide not only an expensive

but an interesting spectacle if they were not shrouded during the greater part of the film in a dim twilight which even the desert sun at midday is powerless to dispel. But as the eye slowly accustomed itself to this mysterious *chiaroscuto* it is possible to discover that an English pantomime is proceeding, and it may well be that the fog is there to make everyone feel at home. Mr. George Robey is unalterably domestic in any disguise and the love affair of the hero and heroine (Mr John Garrick and Miss Pearl Argyle) is admirably prim. The robbers are heartily operatic and their leader (Mr Fritz Kortner) exaggerates his own villainy with an evidently humorous intention.[11]

Wong's performance was especially noted. The *London Times* reviewer continued: "Miss Anna May Wong is rather more suited to the exotic setting but even so, her American rather than her Chinese attributes come to the front."[12] That she was now more American than Chinese made her appearance distinctly different from her first sojourn in European films.

In 1930, just after Wong's completion of *The Flame of Love* (1930), *Hai Tang* (1930), and *L'amour maitre des choses* (1930), the German art director Ali Hubert had been adamant in portraying Wong as exquisitely and exotically Chinese. She was the perfect Other. He wrote:

> She personifies the spirit of the great Li Taipe, and brings to life for us the tales of 1001 nights. On her tender and youthful body, expressing every moment with the indescribable grace of the Oriental woman, towers her head which, although completely Mongolian, is beautiful by European standards. Her eyes, for a Chinese unusually large, deep and dark like a Tibetan mountain lake, gaze with enormous expressiveness. Her well-shaped, slightly voluptuous lips form a striking contrast to the melancholy darkness of her eyes. Her hands are of outstanding beauty, slim and perfectly formed. Only a Van Eyck or a Holbein could capture her on canvas.
>
> Externally, she appears American: smart, confident, and chicly dressed. But inside, she is purely Chinese, wearing long hair, and believing in reincarnation, convinced that in her next life she will swing as a hummingbird on the branches of a pepper-tree.[13]

Hubert's description of Wong epitomized the tortured ideology of "Orientalism," which "depends for its strategy on this flexible positional superiority, which puts the Westerner in a whole series of possible relationships with the Orient without ever losing him the upper hand."[14] As a practitioner of "Orientalism" and therefore an "Orientalist," Ali Hubert subscribed to the proposition that "Europe is powerful and articulate; Asia is defeated and distant. . . . It is Europe that articulates the Orient; this articulation is the prerogative, not of a puppet master, but of a genuine creator, whose life-giving power represents, animates, constitutes the otherwise silent and dangerous space beyond familiar boundaries."[15] Since he perceived her through the ideology of "Orientalism," Hubert spoke for Wong because he surmised that she could not articulate her persona and existence herself.

Deliberately articulating Wong as an "Oriental" and thus an Other, Ali Hubert objectified her as if she were one of the Oriental, objets d'art–like diminutive Japanese ivory carvings known as *netsuke*, a precious commodity and artifact waiting to be acquired and consumed by Western customers.[16] For "Orientalists" like Hubert, Oriental "women are usually the creatures of a male power-fantasy. They express unlimited sensuality, they are more or less stupid, and above all they are willing."[17] For the Westerners peering into a totally different and alien world, bountiful feasts, capricious thieves, corpulent princes, cunning spies, dainty princesses, evil debauchers, outlandish motifs, religious fanatics, slave auctions, sparsely dressed dancers, veiled women in harems, and villainous murderers inhabited the Arabic world. In *The Thief of Bagdad* and *Chu Chin Chow*, Anna May Wong symbolized in the eyes of European and European American males what an Arabic or "Oriental" woman ought to be and how she ought to behave. And she was also objectified by female audiences at showings of *Chu Chin Chow*.

In a *Seattle Daily Times* commentary about *Chu Chin Chow*, the notion of Wong as an adornment and artifact was perpetuated. She was a Hollywood commodity to be acquired and consumed:

> At any rate, not even the beautiful clothes the star of *Chu Chin Chow* wears, fascinating as her wonderful gowns are, particularly to the feminine eye, can distract attention from their wearer. And yet—in one scene she appears, a figure of shimmering light, clad in silken vesture, entirely covered over with shining pearls of price, a literal garment of gems which brings "Ohs and Ahs" of rapt admiration from every member of her own sex who gazes upon it.[18]

Despite the public attention to her body and adornments, Wong was also often depicted as a consummate professional whose major traits were not only true acting ability but also hard work and punctuality. In Britain's *Picturegoer Weekly*, Vivien North commented on her studio presence and preproduction theatrical persona:

> One evening, at her request, I went down to Islington to watch her working in *Chu Chin Chow*. I found her on the edge of a terrific set teaming with Oriental bandits and Negro slaves and on which a barbaric battle was taking place. She was talking calmly, with unraised voice to Edward Knoblock who wrote the dialogue for *Chu Chin Chow*.

There was no high-handed nonsense about Miss Wong. When a harassed assistant bawled across at her, "Anna May! Hi there! We'll want you in this next shot," she just waved a friendly hand and pushed her way through the slaves and robbers.

Mr. Knoblock tells me that he was the first person to give her a big chance. That was when he was working on *The Thief of Bagdad.* "Anna May," he says, "is a dear person. She is the sole of thoughtfulness and consideration. She never forgets a kindness, and she works very hard."[19]

North's description of Wong in *Chu Chin Chow* as an industrious professional did not preclude her from being defrauded or cheated. In addition, her talents were sometimes overlooked when auditions were open for choice roles. The call for parts in *The Good Earth* was one of these occasions.

NOTES

1. "British Film Success in New York, '*Chu Chin Chow*' shown to President Roosevelt," *London Times,* 25 September 1934, 4.

2. "British Film Success in New York," 4.

3. Kinglake, cited in Edward Said, *Orientalism* (New York: Viking, 1979), 193.

4. "A Robust Operetta," *New York Times Film Reviews,* 22 September 1934, 1096–97.

5. Roy Armes, *A Critical History of the British Cinema* (London: Secker & Warburg, 1978), 93.

6. Basil Dean, *Mind's Eye: An Autobiography, 1927–1972,* vol. 2 of *Seven Ages* (London: Hutchinson, 1973), 219.

7. Tim Bergfelder, "Negotiating Exoticism: Hollywood, Film Europe and the Cultural Reception of Anna May Wong," in *"Film Europe" and "Film America": Cinema, Commerce and Cultural Exchange, 1920–1939,"* ed. Andrew Higson and Richard Maltby (Exeter, England: University of Exeter Press, 1999), 315.

8. Sue Harper, "From Wholesome Girls to Difficult Dowagers, Actresses in the 1930s, British Cinema," in *British Cinema, Past and Present,* ed. Justine Ashby and Andrew Higson (London: Routledge, 2000), 139.

9. "Robust Operetta," 1096–97.

10. "Robust Operetta," 1096–97.

11. "'*Chu Chin Chow*' at the Tivoli," *London Times,* 20 August 1934, 12.

12. "'*Chu Chin Chow*,'" 12.

13. Ali Hubert, *Hollywood, Legende und Wirklichkeit* (Leipzig, Germany: E. A. Seemann, 1930; repr. Heidelberg, Germany: Das Wunderhorn, 1988), 106–7, cited in Bergfelder, "Negotiating Exoticism," 318–19.

14. Said, *Orientalism,* 7.

15. Said, *Orientalism*, 7.

16. Sumiko Higashi, "Touring the Orient with Lafcadio Hearn and Cecil B. De-mille: Highbrow versus Lowbrow in a Consumer Culture," in *The Birth of Whiteness: Race and the Emergence of U.S. Cinema*, ed. Daniel Bernardi (New Brunswick, N.J.: Rutgers University Press, 19), 333; Bergfelder, "Negotiating Exoticism," 318.

17. Said, *Orientalism*, 207.

18. "Lovely Oriental Star Adorned in Rich Dress," *Seattle Daily Times*, 28 December 1934, 11.

19. Vivien North, "There's a Secret Anna May Wong," *Picturegoer Weekly* (8 September 1934): 4.

SEVENTEEN

NEFARIOUS PLOTS

LEGAL MATTERS

Asian American women might have reveled in Anna May Wong not only as an industrious actress and a self-directed, proactive woman with a professional career, but also as a cinematic performer who portrayed women of action, power, and substance. In real-life adventures filled with treachery and deceit, moreover, they would have been delighted with her actions. In a tussle probably over money in the *Chu Chin Chow* production, Wong filed legal action through her solicitors, S. Myers and Sons of Wormwood Street (London), against Gainsborough Pictures, Ltd.[1] Ever since she was stung by a potential deal with promoter Forrest B. Creighton to develop "The Anna May Wong Productions" in 1924 when she was merely nineteen years old, Wong had never hesitated to seek redress through legal adjudication.[2] It did not matter if these backroom maneuvers that were damaging to her career were perpetrated by European Americans or Europeans, she would sue and if need be, sue often.

From 1930 to 1939 Wong appeared in seventeen films, of which *Elstree Calling* (1930), *Hollywood on Parade* (1932), and *Hollywood Party* (1937) were more burlesque, vaudeville, and cameos than feature films. But it was still work.

As a Chinese American film actress performing in a predominantly European American or European industry, work and the next paycheck were always on her mind. Between the release of *Shanghai Express* (1932) and *Chu Chin Chow* (1934), Wong became aware of a plum acting part in a film based on *The Good Earth,* a novel written by sinophile Pearl S. Buck (1892–1973).

THE GOOD EARTH

Published on March 2, 1931, this story chronicled the lives of Wang Lung, a Chinese peasant, and his wife, O-lan, as they mastered the intricacies of life in a China ravaged by warlords, conflicts between the nationalist government and communist rebels, and the marauding Japanese military intent on snaring China into its empire.[3] Translated into more than thirty languages, *The Good Earth* was the top-selling novel in the United States from 1931 to 1932. It was translated into Chinese in 1932 and serialized in the *Eastern Mercury (Dongfang zazhi)* for Chinese readers, one of whom was professor Wu Lifu. He criticized the book for its misleading interpretation of the Chinese as one-dimensional characters who were simply avaricious, greedy, ignorant, and superstitious amid drought, famine, thievery, and revolution. Wu questioned the notion that China's salvation could only be achieved through Western benevolence and intervention based on European American and therefore white values.[4] The Republic of China was also critical of the novel.

Despite some Chinese criticisms of *The Good Earth,* many Western readers loved the book and some even took it as fact. It was awarded a Pulitzer Prize in 1935. This was one of the major reasons for Buck's attaining the Nobel Prize for literature in 1938. Film stars signed to play the major roles would not only have their careers expanded but would also be guaranteed a large audience, thereby increasing their celebrity and earning power. By 1932 when Metro-Goldwyn-Mayer Studios purchased the film rights to *The Good Earth* for $100,000, the word was out that it would be casting for the role of O-lan and Lotus.[5]

Wong lobbied hard for the role of O-lan. If she was cast as Wang Lung's wife, the characterization would have been muted since O-lan was the stereotype of what European American males depicted as the typical Chinese woman. She would have been required to play a docile, obedient, unassuming and submissive woman bowing to the wishes of her husband. Thus, in the eyes of Chinese and non-Chinese alike, Wong as O-lan would have perpetuated the notion of the inferior woman in Chinese patriarchy. For an actress who had been entrusted with playing strong, powerful, intelligent, and strategically profound Chinese women who were singularly aggressive in demanding retribution in *Shanghai Express* and *Chu Chin Chow*, the role of O-lan would have challenged all of her acting acumen, cinematic experience, and theatrical presence. But as a consummate professional, she was up to that challenge.

In April 1933 Hollywood columnist Grace Kingsley proclaimed that Wong was the leading candidate for the role of O-lan. Wong herself was enthusiastic about playing O-lan and was "quite sure to if W. S. Van Dyke (1889–1943) directs it."[6] The story even mentioned that her sister, Lulu Ying Wong, who was directed by Van Dyke in *Eskimo* (1933), might also have a part in *The Good Earth*.

If Pearl Buck, who received only $25,000 for the film adaptation for her novel from MGM,[7] had had her way, someone like Wong would have been cast in the title role. In an authorized biography, Buck remarked:

> I remember having lunch at Sardi's with a member of the firm of Metro-Goldwyn-Mayer. He asked me if I had any particular wishes about the motion picture, and I said that I hoped they would use Chinese actors in the leading parts, to which he replied that this was impossible because of the American star system.[8]

No doubt Buck's request was motivated by the fact that the stage adaptation of *The Good Earth* written by Owen Davis and his son, David, had flopped on Broadway. She said:

> When I returned to America, I saw that play in rehearsals, and I knew it would fail. I remember that so well because it was a rehearsal quite near opening day. I was discouraged because the American actors were so un-Chinese, even in the abrupt, ungraceful fashion in which they walked. I was used to the graceful movements of the Chinese. It was a shock to see these awkward Americans dressed in Chinese clothes.[9]

By 1935 MGM had decided that "awkward" Americans would not be cast in the major roles. In fact, "awkward" Europeans would be used instead. While Pearl Buck was dismayed that Vienna-born Luise Rainer (1910–) and Austrian–Hungarian-born Paul Muni (Meshilem Meier Weisenfreund, 1895–1967) were hired respectively as O-lan and Wang Lung and not Asian or Asian American performers, Wong was devastated. Not only was she turned down for the role of O-lan, but after testing for the role of the concubine, Lotus, she was turned down for that part as well. This rejection was substantiated by *New York American* reporter Regina Crewe. After Wong returned from her

China sojourn, Crewe discovered that "while she doesn't say so, it must have been a keen disappointment to Wong, after taking dozens of tests for the role of the second wife in *The Good Earth,* the role was given to Vienna-born Tilly Losch (1904–1974) who had a very short career of only three films. The producer said Anna May Wong 'wasn't the type.'"[10] While in Hawaii on the first leg of her trip to China, however, Wong told Ray Coll of the *Honolulu Advertiser* that "I do not see why I, at this stage of my career, should take a step backward and accept a minor role in a Chinese play that will surround me entirely by a Caucasian cast."[11]

In the casting notes to *The Good Earth,* agents were looking for an O-lan who was not beautiful but was slavelike, with a kind, ordinary face. Lotus was to be a young woman of twenty who exuded sensuality as well as beauty. Casting agents and directors already knew that Wong had performed as a beautiful courtesan, devious woman, hooker, sensuous vamp, and slave spy. She had a reputation playing powerful, proactive, and courageous women. On both accounts, Wong would not have complied with the prerequisites for either O-lan or Lotus. She was too attractive to play a plain O-lan, who epitomized obsequiousness. At thirty, she was ten years older than the young and beautiful Lotus character whom the producers wanted. Too beautiful for one part and too old for the other role were her downfalls in trying to be cast in *The Good Earth.*[12]

Certainly the unwillingness of MGM producers to hire Wong in *The Good Earth* smacked of racist casting, with the notion of "Yellowface" surfacing prominently. But Hollywood never allowed "correct" casting to interfere with the bottom line. After all, Hollywood producers were in the highly profitable business of fantasy, not social reconstruction.

The Good Earth was a major property for its prominence and celebrity. It was on the best-seller list for two straight years. Because it was a highly known product as a novel, this was a positive sign for guaranteeing a large viewing audience for its financial backers. Miscasting would have severely damaged the box office receipts. Thus, two known acting commodities, Luise Rainer and Paul Muni, who had just finished performing in *The Great Ziegfeld* and *The Story of Louis Pasteur* respectively in 1935, were given the opportunity to act in *The Good Earth.*

When the Academy Awards were announced for the best performers of 1936, the winners were Luise Rainer for best actress and Paul Muni for best actor. They were both bankable superstars, and their success at Oscar time would seem to justify MGM's hiring two Europeans for the top roles instead of Asians like Anna May Wong. In 1937 Luise Rainer won her second consecutive Oscar for best actress, this time for her role as O-lan in *The Good Earth.* If a rationale were needed for Luise Rainer being cast as Wang Lung's dutiful wife, being acclaimed the top actress of 1937 was the perfect closer. For MGM, it was just good business to engage "Yellowface" Luise Rainer and Paul Muni for roles that portrayed the Chinese people in stereotypical ways. It was also good business to hire Asian extras who could act. One of them was Wong's younger sister, Mary Liu Heung Wong (1915–1940), who played the part of the Little Bride. Three years after the release of *The Good Earth,* Mary committed suicide by hanging herself in a garage.[13]

The disappointment of not landing any roles in *The Good Earth* did not distract Wong from enjoying and savoring her China sojourn. She also signed a contract with Paramount. The post-China years represented her best period of film work, with starring roles as strong, proactive, and powerful Asian women. One of these was *The Lady from Chungking* (1942).

NOTES

1. "Writ Issued by Miss Wong," *Daily Express,* London, 21 April 1934, 1.

2. "Chinese Movie Star Accuses Film Partner," *San Francisco Chronicle,* 18 July 1924, 9.

3. For a concise analysis of the development of *The Good Earth* from a short story entitled "The Revolutionist," see Paul A. Doyle, *Pearl S. Buck* (Boston: Twayne, 1980), 29–41.

4. Liu Haiping, "Pearl S. Buck's Reception in China Reconsidered," in *The Several Worlds of Pearl S. Buck: Essays Presented at a Centennial Symposium, Randolph-Macon Woman's College, March 26–28, 1992,* ed. Elizabeth J. Lipscomb, France E. Webb, and Peter Conn (Westport, Conn.: Greenwood, 1994), 61.

5. Theodore F. Harris, *Pearl S. Buck: A Biography* (New York: John Day, 1933), 148.

6. Grace Kingsley, "Anna May Wong for Lead in 'The Good Earth,'" *San Francisco Chronicle,* 5 April 1933, 9.

7. Harris, *Pearl S. Buck,* 148.

8. Buck, cited in Harris, *Pearl S. Buck,* 148.

9. Buck, cited in Harris, *Pearl S. Buck,* 148.

10. Regina Crewe, "Frosted Willow," *New York American* (n.d.); Anna May Wong clippings, New York Public Library Theater Arts Collection; see also Michelle Liu, "The Politics of Performing the Chinese Woman: Anna May Wong and Rose Quong," unpublished paper.

11. Wong, cited in Ray Coll, "Anna Scorns Minor Role: Chinese Star Leaves Hollywood Flat," *Honolulu Advertiser,* 30 January 1936, 3.

12. Casting notes, Casting Department, MGM Studios, Culver City, 6 November 1933, 2, *The Good Earth* folder 2, MGM collection, University of Southern California Film/TV Archives.

13. "Anna May Wong's Sister's Suicide," *New York Herald Tribune,* 26 July 1940, 26.

EIGHTEEN

LADIES FROM CHUNGKING
AND SOUTH CHICAGO

Positive roles continued in the 1940s when Producers Releasing Corporation cast Anna May Wong as Lin Ying, an educator, in *Bombs Over Burma* (1942). But the piece de resistance of roles in her distinctly different look was her depiction of guerrilla leader Kwan Mei in *The Lady from Chungking* (1942). Certainly China was at war with Japan, and *Bombs Over Burma* and *The Lady from Chungking* might be called her "patriotic" stage. But Wong had already made a forceful political statement about the Japanese invasion of China with her article "Manchuria," published in 1932. Always a patriot during the early 1930s when that status was not fashionable in the United States and Chinese America, her work in the war films of the 1940s was not only a culmination of her passion for China but also an expression of her overt anti-Japanese feelings. *Bombs Over Burma* and *The Lady from Chungking* were merely the cinematic expressions of her fierce patriotism and political sentiments about China that had begun a decade before. Her determined political dynamics may even have been nurtured during the shooting of *Shanghai Express,* a film depicting a revolutionary China with its clash of ideologies and the influences of Westerners. For Wong, moviemaking during these days of war was now secondary to her antifascist worldview, so much so that she donated her entire $4,500 salary for *Bombs Over Burma* and *The Lady from Chungking* to the China War Relief Fund.[1]

THE LADY FROM CHUNGKING

As a film, *The Lady from Chungking* is a forgettable cinematic work. Because of its low budget, short turnaround production time, and classification as a "B-movie," it lacks the sophistication of a *Shanghai Express* with its mise-en-scène or even *Chu Chin Chow* with its elaborate sets, dancers, and jugglers. William Nigh (1881–1955) wanted a "quick and dirty" film, and it shows in stock footage of the same canons firing not once but twice. Very small sets with phony Chinese statues obviously bought from curio shops in Los Angeles Chinatown were used in the execution scene. Location shooting was kept to a minimum. "Yellowface" is pervasive, with the chief Japanese villains played by Harold Huber (1904–1954) as the flaccid General Kaimura and Ted Hecht (1908–1969) as the obsequious Lieutenant Shimota. Asian American actor James B. Leong, who was cast with Wong as Jimmy Leong in the predominantly Asian production *The Silk Bouquet* (1926) and as one of the rebels in *Shanghai Express,* also performs as Chen, the trusted rebel confidant in *The Lady from Chungking.* Besides Wong, the only other well-known performer is Mae Clarke (Violet Mary Klotz, 1907–1992).

Despite its confinement to the second feature at theaters, however, *The Lady from Chungking* had innovative features. At the heart of the story is Wong's Kwan Mei, leading her regiment of Chinese rebels. Charismatically heroic, she epitomizes leadership, wisdom, and fearlessness reminiscent of such Chinese women warriors as Hua Mulan, Chen Shuozhen, She Saihua, Mu Guiying, Qin Liangyu, and Hong Xuanjiao. Taking control of her anti-Japanese insurgents, Kwan Mei portrays a Chinese woman of action, respect, and substance. In the killing of a Japanese soldier, she commands Chen:

Kwan Mei: *Japanese sentry must die. Don't use the gun.*

In another scene of authority, Kwan Mei exclaims:

Now listen carefully all of you. Kaimura the butcher is here for some important purpose. Wherever he goes, Japanese armies soon appear. Miss no opportunity to destroy the enemy. But be more cautious than ever, until we learn the general's plans! That is all.

In the final command scene, she announces:

General Kaimura's troop train will arrive in twenty-four hours. Choose your objectives and rehearse your men. The bridge must be blown up and the track, the rest ac-

cording to our plans which now include the escape of the American flyers. They will bring much air support for our attack.

These scenes illustrate the role of a heroine in a China now under siege by the Japanese. That Wong is steadfastly heroic in a China of revolution and rebellion led by historical male commanders like Jiang Jieshi, Mao Zedong, and Zhou Enlai places her character, Kwan Mei, in a unique position within a tradition of Chinese storytelling that resonates with heroes and heroines.

What is even more innovative and profound about Wong's Kwan Mei in *The Lady from Chungking* is that she commands a regiment of men. Although there were such historical female commanders as Zhang Qinqiu, who led the Women's Independent Division of about two thousand women soldiers, and Wang Quanyuan, who commanded thirteen hundred women warriors in the Women's Vanguard Regiment of the Red Army during the 1930s,[2] there was never any mention of a woman commander of men in revolutionary China. Only in dynastic China had a woman (Hua Mulan), disguised as a man, led a regiment of male soldiers. Like Kwan Mei, who was killed in the fictional account of the anti-Japanese struggles, many of the women in these two revolutionary units perished or were captured by the enemy in Gansu during the Long March of the Chinese Communists.

The fact that Wong was selected by Producers Releasing Corporation to portray a female commander of men undoubtedly attested more to her box office profitability as a popular movie star than to such an innovative story as a Chinese woman leading a regiment of men. But the war in China was brutal and continuous, and in 1942 when production for *The Lady from Chungking* began, the United States had just entered the war.

Creating a role in which the most popular Chinese American performer was seen as the leader of a revolutionary guerrilla unit was simply good business in the relentless propaganda campaign to depict the Chinese and the Americans as friends and allies and the Japanese as butchers. It was a natural progression to use Wong as the consummate Chinese heroine now fully developed as a revolutionary figure. However, despite her solid leadership and overt self-esteem, Wong also portrays Kwan Mei as a woman with human frailties and uncertainties in her character as she evokes a statute of Kwan Yin:

Kwan Mei: *Goddess of Mercy, give me strength.*

In spite of her strength, intelligence, and cunning in portraying a dynamic revolutionary leader in China's wilderness, her various ensembles throughout the film are quintessential Anna May Wong. While the film's story is a serious matter of life and death, the producers capitalize on the obvious fact that the star is always the beautifully attired and immaculately coiffed Anna May Wong. Even as the rebel leader in the rice fields, Kwan Mei wears a silk suit with handwoven buttons reminiscent of one of Mrs. Pyke's outfits in *A Study in Scarlet*. When she confronts General Kaimura, her evening gown is resplendent with a silk cape that evokes the opening scene in *Shanghai Express*. In the execution scene, Kwan Mei arrives dressed in a shirt with a Mandarin collar and fan-shaped sleeves covered by a sweater with a large peony, which in Chinese tradition signifies "prosperity." This was a bit of cross-dressing that juxtaposes death with a flowery symbol of success and wealth. However, the most provocative costume is Kwan Mei in a tight, high sleeved *cheong sam* with two snakelike dragons grasping her breasts. Many of these dresses were bought when Wong was in China in 1936. Just before the release of *The Lady from Chungking* in 1942, however, she sold many of these costumes made in China and her jewelry in an auction to benefit the United China Relief Fund.[3]

The Lady from Chungking would be Wong's last starring film role. After twenty-four years as a film performer, the role of the Chinese heroine, Kwan Mei, exemplified Wong's final celebrity as a film star. Now thirty-eight years old, she was a woman of agency whose words and deeds empowered not only herself but also those around her.

Her final lines seem to convey a political message that yearns to escape the confines of a European American Hollywood. It is almost as if Anna May Wong is destined to play the role of a fully constructed heroine like Kwan Mei, especially after a suicidal Lotus Flower in *The Toll of the Sea,* the courtesan-heroine Hu Fei in *Shanghai Express,* and the slave spy-heroine Zharat in *Chu Chin Chow.* Famous for the line, "I've died a thousand deaths," Wong's last scene in *The Lady from Chungking* defies death as she reemerges after being shot twice to deliver her soliloquy on the immortality of her heroine and of China:

> *You've not killed me. You cannot kill China. Not even a million deaths could crush the soul of China. For the soul of China is eternal!*
>
> *When I die, a million will take my place. And nothing can stop them. Neither hunger nor torture nor the firing squad.*
>
> *We shall live on until the enemy is driven back over scorched land and hurled into the sea. That time will come soon for the armies of liberty and decency are on the march.*
>
> *For China's destiny is victory. It will live because human freedom will not perish. Out of the ashes of ruin and old hatred, the force of peace will prevail until the world is again sane and pure.*

After the release of *The Lady from Chungking,* if any reporter had sought to ask why her screen characters died so often, Wong would have dredged up her classic answer. When asked by Vivien North in 1934 about her many movie deaths, she exclaimed that "it's a good thing we Chinese believe in rein-carnation,"[4] thus supporting the Westerner's stereotypical notion of Wong as a personification of the "inscrutable *Orient.*" When speaking to journalists, she playfully reveled in her aura of the "mysterious east."

"THE LADY FROM SOUTH CHICAGO"

Anna May Wong was one of the few movie performers who made the transition from silent films to talkies and then to the medium of television almost without any discernible difficulties. Certainly she was the only Asian American film star who transcended those styles of dramatic storytelling production. Although her next film was a small part as Su Lin in *Impact* (1949), she continued to extend her Hollywood persona as a genuine movie star in television.

In the mid-1950s Wong performed in such television shows as *Climax Mystery Theater* and *Producer's Showcase.* On November 2, 1959, Wong was cast in an ABC production. This time she again portrayed a strong, proactive Asian woman who, as a money changer, was the catalyst in trapping the extortionist in one of the ninety-one television episodes in *Adventures in Paradise* (1959–1962). Portraying Madame Lu Yang as a consummate businesswoman in "The Lady from South Chicago" the role was quintessentially Wong in style, appearance, and language. In a classic bargaining scene punctuated with implied sexual overtones between Madam Lu Yang (now fifty-four) and Captain Adam Troy (age twenty-eight), played by Gardner McKay (1931–2001), she asks:

Madam Lu Yang: *You wanted to see me?*
Adam Troy: *Are you Madame Lu Yang?*
Madam Lu Yang: *Yes.*
Adam Troy: *I am Adam Troy.*
Madam Lu Yang: *So I've been informed. What is it that you want of me?*
Adam Troy: *Business!*
Madam Lu Yang: *Your business or my business?*
Adam Troy: *Money!*
Madam Lu Yang: *Money, that is a commodity I do not give away!*
Adam Troy: *I'm sure you don't. There are three million francs there.*
Madam Lu Yang: *Three million francs! That is much money!*

Adam Troy: *I want it converted into English pound notes.*
Madam Lu Yang: *Hmm, there are banks who do that.*
Adam Troy: *There are authorities connected with banks.*
Madam Lu Yang: *Is the money stolen?*
Adam Troy: *I can assure you it is not. Now, do you have this much in English pounds or am I talking to the wrong Madam Lu Yang?*
Madam Lu Yang: *There is only* one *Madam Lu Yang!*
Mr. Troy, I own establishments from Bangkok to Tahiti. Noumea is just one stop in my enterprises that encompass the whole of the Pacific. Three million francs are exactly 2,184 pounds, fourteen shillings and six pence. No, Mr. Troy, if you've come to me instead of going to the banks, you must have a reason.
Adam Troy: *I have, the person I'm representing is . . .*
Madam Lu Yang: *You're not speaking for yourself?*
Adam Troy: *No.*
Madam Lu Yang: *I do not deal with messengers.*
Adam Troy: *Let's call me an interested friend.*
Madam Lu Yang: *Whom are you acting for? I want to know!*
Adam Troy: *She said you might. Victorine Reynard.*
Madam Lu Yang: *Flossie Mulveny? Is she in trouble?*
Adam Troy: *Let's say she's in a difficult situation.*
Madam Lu Yang: *Flossie, that was many years, many years since the old days in Singapore. Once she helped me out of a difficult situation. Mr. Troy, you may take the pound notes.*

As Adam Troy takes the pound notes, Madam Lu Yang holds back a few bills.

Madam Lu Yang: *My commission. I'm sure Flossie will understand.*
Adam Troy: *I'm sure she will.*

This money exchange scene illustrates the continuing European American obsession with exoticism in dramatic storytelling. While casually grasping a long cigarette holder, Wong's Madam Lu Yang assumes an air of mystery in a room filled with ornate Asian fixtures and furniture. Her character is fully dressed in an elaborate Chinese gown with a high neck collar. Her earring and strands of pearl represent women warrior performers in traditional Chinese operas. In demeanor, she resembles Ci Xi (1829–1908), the Empress Dowager of Qing China, holding court with a courtier or retainer by her side. In this scene, the courtier credited as a "Chinese merchant" is veteran Asian American actor James B. Leong, who had been in most of Wong's most memorable films, including *The Silk Bouquet* (1926), *Shanghai Express* (1932), and *The Lady from Chungking* (1942).

After "The Lady from South Chicago," Wong continued playing cameos in such television shows as *The Life and Legend of Wyatt Earp*, the *Barbara Stan-*

wyck Show, and *Danger Man.* By the 1960s, the first Chinese American female film star had survived all odds, especially rampant racism in Hollywood, to become a legend in her own time.

NOTES

1. Wong, cited in Karen Janis Leong, "The China Mystique: Mayling Soong Chiang, Pearl S. Buck and Anna May Wong in the American Imagination" (Ph.D. dissertation, University of California, Berkeley, spring 1999), 165.

2. Lily Xiao Hong Lee, *The Virtue of Yin* (Canberra, Australia: Wild Peony, 1994), 68.

3. Neil Okrent, "Right Place, Wong Time," *Los Angeles Magazine* (May 1990): 96.

4. Wong, cited in Vivien North, "There's a Secret Anna May Wong," *Picturegoer Weekly* (September 8, 1934): 8.

AFTERWORD

The cinema (1919–1961) of Anna May Wong spanned the end of World War I (1914–1918), the Roaring Twenties, the great crash of 1929 and the subsequent Depression, Prohibition, Japan's invasion of China (1928–1945), World War II (1932–1945), the civil war in China (1945–1949), the advent of television, and the beginnings of rock and roll. In all of these upheavals and revolutions that shook the world, Chinese America's first and most famous film actress remained perpetually cool, as if Miles Davis's 1949–1950 recording of detached jazz in his *Birth of the Cool* was meant solely for her and her time on earth.

Wong's sixty-one films reflect a kaleidoscope of the great events that enveloped the United States as a nation in world affairs during the twentieth century and European America as the major ethnic sector behind the national quest for global power and world domination. Throughout this early evolution of the United States into the most powerful international economic and military force on the planet, Wong's films reveal crass consumerism, xenophobia, ethnocentrism, racism, antimiscegenation attitudes, escapism, fantasy, the "Yellow Peril," "Yellow-face," moral bankruptcy, and a heroism not seen again in the film persona of a performer from Asian America. It is as if a screening of her films reveals not only a heart of profound darkness in European America but also a sense of exquisite calm and civility that she brought to an evolving place called Chinese America.

The roles in which she was cast and those given to others, especially the lead in *The Good Earth,* exemplified how European Hollywood visualized China, the Chinese, and Chinese Americans. For many Americans, European, Chinese, or other, Wong represented China, the Chinese, and Chinese Americans. Of all the Asian American performers in film and television from 1919 to 1961, she epitomized the racial politics of representation in European America. But in her work she also was a heroine, a master builder, and a conduit of good fortune.

Wong was a consummate promoter of her career as a performer and celebrity. Her almost endless energy revealed a driven woman bent on mastering her own life and pursuing a film career according to her own needs and values. Her persona as the exotic and erotic Asian woman in films and stage performances was carefully nurtured after she decided to abandon the appearance of a Chinese flapper in Europe. In fact, being Chinese American and a European American flapper was almost incongruous because it seemed to match neither her personality nor her idea of herself. During her first sojourn in Europe, Wong began to see the advantages of cultivating the image of the all-knowing, somewhat mysterious Asian woman. Her earlier films tilted toward the inscrutable, exotic, and erotic as well as the diabolical. In time, she modified the "inscrutable" by revealing her own hint of "mysteriousness" that was often punctuated with mischievous utterances. When asked about dying many times in pictures, Wong declared that "because on the screen, it's very necessary to do something conclusive with any personality that's at all glamorous or exotic. One can't leave them just floating around. They are *too* definite!"[1]

Wong's exoticism was magnified by her legendary playfulness and witticisms. When asked about the potential success of *On the Spot,* she replied that "if the play fails, our work merely goes to the four winds."[2] Not only were reporters susceptible to her charm, but there was also one artist who crafted a bust of the Chinese American star. Felix Weiss recalled that "one of the most interesting women I have ever had sit for me was a Chinese. She was Anna May Wong. She presented an entirely new problem. All the time I was modeling her head, she insisted on doing one of me! And she did it commendably well."[3]

Inquisitive, talented, and a quick study, Anna May Wong was always well read and keenly interested in the politics of the world, to the extent that she voiced her objection to Japan's invasion of Manchuria. Her reading list included the poetry of Edward Arlington Robinson and Li Bo. She favored the fiction of Thomas Hardy in English and that of Orientalist Gustave Flaubert in French. She was also partial to Zone Gale's *Papa LeFleur,* Ernest S. Holmes's *Science of Mind,* and Somerset Maugham's *The Moon and Sixpence.* Her favorite comedians were Groucho Marx and the Beijing performer Hai Yong.[4]

In the early years of her career, Wong was associated with directors Marshall Neilan (1891–1958) and Tod Browning (1882–1962). In 1920, "Mickey" Neilan "was hunting 'types' for his production and one of his discoveries was Anna May Wong. He promptly induced her father to permit her to try the pictures."[5] In fact, Neilan wrote *Bits of Life* (1921) with Wong in mind as Toy Sing, the wife of Chin Chow, played by Lon Chaney. While rumors persisted that Wong at sixteen years old and Neilan at thirty years old in 1921 were contemplating dashing off to Mexico for marriage and a honeymoon, this story of romance was just as fantastic as Toy Sing driving a crucifix into the head of Chin Chow in *Bits of Life*.

Hollywood rumors also persisted about Anna May Wong's love for Tod Browning, who directed *Drifting* (1923) with Wong as Rose Li, daughter of an "Orientalized" physician named Mong. The age difference (Wong at eighteen and Browning at forty-one) and the protective eye of her father probably prevented any liaison even if there was a hint of one.

During Wong's long career in Hollywood, she met many cinematographers. Among them was Charles Rosher (1885–1974). *Los Angeles Times* journalist Ron Russell reported that "there is a fairytale bungalow built by early cinematographer Charles Rosher that has a room said to have been designed for his lover, actress Anna May Wong."[6] She was also linked to fellow Los Angeles High School classmate and Korean American actor Philip Ahn (1905–1978). He responded to the Hollywood rumors of his engagement to Wong with, "Who can tell where love is concerned? It's not serious. At least, not yet." She replied, "I'm very fond of Philip. But marriage—."[7]

Nothing came out of this supposed liaison except feed for the Hollywood gossip machine. But the obvious reason for creating a supposedly intimate relationship between these two Asian Americans, Philip Ahn and Anna May Wong, was that audiences might have perceived her on-screen relations with whites as a natural extension of yellow–white liaisons in actual life. To dispel any hint of miscegenation outside of rape and sexual captivity between the yellow Wong and white European American males, what better romance could have been created than this one between two old high school sweethearts from Los Angeles High School?

Anna May Wong never married. This was a fact that the European American media always stressed, as if a woman without a man in the patriarchal society of European America was incomplete and abnormal. The only male mentioned in her Chicago obituary was Dr. Robert Skeels. As her physician, he stated that Wong was apparently "in good health recently and [had] no history of heart trouble"[8] just weeks before she died.

The European American media argued that Wong did not marry because of her penchant for European and European American males. *San Francisco*

Chronicle reporter Geraldine Sartain in 1937 asked, "What shall an Oriental beauty who prefers western men do? This is the question that plagues the unhappy, much sought film star."[9] Sartain concluded that "our exotic willow-blossom who plays such sinister roles really suffers such pangs. She's in a pretty fix right now, juggling the question whether to risk marrying an American."[10]

If Wong was unable to marry a white European American, what about a yellow Asian or Asian American? She told Sartain:

> If I had fallen in love with a Chinese, all might have been different now. But I don't see why I should start anything I can't finish. A Chinese friend, American-trained, told me he'd never marry anyone except a native Chinese woman "because I want a real wife!" There you have it. The two women are far apart. The men choose the hausfrau, rather than the companion.[11]

For an intelligent woman like Wong who had just returned from China and eventually attained her agency of transcending race, ethnicity, and citizenship and her empowerment as a meaningful human being, the idea of marriage even with an Asian, Asian American, or European American male was simply a fact to be avoided.

Wong was never the conventional Asian American woman. So why should she begin to be a model wife in such patriarchal societies as the United States or China, where men often ruled and women obeyed? If she had obeyed men consistently, Wong would not have had her many lives, which included an improbable and lengthy film career in a European America that abused, demeaned, and subordinated performers of color.

If marriage was on Wong's mind, it was only an afterthought, especially during her career. A student of marriage as an institution, she declared that for two people to have a happy relationship:

> A couple must be able to be silent together.
> They must respect each other's thoughts and personalities.
> They must understand each other's emotions.
> They must enjoy the same things together.[12]

She argued that a "formal written contract" consisting of the items important to the man and woman ought to be drawn up before the wedding day. If the couple agreed to "discuss any annoyances" immediately before "molehills could grow into mountains, that marriage would have a good chance to survive."[13] For the most famous actress from Chinese America, "marriage involves an awful lot of sacrifices."[14] Because she always had other more important ideas and projects than marriage, Wong admitted that she was not inclined to marry a male of any race or ethnicity because, "I still want to rove a bit. I do enjoy my independence."[15] That attitude of freedom and the lack of deference to such conventions as marriage never diminished her stature in Asian America. In fact, it may have even expanded her legend.

LEGACY

Anna May Wong has always had a place in Asian America as the first Asian American female film star. Because of the racist attitudes of many studio bosses, she was unable to land such cherished roles as O-lan in *The Good Earth*. While they might point to the box office potential of Oscar winner Luise Rainer as the logical choice for O-lan, the taboo against intimate relations on-screen between yellows and whites determined many of the roles that Wong could and would take. The regulatory censorship behind former Postmaster General Will Hays's "Don'ts and Be Carefuls" included a prohibition not only against miscegenation but also against "pointed profanity, nudity, drug trafficking, sex perversion, white slavery, sex hygiene and venereal disease, scenes of actual childbirth, children's sex organs, ridicule of the clergy, and offenses against a nation, race, or creed."[16]

With her many films, stage performances, vaudeville acts, revues, television shows, and radio broadcasts, Anna May Wong's career was remarkable. By the time she completed the television series *The Gallery of Mme. Liu Tsong* for Du Mont in 1951, the fact that she was able to transcend silent films, talkies, stage plays, and television attests to her capacity to adapt and constantly reinvent and renew herself.

Evolving into a sophisticated and cosmopolitan woman with a self-contained persona and a global perspective who steadfastly refused to be submissive to males of any race or ethnicity, Wong predated the idea of the independent European American woman of the late 1950s. She was the type of woman that twenty-first-century feminists and women of agency and empowerment would have admired. In 1928, she defied Hollywood and dashed off to Europe and its accolades, celebrity, and fame. She returned to Hollywood in 1930 and took Broadway by storm with her portrayal of Minn Lee in *On the Spot*. By the time she signed to portray Madam Liang in *Flower Drum Song,* she had already lived many lives. It was almost as if her death at fifty-six in 1961 came more from exhaustion after having lived a full and eventful life in many places and time zones than from her health issues. She was one of the few shining stars in a European America that subordinated or dismissed the lives, labor, talents, and thoughts of Asian Americans as simply irrelevant.

Once she returned from China in November 1936, Wong realized that a film career was merely secondary to living well and living fully. What she accomplished in the midst of the social and political difficulties of the times in which she lived opened the way for other Asian American performers. Such demonstrations of respect as the Anna May Wong Award of Excellence have been made annually at the Asian American Arts Awards. Actor Steve Park won it in 1997 for "taking a stand against racism in Hollywood."[17] Ming-Na Wen received it in 1999 and commented that she wished Anna May Wong "was around today to see what is happening in this industry and the path she paved."[18] Of course Anna May Wong would have laughed at being cited as the model for Asian American performers. She was not a model for future generations of Asian Americans, nor was she even a model minority for European Americans.

Like a radiant butterfly fluttering in the wind, her life was short but filled with drama and many changes. If there were any advice she would give to Asian Americans, it would be to "live life to the fullest and live many lives, but always live them with a sense of humor." She defied convention and went her own way as if her path was always clear. With a cool demeanor and detached Daoist bent, she was often heard saying, "Life is too serious to take seriously."

NOTES

1. Wong, cited in Vivien North, "There's a Secret Anna May Wong," *Picturegoer Weekly* (8 September 1934): 8.

2. Wong, cited in "Anna May Wong Combination of East and West," *New York Herald Tribune,* 9 November 1930, 14.

3. Weiss, cited in "Heads and Tales," *Christian Science Monitor Magazine* (18 September 1935): 4.

4. "Anna May Wong Combination of East and West," 14; Marguerite Tazelaar, "Film Folk in Person, a Chat with Miss Wong," *New York Herald Tribune,* 30 April 1933, 3; "All for Mr. Wallace," *New York Times,* 16 November 1930, 3.

5. Marjorie C. Driscoll, "Chinese Girl Becoming Star of Screen," *San Francisco Chronicle,* 28 October 1921, E3.

6. Ron Russell, "An Oasis of the Past: Neighborhood: The Uplifters Club Built a Pacific Palisades Getaway for Its Fun-loving, Influential Members," *Los Angeles Times,* 28 June 1994, 1.

7. "Who Can Tell Where Love Is Concerned?" *San Francisco Chronicle, Rotogravure,* 7 November 1939, 3.

8. Skeels, cited in "Anna May Wong Movie Star Dies at 54," *Chicago Daily Tribune,* 4 February 1961, 11.

9. Geraldine Sartain, "Tragic Real Love Story of Anna May," *San Francisco Chronicle,* 4 July 1937, 15.

10. Sartain, "Tragic Real Love Story," 15.

11. Wong, cited in Sartain, "Tragic Real Love Story," 15.

12. Wong, cited in Sartain, "Tragic Real Love Story," 15.

13. Wong, cited in Sartain, "Tragic Real Love Story," 15.

14. Wong, cited in Sartain, "Tragic Real Love Story," 15.

15. Wong, cited in Tazelaar, "Film Folk in Person," 4.

16. Leonard J. Leff and Jerold L. Simmons, *The Dame in the Kimono* (New York: Doubleday, 1990), 7.

17. Corey Takahashi, "An Actor Speaks for Asians in Hollywood," *Seattle Times,* 17 October 1997, F2.

18. Ming-Na Wen, cited in Jesse Hamlin, "Asians in Art Pick up Awards," *San Francisco Chronicle,* 4 October 1999, D3.

MILESTONES

1848	Discovery of gold at John Sutter's Mill near Sacramento, California.
1850s	Grandfather Leung Chew Wong arrives in Sacramento from *Taishan*. Opens store with four others.[1]
1858	Birth of father, Sam Sing Wong, in Michigan Bluffs, California.[2]
1887	Birth of mother, Gon Toy Lee, in Oakland, California.[3]
1890	Marriage of Sam Sing Wong to first wife in *Taishan*.[4]
1890	Birth of first son to Sam Sing Wong's first wife.
1900	Marriage of Sam Sing Wong to Gon Toy Lee.[5]
1900	Sam Sing Wong and Gon Toy Lee move to Los Angeles.[6]
1900	Birth of first daughter, Liu Ying Wong, or Lulu Wong.
1905	Birth of second daughter, Liu Tsong Wong, or Anna May Wong.
1907	Birth of first son, James Norman Wong.[7]
1913	Birth of second son, Frank Wong.
1915	Birth of third daughter, Liu Heung Wong, or Mary Wong.
1916	Birth of third son, Roger Wong.
1920	Birth of fourth daughter, Meahretta, or Margaretta Wong; dies young.[8]

1920	Birth of fourth son, Richard Kim Wong.
1930	Gon Toy Lee dies in a car accident in front of the North Figueroa Street house, age forty-three.
1934	Sam Sing Wong reunites with first wife in *Taishan*.
1936	Anna May Wong visits China from January to November.
1938	Sam Sing Wong returns to Los Angeles from China.
1940	Liu Heung Wong commits suicide in a garage at her residence.[9]
1949	Sam Sing Wong dies in Los Angeles, age ninety-one.[10]
1961	Anna May Wong dies at home on February 3 in Santa Monica, California, age fifty-six.[11]

NOTES

1. Karen Janis Leong, "The China Mystique: Mayling Soong China, Pearl S. Buck and Anna May Wong in the American Imagination" (Ph.D. dissertation, University of California, Berkeley, spring 1999), 348.

2. Sam Sing Wong's death was announced in October 1949. He was ninety-one years old. Thus, his birth year was 1858. "Funeral for Father of Anna May Wong," *San Francisco Chronicle,* 14 October 1949, 33.

3. For details of Gon Toy Lee's birth and death, see "Injuries Fatal to Mrs. Wong," *Los Angeles Times,* 12 November 1930, 5.

4. "Injuries Fatal to Mrs. Wong," 5.

5. Anna May Wong's sister, Liu Ying Wong, or Lulu, was born in 1900. See "Last Will and Testament of Anna May Wong," *The Silent Film Monthly* 5, no. 6 (June 1997): 1, which lists Lulu as fifty-eight when the will was filed on March 8, 1958. Since Gon Toy Lee was born in 1887, she was thirteen when Lulu was born. She probably married Sam Sing Wong at the age of thirteen (in 1900).

It was unlikely that Sam Sing Wong and Gon Toy Lee moved from the Bay area to Los Angeles in 1892 as suggested by Leong, "The China Mystique," 346. Gon Toy Lee would have been a mere child of five in 1892. Leong, "The China Mystique," 347, also states that Gon Toy Lee was twenty-two or twenty-six years younger than Sam Sing Wong. Born in 1887, Gon Toy Lee was twenty-nine years younger than Sam Sing Wong, whose birth date was 1858.

6. Leong, "The China Mystique," 346.

7. In 1931 when Anna May Wong returned from Europe, she was met by James at the Los Angeles railroad station. He had just received his master's from the University of Southern California, which would have put his age at twenty-four, if the normal duration for the completion of a master's is assumed. Also greeting Anna were Frank, who had just graduated from high school, making him eighteen in 1931, Roger, who was fifteen, and Richard, who was eleven. "Screen Star Has Her Homecoming After Much

Delay," *Seattle Times Daily,* 6 September 1931, 14. In "Last Will and Testament of Anna May Wong," Richard is listed as thirty-eight.

8. A 1920 census recorded a daughter to Sam Sing Wong and Gon Toy Lee named Meahretta, or Margaretta, who was never mentioned by Anna May Wong. She probably died young. Leong, "The China Mystique," 117, n. 6.

9. "Anna May Wong's Sister's Suicide," *New York Herald Tribune,* 26 July 1940, 26.

10. "Funeral for Father of Anna May Wong," *San Francisco Chronicle,* 14 October 1949.

11. "Miss Wong Gave Films Exotic Flavor," *New York World Telegram,* 4 February 1961; "Anna May Wong Is Dead at 54, Actress Won Movie Fame in '24," *New York Times,* 4 February 1961, 19.

FILMOGRAPHY

FILM

1919

1. *The Red Lantern.* Unbilled, as a lantern holder.

Dir. Albert Capellani (1870–1931). Nazimova Productions for Metro Pictures. With Alla Nazimova, Margaret McWade, Virginia Ross, Frank Currier, Winter Hall, Amy Van Ness, Darrell Foss, Noah Beery, Harry Mann, Yukio Aoyamo, Edward J. Connelly, Harry Kolker.

1920

2. *Dinty.* Unbilled, as a Chinatown resident.

Dir. Marshall Neilan (1891–1958). Associated First National Pictures. With Wesley Barry, Colleen Moore, Tom Gallery, J. Barney Sherry, Marjorie Daw, Noah Beer, Walter Chung, Pat O'Malley, Kate Price, Tom Wilson, Aaron Mitchell, Newton Hall, Young Hipp, Hal Wilson.

1921

3. *The First Born.* Unbilled, as a Chinatown resident.

Dir. Colin Campbell (1859–1928). Robertson Cole. With Sessue Hayakawa, Helen Jerome Eddy, Sonny Boy Warde, Goro Kino, Marie Pavis, Clarence Wilson, Frank M. Seki.

4. *Shame.* As Lotus Blossom.

Dir. Emmett J. Flynn (1892–1937). Fox Film Corporation. With John Gilbert, Mickey Moore, George Siegmann, William V. Mong, George Nicholas, Rosemary Theby, Doris Pawn, David Kirby.

5. *Mother O'Mine.* Unbilled, as an extra.

Dir. Fred Niblo (1874–1948). Associated First National Pictures. With Lloyd Hughes, Betty Ross Clarke, Betty Blythe, Joseph Kilgour, Claire McDowell, Andrew Robson, Andrew Arbuckle.

6. *Bits of Life.* As Toy Sing.

Dir. Marshall Neilan. Marshall Neilan Productions for Associated First National Pictures. With Wesley Barry, Rockliffe Fellowes, Lon Chaney, Noah Beery, John Bowers, Teddy Sampson, Dorothy Mackaill, Edythe Chapman, Frederick Burton, James Bradbury Jr., Tammany Young, Harriet Hammond, James Neill, Scott Welsh.

1922

7. *The Toll of the Sea.* As Lotus Flower.

Dir. Chester M. Franklin (1890–1954). Technicolor Motion Pictures for Metro Pictures. With Kenneth Harlan, Beatrice Bentley, Baby Moran, Etta Lee, Ming Young.

1923

8. *Drifting.* As Rose Li.

Dir. Tod Browning (1882–1962). Universal. With Priscilla Dean, Matt Moore, Wallace Beery, J. Farrell MacDonald, Rose Dione, Edna Tichenor, William V. Mong, Bruce Guerin, Marie De Albert, William Moran, Frank Lanning.

9. *Thundering Dawn.* As Honky Tonk Girl.

Dir. Harry Garson (1882–1938). Universal. With Tom Santschi, Charles Clary, Georgia Woodthorpe, Richard Kean, Edmund Burns, Winifred Bryson, Winter Hall, J. Warren Kerrigan, Anna Q. Nilsson.

10. *Mary of the Movies.* As herself.

    Dir. John McDermott (1892–1946). With Maria Mach, Florence Lee, Mary Kane, Harry Cornelli, John Geough, Raymond Carman, Rosemary Cooper, Creighton Hale, Frances McDonald, Henry Burrows, John Mc-Dermott, Jack Perrin, Ray Hanford.

11. *Lilies of the Field.* Unbilled, as an extra.

    Dir. John Francis Dillon (1884–1962). Universal. With Corinne Griffith, Conway Tearle, Alma Bennett, Myrtle Stedman, Crauford Kent, Sylvia Breamer, Charlie Murray, Phyllis Haver, Cissy Fitzgerald, Edith Ransom, Charles Gerrard, Dorothy Brock, Mammy Peters.

1924

12. *The Thief of Bagdad.* As Mongol spy and infiltrator.

    Dir. Raoul Walsh (1887–1980). United Artists. With Douglas Fairbanks, Julanne Johnston, Snitz Edwards, Charles Belcher, Winter Blossom, Etta Lee, Brandon Hurst, Tote Du Crow, Kamiyama Sojin, Noble Johnson, Sadakichi Hartmann, K. I. Nambu, Mathilde Comont, Charles Stevens, Sam Baker, Jess Weldon, Scott Mattraw, Charles Sylvester.

13. *The Fortieth Door.* As Zira.

    Dir. George B. Seitz (1888–1944). Pathe Serial. With Allene Ray, Bruce Gordon, David Dunbar, Frankie Mann, Frank Lackteen, Lillian Gale, Bernard Seigel, Scott McKee, Chief Whitehorse, Omar Whitehead, Eli Stanton.

14. *The Alaskan.* As Keok.

    Dir. Herbert Brenon (1880–1958). Paramount. With Thomas Meighan, Estelle Taylor, John Sainpolis, Frank Campeau, Alphonse Ethier, Maurice Cannon, Charles Ogle.

15. *Peter Pan.* As Tiger Lily.

    Dir. Herbert Brenon. Paramount. With Betty Bronson, Cyril Chadwick, Ernest Torrence, Virginia Brown Faire, Esther Ralston, George Ali, Mary Brian, Philippe de Lacey, Jack Murphy.

1925

16. *His Supreme Moment.* As harem girl in a play.

    Dir. George Fitzmaurice (1885–1940). Samuel Godwyn Productions for First National. With Blanche Sweet, Ronald Colman, Kathlyn Myers, Belle Bennett, Cyril Chadwick, Ned Sparks, Nick de Ruiz, Kalla Pasha, Jane Winton.

17. *Forty Winks.* As Annabelle Wu.

    Dir. Frank Urson (1887–1928). Paramount. With Viola Dana, Raymond Griffith, Theodore Roberts, Cyril Chadwick, William Boyd.

1926

18. *Fifth Avenue.* As Nan Lo.

    Dir. Robert G. Vignola (1882–1953). Producers Distributing Corporation. With Marguerite De La Motte, Allan Forrest, Louise Desser, William V. Mong, Crauford Kent, Lucille Lee Stewart, Lillian Langdon, Josephine Norman, Sally Long, Flora Finch.

19. *A Trip to Chinatown.* As Ohtai.

    Dir. Robert P. Kerr (1892–1960). Fox Film Corporation. With Margaret Livingston, Earle Foxe, J. Farrell MacDonald, Harry Woods, Marie Astaire, Gladys McConnell, Charles Farrell, Hazel Howell, Wilson Benge, George Kuwa.

20. *The Silk Bouquet.* (Also released as *The Dragon Horse*). As the Dragon Horse.

    Dir. Harry Revier (1889–1957). Fairmont Productions for Hi Mark Films. With Fay Kam Chung, James B. Leong, Marie Muggley, K. Namien, Ernie Viebare, Anne Nuttley, William Veigh.

21. *The Desert's Toll.* (Also released as *The Devil's Toll*). As Oneta.

    Dir. Clifford Smith (1894–1937). MGM. With Kathleen Key, Chief John Big Tree, Francis McDonald, Tom Santschi, Lew Meehan, Guinn Williams.

1927

22. *The Honorable Mr. Buggs.* As Baroness Stoloff.

    Dir. Fred Jackman (1881–1959). Pathe, Hal Roach. With Matt Moore, Kamiyama Sojin, Oliver Hardy, Martha Sleeper, Laura Varnie, Tyler Brooke, Priscilla Dean, James Finlayson.

23. *Driven from Home.* As a denizen of a Chinatown hop joint.

    Dir. James Young (1872–1948). Chadwick Pictures. With Ray Hallor, Virginia Lee Corbin, Pauline Garon, Kamiyama Sojin, Melbourne Mac-Dowell, Margaret Seddon, Sheldon Lewis, Virginia Pearson, Eric Mayne, Alfred Fisher.

24. *Mr. Wu.* As Loo Song.

    Dir. William Nigh (1881–1955). MGM. With Lon Chaney, Louise Dresser, Renee Adoree, Holmes Herbert, Ralph Forbes, Gertrude Olmstead, Wong Wing, Sonny Loy, Claude King.

25. *Old San Francisco.* As a flower of the Orient.
    Dir. Alan Crosland (1881–1959). Warner Bros. With Dolores Costello, Warner Oland, Charles Emmett Mack, Josef Swickard, John Miljan, William Demarest, Anders Randolph, Kamiyama Sojin, Angelo Rossitto, Rose Dione.
26. *Why Girls Love Sailors.* As Delamar.
    Dir. Fred L. Guiol (1890–1964). Pathe. With Stan Laurel, Oliver Hardy, Viola Richard, Kamiyama Sojin, Eric Mayne, Anita Garvin, Malcolm Waite, Charles R. Althoff.
27. *The Chinese Parrot.* As Nautch dancer.
    Dir. Paul Leni (1885–1929). Universal. With Marian Nixon, Florence Turner, Hobart Bosworth, Edmund Burns, Albert Conti, Kamiyama Sojin, Fred Esmelton, Edgar Kennedy, George Kuwa, Slim Summerville, Dan Mason, Etta Lee, Jack Trent.
28. *The Devil Dancer.* As Sada.
    Dir. Fred Niblo. United Artists. With Gilda Gray, Clive Brook, Serge Temoff, Michael Vavitch, Kamiyama Sojin, Ura Mita, Anne Schaeffer, Albert Conti, Clarissa Selwynne, James B. Leong, Martha Mattox, William H. Tooker, Claire Du Brey, Nora Cecil, Barbara Tennant, Kalla Pasha.
29. *Streets of Shanghai.* As Su Quan.
    Dir. Louis J. Gasnier (1875–1963). Tiffany-Stahl Productions. With Pauline Starke, Kenneth Harlan, Eddie Gribbon, Margaret Livingston, Jason Robards Sr., Mathilde Comont, Kamiyama Sojin, Tetsu Komai, Toshyie Ichioka, Media Ichioka.

1928

30. *Across to Singapore.* As Bailarina.
    Dir. William Nigh. MGM. With Ramon Novarro, Joan Crawford, Ernest Torrence, Frank Currier, Dan Wolheim, Duke Martin, Edward Connelly, James Mason.
31. *The Crimson City.* As Su.
    Dir. Archie Mayo (1891–1968). Warner Bros. With Conrad Nagel, Myrna Loy, John Miljan, Leila Hyams, Matthew Betz, Anders Randolf, Richard Tucker, Kamiyama Sojin, William Russell, George E. Stone.
32. *Chinatown Charlie.* As Mandarin's sweetheart.
    Dir. Charles Hines (1883–1936). First National Pictures. With Johnny Hines, Louise Lorraine, Harry Gribbon, Fred Kohler Sr., Scooter Lowry, Kamiyama Sojin, George Kuwa, John Burdette.

33. *Song.* (Also released as *Wasted Love, Dirty Money, Show Life, Die Liebe Eines Armen Menschen Kinds, Schmutziges Geld, Argent Maudit.*) As Song.

　　Dir. Richard Eichberg (1888–1953). British International. With Heinrich George, Hans Adalbert Schlettow, Paul Horbiger, Julius E. Hermann, Mary Kid.

1929

34. *Pavement Butterfly.* (Also released as *City Butterfly, Grosstadtschmetterling, Asphaltschmetterling.*) As Hai-tang, a Malayan dancer.

　　Dir. Richard Eichberg. Universum. With Alexander Granach, Elwood Fleet Bostwick, Tilla Garden, Gaston Jacquet, Louis Lerch, Nien Soen Ling, S. Z. Sakall.

35. *Piccadilly.* As Shosho.

　　Dir. Ewald-Andre Dupont (1891–1956). Wardour, British International. With Gilda Gray, Jameson Thomas, Charles Laughton, Cyril Ritchard, King Ho-Chang, Hannah Jones, Ellen Pollock, Harry Terry, Gordon Begg, Charles Paton, Ray Milland, Debroy Somers and his Band.

1930

36. *Elstree Calling.* As herself.

　　Dir. Alfred Hitchcock (1899–1980) and others. Wardour, British International. With Will Fyffe, Lily Morris, Tommy Handley, Teddy Brown, Bobbie Comber, Hannah Jones, Cicely Courtneidge, Jack Hulbert, Helen Burnell, Donald Calthrop, Jameson Thomas, Ivor MaeLaren, John Longden, Berkoff Dancers, Charlot Girls, Three Eddies, the Adelphi Girls, Kasbek Singers.

37. *The Flame of Love.* (Also released as *The Road to Dishonor.*) As Hai-tang.

　　Dir. Richard Eichberg. Wardour, British International. With John Longden, George Schnell, Mona Goya, Percy Standing, Fred Schwartz, Ley On, Alexander Granach, Gaston Jacquet, Louis Lerch.

38. *Hai-Tang.* (German version of *The Flame of Love*). As Hai-tang.

　　Dir. Richard Eichberg. Elstree Studio. With Franz (Francis) Lederer, Herman Blass, Edith d'Amara, Ley On, George H. Schnell, Hugo Werner Kahle, Hay Yung.

39. *L'amour maitre des choses.* (French version of *The Flame of Love*). As Hai-tang.

　　Dir. Richard Eichberg. Elstree Studio. With Robert Ancelin, Marcel Vibert, Yvette Darby, Gaston Du Pray, Francois Viguier, Armand Lurville, Clair Rawan, Mona Goya.

931

). *The House That Shadows Built.* As herself.

Film clips and profiles to celebrate the twentieth anniversary of Paramount. Paramount.

. *Daughter of the Dragon.* As Princess Ling Moy.

Dir. Lloyd Corrigan (1900–1969). Paramount. With Warner Oland, Sessue Hayakawa, Bramwell Fletcher, Frances Dade, Holmes Herbert, Lawrence Grant, Harold Minjir, Nicholas Soussanin, E. Alyn Warren, Harry Lee, Olaf Hytten, Nella Walker, Oie Chan, Tetsu Komai, George Kuwa.

932

. *Shanghai Express.* As Hui Fei.

Dir. Josef von Sternberg (1894-1969). Paramount. With Marlene Dietrich, Clive Brook, Warner Oland, Eugene Pallette, Lawrence Grant, Louise Closser Hale, Gustav Von Seyffertitz, Emile Chautard, Kamiyama Sojin, Willie Fung, James B. Leong, Forrester Harvey, Leonard Carey, Claude King, Minoru Neshida, Miki Morita.

. *Hollywood on Parade.* As herself.

Dir. Louis Lewyn (1891–1969). Paramount. With Gary Cooper, Buster Crabbe, Bing Crosby, Stuart Erwin, Larry Fine, Ginger Rogers, Ed Wynn.

33

. *A Study in Scarlet.* As Mrs. Pyke.

Dir. Edward L. Marin (1899–1951). World Wide. With Reginald Owen, June Clyde, Alan Dinehart, John Warburton, Warburton Gamble, Alan Mowvray, Doris Lloyd, Billy Bevan, Leila Bennett, J. M. Kerrigan, Wyndham Standing, Halliwell Hobbes, Tempe Pigott, Cecil Reynolds, Tetsu Komai.

. *Tiger Bay.* As Lui Chang, a cafe owner.

Dir. J. Elder Wills (b. 1905). Associated British, Wyndham Studios. With Henry Victor, Rene Ray, Lawrence Grossmith, Victor Garland, Ben Soutten, Margaret Yarde, Benn Williams, Wally Patch, Ernest Jay, Brian Buchel.

34

. *Chu Chin Chow.* As Zahrat.

Dir. Walter Forde (1896–1984). Gaumont, Gainsborough Pictures. With George Robey, Fritz Kortner, John Garrick, Pearl Argyle, Malcolm

MacEachern, Denis Hoey, Francis L. Sullivan, Sydney Fairbrother, Lauren€
Hanray, Frank Cochrane, Thelma Tuson, Kyoshi Takase.

47. *Java Head*. As Taou Yuen.

   Dir. J. Walter Ruben (1899–1968). Associate British, Wyndham Studio
   With Elizabeth Allan, John Loder, Edmund Gwenn, Ralph Richardso:
   Herbert Lomas, George Curzon, Roy Emerton, John Marriner, Gr€
   Blake, Amy Brandon Thomas, Ben Williams, Frances Carson.

48. *Limehouse Blues*. As Tu Tuan.

   Dir. Alexander Hall (1894–1968). Paramount. With George Raft, Je£
   Parker, Kent Taylor, Montagu Love, Billy Bevan, Robert Loraine, Jol
   Rogers, E. Alyn Warren, Wyndham Standing, Louis Vincenot, Keith Ke1
   neth, Forrester Harvey, Desmond Roberts, Colin Kenny, Robert Ada:
   Eric Blore, Tempe Pigott, Eily Malyon, Elsie Prescott, Otto Yamaoka, A1
   Sheridan.

1937

49. *Daughter of Shanghai*. As Lan Ying Lin.

   Dir. Robert Florey (1900–1979). Paramount. With Charles Bickfor
   Buster Crabbe, Cecil Cunningham, J. Carrol Naish, Anthony Quinn, Phil
   Ahn, Evelyn Brent, John Patterson, Guy Bates Post, Frank Sully, Ching W
   Lee, Maurice Liu, Wong Wing, Paul Fix, Bruce Wong.

50. *Hollywood Party*. As herself.

   Various directors. MGM. With Clark Gable, Elissa Landi, Joan Benne
   Joe E. Brown, Freddie Bartholomew, Leon Errol, Joe Morrison, Bet
   Rhodes, Charley Chase, Leon Janney.

1938

51. *Dangerous to Know*. As Madam Lan Ying.

   Dir. Robert Florey. Paramount. With Akim Tamiroff, Gail Patrick, Llo⁴
   Nolan, Harvey Stephens, Anthony Quinn, Roscoe Karns, Porter Hall, Ba
   lowe Borland, Hugh Sothern, Hedda Hopper, Edward Pawley, Gar
   Owen, Robert Brister, Stranley Blystone, Pierre Watkins.

52. *When Were You Born*. As Mary Lee Ling.

   Dir. William McGann (1893–1977). Warner Bros. With Margaret Lin
   say, Lola Lane, Anthony Averill, Charles Wilson, Jeffrey Lynn, Eric Stanl€
   James Stephenson, Leonard Mudie, Olin Howland, Maurice Cass, Ja
   Moore, Frank Jaquet, Edwin Stanley, Tetsu Komai.

*939

3. *King of Chinatown.* As Dr. Mary Ling.

Dir. Nick Grinde (1893–1979). Paramount. With Akim Tamiroff, J. Carrol Naish, Sidney Toler, Anthony Quinn, Philip Ahn, Roscoe Karns, Richard Denning, Chester Gan, Charles B. Wood, Lily King, Wong Chong, Alexander Pollard, Charles Lee, Grace Lem, David Dong.

4. *Island of Lost Men.* As Kim Ling.

Dir. Kurt Neumann (1908–1958). Paramount. With Anthony Quinn, J. Carrol Naish, Eric Blore, Broderick Crawford, Ernest Truex, Rudolph Forster, William Haade, Richard Loo, Ralph Suncuya, Torben Meyer, Lai Chand Mehra, Philip Ahn, Philson Ahn, Ethel May Halls.

940

5. *Chinese Garden Festival.* As herself.

Dir. various directors. Republic. With Rosalind Russell, Dorothy Lamour, Rita Hayworth, Cesar Romero, Mary Beth Hughes, Charles "Buddy" Rogers, Mary Pickford, Mary Martin, Beulah Bondi.

941

6. *Ellery Queen's Penthouse Mystery.* As Lois King.

Dir. James P. Hogan (1890–1943). Columbia. With Ralph Bellamy, Margaret Lindsay, Charley Grapewin, James Burke, Eduardo Cianelli, Frank Albertson, Ann Doran, Noel Madison, Richard Loo, Chester Gan, Edward Earle, George McKay.

942

7. *Bombs Over Burma.* As Lin Ying.

Dir. Joseph H. Lewis (1907–2000). Producers Releasing Corporation. With Noel Madison, Leslie Denison, Nedrick Young, Dan Seymour, Frank Lackteen, Judith Gibson, Dennis Moore, Connie Leon, Richard Loo, Hayworth Soo Hoo, Paul Fung.

8. *The Lady from Chungking.* As Kwan Mei.

Dir. William Nigh. Producers Releasing Corporation. With Harold Huber, Mae Clarke, Rick Vallin, Paul Bryar, Ted Hecht, Ludwig Donath, Archie Got, James B. Leong, Walter Soo Hoo.

1949

59. *Impact.* As Su Lin.
    Dir. Arthur Lubin (1898–1995). Cardinal Pictures for United Artists
    With Brian Donlevy, Ella Raines, Charles Coburn, Helen Walker, Ma
    Marsh, Tony Barrett, William Wright, Robert Warwick, Philip Ahn
    Clarence Kolb, Erskine Sanford, Linda Johnson.

1959

60. *The Savage Innocents.* As Hiko.
    Dir. Nicholas Ray (1911–1979). Paramount. With Anthony Quinn
    Yoko Tani, Carlo Giustini, Peter O'Toole, Marie Yang, Marco Guglielmi
    Kaida Horiuchi, Lee Montague, Andy Ho, Yvonne Shima, Anthon
    Chinn, Francis de Wolff, Michael Chow, Ed Devereaux.

1960

61. *Portrait in Black.* As Tani.
    Dir. Michael Gordon (1909–1993). Universal. With Lana Turner, An
    thony Quinn, Sandra Dee, John Saxon, Richard Basehart, Lloyd Nolan
    Ray Watson, Virginia Grey, Dennis Kohler, Paul Birch, Richard Norris
    James Nolan, George Womack, Henry Quan, Elizabeth Chan.

STAGE AND TELEVISION

1925

1. Vaudeville act. As herself.
    Orpheum Theater, San Francisco.
2. Vaudeville tour. As herself.
    Cosmic Production Company. Various Kansas, Iowa, and Nebraska ven
    ues. With Harry Anderson, Jack Daugherty, D. S. Finder, Edna Gregory
    Helen Holmes, Cullen Landis, Ruth Stonehouse, Harry L. Tighe.

1929

3. *The Circle of Chalk.* As Hi-Tang.
    Dir. Basil Dean (1887–1978). London stage. With Laurence Olivier.

1930

4. *Springtime.* As herself.
     Dir. Anna May Wong. Austrian venues.
5. *On the Spot.* As Minn Lee.
     Dir. Lee Ephraim. Broadway stage. New York, San Francisco. 167 shows.
     With Crane Wilbur.

1932

6. Vaudeville tour. As herself.
     With Dick Powell.
7. Vaudeville tour. As herself.
     With Jack Benny, Jean Hersolt, Una Merkel, and Abe Lyman and his
     Hollywood Orchestra.

1933

8. Nightclub act. As herself.
     Embassy Club, London.
9. Variety. As herself.
     Blackpool, England.

1934–1935

10. Vaudeville. As herself.
     Various venues in Italy, Spain, Switzerland, and Scandinavia.

1937

11. *Princess Turandot.* As Princess Turandot.
     Westport Country Playhouse. Westchester Playhouse, Mount Kisco, NY.

1939

12. Vaudeville. As herself.
     Various venues in Australia.

1940

13. *Turandot.* As Turandot.
     Straw-hat circuit. With Vincent Price.

1951

14. *The Gallery of Mme. Liu Tsong.* As Mme. Liu Tsong.
    Dir. William Marceau. Du Mont Television. Television series, eleven episodes.

1956

15. "The Letter." As Mrs. Hammond.
    Dir. William Wyler (1902–1981). NBC. *Producer's Showcase.*
16. "The Chinese Game." (Role unknown).
    CBS *Climax Mystery Theater.*

1959

17. "The Lady from South Chicago." As Mme. Lu Yang.
    Dir. Paul Stanley. ABC. *Adventures in Paradise.* With Gardner McKay, Paulette Goddard, Simon Oakland, Suzanne Pleshette, James B. Leong, Tor Johnson.

1960

18. An episode (title unknown). As an antiracist activist.
    Dir. Paul Landres (1912–2001). ABC. *The Life and Legend of Wyatt Earp.* With Hugh O'Brian.

1961

19. An episode (title unknown). As a housekeeper.
    Dir. Lewis Allen (1905–2000). Robert Florey. NBC. *Barbara Stanwyck Show.*
20. "The Journey Ends Halfway." As Miss Lee.
    Dir. Clive Donner (b. 1926). *Danger Man.* With Patrick McGoohan, Paul Dannerman.

Index

About the Author

Scholar, journalist, filmmaker, and writer, **Anthony B. Chan** is currently a tenured associate professor of communication at the University of Washington in Seattle, where he teaches digital journalism, cinema studies, and Asian media.

He is the author of *Li Ka-shing: Hong Kong Elusive Billionaire* (1996), *Gold Mountain: The Chinese in the New World* (1983), and *Arming the Chinese: The Western Armaments Trade in Warlord China, 1920–1928* (1982). He also coedited *People to People: An Introduction to Communications* (1997).

Before his university career, Tony Chan was a senior producer and television journalist at Television Broadcasts Ltd., Hong Kong, where he anchored *Focus*. He also worked as a television reporter for the Canadian Broadcasting Corporation in Edmonton, Saskatoon, Regina, and Calgary.

As an independent filmmaker, Chan is completing a four-part series on Asian Americans in Vietnam. The first three are *The Insanity of It All* (2002), *Sweet Heat* (1998), and *American Nurse* (1992). He has also produced *The Panama* (1996), *Another Day in America* (1989), and *Chinese Cafes in Rural Saskatchewan* (1985).

He has written for *Cinemaya, Snoecks* (Ghent, Belgium), and the Toronto *Globe & Mail*.

Tony Chan has a Ph.D. in modern Chinese history from York University, a diploma in Chinese from the Beijing Language Institute, masters' degrees from the University of Arizona and Bowling Green State University, and a bachelor's degree from the University of Victoria.